My Dear Old Boys

Remembering George Corner and the fallen of Wellington School, 1914-1918

Kate Hodson

‘The living owe it to those who can no longer speak to tell their stories for them.’

Czesław Miłosz

Dedication

This book is dedicated to all the pupils, colleagues and friends I have been lucky enough to work alongside during the past nineteen years. I have no doubt it is because of them the School has come to mean so much to me. I hope all who read it will find interest in the rich legacy George Corner and his 'dear Old Boys' have gifted us. The stories speak for themselves – I just hope I have done them justice.

ISBN 978-1-9993114-0-7

Permission to use the photo of Captain W. A. G. Moore from the IWM
Photographs of the graves of the fallen courtesy of TWGPP and Steve Rogers.
Book cover design by **www.battlefield-design.co.uk**

Designed and Printed in the UK by The Carly Press Limited, Wellington, Somerset.

Contact **mydearoldboys@gmail.com**
Visit **www.mydearoldboys.com**

Acknowledgements

What seems difficult to a single one may, by the help and effort of all, become attainable. But faith – and effort – and sacrifice – are required for the work. There are, and will be difficulties: if there were none, effort and work would lose their meaning, and joy of achievement there could, and would, be none.

(George Corner)

The Wellington School 'community' has been vital in helping me transform the research into a book and I have no doubt that without the help of various members, the book would not have happened. Colleagues, ex-colleagues and friends have gone out of their way to proof-read various chapters, advise on the best covers and promote the book. My posts on Facebook have never before been read by so many! Particular thanks, however, must go to Kate Trewhella (Storr) whose support and enthusiasm for all aspects of the project have been absolute. Her ebullient emails often arrived at moments of doubt and restored the drive to complete the project that meant as much to her as it did to me. I hope Joe would be proud of what we have done.

I would also like to thank David Suchet who, despite a very heavy work schedule, took the time to share some thoughts in the Foreword. His affection for the School is clear and I am indebted to him.

The research brought me in contact with a number of relatives of our Old Boys who have taken time to speak with me and share their family stories and photographs. I hope we have helped each other bring the stories to life. Thanks must go to the relatives of Percy Clode, Edward Knight, Philip Rowe, Harry Martin, Henry Wadland, Waldo Moore, Robert Talbot, Ralph Zealley, Herbert Shapland, Wilfred Baker and George Corner.

Lastly, I would like to thank my family. They haven't seen much of me in the last three months but have allowed me the room to pursue something they knew I cared so much about without grumbling. I am back now.

Contents

Foreword

By David Suchet

My Memories of Wellington School

I had a terrible time at my boarding prep school, Grenham House, in Birchington on Sea, Kent. I arrived there as a new boy aged 8 years in 1954. The School was very strict indeed and very unfriendly. We were called only by our surnames which was a cold way of addressing a boy of 8 years arriving in a boarding school having left a warm and loving home. There were rules and rules and even more rules. We were allowed to see our parents three times on quarter term, half term and three-quarter term during the summer and winter terms. Only on half term were we allowed to see our parents for two days but had to return to the School each evening. During the Easter term, we only had a half term of two days. Breaking rules meant, for most of the guilty, a caning. If sweets given by parents were found in lockers – a severe caning ensued. I spent most of my time there crying into my pillow. It's called being homesick. For me, the only saving grace was that I excelled in sport – hockey, tennis, soccer and cricket – receiving colours in each.

When it came to my Common Entrance exams I failed, miserably, in most subjects. My parents' hopes of me following my older brother (also a Grenham House boy) into Uppingham public school were, in an instant, dashed. My parents tried a couple of other schools but their quotas were full up and so it was that the headmaster of my prep school suggested that he would try to see if an interview might be arranged for Wellington School, Somerset. In this, he succeeded. On reflection, it was the only good deed he ever did me but one which, unbeknown to anyone, would change my life forever.

The day of my interview arrived and my mother and I boarded a train from Paddington station to Taunton and from there we took a bus to Wellington. Instead of my interview being conducted by the headmaster, James Stredder (he was away) it was the Deputy Head, 'Bert' Nichols, who sat behind a desk in front of me. *"Hello, Old Son,"* he said, smiling at me. *"Hello, Sir,"* I replied, amazed at his friendliness and warmth. Inside my chest, I could feel my heart pounding. We began to talk generally at first and then about what subjects I liked and disliked. I remember thinking, again, how warm and friendly he was. After about forty-five minutes, he suddenly noticed my school cap.

"That's an impressive looking cap, Old Son."
"Thank you, Sir," I replied, *"it's my colour cap for cricket."*

"Do you have any other colour caps?"
"Yes, Sir, I have colour caps for all the main sports – football, tennis and hockey as well as this one."

His smile became a beam!

"I think I should show you and your Mum around the school, don't you?"

Bert Nichols finished the tour of the School in a house called *'The Willows'* of which he was the housemaster. He said his goodbyes and we set off towards London having been told that I would hear very soon. *"I wouldn't worry too much, though,"* he said with another warm smile.

Soon afterwards we received the letter of acceptance and so my time at Wellington School, Somerset was secured.

The School was a revelation to me. From the Headmaster down to the most Junior of masters, there was always a smile of greeting. Yes, of course, there were rules and there was a strict discipline but nothing like the severity I had experienced in my prep school. I had the happiest time during my time at school. There will always be one master and one moment that stands out and will stay with me until I am called, *'on stage, please, Mr Suchet,'* in the theatre in the sky! The Master – Joe Storr, the Precise moment after my last performance as Macbeth in his production –

"Have you ever thought of becoming an actor, David?"

The rest is history.

I will always remember Wellington School with its magnificent grounds and glorious Chapel with great affection. Most of all, I remember being at a school that made us, its schoolboys (not co-ed then), feel welcomed, important, and part of the family that truly cared for each and every one of its 'old sons' as Bert Nicholas would say, smilingly.

Foreword

A Fitting Memorial – The Storr Family

In 1981 my father's Imperial typewriter, with its two-tone ribbon, clacked away, taking down what turned out to be A Fitting Memorial, his play about George Corner's impassioned and tireless efforts to raise money to build a School Chapel specifically to commemorate the Old Boys who lost their lives in the First World War.

The building and how it came to be are down to one man, the then Headmaster whose School thrived on such a strong sense of community that, when his dear boys put themselves second to King and country and paid the ultimate sacrifice, George Corner made it his mission for them to be remembered.

Having been part of Wellington School for over 20 years, my father's desire to mark the Chapel's 50th anniversary became more real with access to School archives, magazines and records. The smell of fusty papers filled our cottage and conversations frequently turned to a new line in the script, possible castings and a storyline update. That said, this was no work of fiction.

At the time, the material available to my father was limited, although I am still not sure he and the internet would have been the greatest of friends. Kate Hodson's research for ***My Dear Old Boys*** has gone much further, yet both authors have shared the same enduring passion (some would say obsession) and respect for the story to live on, the story started by one man who simply sought acknowledgement for those who deserved it.

Anyone who encounters Wellington School knows of the Chapel. Fewer know of its significance. How right it would be that ***My Dear Old Boys*** enables a wider understanding for those of us still able to take our own moment in such a place.

Introduction

World War One with its trenches, mud, brutal new warfare and the sense that it was largely a case of 'lions led by donkeys' has retained a unique position in Britain's consciousness. Whether through depictions such as *'Oh What a Lovely War'*, *'War Horse'*, *'Blackadder Goes Forth'* or the poetry of Wilfred Owen, Siegfried Sassoon or John McCrae, the pervading feel in the public imagination is one of the honest, brave and ordinary Tommy, willing to sacrifice himself for King and country, somehow betrayed or cheated by generals who did not fully grasp the situation and whose orders defied common sense. These orders cost the lives of tens of thousands of men and kept the war alive far longer than it needed to be.

The art installation *'Blood Swept Lands and Seas of Red'*, which adorned the grounds of the Tower of London in 2014 to mark the 100 year anniversary of the start of the war, offered the country and world a hard-hitting visual representation of the scale of loss. Focus moved back on to the human tragedy with every United Kingdom soldier who died in the war, all 888, 246 of them, being represented with a single ceramic poppy. Spilling from a tower window into a wave, a tide of poppies covered the moat outside the Tower, turning it into a sea of red. People flocked to see this Yeatsian *'terrible beauty'*, from all over the country. Queues waited for hours to witness the shocking and humbling sight; almost 900,000 poppies, commemorating 900,000 men from all over the United Kingdom who put their country before themselves and never came home.

The numbers associated with the loss of life in The Great War are almost too large to grasp: 19,240 killed on the first day of the Battle of the Somme; 73,000 missing and commemorated on the Thiepval Memorial; over 400 CWGC cemeteries in the Somme region alone; 365, 375 killed on fronts other than France/Flanders and Gallipoli to name but a few. And within this numerical mass, the individuals have been lost under the weight of horror and destruction. With the 2014 commemoration came moves such as the Imperial War Museum's *'Lives of the First World War'* and the British Legion's *'Every Man Remembered'*, and smaller projects such as 'The Great War Memories Project' to bring back as many memories of these men as possible through sharing family stories, photos, letters etc.. In 2011 the last fighting Tommy, Harry Patch, died and in 2012, the last veteran of WW1, Florence Green, passed away and suddenly the realisation dawned that there were no longer any people left who had experienced the war first hand. As the Great War moved away from us into this silence, it could now only be accessed through memoirs, letters and diaries. Yet public and family interest in those who fell seemed to grow. It fed into the efforts to develop our understanding of what it was like to live at that time, in that world. It has always been the 'voices' of history that have interested me; listening to the words of those reflecting on their experiences and using those to gain a greater sense of 'history'.

In September 2014, in Wellington School, Somerset, we were preparing for the Remembrance Service in the Chapel which was due to take place as part of the commemoration of the 100 year anniversary of the start of the war. Sitting in the Chapel one morning, looking at the red and gold panels of the fallen, I began to wonder just who the men were behind the names. They were here in name, regiment and date of death only, but none of us had any sense of the kind of men they were or the lives they led. We had some information about their deaths, but almost nothing about their lives. It was here that I decided I would like to find out as much as possible about them and tell as many stories behind the names as I could.

The research took around three and a half years to complete and moved back and forth between the Magazines, the Somerset Heritage Centre, genealogy sites, military record sites and forums and burial records at the CWGC. The story of each man grew and developed. Some were mentioned in historical accounts, some on local memorials and some had family members researching them, and I was able to make contact and share information. Other men simply seemed to have almost disappeared; no one appeared to be looking for them. With research, it is almost guaranteed that the destination set at the beginning of the process is unlikely to be where the process ends. I set myself the task of finding the stories of the 37 Old Boys who fell – and I did that. However, during the research, one other story emerged that was inextricably bound to the 37. It became clear that a book about the Wellington School fallen could not be written without telling the story of the man who, some said, 'was Wellington School.'

Most people connected with Wellington School will be familiar with the name George Corner. His bust resides outside of Chapel near the Sunken Garden and the Corner building houses the Music Department. We walk past him every day. Yet few would perhaps claim to know much more about him. He seems to exist in the distant past; a long-dead figure belonging to a different world. I must confess to feeling much the same before I began the research. Yet the more I read the School Magazines from 1911-1922, the war years collected in a few hundred pages, the more I heard his voice, never stronger or more articulate than in his *'My Dear Old Boys'* letters. I wondered who this man was who could be so important to so many serving abroad that they took time to write to him. The warmth and affection felt for him were palpable. It was obvious that George Corner was more than a shadow of the past. In truth, as I discovered, he was extraordinary.

Corner served the School as Headmaster for 38 years. He experienced the years of WW1, the 'nightmare' years as he called them, watching helplessly as huge numbers of his Old Boys went to war to serve King and Country. He felt the anxiety and fear, as well as the pride, that any parent would feel, not just for one or two sons, but for hundreds, as boys he had lived with, played cricket with and trained in the O. T. C. rushed to enlist. He witnessed boys he'd seen grow from childhood to adulthood go to fight, to come home wounded, changed, or not come home at all. And he felt for every one of them; each loss a personal grief.

Though his letters are inspiring, it is in the devotion, dedication and determination he showed in building the Memorial Chapel that I believe his greatest legacy can be seen. The dream he had for the Chapel, given the size of the School and the funds available, was more than ambitious. It verged on the ridiculous. Yet he was driven by his sense of duty to build a 'fitting memorial' for his Old Boys. He led by example, giving his own money when funds ran low. It is reported that he was owed around £8,000 which is around £400,000 today. In George Corner, we can see someone who had a clear purpose, a goal, and even when that goal seemed impossible, he never gave up. Fired by faith and a conviction that this building had to happen, Corner risked his health and his financial security to see it realised. The Chapel was 'ready' on time for its opening, but it was not finished to Corner's specifications. In fact, money was still owed to craftsmen after he retired in 1938. He was both mindful and upset that not all debts to those who worked so hard had been paid.

In the book, the story of George Corner frames those of the 37 who died. **Chapter 1** explores the School in the years before the war: its ethos, the early years of Corner's headship and a sense of everyday life for pupils and masters. **Chapter 2** explores how Corner led the School during the war years through the Editorial of the Magazines and 'The Extracts from the Head's Letter Bag'. As the war progressed, the Magazines changed and Corner saw his role as uniting the Wellington School family with organising news of those who fought around the world. As the letters grew in number and detail, and the Magazines were published less frequently, Corner's tone seems to embody a weariness as the huge task of editing the letters drained him, both physically and emotionally, and good news appeared scarce. The Chapter ends with the memorial service that took place during the Reunion Weekend in July 1919.

Chapter 3 is by far the longest chapter and tells the individual stories of the 37 Old Boys who fell. It aims to put in one place the various documents and 'tales' that relate to each man. Each story includes where appropriate: details of family and school life, experiences of war, letters to Corner, the School Magazine obituary, as well as the various places each individual is remembered. The archive also holds some letters from parents with details for the Memorial Chapel plaques and references to these have been made. The nature of these items means there are occasional repetitions, but the fact that the stories were told in different places seems important in giving the sense of how each man lived and died. There are some stories which convey the human cost of war. The postcard sent by P. A. Clode to his wife and son, *'Daddy off to France – Au Revoir'* is so simple, yet so poignant. Clode's son was only a year or so old when his father left for France – and never returned. There is the terrible plight of Harry Martin's children, orphaned in 1917, and once more thrust into despair when their grandmother, their only living family, died in 1923. They were only 15 and 13 years old.

It is easy to think of those who fell as 'the 37', yet each one was a son, many were brothers, some were husbands and four were fathers. They had lives; they were loved, and their deaths changed the lives of their families forever. I wanted to tell the human stories behind the names.

Chapter 4 returns to George Corner and focuses on the building of the Memorial Chapel and the relentless drive for funds and support. It is an inspirational story of what can be achieved with passion and commitment. The fundraising took twelve years. In 1981 the Head of English, Joe Storr, wrote a moving play called *'A Fitting Memorial: A Tribute to George Corner'* to mark the 50th anniversary of the Chapel. The play provides a sometimes humorous, poignant and moving account of the strain and personal cost, in terms of money and health, to Corner and his family. Storr's play is itself a *'Fitting Memorial'* to George Corner and the legacy of the Chapel. The play stands as a part of our School's history and extracts are used here to help tell Corner's story.

The story of George Corner would not be complete without a sense of what happened to him once the Chapel was built and this is explored in **Chapter 5**. It is a sad story in many ways as Corner found himself increasingly alone as those he loved most passed away but he continued to make the most of life at Ruggin before his death in 1947.

As the commemorations for the 100-year anniversary of the end of the Great War move nearer, it is natural that our attention moves back to the sacrifice of those who fell, the bravery of those who fought and the endurance of those who lived with the absence of loved ones. We cannot imagine how it must have felt to live at this time but the stories in the Magazines and letters, written by those who never imagined we would be reading them 100 years later, offer us an insight. Our Wellington School is a very different place now than it was 100 years ago in many ways, but the legacy of Corner and his Old Boys is all around. The 'community' feel of the School, which makes it so special to many, lives on.

Chapter 1

The School In The Years Before 1914

The Return of George Corner, 1899

The Corner family's association with Wellington School did not begin with George's appointment as Headmaster in 1899. In fact, this appointment marked a return rather than an arrival. In 1848, William Corner, George's father, had taken over the running of the School. At the time he was only 25 years old and unmarried. His eldest sister, Ann Elizabeth, lived with him and helped to run the house. In 1852, William married Susannah Lutley. Aided by Susannah's inheritance, William was able to fund a range of improvements to the School site and buildings. It was an approach that the School would see again fifty years later.

William and Susannah had nine children: five boys and four girls. The youngest of all was George. For the first ten years of his life, he lived on the School site and, we can only assume, had a happy childhood. The family's happiness was shattered, however, in 1879 when George was just 10 years old. As the School began to struggle with numbers and finances, Susannah died of bronchitis at the age of 52. William sold the School, which shut temporarily and moved the family to Nottinghamshire.

The Corner family with George sitting on the left

George Corner

In 1885, Samuel Corner, George's oldest brother, came very close to being appointed as the School's Headmaster after the then Headmaster, Francis Raban, resigned. A casting vote meant Samuel narrowly missed out and J. O. Beuttler was appointed instead. Fourteen years later, when Beuttler stepped down, George Corner was appointed Headmaster.

Whether driven by a desire to further his father's work, or a deep need to 'go back' to the place of happy childhood memories or whether Corner simply applied for an available headship, we can't be sure. What we do know is that George returned to live in the house he had been born in and his bedroom became the room in which he had entered the world.

Some aspects of his headship mirrored those of his father, fifty years before. He sought to improve the School site and buildings so that a better provision could be offered. Like his father when he became Headmaster, George was unmarried and his sister, Mary, came to live with him and run the house. She became a much-loved 'maternal' figure to the School community for the next 39 years.

In 1901, Corner established the Cadet Corps which would later become the O. T. C.. Unlike many Cadet Corps, Wellington had its own cap badge designed by Corner. He became the commanding officer and chose the uniforms. The Cadets were taught signalling, marching and shooting. There does not seem to have been an age limit on those joining the Corps. Many of those in the photo seem very young. One of the highlights of the year was the Cadet Corps Camp where the cadets camped out and practised their skills. It is perhaps due to the popularity of the Cadet Corps and the various skills taught that so many Old Boys went to war so early and their signalling was singled out many for special roles.

The Cadet Corps (c. 1905)

School Production of A Midsummer Night's Dream, Xmas 1907

In the early years of Corner's headship, the daily life of the School does not seem all that different from ours today. The boys were encouraged to play sport and take part in physical activity. Many matches were played against local schools and the Magazines always carried a report of each match and, at the end of the term, the Captain wrote a 'Critique' of his team. Perhaps one of the differences between Corner's School and ours is the tone of the write-ups where unapologetic frankness seems to reign. Those whose performance was lacking were left in no doubt that their limitations had been noticed. This is the case for Henry Wadland whose only mention in the Magazines as a pupil seems inglorious. Wadland was the goalkeeper in a 2nd XI match against Taunton School's B team. It was anything but a success:

'Played at Taunton and resulting in a crushing defeat of the visitors by 14-0. The visitors showing disappointing form, their custodian being especially weak. Team: Wadland: Doubt, Crick.'

It would seem that Wadland was the custodian. Being described as *'especially weak'* must have been humiliating but Wadland seems to have taken it in good part. The appraisal of Colin Gordon's football skills in December 1908, again shows us the accepted honest, but fair approach:

'A very fast wing man. Has not yet learned to control the ball. Plays a spirited game but is subject to off days.'

In the School in these years, pupils could expect to be praised when they had done well and affectionately 'critiqued' when they had not. There were notable triumphs, particularly on the stage and certain performances received a legendary status, held up as most memorable performances years after the boys had left. This is the case for Colin Gordon's 'Henry V' and Percy Clode's 'Puck'.

School days were framed by lessons, obviously, but excellent music concerts, well-attended Debate and Scientific Societies and, of course, the much-loved O. T. C. training gave the boys much to do outside the classroom.

The School Before the Outbreak of War in 1914

In the years preceding the outbreak of WW1 the Magazines show that Wellington School was a friendly and warm place. They record sporting successes, O.T.C. camps, reports from the Science and Debating Societies, exam results as well as schoolboy jokes, poetry and comments on School life.

A cricket team, about 1914.

The ethos of the School set by George Corner is clear from the early Magazines. Here was a Headmaster who took part in cricket matches, helped build the trench to carry water to the swimming pool and who personally invested his own money into securing the build in much the same way he would donate his own money to help build the Memorial Chapel. Corner was dedicated to the O.T.C. and achieved a 'commission'. He was not a head who was aloof or separate from the boys; he believed in them and they rewarded him with loyalty and affection that, as the letters from the war testify, went beyond their days as pupils. When, in 1911, Corner's dog died, the boys were quick to mark his passing with an entry in the Magazine, feeling the loss almost as keenly as Corner:

We regret to record the death of the Headmaster's faithful little dog, 'Garry' on November 11th. He was born at Banchory in 1898. He was a delightfully quaint companion and entered into all the life of the School. He will be missed by one and all, especially next Cricket season, for it was his wont to stroll unconcernedly with a measured step across the field during the progress of every match. Vale carissime.

The trench across School Field: typically, Corner is down with the labourers.

The enthusiasm with which the boys embraced the news of their Headmaster's engagement in 1913 also shows us the esteem in which Corner was held. In April 1913, the boys were astounded and delighted to hear the news, having tried for many years to find a suitable 'wife' for their Headmaster.

We can hardly find words to congratulate Mr Corner on his engagement to Mrs Pound. The news came as a bolt from the blue and quite took our breath away by its suddenness. When we had recovered, we rushed out to the flag post and hoisted the flag and gave three cheers, for first Mr Corner, then for the 'future Mrs Corner'.

Corner was also committed to building a strong relationship with the O.B.A. (Old Boys' Association) which had been formed in 1905, believing that supportive Old Boys and a shared vision for the School were essential in shaping it for the future. The Magazines tell of numerous Annual London Dinners that Corner travelled to London to attend. In the December 1913 Magazine, this meeting centred around how the School was developing and Corner was keen to discuss the issues under consideration, to garner the views and opinions of the O.B.A.. Topics up for discussion included the move from football to rugby, the change of name from 'West Somerset County School' to 'Wellington School', the purchase by the O.B.A. of 'The Gatehouse', the issue of two scholarships for leavers and the question of the Masters' salaries, *'which were totally inadequate'*. This was met with a loud *'Hear, hear.'*

Corner's wedding in 1913 brought all aspects of the School together and shows us how strong the relationships within the School were.

On the day before Speech Day, the Headmaster was presented with his wedding gift from the Present Boys.

The present consisted of an exquisitely beautiful silver tea service and illuminated address signed by all the boys of the School.

The Headmaster was so overcome at the presentation that he could scarcely find words to express his gratitude.

Congratulations to the Headmaster on his marriage to Mrs Pound; all O.W.s. will unite in wishing Mr and Mrs Corner every happiness and joy. It was unanimously felt by the Old Boys that this important event could not be allowed to pass without the O.W.s sending some slight token of their esteem and regard to the Headmaster, and at the same time show that the work he has done at the School has been appreciated by them.

To this end, a pair of silver candlesticks were sent with the following letter:

9th August 1913,

Dear Mr Corner,

We are sending under separate cover a small present from the Old Boys' Association on the occasion of your marriage. We would ask your acceptance of this as a slight token of our esteem and as an indication of our appreciation of the kindly interest you have always shown in the affairs of the Association.

On behalf of the members, we would wish you all happiness and prosperity and would add the hope that you may both be spared to preserve that happy connection with the School which you have now enjoyed for so many years.

Yours very sincerely,

J. W. Spiller, President

F. J. Riddler, Joint Hon. Sec.

In typical fashion, Corner's response was one of warmth and humility:

11th August 1913

My dear Jack and Frank,

The beautiful present of the Old Boys arrived safely here today. It is really awfully good of you. I am so accustomed to receiving kindness at your hands that I will not say for a moment I was surprised.

Will you please convey my warmest thanks to the Old Boys and tell them how much I appreciate their wedding gift and how greatly I shall always prize it.

I think the Candlesticks are most handsome and of exquisite shape and design.

I wish also to thank you very sincerely for the kind expressions contained in your letter, and I hope I may have the strength to carry out my work for some years and enjoy still further the cordial sympathy of the Old Boys.

Believe me, with best wishes to you all,

Yours very sincerely,

George Corner

As much as the boys were delighted that their Headmaster had found happiness, they were as excited by the gift of the Rector of Coombe-in-Teignhead – a new dog, *'a little well-bred fox terrier'*.

'His name is 'Ben' or as one boy said, *"We call him 'Bennie' for short."*

Speech Day, July 1914

When George Corner delivered his Speech Day address on the last day of the School year in July 1914, he was able to tell those present what a successful year it had been. It certainly seems that the School was doing well.

A record number of exam successes, a record number of pupils on roll, new buildings, a new swimming pool and good health were just some of the positives. From the Magazines around this time, it can be seen that this was a time of change and progress. The School changed its name and became Wellington School in April 1914. Though a little long, the account of the speeches gives a very good sense of Corner's principles and, at this time, the vision he has for the School.

The Headmaster, returning thanks, said he wished to define very clearly what that School was in his opinion; what it was aiming at; and what he hoped, as far as he could do, would be realised. During the past 25 years, there had been a great outcry, a great striving for better education, for more education; education within the reach of all. He wanted to see an ideal crystallized throughout the land, and he hoped that School would help in the foundations of that ideal – of a school which was within the reach of people who perhaps by the dispensation of worldly matters were not able to pay the higher fee. Yet at the same time he wanted, if possible, that school to be guided on precisely the same ideal, with precisely the same things in view, as the greater public schools. He wanted them to be considered one of the lesser public schools, but not one wit lesser in the aims that they were striving at with regard to turning out good citizens. He absolutely rebelled against anyone who suggested that there must be a levelling down for a certain kind of education for which some people had invented the name of secondary. Eton was a secondary school, and so was theirs. Every school was a secondary school in the sense that it provided something beyond the three Rs. Years ago, the old grammar schools sprang up to provide an education for the burgesses, and for those who could not command the same opportunity as the sons of the nobility. Thus, grammar schools did a mighty work. In his young days, he was happy to attend one which was founded in the year 1513.

The idea of an aided education was not a new one. Some people seemed to run away with the idea that the giving of a scholarship was something quite new, but it was nothing of the sort. Their great-grandfathers had scholarships; at any rate, they had practically free education as burgesses in some of the great towns of their land. Was it to be wondered at that with the ever-increasing population that there should be aided education nowadays? Was anyone going to be so idiotic as to say there was anything derogatory in aiding a brilliant boy from whatever rank he was derived whose father could not afford to pay? He was proud to say that he had within those walls not only the sons of men who by a happy state of affairs were in a good position, but he had at the same time sons of working men. He was very proud to have them, and very fine fellows he was certain they would make. There were far worse things – if it could be described as such – than having a poor man's son at a school. The sort of person they did not want was the person who aimed at a kind of insipid smartness, a shallowness such as they saw in illustrated magazines. That person was far more dangerous to a school than the person to whom he was referring. He wished them to understand that many scholars, only 50 years ago, at Oxford and Cambridge, who were now looked upon as the proudest members of their universities had to perform quite menial duties. A scholar now took his proper position and was honoured by everyone, even if he was a poor man, and the same thing happened at their schools when the thing was properly understood. As a word of warning Mr Corner pointed out that at the wedding feast everyone had to have a wedding garment, and people who wished their children to take advantage of the higher education and the culture and the general civilising tendency of the School must be prepared to make sacrifices. They must not think it came without effort. They would do whatever they could for them, and they on their part had got to learn that they could not get the culture and good breeding and everything which came from the mixing in a refined home, without effort, and they must be prepared to make effort and sacrifice. In that way, the School and the boy would mutually react for the good of one another. (Applause).

The Dining Hall in about 1900, looking east. The bench on the left appears still to be in use in 1992.

The Headmaster was called upon to give his report upon the work of the School for the last twelve months. With regard to numbers, they had during the past year broken all records, both in day boys and boarders. Their total that term was no so high as it had been earlier in the year, as the summer term was always the lowest, but it was exactly the same a year ago. The health of the School had been splendid during the whole of the year; they had had no sickness worth calling sickness, he was very thankful to say, which showed that the School, with its beautiful grounds behind, was a most healthy spot, and one suited in every way for boys. (Hear, hear).

As to the school work, there had been at the end of that term a most searching examination, concluded partly by the permanent staff and partly by help from outside. He wished to say in passing, a word of thanks to his staff for the indefatigable labour and scrupulous completeness of that examination. The result had disclosed what weaknesses there were, and the knowledge of those weaknesses would be helpful to them in the hard work facing the School next term.

Mr Corner went on to say that in this age of science with its wonderful developments there were certain simple things which were apt to be overlooked. In regard to education, people were dinning this and that system of teaching into their ears and forgetting sometimes that, after all, education begins with the mother's care. At the present moment, if there was one thing that needed to be rubbed into the minds of the people of this country, it was that they should take care of the home training of their children, foster it, and not allow the manifold distractions of everyday life to interfere with it. Nothing could take the place of a mother's care in the first twelve years of a boy's life it was the structure upon which schoolmasters had to build, and if that foundation was not there it made their work extremely difficult. He hoped that parents would do all they could in the early years of their children's lives to make them readers, and regular readers of the Bible. He was sorry that he sometimes had to discover a most extraordinary want of care in that direction. After all, the fear of God was the beginning of wisdom, and though he had tried many, many times in his leisure hours to make the deficiency good, he found it could never be done in the same way as it could be done at home.

The Bishop, who was received with very much enthusiasm when he rose to speak, said it was very kind of them to welcome him in the very cordial manner that they had, but it had been a very great happiness to him to come to a school which, he understood, had made a very considerable advance in the last few years. When their present Headmaster came there the School had, he believed, only some 25 boarders, and now it had at least 80, and the day boys had increased from a very small number to 44. There were he thought, two lessons which their dear old England was in great need of learning today, lessons which had equally to be learned in every school. One of these lessons was to be not always in a hurry. He was quite sure that the mistakes which were being made, and had been made in England in all its history, were caused generally by people being in too great a hurry. He was convinced that even in the present time because they were in a hurry they made many mistakes, politically, socially, commercially, and in other directions. In the matter of education, if people were not in such a hurry to see immediate results of school work it would be better for the masters and better for the boys.

The other lesson which old England had to learn, and which every boy and every person for that matter needed to learn, was the lesson of self-discipline. He was quite sure that until they learnt something of that self-discipline by which they could train themselves they would never really achieve what they might achieve or what they ought to be. For this reason, he was very pleased to hear the Headmaster's reference to the Officers Training Corps of the School and to know that with one or two exceptions every boy qualified belonged to the Corps and was going to camp. There they would learn that spirit of discipline which helped so much in the formation of character. Drill and discipline undoubtedly had a wonderful effect upon character, and for that reason alone he was glad indeed that they in that School encouraged their boys to go to camp and join the Officers Training Corps (Applause). In conclusion, his lordship wished the boys a very happy holiday and hoped they would return to their studies with a renewed determination to do their best for the School and for others, as well as for themselves. Those who were leaving School now would leave it with regret but would take away with them the resolve that wherever they were or whatever they might do, they would be worthy of their good old School at Wellington (Applause.)

OTC Signallers, probably pre-1914.

No doubt, the boys left for the summer holiday with excitement, looking forward to weeks of relaxation and no school work. There was no reason to think at this time that the next academic year would be any different to the last, but history tells us that this summer would be very different indeed.

Many of the pupils left for the O. T. C. Camp towards the end of July. Pupils included Sergt. S. W. Baker, Lc.- Cpl. E. R. Zealley, Cadet Shapland and, of course, Capt. Corner. It was being held 'amidst the trees of Mytchett Farm, near Aldershot'. Whilst the boys were practising signalling and learning new drills, tensions across Europe were intensifying. Though on a much smaller level, the boys had their own challenges to face. The night operations on Saturday 1st August were not a success. An account in the July 1914 magazine states:

The intense heat and thick dust were at times rather trying, but we were amused rather than otherwise at our dirty appearance after long dusty marches.

The innocence of the above remark, given the seriousness of what would happen just days later, is striking. As the nation waited to hear whether Germany would back down and stop its troops marching through Europe, Britain 'held her communal breath'. Sir Edward Grey, the foreign secretary, warned on the eve of the declaration of war, *'The lamps are going out all over Europe, we shall not see them lit again in our lifetime,'* but those running the camp had already made the decision on Monday 3rd August to dismantle the camp three days early and not to wait for the German response:

The first intimation we had of any possibility of an early return was an order to give in all water-proof sheets on Monday morning, August 3rd. We arose at reveille, Monday morning, looking forward to three days of hard work, but at seven o'clock we were ordered to return by the 11 o'clock train.

Strange to say, no one was at all surprised. There as an atmosphere of mystery and all were expecting something, no one knew what, to happen. The corps is to be congratulated upon the orderly way in which packing and departing were carried out.

This account written weeks later when the war still hadn't really impacted on those at the School suggests a lack of awareness of what was to follow. There was no reason for those writing to think either the war would last four years or that the type of fighting that would be seen would be new and so devastating. On 4th August, as the bells of Big Ben rang out to signal the failure of Germany to respond to Britain's ultimatum, the nation exhaled. David Lloyd George's remark, *'The big clock echoed in our ears like the hammer of destiny'*, suggestive of a Blakean forge, encompassed the enormity of the conflict about to begin, yet the mood was buoyant in London, as it was across the country, as people responded to the announcement of war with a mixture of excitement, jingoism and naïve enthusiasm. For more cautious citizens, the fact that the German army consisted of two million soldiers and was already mobilizing and that the British army only had, at this time, 120,000 soldiers, was a reason to be more anxious than excited; the war was not something that would be over soon.

When the boys returned to Wellington for the new academic year, Britain was adapting to war and great changes were afoot. Though the direct impact of the war would not be felt for some months, everything had changed.

The Editorial for July 1914, written perhaps by Corner, shows the shock and worry that now was felt both in Wellington and in the country.

Editorial July 1914

We turn our thoughts back to August and to Camp when we are wont to look forward to the leisure and delight of glorious summer holidays. At such time it is our custom to edit sundry pages of our chronicle in the interval of sea-side joys – but banished quite were all such thoughts by the ever-growing clouds of war.

We offer no apology for our lateness; we think none is due, for it seemed better to wait a while to tell, in part, at any rate, the doings of our old Cadets and so we here present our readers the doings of two terms under one cover, feeling sure that our readers will readily recognise the necessity of this. The glory of this page hurries us on – gladly we would have stayed a while longer to linger over a useful and delightful Summer Term and to recall many praiseworthy deeds on the cricket field or the Training ground – but play gives way to grimmer work.

At another time, too, the football would have claimed a longer word in our opening column, but we cannot bring ourselves to dwell longer on these events. In what horrid nightmare we are living. Europe, aye, the world at war – does anyone yet realise what this means – it is but another of those mighty restless wanderings of peoples such as we have seen in ages long since gone, movements indeed which account for our own presence in this Island.

There is a difference – the strife, inevitable in our opinion has been long delayed by diplomatic dallyings, sincere indeed perhaps, some of them, but deadly and dangerous too, for they only served to bide, aye and foster the irreconcilable jealousy of the Teuton. Many had foreseen the struggle but to many, it came as a great shock. Now as we write the enemies' guns have dared to bombard our beloved shores – vain effort of mingled hate and rage.

What our School has done is told on another page. We feel sure that every old boy and particularly every old Cadet will feel his pulse beat faster when he sees the noble effort his old schoolfellows are putting forth to do their part in the defence of their land – another page may tell of loss sustained as days go on. We must steel our hearts to bear it – what must we not endure before the tyranny is overpast?

Not only have we given of the past, but our present boys are leaving us prematurely in the flower of their Schooldays and some have exchanged the prefect's cap for the officer's sword. We are losing temporarily many of the staff. So, as they, boys and Masters, have played games together they will now fight together, and may they all return to feel that they have done their duty and taste the sweets of peace restored.

In December 1914, the 'List of Old Boys Serving Their Country' was printed. In total 85 Old Boys were serving their country including 11 of the men who would eventually fall.

For those at home, thoughts of those serving were never far away. The mood was positive, infused with the assumption, mistaken though it would clearly be, that a quick victory would be secured. Nobody could have imagined that four years would go by before peace was restored. The December 1914 Magazine ends with a message in the form of a Christmas Card from the Old Boys' Association to those fighting. All Old Boys serving with His Majesty's Forces were sent a card which read 'Hearty Xmas Greetings and all Good Wishes For the New Year'. The card bears the School Crest and the flags of the Allies, and the words:

"To count the life of battle good,
And dear the land that gave you birth,
And dearer still the brotherhood
That binds the brave o'er all the earth.' (Newbolt).

Six months or so would go by before the horror of the war reverberated in the School community.

Chapter 2

The War Years 1914-1919

The School Magazines are the most important source of information about the School in the years before, during and after the war. Before the war, they had been published three times a year, in April, July and December. Each Magazine reflected on the successes of the previous term and would be printed two months or so after the term's end. During the war, publication of the Magazine became a little erratic and sometimes two issues were printed together; sometimes there was a significant gap between them. For this reason, the Magazines' dates become a little confused and some 'news' and 'letters' appear to be out of sequence. Up to July 1915, the first war editions of the Magazines had been published termly but things changed when the December 1915 was published in a double edition with the April 1916 issue. The July 1916 Magazine was printed as normal, but the next 'issue' combined three editions (December 1916/April 1917/July 1917) and came out in Sept./Oct. 1917. The Magazines were not officially issued for four years and Corner published them all together early in 1922. This meant news of the Armistice in 1918, the Reunion in 1919 and the Chapel Supplement all appeared in 1922.

July 1915 – (distributed in October 1915)

Although the School had suffered its first fatal casualty of the war in October 1914 when Captain Waldo Alington Gwennap Moore was killed, the devastating impact of the war only really took hold during the summer and autumn of 1915. Moore was a professional soldier and had served in many wars. He died at the age of 38, having left the School before George Corner became Headmaster and so the connection between the School and Moore was not an intimate one. It was only in the July 1915 Magazine when the death of James Merson Kidner in the Dardanelles in May was reported that the inescapable reality of the war hit the School. As the vicious fighting took place in Gallipoli and the Dardanelles, and the Battle of Loos marked a change in fighting in Europe, it is perhaps fair to say that the 'innocence' of the School and its wider community was destroyed as some of its most revered Old Boys were taken.

The Editorial of the July 1915 Magazine

'The present is nothing but as it appertains to what is past and what is to come.' Landor

It has become customary of late years for the Editor to write his opening pages in a vein of what he fondly imagines is light humour. We have tried and tried and literally made light of our attempts ("how every fool can play upon the word"): now in despair we fall back on the older form of Editorial – a brief resume of past events and hopes for the future.

This term has brought us the sad news of the death of the first of our Old Boys to fall for his Country in the present War. J. M. Kidner, who left five years ago, died early in May of wounds received in the fighting at the Dardanelles; and the deepest sympathy of us all will go out to his mother and brothers in their loss.

Three other O.W.s have been wounded, but we are happy to congratulate them all on their recovery.

With the war-cloud still overshadowing everything we did, our efforts this term have naturally been turned to the improvement and efficiency of the O.T.C.. A tremendous amount of work has been done and the Corps, although more of the older fellows have gone, still reaches a high standard in all the different branches. Early morning parades have in the time-honoured way made life miserable (until breakfast), and at last, we have a band. We hope the youngsters will keep it going.

Inspection brought a good report and the term's work was pleasantly terminated by a private Camp at Bude, Cornwall.

At the beginning of the term, great difficulty was experienced in School life owing to our lack of masters and prefects. Enthusiastic persons however soon stepped forward to take the places of those who had gone and made up for lack of knowledge by extra energy.

Cricket was unfortunately brought to an untimely end owing to a visit of measles, but the team certainly showed promise, (and O.B.'s please note) actually beat Wellington Town.

The Bath has been in great favour and many of the smaller fellows should make good swimmers. Very successful Sports were held which are described on another page.

The well-worn cry for copy must close our remarks. What a surprise for the next Editor should he receive were it only one original article!

The light tone at the end of the Editorial is immediately quashed by the Roll of Honour listing Kidner as 'Killed' and de la Bere, Hancock and Rowe as 'Wounded'.

The magazine also presented another 'List of Old Boys Serving Their Country'. At this point in July 1915, 165 Old Boys were serving their Country including 17 of the 37 who would eventually die. Two had already died.

The July 1915 edition also saw the publication of Corner's first letter to his serving Old Boys.

July 1915

My dear Old Boys serving in the Forces,

I hope that this Magazine will fall into your hands. It will reach you in many different lands and will be addressed to almost every kind of unit of His Majesty's Forces, and I know how deeply interested you will be in one another's doings in the different lands, from India to the Dardanelles, and from the Dardanelles to France and Flanders.

The bulk of our boys are naturally in the New Armies, so that from now on the news becomes increasingly of more and more absorbing interest and deepening anxiety. Remember we are all mindful of you and very proud. How often does one wish that we could share the same fields of action and tread the same paths of danger and of honour? As we write we have but now heard of the loss of J. M. Kidner, who died of wounds received in the Dardanelles, the first O.T.C. boy to lay down his life for his country's honour – the news is all too meagre thence. We are also waiting in anxious hope to hear good tidings of Capt. Aplin, reported wounded in the recent desperate fighting in the Dardanelles towards the end of August. One turns back in memory to the many times when these and all you others have taken part in mimic warfare in the old training days and wishes that we could have been altogether fighting side by side, but different fields are ours though we trust and know that the old keen spirit is the same. Another old O.T. C. officer, Capt. J. N. Treble is in the trenches in Flanders, and another, Lieut. J. Baker, in the Dardanelles, and many are going out from day to day now as the new armies mobilize. May they in defending their country be spared and defended themselves and bring glory and honour to their Homes, their Country, and their old School.

Another Homer will surely arise to tell of the heroic deeds of our men in the fields so near the land of Troy that we read of in the happy days gone by. May you be cheered by the Home news and be spared to return and gladden the homes left at such sacrifice. This is the prayer of your old friend and Master.

G.C.

References to *'heroic deeds', 'Troy'* and *'Homer'* give the War an almost classical heroism, a glorious and epic quest. No doubt Corner wishes he was there with them, that *'we could share the same fields of action and tread the same paths of danger and honour'* but he knows he is unable to. Instead, his role is to support them. To this end, Corner makes references to the *'old'* days where war was almost a game played by the O. T. C.. This sense of the happier, safer days in School, fondly remembered, connects them still. It is a place of shared experience now they endure life in two very different *'fields'*. He is keen that his boys know how *'proud'* the School is of them. At the end of the letter, Corner refers to himself as *'your old friend and Master'*. The use of *'your old friend'* shows us much about the high regard he held these men in and the closeness he felt to them. In later letters, Corner's tone changes as the realities of unending conflict took their toll on the School and country at large.

As the July 1915 edition of the Magazine was going to print in October, news came through that two of the School's brightest and most able pupils, Silvanus Wilfred Baker and Edward Franklin Corner, were casualties of the Battle of Loos, 25th - 27th September 1915. It is difficult to overestimate the impact of this news on the School. Not only was E. F. Corner Corner's nephew, but he and Baker had also been the most able of the O.T.C., prefects, sportsmen and academics. Together they embodied the very essence of the spirit of the School.

A small piece of paper carrying the following information was attached to the Magazine. There had been no time to elaborate.

We deeply regret to record the two following casualties,
of which we learn as we go to press.
Killed September 25th–27th
2nd Lieut. S. W. Baker, 8th Somerset Light Infantry

Missing believed killed, September 25th–27th
2nd Lieut. E. F. Corner, 8th East Kents

After the Autumn Magazine was sent to Old Boys around the country, many wrote to express their upset at the terrible loss. It is clear from the number of letters Corner received that many found the deaths of Baker, Corner and Kidner hard to comprehend. Many had lived with them in the boarding houses and had spent years as schoolfellows. The sense of communal grief is palpable, even in the letters that arrived dated 1916. Some Old Boys received the Magazines months after they had been published and so the letters of commiseration seem a little out of date. People were writing to George Corner to express their sympathy almost a year after Kidner, Baker and Corner had died. In this way, the School community experienced the deaths of the Old Boys in an almost staggered way. The slight confusion was compounded by the collation of the letters in the 'Extracts from the Head's Letter Bag'. They were not always in chronological order and sometimes there could be a year's difference in letters published next to each other.

2nd Lieut. C R Price, RGA writing from Portsmouth in November,

'It is hard to realise that S. W. Baker was training with us last February in the School Corps.'

2nd Lieut. L. G. Dawe (School of Signalling and Telephony) writes:

'I am grieved to see the sad news in it (of S. W. Baker, E. F. Corner and Kidner). At this time, when so many families are going stricken, one's sympathy is transformed into a grim determination to make any sacrifice to help in avoiding a disaster that would render previous sacrifices vain.'

2ND LIEUT. L. G. DAWE, 5TH DURHAMS.
Wounded, Summer, 1916.

Capt. J. BAKER, M.C. (wounded).

Lieut. J. Baker (Nov. 25th) from the Dardanelles:

'I am deeply grieved to see that Teddy is on the list of the missing, and Baker and Kidner have given their young lives for their Country. It is too sad that such young people should be taken away like this.'

2nd. Lieutenant. S. Male, 7th Som. Writes from France, Dec. 19th:

'I was very sorry indeed to hear of S. W. Baker's death. He was one of the best-tempered fellows I have ever met. Has anything further been heard of Teddy Corner? I heard that he was reported 'missing'. I do hope that he has turned up or that something satisfactory has been heard of him.'

LIEUT. S. F. MALE,
Dangerously Wounded Easter Monday, 1917

A. W. HARMAN, Dorset Yeo (wounded.)

Trooper Harman, Dorset Yeomanry, Dec. 29th from Alexandria:

'Very sorry to hear of the news regarding Berry minor and S. W. Baker.'

Lieut. J. V. R. PASTFIELD
(*killed Sept. 9th, 1918*).

2nd Lieut. J. V. Pastfield writes from Tenedos, Jan. 10th, 1916:

'I am very sorry to read about Lieut. S. W. Baker. Hope the news concerning Lieut. E. F. Corner is false. It is rotten to think of so many Old Boys being lost.'

Bisset Halliwell, writing from South Africa: *'I am more than pleased to see so many O.W.s going to the front and keeping the reputation of the School even in the battlefields. I am longing to go and enlist. I was very sorry to see that poor Teddy had been killed, also poor Baker – still it is for King and Country and I only wish I could go out and do my bit for my country.'*

H. F. Marks – from Kenneth Goffe: *'I met Victor Pastfield 'mirabile dictu' out here about two months ago. He was attached to the Essex Regiment for the time being. My brother sent me out the School Magazine a few days ago, which as you know I was delighted to receive. I was deeply grieved to see Baker and Teddy Corner had fallen.'*

2nd Lieutenant A. L. G. Price, 1/5 Somerset L. I. writes from India on May 14th:
'I was more than sorry to hear about young Baker and Teddy.'

Lieut. O. S. Hughes.
Wounded, May, 1917.

2nd Lieutenant O. S. Hughes, 10th Royal Welsh Fusiliers writes on June 16th: *'I must offer you my sincere sympathies over Teddy's death. I am afraid that I cannot write all I would, but I trust you will understand that I feel his death very strongly. Also, of the news of poor old Treble, S.W. Baker and Kidner, who have all given their lives for their country.'*

2nd Lieut. L. A. E. S. Bilton,
Killed Spring, 1917.

L. A. E. S. Bilton, R. E., Harwich, writes July 4th (1916):

'The School Magazine came the other day, and I was awfully sorry to see about "Teddy" and Baker. It makes me mad to think that I am kept here when I so want to go out and try to revenge those of my school-fellows who have fallen. It seems my fate to have to stay in this company, which is very little good at all. But I mean to have another good try and get out of it. Will you please do me the favour of signing the section regarding my education? I hope my O. C. will let me go.'

A. H. W. PALFERY, Warwick Regt (*killed April 15th, 1918*).

A.H. W. Palfery, in Hospital at Salcombe, writes on June 23rd, 1916:
'I have just received the School Magazine. Please accept my best thanks for the same. I was very glad indeed to get some news of the Old School. I was sadly reminded by the photographs of those who have given their lives in this war. It is cruel to think that such splendid fellows as Wilfred Baker and 'Teddy' have passed to the great unknown. I was also very grieved to hear about Mr. Treble.'

Lance Corporal C. E. Talbot, 1/5th Somerset L. I., writes from Meerut, India on 24th July 1916: *'I need not tell you how sorry I was to hear the sad news of Mr Treble, 'Teddy' and Baker, but we must remember that they died doing their duty as brave men, and hope that when our time comes we shall do the same unshrinkingly.'*

B. L. Haddon :
'We were awfully sorry to see the sad news about Ted Corner'.

CAPT. L. C. STEVENS, Wounded, Spring, 1917.

Capt. L. C. Stevens, R. A. writes from Multan, India, Dec. 3rd:
'I must offer my sincere sympathies. I know how you must have felt Teddy's death. We all do – all Old Boys who knew him. But we also feel very proud of him, and the fact that we were at School with him. I am afraid I cannot write all I would, but I trust you will understand that I feel his death very strongly and offer you my sympathy.'

2ND LIEUT. G. W. DIBBLE, twice

2nd Lieut. C. G. S. Follows, 12th King's Liverpool Regiment, writes from France: *'I was very sorry to hear about Teddy Corner.'*

Geoffrey Dibble writes to Miss Corner from France on January 10th: *'I was awfully sorry to hear of the death of Mr Treble; Tom said he thought he was killed near here but I never saw his battalion.'*

W. H. DUNN (*wounded in Palestine, Nov. 6th, 1917*)

Sergeant. W. H. Dunn, West Somerset Yeomanry, Egypt, January 1916: *'I was so sorry to see in the papers some time ago that poor Teddy had been killed in action in France. He will, I'm sure, be severely missed by all who knew him, as he was of such a loving disposition. You have my sympathy.'*

Major H. Aplin, 7th Munsters, D.S.O.
Chevalier Legion d'Honneur.
Twice Mentioned in Despatches. Wounded at Suvla.

Captain H. Aplin wrote from Salonica, Nov. 30th, 1915:

'The news about Teddy is appalling – one can still hope he has been picked up somewhere by one side or the other and is still safe.

I do trust that the news of Teddy is at least not so bad as it sounds. Your anxiety must be terrible. It is a hard price we have had to pay for German ambition – may their collapse come sudden and very complete. Hardest of all when promising youngsters have to go; Heaven knows I have seen enough of that out here. You all have my deepest sympathy. I cannot say more.'

Major H. Aplin writes from Salonica on December 12th to Miss Corner:

'Have you any news of Teddy? I know he was reported missing and I know how futile it is to build up much hope on that. Yet there is always hope. And dear old Treble. I wish I'd been with him. How one's friends go! I am now the only officer in the battalion who has been right through the show.'

For George Corner, the challenge of the war years became one of keeping the School running as it always had, minimising the impact of the loss of masters, senior prefects and pupils who had left to serve, whilst supporting and offering encouragement to 'his' many Old Boys serving the country. It would be naïve to think that the pupils were unaffected by the fighting but it must have been very hard for them to really appreciate the conditions experienced overseas. Corner encouraged them to write to the serving soldiers and to send gifts such as food and socks. Much emphasis was also placed on the O.T.C. and training the boys in military skills. The Magazines during the war years were not published every term as they had been in the years preceding the war. Now a balance had to be struck by the need to record and reflect on School life and achievements and the many letters from serving Old Boys Corner and his sister received. Only extracts were published, and we have no recourse to the originals, sadly, but the volume and nature of these 'extracts' suggest the sheer number Corner must have been sent. No doubt reading them would have been an emotional experience; a mixture of pride, joy and sorrow. The letters came from all over the world and communicated a range of experiences in, and away, from the fighting. They brought the war closer to those at home. By 1916, the Magazines were dominated by the war, particularly the 'Jottings of Old Boys' and 'Extracts from the Head's Letter Bag'.

By the end of 1915 eight Wellington School Old Boys had died serving their country: Capt. W. A. G. Moore; Pte. J. M. Kidner; Pte. F. H. Ford; 2nd Lt. S. W. Baker; 2nd Lt. E. F. Corner; Capt. J. N. Treble; Pte. H. J. Martin and Corporal F. F. Yeandle.

Double Edition December 1915/April 1916

These editions were published together, probably in June 1916. As with all Editorials, a balance needed to be struck between reflecting on current School events and acknowledging the Old Boys serving in the war. Whether Corner wrote the Editorial, we are unsure. There are flashes of his rhetoric with emotive language such as *'desolating war'*, *'Titanic contest,' 'another country lies ravaged', 'powerful and relentless enemy,'* and 'year of horror'. Yet the Editorial makes clear that the School's history is being written every day by the actions of its Old Boys overseas. After focusing on the war, the Editorial moves onto the current School and how it is adapting to a different every day life. For the Old Boys reading it, a sense of nostalgia would have likely been engendered; the sense of safe School routine, reminders of happier times would, perhaps, have given comfort and hope. The mood of the Tennyson poem is one of optimism and hopefulness that Peace will soon 'ring out'.

Editorial

'Ring out, wild bells, to the wild sky,
The flying cloud, the frosty light:
The year is dying in the night;
Ring out, wild bells, and let him die.

Ring out old shapes of foul disease;
Ring out the narrowing lust of gold;
Ring out the thousand wars of old,
Ring in the thousand years of Peace.'

Tennyson

The above lines, chosen from In Memoriam, might have been written expressly for the end of the year 1915, so suited were they both to the season and to the present situation.

Last year, like its predecessor, drew to a close on a scene of desolating War. The Titanic contest continues, other nations have been drawn into the struggle, yet another country lies ravaged by an invader; but still our Soldiers and those of our Allies fight on against a powerful and relentless enemy.

It is not for us to dwell here upon the doings of the Allied Armies, except so far as the School itself is concerned. This year, though a year of horror, has witnessed deeds which must be writ large in the School's history.

On another page of this Magazine will be found the tale of the sad but noble deaths of five of our Old Boys. Meanwhile, the list of those serving is continually growing, more names are being added to it every day.

To turn to the present work of the School, the same changes as were indicated in our last issue are still noticeable; it could not be otherwise. Football to a large extent has given place to O.T.C. work.

The numbers of the Corps are larger than ever and in this Easter Term, we have a hundred Cadets on parade.

On the other hand, the 1st XI, although lighter than usual, has proved keen; and had not a trifling epidemic intervened, no doubt the School matches would have proved interesting as of yore.

The Xmas term, as usual, ended with the Cambridge Local Examinations. In conclusion, let us echo the words of the poem and hope that 1916 will

'Ring in the thousand years of Peace.'

In this issue soon after the Editorial, the second letter from George Corner to the Old Boys serving around the world is printed. In this letter, Corner refers to the loss of some of the Old Boys as something noble but the pain behind his words is clear. The letter is perhaps avuncular, giving those fighting important news from home and a reminder of happier memories. The words *'devotion'*, *'duty'*, *'silent sacrifice'*, *'valour'* and *'constant prayer'* give a real sense of the pride Corner feels as his Old Boys risk their own lives in service of their country. Yet there are clues that getting the letters ready has been emotionally draining, *'no light task, a task of mingled joy and sadness'* Corner writes. He does not dwell on the *'scenes of horror'* but one senses the impact some of the letters have had.

Letter From The Head **December 1915**

My dear Old Boys serving in the Forces,

I trust sincerely that this number of the Mag. will fall into your hands because it will I know be full of interest for you. You will be glad to hear news of many of your old comrades from every Front. I trust also that this number will to some extent explain my silence – amidst a press of work it has been no light task, a task full of mingled joy and sadness. You will find in the letters pictures of many shades and colours – pictures of devotion, of duty done and silent sacrifice – scenes of horror and interesting snatches of a happier lot. Your old School is very proud of you all. May the time come quickly when we may all hear your tale face to face once more in the old Hall. We have included in this number some photographs of Old Boys who have played their parts on this worlds' stage: noble parts which will never be forgotten. You quickly answered the call of your country's need – you did not await a second summons – all honour to you. You will be glad too to see the photographs reminding you of your old Schooldays and know that the old School life still runs, in part at any rate, its old familiar course though shorn, of course, of some of its old-time amenities – no plays now – the stage is a sterner one – no prizes save the due reward of work – no break up suppers: we await your return for those. The Sports you will note were run without prizes, and you would have liked to see the keenness – there is much young promise – but there was no Old Boys' race; that is being run on a greater course.

That you may all safely gain the winning post and receive the due reward of sacrifice and valour is the constant prayer of all those who cannot now be with you.

Your old friend and Master,

G. C.

The picture Corner paints is of a school almost holding its breath, waiting for the war to be over. The Old Boys' absence is marked by the changes to the traditional school year: *'no plays now – the stage is a sterner one', 'no prizes save the due reward of work', 'no break up suppers; we await your return for these,' 'no Old Boys race – that is being run on a greater course'.* This paring back of the School events is an acknowledgement that things are different; the boys at home may not be fighting but life does not go on as normal; only when the war is over will things be restored. The School is waiting. It is also clear how much Corner believes news of the School and School Life will encourage those away at war both in terms of the sense of continuation but also in the respect that each soldier's absence is so marked, it is the duty of the School to acknowledge their service by putting the events traditionally associated with the Old Boys on hold. The Old Boys are, in absence, as much a part of the School as they are when present.

In this edition of the Magazine can be found an article entitled 'Notes from the Front'. In it, an anonymous narrator gives a breakdown of the daily life of an officer in the trenches. The tone is reminiscent, particularly towards the end, of *The Wipers Times* or *Blackadder*. Who wrote it, we do not know; neither do we know if it was written by an officer at the front line or whether it was a purely creative enterprise. What it does show, however, is that not everything in the Magazine was serious or sorrowful. Here in a gently humorous way, we can see the ridiculous instructions offered by the Adjutant. It has a very funny and contemporary feel.

Notes From The Front

One day of crowded joyous life in the trenches
(exclusive of Huns, shells and bullets)

5.00 pm. *Arrival in trenches. Temper normal. Half an hour spent in trying to appear interested while outgoing officer explains to you the enormous amount of work he has done during his time there.*

5.30 pm. *Outgoing officer departs. Half an hour spent in commenting with your own officers on the utter and complete absence of any signs of any work whatever having been done since you were there last.*

6.00 pm. *Start your own work for the night.*

6.15 pm. *Telephone operator reports he has got connection with Battalion H. Q. (N.B. – Life in the trenches has now started.)*

6.45 pm. *First instalment of messages handed into you:*

No. 1. You will hold your respirator and smoke helmet drills frequently during your tour. The signal for respirators to be put on will be two G's on the bugle – Adjutant.

No. 2. Report at once if you have a fully qualified Welsh miner in your Company who can speak French and German. Age not under 18 years – Adjutant.

No. 3. All respirators will be immediately withdrawn. The signal for putting them on will be two blasts on the whistle and not as per last part of message 1 of this date – Adjutant.

No. 4. A French aeroplane with slightly curved wings giving it the appearance of a German one is known to be in your vicinity. Use your discretion in accordance with Anti-Aircraft Regulations, para. 1, section 5 – Adjutant.

No. 5. Report at once number of windows of smoke helmets broken since you have been in the trenches. The signal will now be two beats on a shell gong and not as per message 3 in correction of my message 1 – Adjutant.

No. 6. Re. my message No. 4 for the word French read German and for the word German read French. You will still use your discretion.

7.30 pm. *Messages dealt with. Dinner.*

8.30 pm. *Arrival of C. O. Suggests politely that your men would be better employed doing some other kind of work. Assent enthusiastically. All working parties changed over to different work. (Temper indifferent.)*

9.00 pm – 2.00 am. Answer telephone messages.

2.30 am. *Stand up to arms. Walk round and survey result of the night's work. Find the majority of it has been blown in by trench mortars in the early morning.*

3.30 am. *Try and sleep.*

4.00 am. Waken up to receive the following messages:
No. 115. All smoke-helmets are to be immediately marked with date of issue. If no date is known, no date should be marked and the matter reported accordingly – Adjutant.
No. 116. R. E. require a working party from your company tomorrow from 8 am. to 7 pm. Strength 150 with suitable proportion of N. C. O.'s. Otherwise, your work is to be continued as usual – Adjutant.

5.00 am. Waken up to send in "Situation Report". Report situation normal.

9.00 am. Breakfast.

9 – 11 am. Scraping off mud in Oxford Street. Removing bits of bacon in Bond Street. Reburying Fritz, who owing to night's rain had suddenly appeared in Regent Street.

11.15 am. Arrival of Brigade Staff. Orders given for everything that has been dug out in the night to be filled in and everything that has been filled in to be dug out.

11.16 am. Departure of Brigade Staff. Brain now in a coma. Feel nothing except a dull wonder. Rest of day spent in eating chocolate, writing letters home to children and picking flowers off the bank.

Final message can remember receiving is about 12 noon:

No. 271. The Brigadier General and Staff will shortly be round your trenches. – Adjutant.

The value of the School Magazines as carriers of 'news' was high and people relied on them to keep them up to date about the experiences of their schoolfellows. In our age where news is immediate and available online every minute of the day, it seems impossible that 'news' could filter through so slowly. The Magazines served a vital role in connecting the School community and strengthening the sense of 'family' yet the length of time between the news arriving, being printed and being read meant that news was spread in almost slow motion. The experience of time was very different. Men were wounded but by the time their injuries were reported in the Magazine, they could be back on active service. Men reported missing in the Magazine were sometimes confirmed dead before the Magazine reporting them missing was published. Still, the news in the Magazines was vital.

In April 1916, the 'List of Old Boys Serving Their Country' (the third list) was published. Although there were mistakes, over 208 Old Boys were engaged in the war effort around the world. Of the 37 Old Boys who died, 26 are signed up for military service. Many were in training in England, awaiting instructions to go to the Front.

This edition of the Magazine ends with the 'Roll of Honour' for the five confirmed deaths: Capt. J. M Treble, 2nd Lieut. E. F. Corner, 2nd Lieut. S. W. Baker, Cpl. F. F. Yeandle and Pte. J. M. Kidner.

July 1916 Magazines (distributed October 1916)

When the July 1916 Magazine came out, the horrors of the Battle of the Somme would have been known to the British public. With 19,240 men killed on the first day alone, warfare had entered a new and brutal phase. As many thousands of men joined up in the 'new armies', the number of Wellington Old Boys serving grew. The Editorial refers to the Old Boys' letters forming a *'splendid record of the part the School and more particularly the O. T. C., have been playing in the Great War'* and it is true that reading them 100 years after they were written gives us an invaluable insight into the School and the war. There is much less emotive language in this Editorial. News of C. G. Gordon's death on the first day of the Battle of the Somme feels almost subdued.

Editorial, July 1916

With the close of another summer term comes the time for the publication of a new number of the magazine. Like previous War-time numbers, it contains numerous letters from Old Boys at present on active service. These form a splendid record of the part the School and more particularly the O. T. C., have been playing in the Great War.

We deeply regret the addition of another name to the Roll of Honour – C. G. Gordon, who was killed in action on July 1st, will be remembered by many who read these pages.

To turn to the work of the School during the term, the chief extra work done was of course with the Corps. Morning parades and N. C. O.'s classes were held, and in addition, squads were instructed in shooting and signalling each day. The Inspection by Col. Earle, of Taunton Depot, passed off successfully.

It must not be thought that Cricket was abandoned altogether. Several School matches were played, and the lack of success was not due to lack of keenness in the teams. Excuses could be offered, but we will rather be content with reminding those who are dissatisfied that many who would have represented the School are at present playing a more serious game for their country.

The health record has been excellent. A stray case of German measles was promptly interned and suppressed.

Our numbers are still increasing, and further extensions will soon be rendered imperative.

Shock and dismay continued to reverberate as the list of the Roll of Honour grew.

LIEUT. S. F. MALE,
Dangerously Wounded Easter Monday, 1917

2nd Lieutenant S. F. Male writes from France on August 1st:

"Do you know that Colin Gordon has been killed? He wrote to me when he came out but did not mention which division he was in. I found afterwards that he was very close to me and I could easily have managed to go and see him. He was with 2nd Gordons. We were great friends. Since he left Wellington we have written regularly, and I have met him several times.

When I went to the School he was a great hero to me – as Colour Sergeant and Senior Prefect and later as Henry V. I am afraid that many, many thousands must die yet before this war is concluded."

It is, perhaps, a little too easy to talk of the community of Wellington School, but the Magazine editions carry a list of Old Boys who visit the School each term and in this edition, there were fifty names on the list. Of the Old Boys who died, H. G. Shapland, W. J. C. Brown, G. W. Powell, E. R. Zealley and W. E. Chave are mentioned. Maybe in a time of great anxiety and a sense of powerlessness, boys returned to the School to connect with happier times. Due to the lapse between the publication of the Magazine and the happening of the events it describes, it is not uncommon to have very different 'news' about individuals. On the page after the list of 'Old Boys Visiting the School', G. W. Powell is recorded as wounded and missing, *"We regret to say that we have no news of Winton Powell reported wounded on April 28th."*

It is not easy to imagine the frustration and strain of waiting for news of those wounded or missing. Perhaps the four words used to describe hearing of the death of Jack Annal, *'it is very hard'* show best the pain and sense of powerlessness that was endured as bad news kept arriving. There seems to be a very real sense of despair, an honest and genuine response to the loss of a life and all its potential, but the helplessness of only knowing a little of what happened and sometimes less than that would have been hard to bear. In the July 1916 Magazine we read:

Jack Annal after being wounded died of dysentery in Turkish hands.
This is all we know – it is very hard.

News was not always delivered in a predictable and ordered way. On occasions, eyewitness accounts filtered through different publication routes and the pain of 'new' information about the loss of loved ones could not be avoided. This was the case as an 'account' in the War Dragon gave an insight into the final moments of Corner's nephew, 2nd. Lt. Edward Franklin Corner. Published in the July 1916 issue, almost nine months after his death, the account is amongst the Old Boys' Jottings:

From the 'War Dragon' under the initials C. H. C., we find the following, describing an incident in the Battle of Loos. *'Young Corner, one of our machine gun officers, a boy of about nineteen, was leading a platoon not far from me, looking deadly serious, with his revolver held well out in front of him and a man carrying the machine gun alongside him. I shouted out some ribald remark, to which he responded with a laugh and a wave of his revolver over his head. Poor boy, he never returned from that adventure, and died with his machine guns, of which he was so proud.'*

December 1916, April 1917, July 1917 –
Published together probably in Sept./Oct. 1917

In the war years, outside influences often impacted on the publication of the Magazines and created a tension between 'reporting' the words of Old Boys and informing the reader about everyday School life. This is the case for the next edition which was published in the Autumn 1917, a year later than expected. The Editorial explains why:

Editorial Autumn Term, 1916

The 'chair of excuses' would form an excellent title for the chair we now occupy. The chief point of this exordium will be its brevity. We only want to tell our year-long patient reader that this time considerations of the censorship forbade the earlier publication of this journal – "Our Mag." Censored! Strange, but true it is in this troubled world! Briefly, to explain, it contained too much information in its pages, in the letters and in the list of those serving. Had we complied with the censor's requirements at that time, the Mag. would have lost more than half its interest.

The great preparation for the Battle of the Somme gave rise to this necessity. That is now past, and so are Arras and Messines, and some of our bravest fellows have fallen and many have been wounded. They have achieved undying glory for their native land, and laurels which in the annals of their School will never fade.

We have thought it better to put all the Extracts of O. B. letters, and the jottings, at the end of the four numbers. We crave pardon for omission and inaccuracies. We would have liked more time to do justice to them, but rather than another holiday should begin, we send you what we can.

It seems remarkable that the School Magazine was considered so 'dangerous' that it was subject to censorship and kept out of circulation for a year. It shows us just how much of interest was in the 'Extracts of Letters from the Head's Letter Bag', not simply for readers in the School, Old Boys and the community at large. The Magazines contained too much information and detail.

As already stated, the December 1916, April 1917 and July 1917 editions were published together. The first two were very short and contained little but the July 1917 edition was large. Here were included obituaries for those boys lost since 1915 and not yet remembered, an updated, and much enlarged, 'List of Old Boys Serving Their Country' as well as a large number of 'Extracts of Letters from the Head's Letter Bag'. The Somme and Battle of Arras had been and gone, but the impact of those battles was clear. Whereas the deaths of Kidner, Corner, Baker and Treble had been met with shock and almost disbelief that the war could intrude in this way, there seems to have been a pervading sense of weary acceptance as news was brought of casualties and deaths almost daily.

Editorial, July 1917

If one editorial was short, this must be shorter, for see how the volume swells! To present boy readers we will say "we are proud when we see what our old boys are doing in every part of the Front – and the Front is almost the world now. It behoves us then to emulate them and keep the Old School going strong in its best traditions, for so shall we do our bit best." Our cricket has been knocked to pieces, but we can truly say that what cricket there has been, has been very keen. The O.T.C. was probably never more flourishing.

To Old Boy readers we say, simply and truly, "We are very proud of you and wish you God-speed and trust that this volume, long delayed, will bring you some pleasure if also, alas, some pain. It will remind you of home and show you that, at any rate, you are not forgotten."

The Editorial is immediately followed by George Corner's third letter to his 'dear Old Boys'. The tone feels much more sombre than the previous letters. Perhaps emotional exhaustion has played a part. It is interesting to note that the Headmaster refers to the Magazine as being *'a message and a newspaper of many of your schoolfellows.'* In this letter, there is a sense that Corner feels a little despondent that he is not fighting alongside 'his' boys. The routine of running a school remains his focus but there is, perhaps, a wistful regret that he could not contribute more effectively to the war. He refers to his not choosing a life of *'tame security'* and acknowledges his role as that of the chronicler, *'We will applaud your deeds and chronicle them with affection since equal them we cannot.'*

The Head's Letter to Old Boys **July 1917**

My dear Old Boys,

My chief concern in handing to you a copy of the Magazine in which you find these words, is the incompleteness of the volume, and the somewhat barren reference to your heroic deeds and sufferings. These pages chronicle in meagre fashion the doings of some of you for nearly a year. I know how inadequate they are. Many of you could fill a book of absorbing interest with the story of your own experiences. Still, for all that I know that you will welcome these pages as being a message, I had almost said from home, and as a newspaper of many of your old schoolfellows.

A busy year of routine work has not allowed me to devote a small fraction of the time that the work demands. With some help from Dibble, and from Miss Corner, I have just thrown together such material as has come into my hand. You will, I know, be interested, sadly interested, in many of its pages, as I indeed am deeply touched in the compilation of them. We labour on in the same old groove – you are cutting new ones; some of us, apart from the absorbing interest in the doings of all those who are fighting our battles, are living lives from which the deeds of which most of you are now daily witnesses, are strangely distant. Some of you have crowded into one brief year experiences that but three years ago would have more than filled a lifetime – we here add one slow deed to another in life's long course, but you sadly achieve the glory of immortal need in one short, quick life of energy, thronged with high tensed action.

We may both have our goal, but it is hard to understand why you do battle – many of you are hardly hit – but we labour on in ordinary toil.

It is not for us to know perhaps, hardly wonder why – one thing we feel – we would not compare our inconspicuous lot with yours, but rather regard you as chosen spirits born to free the earth from tyranny. Be it so – our hearts throb with yours; it is not our choice to live a life of tame security. We will applaud your deeds and chronicle them with affection since equal them we cannot. That you may all be spared to see your well-loved ones once more is the sincere wish of

Your old master and friend,

G. C.

The 'Roll of Honour' of eleven of the Old Boys who fell can be seen towards the end of the Magazine. With pages of photographs, those killed, wounded and serving are 'chronicled'. We can only assume that Corner himself wrote the obituaries – the last act he could do for his dear Old Boys. The Old Boys remembered in this Magazine include Gordon, Brown, Bilton, Annal, Farrant, Ford, Bowerman, Rowe, Brooks, Powell and Clode. Before the obituaries, the Latin "Procul hinc ante diem periere. Sed milites sed pro patria" appeared – it roughly translates as "A man who died young far away, but a soldier and for his country".

After the Obituary Notices, a more holistic view of the Old Boys serving is presented. It starts with the 'Decorations and Mentions' (there are eight in total), the current 'Roll of Honour' (17 men) and those wounded (30 men). Next follows an updated 'List of Old Boys Serving Their Country'. Over 280 Old Boys were serving or had served. In a school of just over 100 pupils at any one time, this figure is high.

School Magazines from December 1917 to December 1921 – Distributed in January 1922 as one collection

There seems to be a little confusion over the next Magazines and when they were published. The next volume opens with a Preface and this is immediately followed by a letter from George Corner, dated November 1921 and January 1922 respectively. It is perhaps best, therefore, to look at the next issues as a collective as editions from 1918 to 1922 seem to have been published at the same time. Given the assiduous detail seen in other Magazines, it seems a little strange that four years have gone by before the editions examining the end of the war are published. Corner's letter shows how School business has occupied him and it could very well be that the task of sorting and editing the letters from Old Boys was a 'duty' that demanded to be done well and to do this both space and time were needed. Corner appears to be exhausted, both physically and emotionally, in this letter. Constant striving for new buildings and funding initiatives to carve a future for the School together with the sheer size of the 'serious job' of doing his Old Boys justice have taken their toll. Though there are April, July and December editions for each year, they were read together.

General Editorial Letter **January 1922**

My dear Old Boys,

At last this volume long expected, patiently awaited, is in your hands, and I trust that the pleasure of having it in your hands will banish all feelings of disappointment, which I know very many, indeed all of you, must have felt during the past four years – you have asked again and again for it and you have received nothing; no doubt you have groused a little. I do not wish to stand long between you and the following pages – but I must say just this. It will be plain to you on scanning the pages that no small portion, and not the least interesting, consists of extracts from my Old Boys' letters. These letters had to be read and searched for news and I could not give this task to another. This August-September of 1921 is the first uninterrupted leisure I have had, in which I could grapple with a task, which by mere accumulation, had become a serious one. The summer Holidays of 1918 were claimed by The Willows. Overside consumed the leisure of 1919 and the Building of the Engine House, rendered imperative by the large extensions, absorbed 1920. These three jobs in which I was busy in a way in which it is difficult to explain, and could not avoid, constituted a tax on my energies and time which I could not easily face again. One was indeed 'all out': and that is one's only 'apologia'.

To those who had to build, with limited means, during those trying years, some of my meaning will be clear, but why need I stay you longer? The Mag. is out.

I am,

Yours sincerely,

George Corner

1918

The Magazines record events and responses to them from 1918. The British had experienced brutal fighting and losses and these setbacks affected the mood of the School. Those writing the Editorial in July 1918 refer to the response of the pupils as news of retreats and lost battles were reported. The language conveys the mood clearly: *'gloom', 'reverse of our forces', 'furious attacks of the Germans', 'struggles' and 'raids, rations and restrictions'.* Mention is made of the American forces that used the School facilities and there seems to be a more positive outlook from July although the cricket season was impeded by potatoes in the field and an outbreak of influenza meant the O. T. C. Camp was cancelled. Given the huge loss of life around the world from influenza, there doesn't seem to have been any serious complications in Wellington.

Editorial July 1918

The gloom engendered by the great reverse of our forces at St. Quentin was largely dispelled when we met for the Summer Term. The furious attacks of the Germans had been held. The Channel ports were saved. The struggles around Mount Kemmel and Bailleul had greatly told on the enemy's morale. The French and English had seconded one another with splendid spirit and the new American forces had been brigaded with us. At home, the talk, when it was not of the deeds abroad, was ever more of raids and rations and restrictions.

It was not until mid-July that buoyancy was restored. The great summer attack of the Germans was failing, Rheims was saved, although its sacred shine bore grievous mark of shot and shell and bomb, and the immortal and final counterattack of the Allied Armies was beginning under Foch.

In the Cricket Field, we still had to contemplate a large portion tilled for potatoes, and tennis racquets were put away, and garden tools alone were of any use upon the Lawn.

We were all looking forward to the restoration of camp when a wave of influenza caused the War Office to cancel this, and with it went Camp and all End of Term celebrations. It was not the best of Terms. We were greatly delighted to hear of the honour paid to 'Gillie Garnsey,' and an appreciation of the work of Sir Gilbert Garnsey will be found in our pages.

After four long years at war, the December edition of 1918 was written after the Armistice had been declared and a newfound sense of relief and jubilation can be seen in the Editorial, *'a mad orgy of delight such as none could ever remember or is ever to see again.'*

Editorial December 1918

When we returned from our holidays the British Armies under Haig were beginning to make their influence felt in the northern sectors. The Hindenburg Line had crumbled, and eyes were already being turned to Mons and the Rhine beyond, but probably few realised the end of the struggle was so near. After the four long years of ceaseless effort and bitter struggle, it was difficult to understand the meaning of "cease fire". The word Armistice was so strange a word that one almost dreaded that some hidden terror lurked behind it. But no, it was true, the Great War was over, submarines would no longer be the peril of the seamen, the infantryman would ground his arm, the deadly aeroplane would sail the night

THE WILLOWS, 1918.

no more. It was true, and England, and indeed the world, gave vent to a mad orgy of delight such as none could ever remember or is ever like to see again. The Germans had sued for peace.

In School Life proper the chief event was the institution of 'The Willows,' the new house, which, in spite of all difficulties, had been slowly taking shape during the late summer and the following months. Our columns must tell the other news.

In this edition, an unknown pupil writes about the experience of 11th November 1918. After four years of war, jubilation and celebration accompanies the news that it has finally ended.

November 11th, 1918

We had paid our usual break-time visit to the tuck-shop, and the Upper V. Form was settling down to "practical chemistry" when the fire hooter at the Gas Works began to make itself heard. Chemistry lost its usual interest, and one began to hear whispers of "wonder where it is?" and similar enquiries. Suddenly an excited youth burst into the labs and informed all and sundry (at the top of his voice!) that the Armistice terms had been agreed to and signed by the Huns.

By this time our interest in Chemistry had really disappeared; some people even forgot themselves to the extent of shouting and being 'rowdy' in class!!

We then received the order to fall in in front of the New Buildings, and this having been done, we moved off in two squads to the corner of the field in which the flagstaff had recently been re-erected.

Cheers were raised as the flag was hoisted, for the King and the Allied Generals, and immediately afterwards the Headmaster made a short speech, in which we were reminded that in the midst of our joy we ought not to forget those who had fallen.

School was then dismissed, and we proceeded in a body to inspect the decorations of the town. Having done this we decided that things were not quite as they should be, so we returned to School, and the band prepared to march.

Wellington then realised that there was an "Armistice on"; we paraded the principal streets, our ranks stretching across the whole width of the street, with a large flag borrowed (?) from the front of the shop, at our head. Our band (assisted by various "amateurs" armed with tin cans) played lustily, and those who were not members of the band gave vocal assistance.

This went on until after our usual dinner time, but at last everyone returned to School, and it was announced that the Corps would parade at three o'clock.

We fell in accordingly at the appointed hour and marched to the open space in front of the Post Office. Speeches were made by various prominent people, between which, the Town Band (spurred on doubtless by our efforts of the morning) played patriotic music. Our Corps and the V.T.C., who were also present, then "fixed" and "presented arms", while the buglers sounded the "General Salute". The meeting was concluded by the firing of a "feu de joie" by the Corps and the V.T.C.

In the evening a Church Parade was held to attend the thanksgiving service in the Parish Church. It may be noted that the band is not praised in this account, but the writer objects to blowing his own trumpet (or bugle). Nevertheless, the band certainly did its fair share in making the Armistice celebration a success.

1919 - The Move to Peace

The transition from War to peace was immediate in some respects but in others, it was a process that had only begun with the Armistice. The Magazines still carried 'Extracts from the Head's Letter Bag' and 'Jottings of Old Boys' but attention was, under Corner's desire to find a 'fitting memorial' to the fallen, turning to how best to recognise and remember the sacrifice of the 37 Old Boys. Those who served were 'Welcomed Back' and it was hoped that the adjustment back to life in peacetime would be smooth.

April 1919 Editorial

WELCOME TO OUR SOLDIER OLD BOYS

"Cedant arma togae." Let warfare give place to the duties of peace – such was the war-tired wish of the ancient Roman, and surely if anyone has a right to express that wish, it is our brave returning soldiers, men who have hazarded their lives for right and reason, for hearth and home and their country's liberty. We welcome you all back, brave soldiers, and may it go well with you. Some of you are now exchanging the ceaseless jar of march and camp and fire of more than four years' war for works of peace and you are turning your faces homewards. Oh, it will be good to be at home once more, and we welcome you. You have been sorely tried and splendidly you have stood the test. We are very proud of you. You are returning to your old labours, but we will never forget your deeds in war. Well may England be proud of you, brave soldiers, and may she never prove unmindful. We hold out our hands to you and welcome you and wish you well wherever fortune calls you.

Some of you return this term to our midst to take up the trail of your work where you left it. Strange faces you may find, but the hearts are right and all the same old sort, and you have never been forgotten. So welcome again to the Old School, welcome and well done!

The July 1919 Magazine reported on the reunion that occurred on July 16th. Old Boys and the present pupils gathered together at the Parish Church for a Memorial Service. There was a slow march to the church. Not everyone who wanted to attend was able to, but many who were not there were remembered.

"Breathes there a man with soul so dead
Who never to himself hath said:
This is my own, my native land!
Whose heart hath ne'er within him burned
As home his footsteps he hath turned
From wandering on a foreign land?"

THE REUNION, 1919

Editorial

Last term we bade our Old Boys welcome from afar; this term we have seen many of them again in our midst and wished them Godspeed. If the reunion did not gather all whom we had hoped to see, we must remember that life is difficult and homes are distant. Yet none the less we had a notable gathering and we remembered those who wished to be with us but could not be, and they were many. We remembered too those who return to us no more. The service in the Chapel was all that we could desire for such a service; of this and the other meetings, we give a full account.

The Reunion Sermon

'HE THANKED GOD AND TOOK COURAGE'
ACTS XXVIII. 15.

"This is what St. Paul did after he had been through a very rough time. Christianity at that time had existed for some twenty-eight years and the sound of it had gone through all the world. It had only begun and there was a tremendous lot more to do, but there at that spot on the Appian Way, was held as it were, a rally of the brethren, and the Apostle "thanked God and took courage." Is it forcing it too far to say that that meeting on the Appian Way has in a degree its counterpart here this morning? I do not know what these brethren talked about, but no doubt with St. Paul they all thanked God and took courage. You will notice the expression used, "The Meeting of the Brethren." Whether past or present members, the old School does knit us into a brotherhood; so here in Wellington Parish Church, the Church that brings back old associations and memories to many of us, we today gather for the dual purpose, viz: to thank God and take courage. First to thank God. It is doubtless with mingled feelings we join in such a service as this; we remember before God those of the School who have laid down their lives in the great cause of Right versus Might, and while we remember those who died, there is our sympathy with those to whom they were bound by close ties of relationship and affection. That personal loss is not to be talked about; we stand by in respect for their sorrow;

but we would say this; may they realise more and more fully with so many who have been bereaved during these past years of war, that those who pass from our sight do not pass out of the love and care of our Heavenly Father, that though the gulf seems so deep, and the veil so impenetrable, there is no separating loss or veil in His sight between the living and those whom we call "dead" for all live unto Him. These lives that we today remember before God, were laid down for us so that no invading Army landed on our shores – why? Because those gallant lads at the Front, Soldiers, Sailors, and Airmen, so tied the enemy up that they could not carry out their purpose of invasion of these shores; this we owe to those gallant fellows who have as truly fought for the defence of England as if the battle had been on English ground. The sights witnessed by those who have been on the battlefield or at the collecting stations, who have stood by a soldier's grave over there, the cruelties and brutalities of the foe, the sights seen even in London or in some of the East End districts during the air raids, those sights, I say, we shall never forget. These were sights which those who live in quiet towns like Wellington and have slept by night in peace have been spared. These memories stir our minds surely to acknowledge the debt we owe to those between forty [sic] members of our School who have fought and died for us. To them, we would bring our wreath of grateful memory to lay upon their graves, and thank God for them, for they were true to the traditions of our race. What can we do then today but speak out our thanks to those of the old School who laid down their lives with a smile, and for their sufferings cheerfully borne, for the sacrifice of which we who are alive feel we are hardly worthy. Could we speak now face to face with them, we could not utter better words than those used by the Head Master in one of his letters to the Old Boys: - "It is not for us to know, perhaps hardly wonder why. We feel we would not compare our inconspicuous lot with yours, but rather regard you as Chosen Spirits, born to free this earth from tyranny; be it so, our hearts throb with yours. It was not our choice to live a life of tame security: we would applaud your deeds and chronicle them in affection, since equal them we cannot." They loved not their lives unto the death, those members of the old School, and they have shown us that there is something more precious than life – precious as life is – there is witness to the faith, upon which the future depends. It reminds us of the faith and patience of the Saints. Saints! Probably when they were boys at School, as we all were, they were called anything but Saints by those in authority, perhaps the old "Detention Book" was anything but a record of the names of Saints, but there was the stuff in them that comes out, as it always does come out in the healthy-minded Schoolboy, in times when pluck and endurance is called for, and they were found worthy. Perhaps they were not all Saints, but they were all Souls, worthy Souls, every one of them in the hand of God by a baptism of blood. In our sight today, they climbed the steep ascent of duty, patriotism, and honour, so we thank them, and we thank God for them.

It is part of the goodly heritage of the School, and of the Town, and in the hearts of all associated with the School is the triumphant thought that the lives of our Old Boys of Wellington, so ungrudgingly given, will live forever not only in the old School, but in our Country's Roll of Honour; so for them and for the peace they died to win, we thank God, and not only do we thank God, but we take courage. Through these long years of war, anxiety and sorrow, we believe that God has been guiding and leading us onwards and upwards, and now he has given us peace. He has given us the greatest Victory ever won by Freedom over Tyranny, by Right over Wrong. The mighty German Army which had been preparing for forty years to dominate the world lies in the dust. The German Navy is at the bottom of the sea. This has been brought about by the help of God to whom we cried in our trouble, and He delivered us in our distress. We may be certain that God has some great purpose in protecting our Nation and Empire, and

THE RETURN FROM THE MEMORIAL SERVICE.

dull will be the heart and feeble the mind that will forget the lesson we have learned in the past years. Realising then what God has done for us in the past, and having sufficient faith in His goodness and mercy, we may take courage to meet the future with its pressing problems in a wise, patient and unselfish spirit. Upon us all, a very heavy responsibility is resting now that the war is over, and each individual must bear his share in that responsibility. There is work for everyone to do, and those who at this time and during the coming years slack and grouse and criticise will do the country a great disservice. Our foe is only waiting for a division amongst us, or for the country to go to sleep. A special responsibility rests upon schools and their work, and upon every member of every school, and I know full well that all connected with our own School will willingly and cheerfully bear their part. The Old Boys of the School tried to show a good record during the past years, for their Country and the Honour of the School, and those who have been spared will continue to do so, each in his degree, and to you present members of the School may I, not simply as a stranger, but as an Old Boy myself, and therefore I hope as a friend, may I exhort you to remember that you have responsibilities now still greater than ever before to your School and to your Country. Some of you were at School during the war years; you could not join the ranks of fighting men, but you can join the ranks of the Army of Reconstruction by equipping yourselves physically and mentally for the work that lies before you as citizens of our Country and Empire; therefore, take courage. You know sometimes we are apt to get discouraged because our Army does not seem to count for much. A taper lay in a drawer when its owner took it out and carried it away, "Where are you taking me?" asked the taper, "To show big ships their way across the sea," was the reply. "but no ships could see by means of my tiny light," "Leave that to me," said the owner, as he lighted the lantern and blew the taper out. Great days and great work lie ahead, work in which the Public Schools – and Wellington School by its keenness, its games, its patriotic spirit, is to build up, to consolidate today, and grow firm and strong, in purpose. That magnificent thing which we can hardly describe, but whose efforts can be seen, that magnificent thing, which has so splendidly shown itself in the past, and will again in the future, "THE PUBLIC SCHOOL SPIRIT," will be a strong help and guide to us. As long as we can keep this spirit alive and bright, we may take courage. The Public Schools may have their faults, but they are gloriously redeemed today by shining virtues. No need was there of conscription or compulsion; those who learned to play the game at School, rushed to play it in the field of battle, and sport is not merely the dissipation of the idle, but is, as has been shown, part and parcel of the philosophy of life. We may take courage then, as we face the future. We for our School and for our country nourish and foster the secret underlying soul of the Public School Spirit, which is so finely interpreted by Sir Henry Newbolt: -

"To set the cause above renown,
To love the game beyond the prize,
To honour, while you strike him down,
The foe that comes with fearless eyes;
To count the life of battle good,
And dear the land that gave you birth,
And dearer yet the brotherhood
That binds the brave of all the earth."

Thank God and take courage, peace will have her victory not less renowned, and in a way a victory more glorious, because it leaves no aftermath of sorrow or of pain, and if we all put School first, and self, last, Country first and self, last, giving our very best in our work, in our games, in our prayers, if we are faithful to God, and faithful to one another, we shall help the life of every day to move to grander music than has ever yet fallen on the listening ears of men. This, my brothers and comrades remains for you and for me to do, and this will be the best tribute we can offer to those who have laid down their lives for us, and those of our old School boys whom we remember today in Wellington Parish Church.

Forget them not, O land, for which they fell,
May it go well with England, still go well,
Keep her bright banners without block or stain,
Lest they should dream that they have died in vain.

'Per aspera ad astra, per augusta ad augusta.'

Rev. J. E. D. Pratt

Chapter 3

Remembering The Fallen Of Wellington School, 1914-1918

"We feel we would not compare our inconspicuous lot with yours, but rather regard you as Chosen Spirits, born to free this earth from tyranny; be it so, our hearts throb with yours. It was not our choice to live a life of tame security: we would applaud your deeds and chronicle them in affection, since equal them we cannot." (George Corner)

Poppy found by the roadside in the Somme, July 2018.

PTE. J. G. ANNAL, 4TH S.L.I.
Wounded in Mesopotamia, died a prisoner in hands of Turks June 15th, 1916.

Private John Gerard Annal

b. 1892 – died 15th June 1916, aged 24

'He worked well, and his spare time was chiefly spent reading, to which he was devoted.'

School Magazine, July 1916

John Gerard Annal is Remembered with Honour on the Basra Memorial. On 9th November 2008 he was remembered by Darks House and flowers were placed in Chapel in his memory.

John Gerard Annal was born in St. Ives, Huntingdon to Henry Sinclair (b. 1859) and Caroline (nee Jowitt) (b. 1859). At the time of his birth, he had two older sisters: Annie Dorothy (b. 1889) and Grace Elizabeth (b. 1890). His father was a chemist.

The years between 1894 and 1897 must have been very traumatic for the Annal family. Twins Mary and Maud were born in 1894 but died the same year. Geoffrey was born in Melksham in 1896 but passed away in 1897. Henry Norman was born in 1897 but also died shortly after birth. Out of seven children, only three remained alive after 1897.

The 1901 census placed the family in Melksham living in Bank Street. Henry was still a chemist and the children were aged 12, 10 and 9 respectively.

By 1911, there had been some movement. John was living with the Shepherd family at Malvern House, Hill Road, Clevedon and training to be a chemist. Annie was living with her parents in Melksham and Grace was living in the West Riding of Yorkshire and noted as a student in training.

John Gerard Annal's War

In the 'List of Old Boys Serving Their Country' published in the December 1914 edition of the Magazine, Annal is recorded as follows: **Annal, J. G. Pte. G Co. 5th Battalion Somerset Light Infantry, India**. He joined up in Bath soon after war was declared.

As part of the 1/4 Battalion of the S. L. I., it seems that Annal left Southampton on 9th October and disembarked at Bombay on 9th November 1914. The Division was to stay in India for the duration of the war.

Annal was one of the more prolific letter writers and his correspondence with George Corner shows us much about life for the troops in hot, foreign climes.

Pte. J. G. Annal, of the Somerset Light Infantry, writes on November 9th 1914, from Bombay as follows:-

At last, we are really here, we left on Oct. 9th and it is now Nov. 9th. We arrived here at about 2 pm today and it is now 6.30pm. It is a beautiful sunset and from where we are Bombay looks a splendid town. The first boat to welcome us was a Y. M. C. A. boat. They really do splendid work amongst the troops. Towards the end of this voyage, we had several games of cricket which were ripping. We have just received a rotten order. The whole of the battalion was going to Bangalore, but now we are to be hopelessly split up and sent to various small stations.

As far as Gibraltar there were 11 transports and two British cruisers, we came on to Malta without an escort. From Malta to Port Said we were escorted by two French cruisers, "Charlemagne" and "St. Louis". We had three days at Suez and then proceeded with a French cruiser, the "Dupleix," together with one or two scouts.

We have over 1500 men on our boats, 800 men of the 4th Somersets and 4 batteries of Artillery of Wilts, Devon, Hants and Dorsets.

Tuesday morning 8 a.m.

We are now in a huge dock, "The Alexandra Dock," and enjoying a huge feast which I can assure you is well earned.

Pte. J. G. Annal also writes on Nov. 16th 1914, from Wellington Barracks, Nilgiri Hills, the following:-

We arrived in Bombay on Monday and came into harbour on Tuesday morning. One or two of us managed to get into the town and it was really of absorbing interest. On Wednesday morning we entrained and started about noon. We were in the train, excepting a stop every few hours, until we arrived here on Sunday, Nov. 15th, so we were in the train 4 days. There were fourteen in our carriage but there was room for us to lie down. For food, we had tea, tinned beef, bread and jam and cheese. We went within 20 or 30 miles of Madras and then branched off to here. "The Buffs" (or East Kent Regiment) were here at Wellington. We also passed the Dublin Fusiliers who came from Madras. Also in Bombay harbour, we passed quite 50 transport ships, which are to take British and Native troops over. "The Buffs" will have a few days leave and then go to France. They are a splendid lot of fellows and are all eager to get at the Germans.

The Nilgiri Rock Railway is a marvellous engineering achievement and it took us from the plains to here. We are 6,500 feet above sea level. The scenery along this railway was grand. It resembled that of North Wales, but on a far larger scale. One could look out of the carriage window on a sheer drop of 600 or 700 feet. There are 21/2 companies of us here, the remainder of the Battalion having gone to Madras and Malappuram. We are all delighted with our surroundings. The country here is like a large estate, pretty bungalows, well-kept roads, splendid scenery and an English climate. I feel in the pink of condition. All the work is done by the natives and seriously, I think I shall get generally slack.

Pte. J. G. Annal, F Co., 4th Somerset Light Infantry, Amritsar, N. India, writes on April 5th 1915:

On Wednesday is the Anniversary of Jellalabad (the most important "honour" of this regiment) and they are holding battalion sports at Jullundur. We sent two men from each company for each event. I have entered for the high jump. I don't expect to get anything as there is some hot stuff in one or two of the companies.

I have to go to the Orderly Room tomorrow for the first time for a petty offence. I may get off or I may get three days C.B. I really don't care a straw what happens only C. B. is a bit of a nuisance, as you have to report yourself to the Guardroom at 12.30 p.m., 2.30 p.m. and every half hour until 9 p.m. A whole crowd of our company got 14 days C. B. last week for playing Canker after "lights out." At present, the Regimental Bazaar is out of bounds owing to the plague. Plague is a fearful disease out here and people die like flies. It is carried chiefly by the fleas found on rats.

April 13th. *Last Tuesday 25 of us went to Jullundur for the Sports. There were a large number of entries for every event, and all were well contested. On the Tuesday evening the heats were run (and jumped). There were about 20 entries for the high jump and 4ft. 9ins. saw 9 of us left in.*

A violent thunderstorm caused the sports proper to be postponed until the Thursday evening. I was fourth in the high jump, so got no prize. Two of them cleared 5ft 1 in. which is remarkably good jumping. We brought back 3 second prizes and 2 thirds. It is much cooler at Jullundur during the night and we all slept well for the first time in some weeks as there were very few mosquitoes.

April 21st. *Well, we've stuck[sic] the heat right enough now. It was 96° in the shade and 126° in the sun today, but they tell us that we shall get it hotter by 20° yet. We have got our mosquito curtains now. They are a great boon, as they keep off the mosquitoes by night and the flies by day. We have had several cases of sunstroke, nothing really serious though.*

May 10th, 1915 *The probable has happened, and we are leaving for the Gulf on Friday, May 14th. We leave here for Karachi on Friday evening, when we shall embark together with similar units from various battalions. Our unit comprises one officer, a sergeant, one corporal, two lance-corporals and I think 28 men. There are about 24 of F Company, so we shall be pals together. We have been issued with various equipment, and on Sunday last the Colonel and Lieutenant-Colonel came to inspect us. He made a very impressive little speech, telling us he wished that he might come with us, and giving some very sound advice. I'm afraid the sun is a greater peril than the Turks. However, we have padded spine protectors and helmets with back flaps. It is to my mind rather a scandal that though we have only been issued with one shirt and one pair of socks in India, we are obliged to have three sound shirts and pairs of socks and have to pay for the remainder out of our princely screw.*

We shall now receive service pay which is 6d. a day extra, and I believe we are entitled to £5, blood money. So it is a case of either a medal or a bullet now. I have often read accounts of fighting there in the Indian papers and it seems that on the whole, it is not severe. At present, the Turks are concentrating their efforts on the Dardanelles where the British force is very strong so that I think our term of active service there will not be lengthy. It is quite likely that we may have to escort prisoners or ammunition from the base to the firing line. It will not be a picnic, but we are all looking forward to seeing a little of the real thing.

Forces War Records show that on 5th November 1915, Annal is 'Listed as "Wounded" on the Casualty List issued by the War Office.' He explained the situation to George Corner in his next letter.

Pte. J. Annal, ¼ Som. L. I., attached 2nd Dorsets, writes from Mesopotamia, October 8th 1915:

Am writing this in hospital in Amarah, which is a perfect heaven to our previous surroundings. I dropped you a line recently just to say that my wound was not serious. The Bishop of Lahore, who was visiting the troops, took the letter so you ought to have received it before this one. Apart from this, I haven't written since leaving Ali Al Garbi, so I'll try and give you a brief account of our doings since that date. Our brigade (censored) left (censored) on a Sunday and for 5 days we trekked it, keeping near the river. The marching was of the most fatiguing sort as the whole district near the river is traversed by great dykes used for irrigation purposes. Most of the ground has also recently been under cultivation but is now barren and like cement plough fields. The chief discomfort, however, is the sun, which made marching impossible after 9 or 10 am. We only averaged about 9 miles a day. The first day's march killed 3 men apart from dozens who were knocked up. The end of the fifth day's march brought us within 8 or 10 miles of the enemy's position and there we encamped at a place called Sannaiyat for 9 or ten days. The average day on the march was something like this – reveille 3 a.m., breakfast (so-called) 3.30 a.m., march off. Halt and pitch tents 9.30 a.m. or thereabout. We would then make slight entrenchments and do various fatigues. Tents were struck each evening at 6 p.m., and we slept in the open and were tormented by sand flies not to mention an everlasting dust.

At Sannaiyat, of course, it was unnecessary to strike tents each night, we merely found outposts, whilst each morning we had to "stand to arms" from 4 a.m. till 5.30 a.m. It was bitterly cold. On arrival at Sannaiyat, we had the misfortune to lose an aeroplane, which was compelled to descend in the enemy's lines. The pilot and observer were evidently unhurt as the Turks sent down for their belongings on the following day. Whilst standing to arms one morning when we were all half asleep and cold as you lie, we were startled by a huge explosion. It was a shell almost directly overhead. For 5 or 10 minutes they came in rapid succession from various places. By wonderful stroke of luck, nobody was touched as they all burst just beyond us. It appears they brought the guns down on a fast boat and re-embarked them and scouted at the first sign of dawn. We left Sannaiyat on a Friday and a short march brought us within 4 miles of the enemy's advanced position. No sooner had we halted and made a trench than they commenced to shell us, the first shell finding the range perfectly. Again, thanks to luck, our casualties were next to nothing. There was one incident however which I shall not easily forget. That was when a Sergeant of our platoon working on a bank with his entrenching tool trod on a mine and was terribly mutilated. He died a few minutes later. I was only a few yards from him at the time. I don't know if I am allowed to write of our doings, but I can hardly see how the information could influence anyone in the least.

On Saturday we remained in our position whilst the (censored) attacked and drove back their advanced post and entrenched themselves 300 yards from the enemy's main position. Our brigade moved off at 5 p.m. on the Sunday. We firstly advanced some way on the left bank of the river and there made ourselves conspicuous and raised a big dust with the intention of deceiving the enemy into believing that we were entrenching ourselves. As soon as the sun set, we retired, crossed the river by a pontoon bridge, and after a weary march halted at 10 p.m. and lay down until 2 a.m. The enemy had a wonderfully strong position on either side of the river, their front extending 4 or 5 miles. Our entire attack was launched from the right bank, and from the river itself by the heavy guns on barges. The Dorsets were in "General Reserve," that is, the last troops to be called upon. When after a circular route, the attack commenced we were left with the artillery and consequently were incessantly shelled. The Oxfords took the lead.

For a couple of hours, we did nothing but dig ourselves in and move round with the battery.

Then the Dorsets' C. O. was called for and we were informed that we were to reinforce the (censored). We fell in, and A and B Companies advanced after having extended 4 paces, and almost immediately we were under rifle fire. It is not much use trying to describe in detail what happened. Enough to say that we made some sort of record in taking a position strongly defended by barbed wire entanglements, landmines and cleverly constructed trenches, over 1,500 yards of perfectly open ground, in 20 minutes. As we took one they retired (or some of them did) to the next; there were in all 4 redoubts. Our regiment sustained (censored) casualties. Of the whole force engaged there were about (censored) casualties, of these the Dorsets claimed (censored). Many have since died of wounds. About half the 4th Somerset men were wounded, and of those 3 were killed. I was wounded about 200 yards before the first redoubt and was compelled to lie there in a perfect hail of bullets. I made a hole with my entrenching tool and buried my head and covered myself as far as possible with my equipment. The wound bled a good deal before I was able to bandage it. I then hobbled back with a few more unfortunates to the first dressing station. The retiring enemy kindly shelled us all the way back, and to me, it seems a marvel that we were not wiped out. I can fully appreciate some of the difficulties of the ambulance people, so the less said of our treatment the better. However, after 10 days of misery, we are now safely in hospital where we have the luxury of a bed and blankets to keep us warm and food which is rather an improvement on mouldy biscuits and salty bully beef. Yes, we are very comfortable here and already there is a great improvement in the fellows. The doctors have been busy extracting bullets and dressing wounds. Am glad to say that my wound is practically healed though I am quite unable to walk on my left leg. However, the bone can't be badly smashed as I walked a mile or so on it after I was shot. We each have a diet sheet.

Disease – G. S. W. ix 4 Tibea, left, slight.

Notes by Medical Officer – Wound in Action, 28/9/15, at Kut-al-Amara. Entrance wound, just below knee joint, slightly to inner side of middle line at level of insertion of patella ligament. Exit behind, 2" below level of entrance wound, inner side.

We are well off for smokes and reading material and have a topping tent which holds 9 of us. I must not tell you what the force is doing at present but I can assure you they are not idle. I wish I were with them. Of the enemy's casualties, I know little except they were considerably more than our own. We had 11 officers wounded, none killed, and only 2 seriously wounded, namely the C.O. and Adjutant.

This appears to be the last time Annal wrote to the School. At some point, he was a Prisoner of War and it is here he met his death. As the country reeled from the huge loss of life on the Somme, news broke of Annal's death. It is clear what an impact this had on the editors of the Magazine: *Jack Annal after being wounded died of dysentery in Turkish hands. This is all we know – it is very hard.*

Remembering John Gerard Annal

School Obituary

Pte. J. G. Annal, 4th S.L.I

Wounded in Mesopotamia, died a prisoner in hands of Turks June 15th 1916.

John Gerard Annal, only son of Mr Annal, of Melksham, Wilts, entered the School in September 1906, leaving in July 1908. He worked well, and his spare time was chiefly spent reading, to which he was devoted. At the outbreak of war, he joined the 1/4th Som. L. I., proceeding to India in 1915. In May of that year the Somersets, who had been attached to 2nd Dorsets, were ordered to Mesopotamia, and in October Jack Annal wrote from Hospital at Amarah giving a graphic description of the onward march and the hard fighting and privations of the gallant army. He was badly wounded in the left leg, and says, "I can fully appreciate the difficulties of the ambulance people, so the less said of our treatment the better. However, after 10 days of misery, we are now safely in Hospital." Having recovered he re-joined and unfortunately was taken prisoner by the Turks and was ultimately reported as having died in prison. Re-reading his letters which appeared in the Magazine, one realizes what a brave, adventurous soldier he was. All who remember Jack Annal sympathize deeply with his family.

Memorials

John Annal has two memorials: one in Melksham and one in Basra. The memorial in Melksham appears to be his parents' grave. Annal's name is entered at the very bottom of the memorial. As well as here, Annal's name is featured on the Malvern memorial, the Melksham town memorial and the memorial at St Michael's Church, Melksham.

The Basra Memorial - TWGPP

John Gerard Annal. Died while a Prisoner of War and is buried at Mosul 15/06/16 Panel 12.

PLEASE NOTE: Basra Memorial was originally erected in the city of Basra but was dismantled and re-erected in the Desert under Saddam Hussein's regime. The panels were poorly fitted and, in some cases, have now been destroyed. Many names are obscured by cement or damaged.[1]

Jack Annal's name is missing from the memorial.

[1] The War Graves Photographic Project.

2ND LIEUT. S. W. BAKER.
8th Batt. Som. L.I.
Killed in action at Loos, Sept. 26th, 1915.

2nd. Lieut. Silvanus Wilfred Baker

b. 1897 – died 26th September 1915, aged 18

"His loss was keenly felt by all. A brother officer writing to us refers to him as a most popular officer of the regiment, and we can well understand this; for at School he was always one of the most cheerful nature and always the same." School Obituary

Silvanus Wilfred Baker is Remembered with Honour on the Loos Memorial, Panel 38 and 3. In November 2018 he will be remembered by Beech House and a poppy will be placed in Chapel in his memory.

Silvanus Wilfred Baker was the second son of Silvanus Baker (b. 1866) and Kate Bishop (b. 1866). The couple married in July 1887 in Wellington and had three children: Conrad William Anthony (b.1896), Silvanus Wilfred (b. 1897) and Cecil Mary (b.1900).

In the 1901 census, the Baker family was living in 187 Western Road, Wellington. Silvanus Snr. was recorded as a Drapers Assistant. In 1911, the family moved to 64 Waterloo Road, Wellington. The three children were all in school and Silvanus's occupation was listed as Woollen Merchant's Assistant.

There does not appear to be much information about the family between 1911 and 1915, but it seems clear that tragedy struck in 1915 with the death of Silvanus and just a year after that, on 22nd October 1916, the death of his father.

Silvanus Wilfred Baker entered The County School in September 1909 and left in February 1915, to take up a commission in the Somerset Light Infantry. The number of times he is mentioned in the School Magazines show us what an influential and important role he played in the School.

Virtue Functi More Patrum Duces (July 1915):
Baker, S. W. entered September 1909, left Feb. 1915; VI Form Prefect, Spring 1913; Hon. Sec. Scientific Society, Spring 1913; Serg. in O.T.C., Spring 1914; Swimming Colours, Spring 1914; Cambridge Junior, 1910 (3rd Class Honours); Cambridge Senior 1912 (3rd Class Honours), 1913 (2nd Class Honours); 2nd Lieutenant 8th Somerset L. I. Feb. 1915; Address: 64, Waterloo Road, Wellington, Somerset. S. W. Baker ably edited the Christmas Mag.

Silvanus Wilfred Baker's War

Forces War Records tell us that the 8th Somersets completed their training towards the end of August 1915. ***"The 21st Division then received orders that it was to move to France. Advance parties left on 2nd September, the troops began to entrain on 7th September, and by 13th September the Division had concentrated in the Tilques area."*** [2]

[2] Forces War Records, https://www.forces-war-records.co.uk/records/1677708/second-lieutenant-silvanus-wilfred-baker-british-army-somerset-light-infantry/

Having been in France since only the 13th September, the 21st Division had not yet seen the trenches when it was involved in the Battle of Loos. It was stationed at Noeux-les-Mines as part of the General Reserve for the attack on Loos.

As part of the 21st Division, it appears that Baker would have been involved in a failed attack on Hill 70. The Division was fighting alongside 45th Infantry Brigade and was supported by 62nd Infantry Brigade, 10th Yorkshire Regiment and 12th Northumberland Fusiliers. They suffered *'considerable casualties from the Redoubt at the summit.'*

> ***"At 11.00 am, 63rd Infantry Brigade having re-grouped to the West, moved forward to attack trenches north of Loos but again lost direction. Turning south-east towards Hill 70 they came under flanking fire from Chalet Wood and Bois Hugo before retreating back to their start line.***
>
> ***Hill 70 having been captured by 21st Division, the remaining battalions of 64th Infantry Brigade, 9th King's Own Yorkshire Light Infantry and 10th King's Own Yorkshire Light Infantry were sent forward to support 21st Division, but instead began to charge on them, before being cut-down by German machine-guns. In its disastrous first action, the 21st Division suffered 4,501 casualties."*** [3]

Silvanus Wilfred Baker, aged just 18, was, tragically one of them. He had been in France for only a matter of weeks.

Silvanus Wilfred Baker's Death

For those receiving the July 1915 edition of the Magazine, news of the death of Silvanus Wilfred Baker and the 'missing' Edward Franklin Corner, would have come as a huge shock.

The Battle of Loos was a terrible confrontation and thousands would lose their lives. The edition already in print, had a note placed at the front, a small piece of paper to show that two of the School's most popular and promising pupils were lost.

Local newspapers printed the news:
News has just reached Wellington of the death of Lieut. Wilfred Baker, second son of Mr Silvanus Wilfred Baker, who was killed in the action during the recent advance of the British troops in France. Lieut. Baker was leading his men to what proved a successful issue when he was struck down by a shrapnel shell and killed instantly. Special reference was made to the sad event by the Rev. W. Hogan, at the South-street Baptist Chapel, on Sunday evening. He announced that next Sunday evening a memorial service would be held at the chapel with which Lieut. Baker was associated. He was only 18 years of age and left the Wellington School Cadet Corps to join Kitchener's Army. He could only have been in France a few days when he met his death. Widespread sympathy is felt locally for the family.[4]

[3] Forces War Records, https://www.forces-war-records.co.uk/records/1677708/second-lieutenant-silvanus-wilfred-baker-british-army-somerset-light-infantry/

[4] Western Times, Weds. 6th October 1915, British Newspapers Archive.

And a write up of the Memorial Service:

Memorial Service
There was a crowded congregation at the South-street Baptist Chapel on Sunday evening, when a memorial service to the late Lieut. Wilfred Baker of the Somersets was held. The service was conducted by the Rev. W. Hogan (pastor), and the front of the rostrum was draped with a Union Jack. In the course of his sermon, Mr Hogan asked why men should die in the name of duty. It was because they felt duty was higher than life itself. There were men too great to come down to the level of abject cowardice. He believed that was true of their brother who had been promoted to the Homeland. It was not easy to be true to one's principles in the Army, but they had those who, like their brother, would walk miles on a Sunday to go to a small Baptist Chapel. It had been said the loss of their brother, was a terrible thing, and so it was, but how often since he had been taken away had they heard words "How can a man die better than facing fearful odds?" or the saying of the old Greek "Those whom the Gods love die young." Behind the fighting line in France were great heroes, men of extraordinary fine character, and behind them was another fighting line that went to bed with wet eyes and a crying heart and spent the day in prayer for the boys. Their heroines were as great as their heroes at the Front, and he commended them to their prayers. At the conclusion of the service, Mr H. J. Passmore played the "Dead March".[5]

Remembering Silvanus Wilfred Baker

School Obituary

2nd Lieutenant S. W. Baker

8th Batt. Somerset Light Infantry

Killed in action at Loos, September 26th 1915.

2nd Lieutenant S. W. Baker was also killed in the terrible fighting of September 25th, 1915. The news of his death was conveyed to his mother by his old Schoolfellow, Lieut. W. H. A. Thorne, who was in the same regiment. He fell whilst gallantly leading his platoon in an advance. Wilfred Baker was only 18 and obtained his commission whilst still at School and was immensely liked by all. His career at School was most promising. Always a worker he carried off many prizes – amongst them the Senior French and Science. He was a Prefect of the School, Editor of the Magazine and a Platoon Commander in the O.T.C.. He also held a Certificate A. He was gazetted to the 8th Somersets in March and went to the Front in the following September – almost from the Classroom to the Front. He was a good scholar, one of the best French scholars we ever turned out, and indeed everything he did was characterized by thoroughness. His loss was keenly felt by all. A brother officer writing to us refers to him as a most popular officer of the regiment, and we can well understand this; for at School he was always one of the most cheerful nature and always the same.

Remembered In Wellington
In Wellington, S. W. Baker is remembered on the memorial in the town park and in St John's Church. He is also featured in the publication *Our Boys* by Mike Perry and Ray Hitchcock.

[5] Taunton Courier, and Western Advertiser, Wednesday 20th October 1915, British Newspapers Archive

2ND LIEUT. L. A. E. S. BILTON, Killed Spring, 1917.

2nd Lieut. Lewis Albert Edward Sam Bilton

b. 1895 – died 23rd April 1917, aged 22.

"Seeing no chance of active service, he applied for a commission to get the chance to go to France and was gazetted with the Buffs, being sent to France at once. Writing home, he said that he felt that at last, he was in the right place. His loss to his home is irreparable."

School Obituary

L. A. E. S. Bilton is Remembered with Honour in St. Patrick's Cemetery, Loos. In November 2018 he will be remembered by Fox's House and a poppy will be placed in Chapel in his memory.

Lewis Albert Edward Sam Bilton was born in 1895 in Cardiff. He was the only son of George Albert Bilton and Annie Bilton. He had one sister, Mary Margaret Bilton, born in 1893. In 1901, the family was living in Leyton, Essex. In 1911, all were living in Teignmouth and running the London Hotel, except Lewis, who was boarding at Wellington School. Lewis, aged 15, is listed in the census alongside Edward Franklin Corner (15), Herbert George Shapland (14), John Henry Gent (15), Joseph Victor Pastfield (12), George Winton Powell (13) and Victor Tarbet (13).

Lewis Bilton played a very active part in School life and was successful in drama productions, music, sport and shooting. The Magazines record many of his achievements.

Bilton's School Departure

In April 1912 Magazine, Bilton's departure from the School is recorded: *'Entered May 1907, left December 1911, Form IV; Prefect, Autumn 1911; Cambridge Junior, 1910; 1st XI Colours, Football, Spring 1911; Sergeant in O.T.C., Autumn, 1910.*

The School remained very important to Bilton and he was recorded as visiting in July 1915.

Lewis A. E. S. Bilton's War

Bilton signed up for the War in 1914 and we know from the Magazine of December 1914 that he was a Sapper in the Essex Royal Engineers, based at Landguard Fort Camp, Felixstowe. He wrote to George Corner and two of Bilton's letters were published in the war editions of the Magazine. They are slightly short and do not tell us much about fighting, but the desire and almost desperation to get to the front line are clear. He is very keen to do his duty, to *'revenge those of my school-fellows who have fallen'* and the frustration that he may not go, *'makes me mad'.* The letters are dated 4th July 1916 and February 5th 1917, just a couple of months before he was killed.

L. A. E. S. Bilton, R. E., Harwich, writes July 4th (1916):
You will see by the enclosed form that I am having another try for a commission.

The School Magazine came the other day, and I was awfully sorry to see about "Teddy" and Baker. It makes me mad to think that I am kept here when I so want to go out and try to revenge those of my schoolfellows who have fallen.

It seems my fate to have to stay in this company, which is very little good at all. But I mean to have another good try and get out of it.

Will you please do me the favour of signing the section regarding my education? I hope my O. C. will let me go.

Bilton was successful in joining the 1st Battalion, The Buffs, East Kent Regiment.

2nd Lieut. L. A. E. S. Bilton wrote shortly before he fell, February 5th, 1917:
I am gazetted as a regular officer in His Majesty's [the Buffs] (awfully pleased to get into them). I reported to Dover and was there a week with the 3rd Battalion. The adjutant then sent me home on five days' expeditionary leave. I reported on Saturday night. On Sunday afternoon the adjutant told me I was for France, so I packed up and rushed home. I leave for Folkestone tomorrow morning and cross on Wednesday. I will let you know how I get on if I have the chance.

Bilton's Medal Index Card says that he disembarked in France on 6th February 1917. Forces War Records tell us that at this time the 1st Battalion of the Buffs was around Hill 70, Lens, where it was involved in fighting from 13th April 1917. It is likely that Bilton was involved in this. The Battle of Hill 70 was 'inconclusive.'

On 16th April, a counter-attack drove 1st The Buffs (East Kent Regiment) back slightly but was unsuccessful against the 8th Bedfordshire Regiment on the right.

As was a further attack on them the following day. On 18th and 19th April, the 1st King's Shropshire Light Infantry and 8th Bedfordshire Regiment staged their own attack on the trenches of Hill 70 but weather conditions and strong defence allowed little gain.

On 20th April, battalions were rotated and 18th Infantry Brigade, 14th Durham Light Infantry and 11th Essex Regiment replaced 16th Infantry Brigade. On 21st April, 14th Durham Light Infantry staged an attack on a machine-gun post capturing 35 prisoners and 2 machine guns, in co-operation with 46th Division.

On 22nd April, both battalions attacked. 14th Durham Light Infantry securing the whole of their objective, with 46 prisoners and 3 machine-guns, although 11th Essex Regiment was unable to gain any ground.

A German counter-attack recovered much of the lost ground later that day and 6th Division was relieved that evening. Hill 70 was to be the scene of a major operation by Canadian forces in August 1917.[6]

Although there is no mention of fighting on 23rd April, the day Bilton was killed, it is very likely that he fell during this fighting. In a letter written to George Corner by his father, it appears that he was *'killed as he came out the Staff tent with one or two others.'*

[6] Forces War Records, https://www.forces-war-records.co.uk/records/1869906/second-lieutenant-l-a-e-s-bilton-british-army-buffs-east-kent-regiment/

Remembering 2nd. Lieut. L. A. E. S. Bilton

School Obituary

2nd Lieutenant L. A. E. S. BILTON

Killed Spring 1917.

L. A. E. S. Bilton, 2nd Lieut. East Kent Regiment, The Buffs, was the only son of Mr G. Bilton, of Teignmouth. He entered the School in May 1907, leaving in December 1911, and was at all times an earnest and steady worker. His special bent was engineering and his work in the Power House was his greatest pleasure. Lewis was much beloved by his schoolfellows, being not only of a happy disposition but absolutely reliable in matters of daily life. He was very smart and useful in the Corps, attaining the rank of Sergeant, and his shooting was excellent, shooting in the Jacoby Cup competition, scoring a fine 65. He was a keen footballer, becoming goal-keeper for the 1st XI. and always maintaining a sound, cool defence. In the cricket he was in his element with the gloves, thoroughly earning his colours. On leaving School he was at once apprenticed to Messrs. Crompton, of Chelmsford, electrical engineers and joined the Special Reserve of the R. E. On the outbreak of war he was offered a commission, which he declined, and was drafted to Harwich for two years being in charge of a section of the searchlights. Seeing no chance of active service, he applied for a commission to get the chance of going to France and was gazetted to the Buffs, being sent to France at once. Writing home, he said that he felt that at last, he was in the right place. His loss to his home is irreparable, and profound sympathy is felt for his parents, who have lost a brave, devoted son of whom, in the midst of their sorrow, they can be rightly proud.

Bilton is buried in St. Patrick's Cemetery, Loos.

Bilton's father decided the following words should be inscribed on his gravestone:

FOR EVER WITH THE LORD

He is commemorated on the Memorial Window of St James the Less Parish Church, West Teignmouth. The names of all 111 men from the parish who fell between 1914 and 1918 are represented in the window. Bilton was one of the 16 officers who died.

THE BUFFS
SECOND LIEUTENANT
L. A. E. S. BILTON
E. KENT REGT. (THE BUFFS)
23RD APRIL 1917 AGE 22

Wellington School Memorial Chapel – Letters to George Corner

In the papers of George Corner at the Somerset Archive, we found a series of letters addressed to Corner from the parents of those killed in the war, regarding the planned Memorial chapel. George Bilton wrote twice and the letters are copied here. The first shows the desperation of not knowing how exactly his son died as the War Office regarded the information as 'classified'. Dated in 1929, 12 years after Lewis Bilton fell, the pain is still raw.

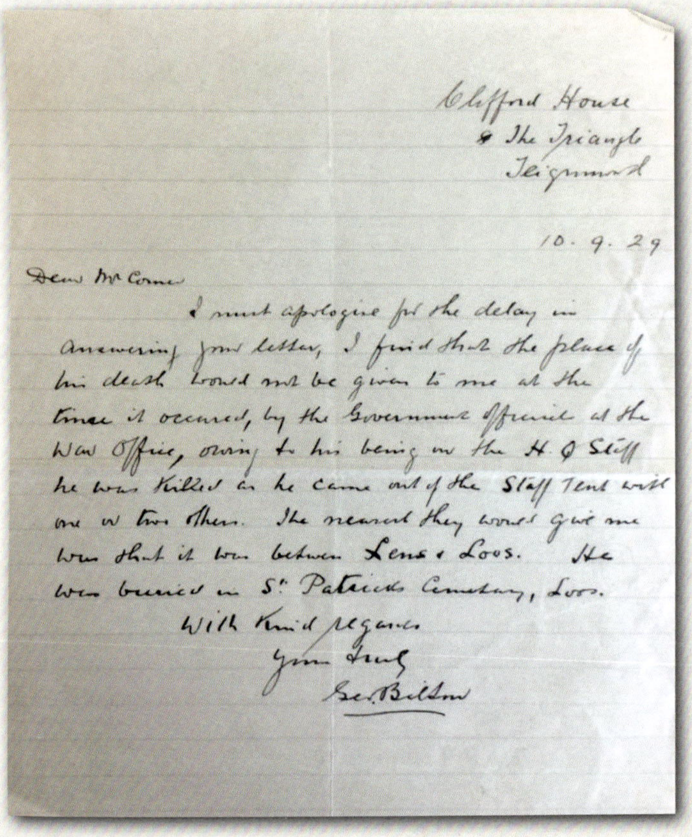

Clifford House
& The Triangle
Teignmouth

10. 9. 29

Dear Mr Corner

I must apologise for the delay in answering your letter, I find that the place of his death would not be given to me at the time it occurred, by the Government official at the War Office, owing to his being on the H. Q Staff he was killed as he came out of the Staff Tent with one or two others. The nearest they would give me was that it was between Lens & Loos. He was buried in St Patrick's Cemetery, Loos.

With kind regards
Yours truly
Geo. Bilton

Bilton's second letter outlines the exact names of his son. There is something very moving in this letter when Bilton's father refers to him as 'my boy' and 'were' not 'are'.

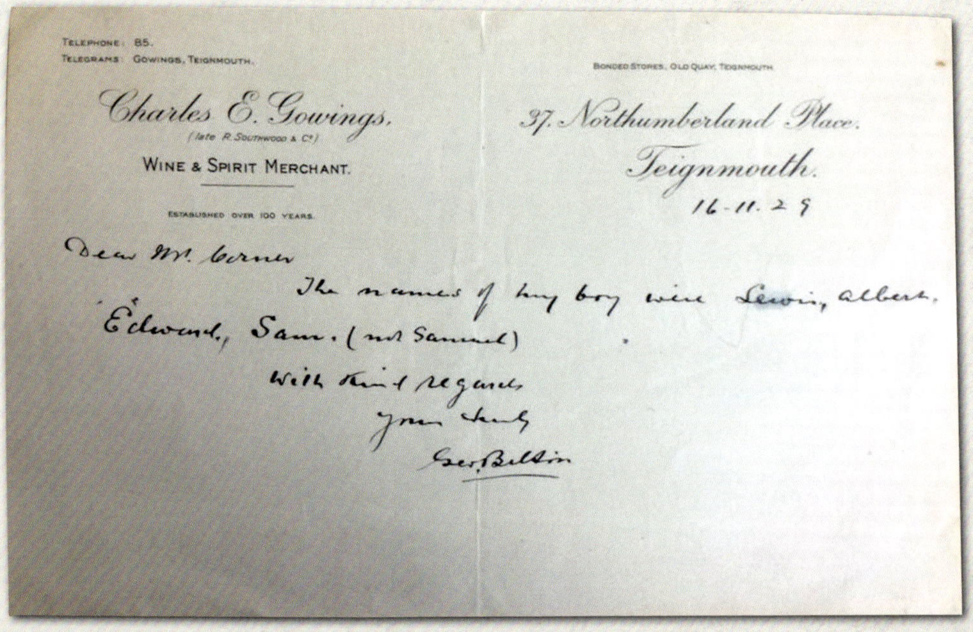

Telephone: 85.
Telegrams: Gowings, Teignmouth.

Bonded Stores, Old Quay, Teignmouth

Charles E. Gowings.
(late R. Southwood & Co)
Wine & Spirit Merchant.
Established over 100 years.

37. Northumberland Place.
Teignmouth.
16-11-29

Dear Mr Corner

The names of my boy were Lewis, Albert, Edward, Sam. (not Samuel)

With kind regards
Yours truly
Geo. Bilton

LIEUT. A. J. BOWERMAN,
illed whilst flying, Sept. 9th, 1916.

Lieut. Arthur James Bowerman

b. 1896 – died 9th September 1916, aged 20

"He was a most promising young officer, keen and energetic and very efficient at his work, and was a general favourite." His General.

Arthur James Bowerman is Remembered with Honour in Allonville Communal Cemetery. On November 9th 2008 he was remembered by Avenue House and flowers were placed in Chapel in his memory.

Arthur James Bowerman was born in Wellington, Somerset in the early part of 1896. He was an only child. His parents Frederick Robert, a clerk in a woollen mill, and Florence Mary (nee Stevens) lived for much of their married lives in Wellington.

In 1901 the census recorded them living at Grangemount, Station Road, Wellington. In the 1911 census, Arthur was not living at home with his parents, but, instead, seemed to be a boarder at Queen's College. We know he left Wellington School in 1910 and obviously spent a few years at Queen's College before joining the Artists' Rifles in 1914.

Arthur Bowerman joined the School in 1905 when he was 11 years old and left in July 1910. The first official mention of him is in the December 1907 edition of the Magazine where he played the role of a fairy attending the King and Queen in *A Midsummer Night's Dream*. In this production were also Gordon, Corner, Bilton, Gent and Bown. At this time Bowerman was also a treble in the Choral Society.

Arthur J. Bowerman's War

In December 1914 Bowerman received a commission with the 8th Somerset Light Infantry. He went to France in 1915, arriving at the Tilques area on 13th September. The 8ths Somerset Light Infantry was part of the 63rd Infantry Brigade of the 21st Division. Less than two weeks later, the Division was involved in the Battle of Loos. This Battle witnessed the first use of poison gas and the first engagement of large numbers of troops from Kitchener's Army. On the 25th September, the 63rd Infantry Brigade was sent to reinforce the line in the same area, taking up positions around Bois Hugo, between Hill 70 and Chalk Pit Wood.

The 8th Somerset Light Infantry's next main battle was the Battle of Albert which took place on 1st July 1916 in a place called Shelter Wood. Here the 8th Somerset Light Infantry was one of the lead battalions, but it was halted by machine gun fire when it reached the German first line trenches.

The 21st Division was also involved in The Battle of Albert on 11th July 1916 at Mametz Wood and the Battle of Bazentin Ridge on 14th July 1916.

Bowerman's direct involvement is unclear, but it is known that he was attached to the Royal Flying Corps in July 1916. On 9th September, 22 Sqn mounted a five-strong photo mission; two photo m/c and three escorts flying higher. Over the German side, they encountered enemy aircraft. One of the enemy planes targeted FE2b 6366 and attacked it causing it to catch fire and glide to British lines near Thiepval. Reports suggest it began to smoke over Martinpuch (German side) and then fell in flames in Contalmaison – on the British side. The dead crewmen were pulled from the wreckage by members of the 15th Scottish Division. They were named as Lieut. Arthur James Bowerman and Lt. H. Strathy Mackay observer.[7]

Local newspapers reported Bowerman's death.

LOCAL OFFICER KILLED – Lieutenant Arthur James Bowerman of the Somerset Light Infantry and Royal Flying Corps, who was killed in action on the 6th Sept., was 20 years of age, and the only child of Mr and Mrs F. R. Bowerman of Grangemount, Wellington. He was educated at Wellington School and Queen's College, Taunton. He was always most keenly interested in all sports and whilst at Queen's was captain of the football team during the season 1912 – 1913. After leaving school he joined the staff of Sedgwick & Collins, insurance brokers, at Lloyds. Early in September 1914, he joined the Artists' Rifles and received a commission in the Somerset Light Infantry in December of the same year. In the following spring, at the School of Musketry, Hythe, he passed the examination with distinction, gaining every possible mark, and in consequence, was appointed Musketry Officer to his Battalion, and gazetted full Lieutenant. He went to the Front in September 1915 and immediately took part in the Battle of Loos, very soon after which his name was sent in for a captaincy, but before he could be gazetted he was appointed to the Brigade Staff as Grenadier and Intelligence Officer. After the Battle of the Somme, his name was sent in by the General of the Brigade for mention in despatches. His work on the staff brought him closely in touch with the Royal Flying Corps, in which he was very keenly interested, and at the end of last July he was attached to it and having passed the examination was graded as a Qualified Observer.[8]

Remembering Arthur James Bowerman

School Obituary

Lieutenant A. J. Bowerman

Killed while flying, Sept. 9th 1916.

Arthur J. Bowerman, only son of Mr F. R. Bowerman, of Wellington, entered the School in Sept. 1905, leaving in 1910. From his days in the First Form, he is remembered as very keen in all that had to do with his school life, becoming as soon as old enough a member of the Cadet Corps. In September 1914, he joined the Artists' Rifles and received a commission in the Somersets at the end of the year. He then went to the Hythe School of Musketry and passed out with distinction, being appointed Musketry Officer to his battalion and gazetted a full lieutenant. He took part in the Battle of Loos and was then attached to the Brigade Staff as Grenadier and Intelligence Officer. After the Battle of the Somme, his name was sent in for mention in despatches. At the end of July, he was attached to the R. F. C. and was graded as a qualified observer, and it was while doing his duty with this branch that he met his death. His general wrote: "He was a most promising young officer, keen and energetic and very efficient at his work, and was a general favourite." His bereaved parents have been the recipients of very widespread sympathy in the loss of their only son in the service of his King and country.

[7] http://www.theaerodrome.com/forum/archive/index.php/t-53301.html
[8] Taunton Courier and Western Advertiser, Wednesday 27th September 1916.

Remembering Lt. A. J. Bowerman in Wellington

Bowerman appears on the town's memorial in Wellington Park. He also has a plaque in St. John's Church.

Bowerman was also featured in the publication *Our Boys* by Mike Perry and Ray Hitchcock. Here they print extracts of a letter from his colleague Major Martyn to Arthur's father: *'Your son was acting as an escort to another machine and when some way over the lines was attacked by a hostile machine. His machine was seen to glide down and catch fire. The ground it landed on was very rough owing to the number of shell holes and both occupants were hurled out. His death must have been instantaneous."*[9]

Bowerman was buried at Allonville Communal Cemetery, France.

[9] Perry, M. and Hitchcock, R. Our Boys: The First World War listed on the Wellington War Memorial Wellington: The Carly Press, 2014.

PER ARDUA AD ASTRA
LIEUTENANT
ARTHUR JAMES BOWERMAN
SOMERSET LIGHT INFANTRY
AND ROYAL FLYING CORPS
9TH SEPTEMBER 1916
OF GRANGEMOUNT
WELLINGTON, SOMERSET
AGED 20 YEARS
IN GODS KEEPING

The inscription on his gravestone reads:

OF GRANGEMOUNT
WELLINGTON, SOMERSET
AGED 20 YEARS
IN GOD'S KEEPING

Wellington School Memorial Chapel – Letters to George Corner

Florence Bowerman responded to George Corner's letter about the Chapel as a memorial to those who died in WW1. Her words show the esteem in which Corner was held. Bowerman had left in 1910, but he was still very much a part of the School.

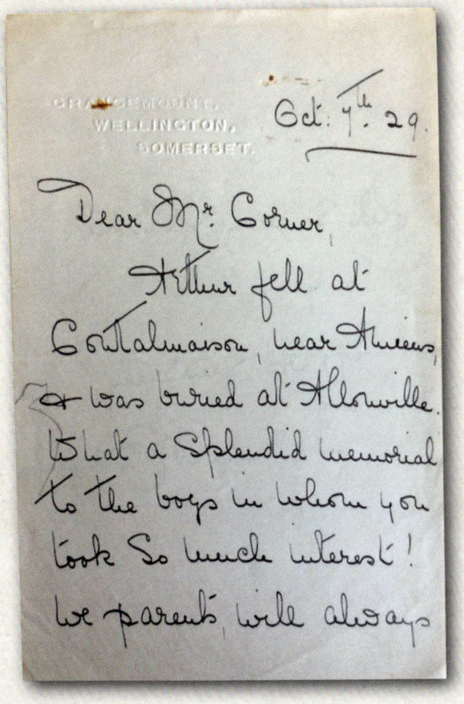

GRANGEMOUNT,
WELLINGTON,
SOMERSET.

Oct: 7th. 29.

Dear Mr. Corner,

Arthur fell at Contalmaison, near Amiens, & was buried at Allonville. What a Splendid memorial to the boys in whom you took so much interest! We parents will always

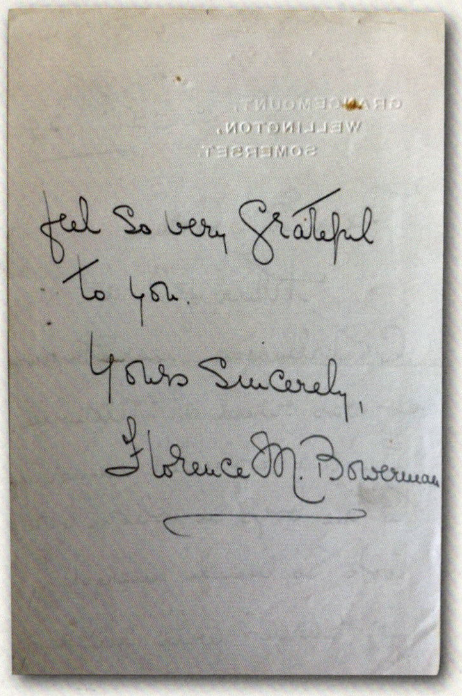

feel so very grateful to you.

Yours Sincerely,

Florence M. Bowerman

Lieut. C. W. BOWN
(Killed at Cambrai, Dec. 1st, 1917)

Lieut. Cyril Walter Bown

b. 1894 – died 1st December 1917, aged 23

"Thus ended the life of 24 short years. It had been one of loving service and duty – in his home, his School, and for his country." School Obituary

Cyril Walter Bown is Remembered with Honour on Cambrai Memorial, Louverval. On November 9th 2008 he was remembered by Lights House and flowers were placed in Chapel in his memory. He was also remembered by Beech House in 2017.

Cyril Walter Bown was the second son of Walter Bown, a farmer and yeoman, and his wife, Clara Beatrice Gullidge Bown (nee Richards). In 1911, the family was living in Mudford, Yeovil and had twelve children. Herbert, Cyril's older brother, was no longer living at home, but all the other children were still there. Cyril was 17 years old and an assistant on the farm.

Herbert and Cyril were pupils at Wellington School, but we know little about the education of the other children. Herbert, Cyril and Leslie enlisted during the War. Leslie was only 18 and went into the Army Veterinary Corps. Herbert and Cyril both entered the Tank Corps. and were involved in the first tank actions.

Cyril Walter Bown's War

Records show that Bown joined the West Somerset Yeomanry shortly after his sixteenth birthday in 1910 although he is listed in the 1911 census as being an assistant on his father's farm.

The December 1914 'List of Old Boys Serving Their Country' tells us that Bown was now a military man: **Bown, C. W. Cpl. D Squadron, West Somerset Yeomanry, 2nd South Western Mounted Brigade, Tendring Wheeling, Essex.**

He was reported as being with the 2/1 West Somerset Yeomanry at Colchester. In October 1915 he was gazetted 2nd Lieutenant but was still in England training.

In 1916, December 3rd, Herbert sent a letter to George Corner updating him on his and Cyril's progress. At this point, Herbert has been awarded the Military Cross:

**Lieut. H. G. F. Bown, M. C.,
writes from Home, December 3rd, 1916**

CAPT. H. G. F. BOWN, mentioned in despatches, Wounded, Military Cross, Summer, 1916.

Very many thanks for the wire of congrats. Have been home now just a week and have sick leave until December 22nd, when another board sits to decide whether it will be necessary for an extension of leave. Am hoping to stay home till after Xmas.

Cyril is still in the 2/1st W. S. Y. He has just finished an extensive signalling course at Cambridge.

Expect he found the grounding he got at Wellington a great assistance. He has also taken courses in physical training, bayonet fighting and machine gun, and did very well in all of them.

Had a nice ride or two since I came home, and an excellent hunt with the B. V. H. yesterday – consequently am feeling very stiff today. Have you still got Tommy and Lorna?

In early 1917, Cyril Bown was gazetted Lieutenant and joined the Tank Corps. He arrived in France in August 1917 and was involved in the fighting almost immediately.

Bown and the First Tank Crews

Herbert and Cyril both belonged to the Tank Corps and were some of the first officers to take tanks into battle. As tanks were very new to warfare at this time, the Bown brothers experienced the ups and downs of using them in such battles as Courcelette and Cambrai. The website www.firsttankcrews had a deal of information on both brothers, particularly Herbert, who took part in the Battle of Courcelette. One post, however, focused on Cyril:

"Lieut Bown was commander of this tank on Dec.1st 1917 when it was hit several times by artillery. He and several crew members were burned to death. Capt. Hickey in his book "Rolling into Action" mentions that as he was bringing Hermosa and another tank through Ypres he thought he was captured in a photograph taken by an Australian official photographer.

Believe it or not, I found the actual photograph on-line. Lieut Bown had just 4 weeks to live.[10]

[10] www.firsttankcrews.co.uk, website 2016.

Rolling Into Action – Memoirs of a Tank Section Commander

Captain D. E. Hickey

Extracts from the above book show what life was like for a member of the tank crew in battle and how difficult it was to operate such huge machines on terrain that was so pock-marked and hostile. The tanks were named and the men had great affection for them. It is also hugely significant for it tells the last days of Cyril Bown's life, how brave he was and how much upset was caused by his death. On 21st October an attack was planned and two tank crews were to take part.

Gerrard had the unenviable honour of being chosen as section commander to undertake the show, with Bown and Glanville in charge of the tanks. Two more capable tank commanders it would have been hard to find. Both had the highest ideals and a strongly developed sense of duty. Bown was not yet twenty, a fresh-looking young fellow of hefty build. Glanville was about ten years older, neat and active. [11]

Hermosa being driven through Ypres.

[11] Hickey, Capt. D. E., Rolling Into Action: Memoirs of a Tank Corps Section Commander Sandhurst: The Naval and Military Press, 2007 pgs., pg. 75.

On the 24th November, the unit moved to Ribécourt where one of the tank commanders was taken to the Casualty Clearing Station and invalided back to England. This left a tank without an officer. On their way to Winter Quarters at Bray-sur-Somme, near Albert on 30th November news came through that the Germans had broken the line in a counter attack. The tanks were needed:

We went round to see what tanks could be pushed in. Bown, one of Gerrard's tank commanders, was working hard at his machine, but could not get the sponsons out. They had jammed. He volunteered to take another tank in. 'Hermosa' was without an officer since Keay's departure and was ready for action, since being a female tank its sponsons had not had to be pushed in for entrainment. Bown with his crew took over his tank. Seven others were comparatively ready and were hastily got into fighting trim. [12]

Bown was one of four tank commanders under Gerrard ordered to counter attack at Gouzeaucourt, almost four miles away. Hickey fought elsewhere but was informed what had happened to Bown later that evening. It wasn't good news.

At Fins, I heard what had happened when the tanks under Gerrard and Grounds had attacked east of Gouzeaucourt, at the same time as we attacked Gauche Wood, on the 1st December. All Gerrard's tanks had been disabled, three having been knocked out. The attack had proved to be 'Hermosa's' last fight, and she had come to a gallant end. Bown, her voluntary commander, and four of the crew had met their death, and the other three had been severely wounded.

Just before they started off at dawn, Bown, evidently ill at ease, had gone to Gerrard and asked him to join his tank, as he had done on the first day, November the 20th. Gerrard replied that he would willingly have gone with him but that he must go with the young McCleod, who had never been in action before.

The tanks advanced against the St. Quentin Ridge. McCleod's tank, which was leading, got ditched, and in spite of repeated efforts to get it going again, it could not be freed. Gerrard ordered the machine-guns and ammunition to be taken out and formed the crew into a Lewis gun section. He took them up to a suitable place at which to form a strong-point. Having established them there, he went off towards his other three tanks. Before he reached them, he saw first one then another, then the third, receive direct hits from a battery on the other side of the ridge, and put out of action. While he was going towards 'Hermosa', eight or nine shells struck her in rapid succession; she burst into flames and soon became a roaring furnace.[13]

Hickey goes on to talk about how the men were discussing whether to hold a burial service for Bown and his comrades when a shell burst on one of the tents. Fortunately, no one was injured. Gerrard took Bown's death hard and wanted the service even though they were in a very dangerous position. It was decided no service should be held much to 'Gerrard's eternal regret'.[14] The effect of Bown's death on Gerrard gives us an insight into the strong bonds felt between the tank crews. Bown was respected and reliable but his death was brutal and affected all.

[12] Ibid. pg. 135.
[13] Hickey (2007), pg. 137.
[14] Hickey (2007) pg. 142.

The De Ruvigny Roll of Honour

BOWN, CYRIL WALTER, Lieut., Tank Corps, *s.* of Walter Bown. of Mudford Manor, Yeovil, co. Somerset, Agriculturist, by his wife, Clara, dau. of G. Richards; *b.* Yeovil, 15 Jan. 1894; educ. Wellington County School, co. Somerset; joined the West Somerset Yeomanry some years before war broke out; transferred to the Tank Corps in the spring of 1917; gazetted 2nd Lieut. at the end of 1915, and Lieut. early in 1917; served with the Expeditionary Force in France and Flanders from Aug. 1917, and was killed in action in the Cambrai battles 1 Dec. 1917. His Commanding Officer wrote: "In the actions of 20-21 Nov. his excellent work and his cool, unselfish bravery were most conspicuous. A great favourite with his men, he was looked upon as one of the very finest of Tank Commanders, and greatly loved by his brother officers, who mourn his loss exceedingly." *Unm.*

Remembering Lieut. Cyril Walter Bown

The obituary in the School Magazine expresses genuine warmth for. The sense of loss is profound.

School Obituary

Lieut. C. W. BOWN

Killed at Cambrai, December 1st 1917.

C. W. Bown, second son of Mr and Mrs Bown, of Mudford Manor, entered the School with his elder brother, H. G. F. Bown, in May 1904. Cyril's fine qualities were evident from the first. Always in earnest and deeply sincere in School and in Sport Bown ii held a place all his own with Dark Blues. His work in the O. T. C. was keen and he was a proficient signaller. One remembers him riding off enthusiastically with his flash lamp to the hill, mounted on Lorna, of an autumn evening. On leaving School in 1908 he took up farming and joined the Somerset Yeomanry. At the outbreak of War, after training in the S. W. Mounted Brigade, he joined the newly formed Tank Corps with a commission as Lieut. in the H Divison, proceeding to France in August 1917. His record of service and good fellowship continued during the severe fighting and deprivations of the months that followed. After the end came the O. C. wrote to Mr Bown, when informing him of Cyril's gallant death, saying – "In the action of Nov. 20 and 21 your son's excellent work and cool unselfish bravery were most conspicuous. He had patrolled the ridge above Ribecourt when the infantry got under short-range fire from a battery of howitzers. But Cyril never wavered and pushed right on and did his job, seeing the Infantry safely into the trenches, thus vindicating the faith of his men in him. On that fatal Dec. 1st, Cyril being so sound an officer, was given another tank and crew, as his own tank had been put out of action. On reaching the St. Quentin Ridge, the Tank was hit simultaneously by three shells, causing his instant death." Continuing, Captain Spray said "A great favourite with his men, he was looked upon as one of our very finest Tank Commanders and greatly loved by his brother officers, who mourn his loss exceedingly. Please allow me to express our very deepest sympathy with you in your great grief." Thus ended the life of 24 short years. It had been one of loving service and duty – in his home, his School, and for his country. Ever faithful in devotion from his earliest days, he lived his life on earth; it falls to few to be so universally loved and respected. Cyril Bown's word was never questioned.

"As ever in his great Taskmaster's eye."

Mudford Church Memorial Window

In the village of Mudford, where Cyril grew up alongside his 11 siblings, his family paid for a memorial window to be placed in the church in his memory. The window depicts Jesus giving His blessing to the world, flanked by St. Martin and St. George.

In 1922, in response to George Corner's initial quest for the 'most fitting memorial' to remember the fallen, Walter and Clara Bown wrote:

"Your idea is excellent: Surely nothing could be more suitable as a memorial to our honoured lads than a School Chapel. I do hope you will be able to carry it out."

They gave money to help the fund although there are no actual letters from them regarding Corner's appeal of 1929 in the archive.

Major E. J. Brooks, Killed, Sept. 15th, 1916.

Major Ernest John Brooks

b. 1878 – died 15th September 1916, aged 38

"He inspired his men by his coolness and decision."
A brother officer

Major Ernest J. Brooks is Remembered with Honour on the Vimy Memorial. On November 10th 2013 he was remembered by Willows House and flowers were placed in Chapel in his memory.

Ernest John Brooks was the youngest son of William Tuke Brooks (b. 1840) a Reverend, and Mary Harris Brooks (b. 1840). The couple had six children, two sons and four daughters. The family grew up in West Buckland, Nr. Taunton.

In the 1891 census, Ernest was 12 years old and lived with his parents, brother William, a draper's assistant, and sister, Mabel (aged 18). At this time, Gertrude (aged 9), Ernest's youngest sister, was a visitor, visiting her two sisters, Florence and Bessie, who were living with the Garnsey family in High Street, Wellington. Both Florence and Bessie were bookkeepers' assistants.

Mary Harris Brooks died in West Buckland in 1915 and her death was registered as being between January and March. Her husband, William Tuke Brooks, died in 1920.

Ernest John Brooks's Life Before the War

Ernest John Brooks appears to have left Wellington School in 1893 so he doesn't appear in any of the Magazines. Little is known, therefore, about his schooling.

In the 1901 census, Ernest was registered as working as a Draper's Assistant in London. He was 22 years of age. By 1911 he appears to be on a Canadian census, working as a clergyman. He married Kathleen Montie McNichol in Nova Scotia, on July 23rd 1906. They appear to have had no children. Kathleen died in Chichester, Sussex, aged 64 in 1945.

Ernest John Brooks's War

Records show that Ernest Brooks enlisted on 7th January 1915 in Halifax, Nova Scotia. He was a 'Minister of the Gospel' when he enlisted and stood 6ft tall. He joined the Canadian Infantry and served with the 25th Battalion. Notes show that prior to serving as Lieutenant with the 25ths, he served with the Calcutta Rifles, but we have no further record of this. The Battalion embarked for Great Britain on 20th May 1915.

The 25th Battalion served in Belgium and France as part of the 5th Infantry Brigade, and then the 2nd Canadian Division from 16th September 1915 until the end of the war. Of the 1000

Nova Scotians that started with the battalion, after the first year of fighting, 100 were left in the battalion while 900 men were killed, taken prisoner, missing or injured.

On September 22nd-23rd 1915, the 25th arrived at Ypres, Belgium, becoming the first Nova Scotian battalion to see combat in the war. The Battalion spent 339 days in the Belgian trenches, 164 of which involved front-line duty. It fought in actions at St. Eloi Craters (27th March - 16th April 1916) and the Hill 62, Mount Sorrel and Sanctuary Wood. Brooks' contribution can be seen in this extract found in the School Archive:

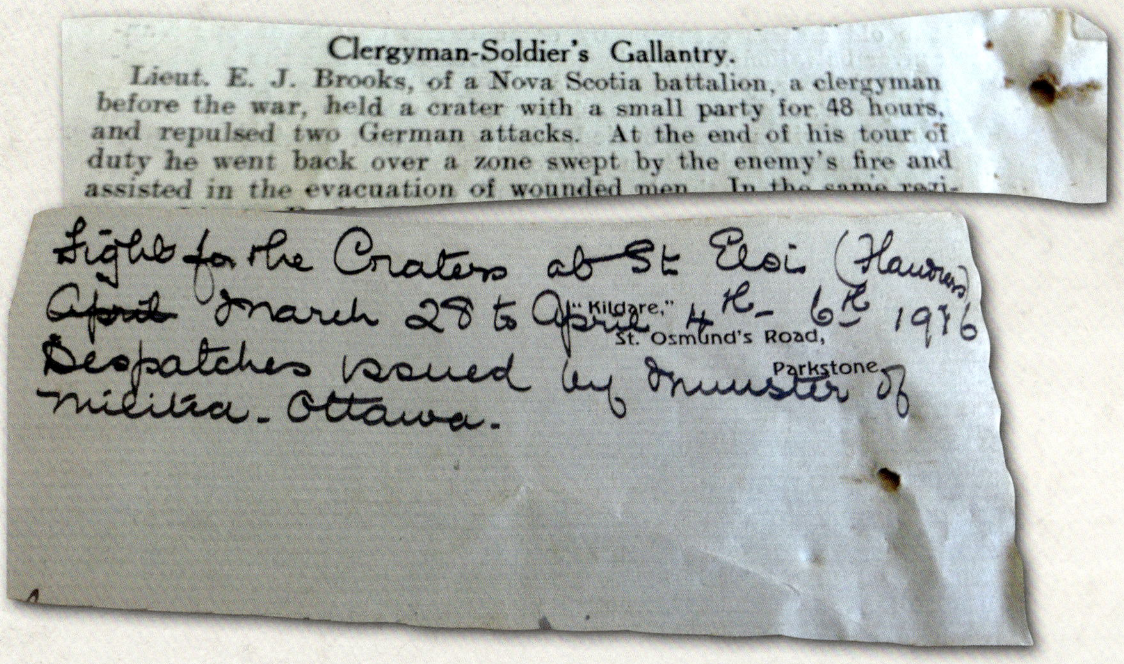

Clergyman-Soldier's Gallantry.

Lieut. E. J. Brooks, of a Nova Scotia battalion, a clergyman before the war, held a crater with a small party for 48 hours, and repulsed two German attacks. At the end of his tour of duty he went back over a zone swept by the enemy's fire and assisted in the evacuation of wounded men. In the same regi-

Fight for the Craters at St Eloi (Flanders)
~~April~~ March 28 to April 4th - 6th 1916
Despatches issued by Minister of Militia - Ottawa.

"Kildare,"
St. Osmund's Road,
Parkstone

On 1st July 1916, Brooks was made Temporary Major having been in the post of Temporary Captain for two months. The 25th Battalion took part in the Battle of the Somme.

In September 1916 it took part in the Battle of Flers-Courcelette. The battle began on 15th September and concluded on the 22nd September. Major E. J. Brooks was killed on its second day.

The account of his death comes from the Canadian Casualty records and reads as follows:

'Killed in Action: This Officer was standing up looking at a map, prior to his Battalion making an attack, when an enemy shell burst nearby, a piece hitting him in the head and killing him instantly."[15]

There appears to be a little confusion with regard to Brooks' burial with some sites stating he was buried in the Albert Communal Cemetery. This cemetery was destroyed by the Germans in 1918 and it is possible that he was commemorated on the Vimy Memorial because there was no longer any grave. It is not certain.

[15] Canadian Casualty Records, Ancestry.co.uk

Remembering Major Ernest John Brooks

School Obituary

Major Ernest John Brooks

September 15th 1916.

Major Brooks, of the Canadian Infantry Contingent, was the youngest son of Mr W. T. Brooks, of The Crossway, West Buckland. He was educated at the School, leaving in 1893 and settling in Nova Scotia. Devoted to his country and prompted by a keen sense of the duty which he owed to it he volunteered for service on the outbreak of war, receiving a commission – being gazetted Major in July last. His sterling qualities and gifts as a leader caused him to be greatly beloved by his men. A brother officer writes of him: 'He inspired his men by his coolness and decision.' His Colonel adds: 'He was close to me when he fell, leading his men, at the moment of victory. His loss to me and the battalion can never be replaced.' Widespread sympathy has been felt for his widow and his father and family in their great bereavement, and his memory will be forever cherished in the records of his School.

Wellington School Memorial Chapel - Letters to George Corner

Though we have no letters from Brooks himself, the archive has letters to George Corner from Brooks's sister, Mabel, and wife, Kathleen.

Dear Mr Corner,

I am very sorry you have had difficulty in getting details as to my brother I cannot in the least understand why my sister-in-law has not answered your letters – it is quite unlike her to be remiss in this matter – she travels a good deal and I have not heard from her quite lately but I should imagine she has letters forwarded wherever she may be.

I hope the paper etc. I am providing will give all you require – please do not hurry, but at some time when you have quite finished with them I should be grateful if you would kindly return them as they are the only copies I have – I shall like to come to see the Chapel when I come to Wellington – it is a great achievement and such a fitting memorial to our precious dead – I'm sure you must have given a tremendous amount of time and effort to it and the size also of the undertaking must be very gratifying to you – In haste – I want you to get this immediately.

Sincerely yours, Mabel Brooks

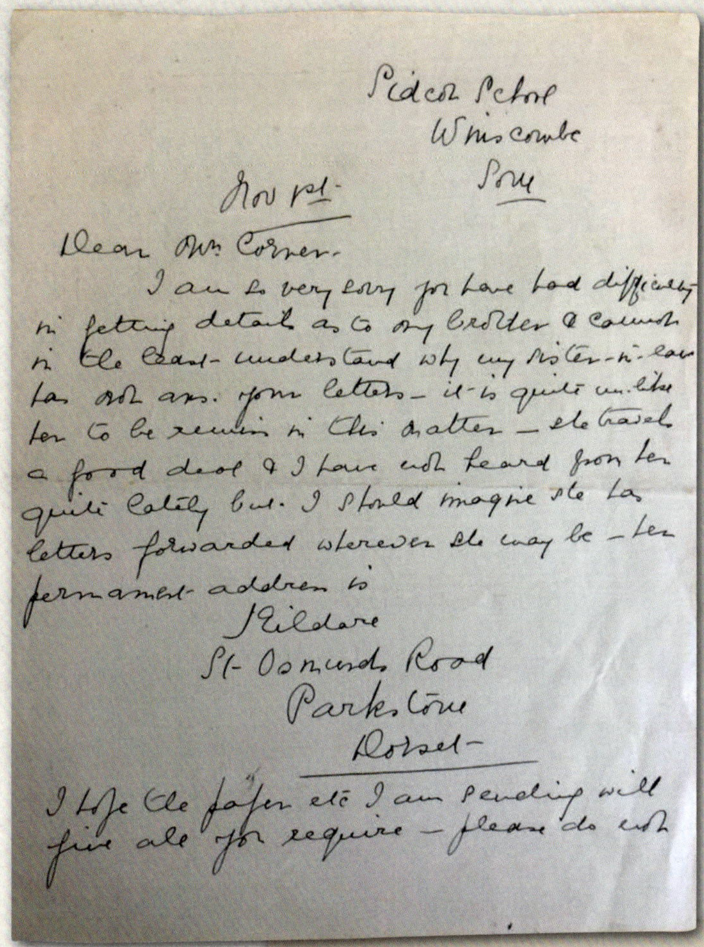

Sidcot School
Winscombe
Som

Nov 1st

Dear Mr Corner.

I am so very sorry you have had difficulty in getting details as to my brother & cannot in the least understand why my sister-in-law has not ans. your letters — it is quite unlike her to be remiss in this matter — she travels a good deal & I have not heard from her quite lately but I should imagine she has letters forwarded wherever she may be — her permanent address is

Kildare
St Osmunds Road
Parkstone
Dorset

I hope the paper etc I am sending will give all you require — please do not

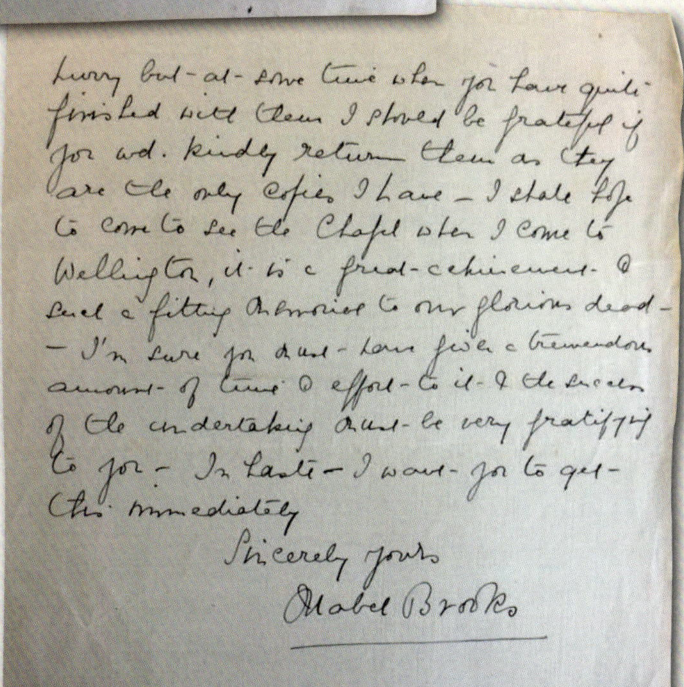

hurry but at some time when you have quite finished with them I should be grateful if you wd. kindly return them as they are the only copies I have — I shall hope to come to see the Chapel when I come to Wellington, it is a great achievement & such a fitting memorial to our glorious dead — I'm sure you must have given a tremendous amount of time & effort to it & the success of the undertaking must be very gratifying to you. In haste — I want you to get this immediately

Sincerely yours

Mabel Brooks

Nov 4/29

Dear Mr Corner,

I understand that you have written me three times for particulars of Major Ernest Brooks's regt. etc. – for inscription on memorial tablet. These letters have not reached me and I should be greatly indebted to you if you will tell me to what address they were sent, and I will make enquiries, as they should have been returned to you via Dead Letter Office.

I must ask you to accept this as a profound apology that you should have been put to this trouble – I have travelled about so much of late years.

I enclose a cutting of 'mention' in case you are including such details in any records, and I regret that you must have received an impression of faithless neglect of a very precious duty – the remembrance of a very brave and good man – my husband.

Yours faithfully,

Kathleen Brooks

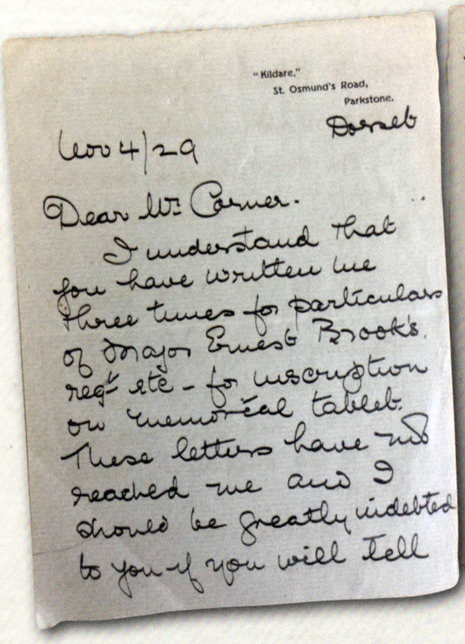
"Kildare,"
St. Osmund's Road,
Parkstone.
Dorset
Nov 4/29
Dear Mr Corner.
I understand that you have written me three times for particulars of Major Ernest Brooks regt etc – for inscription on memorial tablet. These letters have not reached me and I should be greatly indebted to you if you will tell

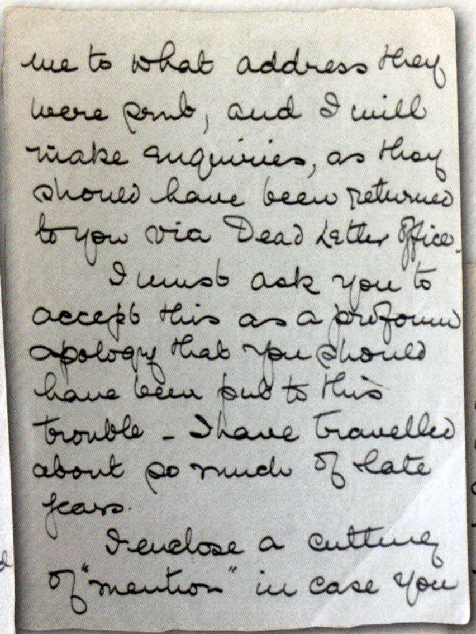
me to what address they were sent, and I will make enquiries, as they should have been returned to you via Dead Letter Office.
I must ask you to accept this as a profound apology that you should have been put to this trouble – I have travelled about so much of late years.
I enclose a cutting of "mention" in case you

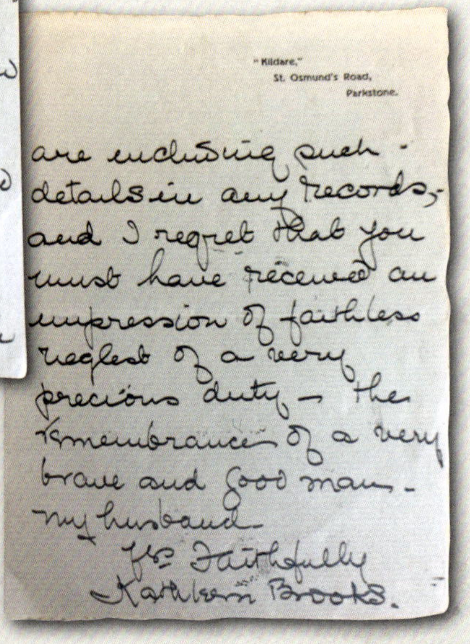
"Kildare,"
St. Osmund's Road,
Parkstone.
are including such details in any records, and I regret that you must have received an impression of faithless neglect of a very precious duty – the remembrance of a very brave and good man – my husband.
Yrs faithfully
Kathleen Brooks.

W. J. C. BROWN,
Killed on the Somme, 1916.

Pte. William John Crofton Brown

b. 1892 – died 8th October 1916, aged 24

"I've never had many particulars as to just where he fell – although I've written so many letters asking for details – I'm sorry this is all I can tell you."

Bessie Brown, Letter to George Corner

William John Crofton Brown is Remembered with Honour on the Thiepval Memorial, France. In November 2018 he will be remembered by Gillard's House and a poppy will be placed in Chapel in his memory.

William John Crofton Brown was the second oldest child of John Brown (b. 1865 in Porlock) and Elizabeth Jane Brown (b. 1864 in Bridgetown, Somerset). The family lived in Wellington where John was a watchmaker and traveller.

In 1901, the Brown family was living at 123 Fore Street, Wellington. The family consisted of Cuthbert (b. 1887), William (b. 1893), Sidney Spencer (b. 1895), Geoffrey Milton (b. 1901). In the census, Geoffrey was recorded as Infant Brown, being only 8 months old.

By 1911, the family had moved to 11 Fore Street, Wellington. Cuthbert does not appear on the census, but the rest of the family do and there has been an addition of a daughter, Elwyn E. Brown. In this census, William was a student at the Grammar School (Wellington School) and Sidney was a shop assistant.

School Life

William John Crofton Brown entered the School in 1904 at the age of 12 years and left in 1911. In the Magazines, he is one of the most frequently mentioned of the fallen where his academic, sporting and musical skills would often elicit praise. He won a scholarship to the School and clearly did his best in every area of School life. He is often mentioned playing the piano at various School events after he left. His memory lives on today with the annual award of the Crofton Brown Music Prize.

Virtue Functi More Patrum Duces

W. J. C. Brown, entered September 1904, left summer 1911.

Prefect, Spring 1909; Captain Dark Blues, Spring 1910; Hon. Accompanist Choral Society 1906-1911; Captain Football, 1910-1911; Vice-Captain Cricket – 1910; Cricket Colours – 1907; 1st X1 Football Colours, Spring 1908; Cambridge Junior, 1907; Cambridge Senior, 1908; 3rd Class Honours 1909; Associate Royal College of Organists, 1911; Intermediate County Scholarship, 1908. Address: 40, Coniston Road, Muswell Hill.

William John Crofton Brown's War

Brown did not join up immediately. At the beginning of the War, he was based in Muswell Hill and teaching music. In the December 1915/April 1916 edition of the Magazine, he was recorded as being part of the London Rifles: *'W. J. C. Brown F.R.C.O. (London Rifles), has sent us some of his musical compositions, including a glee and a new tune for No 576 Hymns A and M.'*

In July 1916, the School was visited by many Old Boys including H. G. Shapland, W.J.C. Brown, G. W. Powell, E. R. Zealley and W. E. Chave.

Army Service Numbers show that Brown joined up between November and December 1915. He joined the 1/5 London Rifles which in turn became part of the 169th Brigade in the newly reformed 56th (London Division) in February 1916. Records show that Brown started in the 'Theatre of War in France' on 14th July 1916, two weeks into the Battle of the Somme.

We do not know exactly what fighting Brown was involved in, but it is likely to include some or all of the Battle of Ginchy on 9th September, the Battle of Flers-Courcelette (15th -22nd September), the Battle of Morval (25th – 28th September) and the Battle of Transloy Ridges (1st – 20th October). Here on 7th – 9th October the 167th the 5th London Regiment was sent to reinforce the 168th Infantry Brigade. It is likely that in this conflict Brown met his death along with 97 other missing riflemen. 55 were killed outright and 166 wounded.

Remembering William John Crofton Brown

School Obituary

W. J. C. Brown, London Rifle Brigade

October 8th, 1916

Crofton Brown was the second son of Mr J. Brown, of Fore Street, Wellington, and entered the School in 1904, at the age of 12 years, leaving in 1911. During this time he was a steady worker and gained many successes, matriculating in 1909. He made a serious study of music and took his A. R. C. O. whilst still at School. He was for some years the mainstay of the School music and was never happier than when at the piano, accompanying the Choral Society. In athletics he excelled in cricket, being a brilliant all-round bat and safe field. In 1910 he was Captain of the Dark Blues, and Captain of Football, playing at all times a grand game. C. G. Gordon and Crofton Brown were close friends and they both fell bravely in the advance on the Somme. On leaving School Crofton Brown held a Mastership at Muswell Hill and was known as an inspiring teacher of music. Having taken his F. R. C. O. he fulfilled his early promise and all who knew him deplore his loss and deeply sympathize with his bereaved parents. His contemporaries at School will remember him always with affection and appreciation of his unselfish and loyal character.

Memorials: Thiepval and Wellington

Crofton Brown has no known grave. He, like so many, is 'missing' and commemorated on the Thiepval Memorial, Pier and Face 9D. This memorial is dedicated to the memory of over 70, 000 men whose bodies were never identified for burial. Brown's entry is as Brown, J. C..

Thiepval Memorial, July 2018

In Wellington

Brown is remembered on the town memorial in Wellington Park and there is a memorial plaque to him in Wellington Methodist Church, Waterloo Road. He is also featured in the publication *Our Boys* by Mike Perry and Ray Hitchcock.

Wellington School Memorial Chapel - Letter to George Corner

We do not have any letters written by Crofton, but there is a letter from his mother, written to George Corner in relation to the wording to be placed in the Chapel. Bessie's torment at not only losing her son but not knowing or being able to find out how he died, is very moving. Parents and loved ones of the missing must have endured months of anguish, simply not knowing what had happened to their loved ones and where they lay. News was scant and often slow in arriving.

Dear Mr Corner,

In reply to your letter respecting Crofton – I had notice from the Director of War Graves that his is at Bernafay Wood – nr Albert – I've never had many particulars as to just where he fell – although I've written so many letters asking for details – I'm sorry this is all I can tell you.

Yours sincerely,

B. Brown

Mrs Brown's letter suggests that Crofton has a grave and is buried but this does not appear to be the case. The letter does suggest how difficult it must have been for the War Graves officials to actually know the whereabouts of all the men. Whether the assertion Brown was at Bernafay Wood was a genuine mistake or whether it was the last place he was known to have been is unclear. To discover he was missing after being told he had a grave must have been very hard to hear.

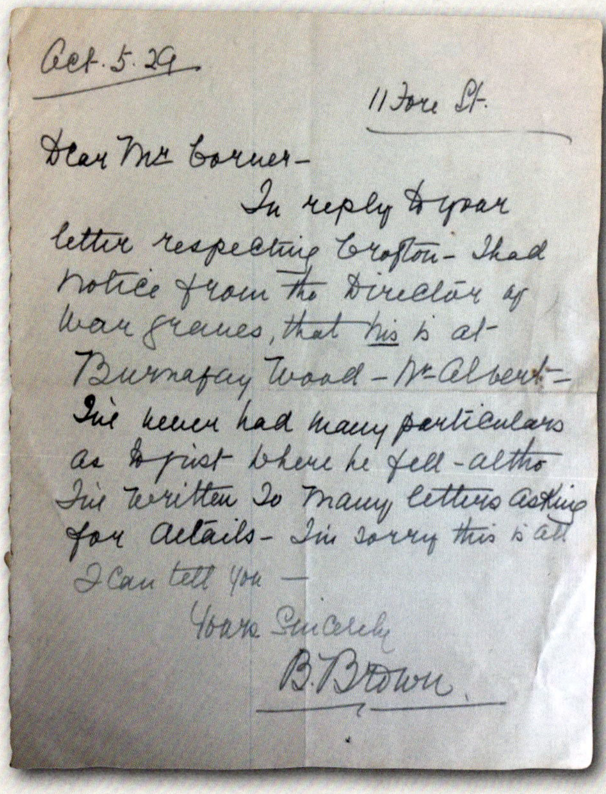

Oct. 5. 29

11 Fore St.

Dear Mr Corner -

In reply to your letter respecting Crofton - I had notice from the Director of War Graves, that his is at Bernafay Wood - Nr Albert - I've never had many particulars as to just where he fell - altho I've written so many letters asking for details - I'm sorry this is all I can tell you -

Yours Sincerely

B. Brown

Cadet W. E. CHAVE,
(*died March 23rd, 1918*).

Cadet William Edward Chave

b. 1900(ish) and died 23rd March 1918, aged 18

"He was a promising and gallant little fellow and a general favourite on board. At the time of our accident, he behaved splendidly and showed great courage and ability for one so young." ***Master of the Tyndareus***

Cadet William Chave was buried in Mount Pleasant Cemetery, Seattle, Washington State, USA. The War Office did not believe he qualified for a War Grave. He was remembered by Avenue House on November 11th 2007 and flowers were placed in Chapel in his memory.

William Edward Chave was a Wellington boy living in different houses in Mantle Street in the 1901 and 1911 censuses. He appears to have had two older brothers and one younger one. Fred and James Chave were both living at home in 1901 (aged 8 and 6 respectively) but neither were living at home in 1911, where Samuel was recorded as being 6 years old and William, 11. James Chadwell Chave (William's father) died in 1913 and it is this event which may have precipitated William's exit from school.

F. CHAVE
(*dangerously wounded, Aug.* 1917

Fred Chave (William's eldest brother)

A picture of Fred Chave, a private in the Somerset Light Infantry, appeared in the School Magazine. Underneath the photograph, it says that Chave was 'dangerously wounded'. He received multiple gunshot wounds to his left leg and knee in August 1917 whilst fighting at Arras. As a result of his injury, his left leg was amputated about 6 inches below the knee. He was discharged from the Army on 14th November 1918.

William Edward Chave's War

The December 1915/April 1916 Magazines note that Willie Chave had joined the merchant navy and was currently onboard SS India, training as a midshipman. Later, he served on SS Tyndareus.

We know little of what happened to Chave between this time and his death in March 1918. What is known is that he arrived at Seattle and was immediately taken to Firland Hospital, Seattle, with Rheumatic Fever. At this time, Firland was the leading hospital for infectious diseases and had many patients suffering from T.B. Sadly, Chave passed away on the 23rd March 1918. He was buried on 24th March 1918 at Mount Pleasant Cemetery in Seattle. We do not know who took the service or whether there were any mourners. He lies at **Grave no.1, Lot 89, Row 2, Section A**. The grave is unmarked and, due to its age, is in a section that is very overgrown and unkept. He is the only one of the 37 Old Boys to die in WW1 not to have a war grave/memorial; neither was he awarded any war medals.

Remembering William Edward Chave

School Obituary

W. E. Chave

23rd March 1918.

W. E. Chave, son of the late Mr James Chadwell Chave, of Wellington, entered the School in September 1913. Messrs. Holt, the owners of the Ocean Steamship Co., sent him to H. M. Transport "Tyndareus," and when that ship was mined off Cape Agulhas on Jan. 6th it was Willie Chave's duty to handle one of the lifeboats engaged in moving the troops on board. The report received by Mrs Chave of his conduct on that occasion is as follows. Messrs. Holt wrote – "Your boy was reported by the military officer in charge of the men as having moved the troops from the ruined ship in a considerable sea and to have behaved with great coolness and courage. For this, and in helping his master and officers in the salvage of the ship, having brought his boat back – the only one that did get back to the Tyndareus – he has been awarded a silver medal and illuminated certificate by the Liverpool Humane Society." When the ship reached Seattle young Chave had fallen ill of scarlet fever and to the sorrow of his shipmates died and was buried there. When at School he had many friends amongst his schoolfellows as he was so full of energy and good temper. The master of the Tyndareus wrote to Mrs Chave saying "I learn to-day with deep regret of your sad loss and hasten to offer you my sincere sympathy. I was very much interested in your son. He was a promising and gallant little fellow and a general favourite on board. At the time of our accident, he behaved splendidly and showed great courage and ability for one so young." Willie Chave was only 18 at the time of his death and leaves a memory of which his family must be proud.

George Corner and W. E. Chave

W. E. Chave never fought in the war or signed up for battle but George Corner felt Chave's death should be recorded as a War death and wrote to the War Graves Commission outlining his views. They replied that Chave had not died within 45 days of attack/enemy action and his death, therefore, could not be counted as a war death. Undeterred, Corner included him in the Chapel memorial, as did the people of Wellington on the town memorial.

W. E. Chave is also featured in the publication *Our Boys* by Mike Perry and Ray Hitchcock.

SERGT. P. A. CLODE,
Killed, July, 1917.

Sgt. Percy Alfred Clode

b. April 1889 – died 21st July 1917, aged 28

'In his last letter to Mr Corner, he wrote, 'I hope I shall be spared once more to wield the willow in the dear Old School field.' School Obituary

Serjeant Percy Alfred Clode is Remembered with Honour in Dozinghem Military Cemetery, Belgium. On November 8th 2009 he was remembered by Darks House and flowers were placed in Chapel in his memory.

Percy Alfred Clode was the eldest son of Alfred Clode, a fishmonger, and Elizabeth Wilkins. The couple married in 1888 on 10th June in Taunton. In the 1891 census the Clode family was living at 3 North Street, Taunton; the family consisted of Alfred, 29, Elizabeth, 25, and Percy, 1. Tragedy struck the family before the next census with Alfred, Percy's father, passing away on 23rd July 1898. At the time of his death, the family had expanded. William, now 6 and Winifred, now 3, had joined the family, and it seems Elizabeth was pregnant.

In 1901, Percy was 11 years old and a boarder at The County School, Wellington. His family was registered as living at 17 North Street, Taunton. Elizabeth was head of the family, a widow, and a fish merchant.

By 1911, the family was still registered as living at 17 North Street, Taunton. Elizabeth, aged 45, was now a fishmonger. Percy, aged 22, had returned home and was an accountant student.

Percy married Mabel Ann Burridge on 25th March 1915 in Tiverton, Devon and the couple moved to Kilkenny Avenue in Taunton. They had a son, Anthony Hamilton Clode, born on 23rd December 1915. He would have been around eighteen months old when his father was killed.

Mabel, Percy's wife, continued to live in their house Cranmore, Kilkenny Avenue, Taunton where she died in 1957. She was 69 years old. Their son, Anthony, appears to have married in Watchet. He died in Taunton in May 2004, aged 88.

Percy Alfred Clode's War

Clode was working for Albert Goodman, the Taunton accountants when war broke out. He had been there since leaving School in 1905. The Magazine records that in July 1915 *P. A. Clode has joined the Benedicts*. More news came in the December 1915/April 1916 issue:

Congratulations to P. A. Clode on the birth of a son and heir

Records show that Clode enlisted on 9th, August 1916 as a Gunner for the 244 Siege Battery. He was promoted to 'Lance Rank' on 4th October. He was promoted to Serjeant before he left England on 16th, January 1917. On 29th January he left Southampton to sail to France, arriving on 30th, January. Here he took on the role of the Battery Accountant. An account is as follows:

Percy had been promoted Serjeant on 16/1/17 and followed his profession prior to enlistment, becoming the Battery Accountant of 244 SB and as such likely to be attached to the battery HQ. In July 1917 the battery was part of 81 HAG (Heavy Artillery Group) under XVIII Corps. HAG was a higher formation grouping of batteries under command of a Lieut Colonel. The battery participated in the preliminary bombardment build up to the taking of Pilckem, which was the start of the Battle of Third Ypres. 244 were armed with 6in Howitzers (26cwt) and the 21st was 'S' day of the bombardment build-up, (of the countdown to 'Z' day) and 81 HAG WD records "batteries in the group suffered heavily" from enemy counter bombardment. The Corps WD shows their position at B28d.0.8 (Sheet 28 NW1) and his service records which have survived indicate Sgt. Clode suffered a shell wound to the left buttock, subsequently dying of his wounds.[16]

News of Clode's Death Breaks

Clode was from a well known Taunton family and his death was reported in the local paper.

SERGT. PERCY CLODE KILLED – The sad news was received in Taunton on Thursday that Sergt. Percy Clode of the Royal Garrison Artillery had been killed in action in France. Sergt. Clode was a member of a well-known Taunton family and was in peacetime a popular cricketer and member of the Taunton team. He was, until he joined the Army, engaged in the offices of Messrs. Goodman, chartered accountants, Hammet Street, and had many friends in the town. He leaves a widow and infant child, and his loss will be mourned also by his mother, sisters, and brother. Much sympathy is felt for the bereaved family. [17]

THE LATE SERGT. PERCY CLODE – The late Percy Alfred Clode, a serjeant in the R.G.A., whose death in action was briefly announced in our last issue, was the eldest son of the late Mr Alfred Clode and of Mrs Clode of East Street. He was only 28 years of age and was educated at Wellington County School, from which he got his colours for cricket and football. He was a serjeant in the School Cadet Corps and was exceedingly well liked by the boys. His keenness and interest in sport were also shown in his professional career after he left school, and during the time he was with Messrs. Goodman, Sons, & Pollard, accountants, until the outbreak of war, he regularly played cricket and football for Taunton. He was an excellent bat, and in his most successful season scored over 1,000 runs for Taunton. Both in the sports' field and in his private life his bright, genial personality won for him many friends, and his loss is deeply regretted on all hands. He enlisted in the Royal Garrison Artillery in July 1916, and in a very short time was promoted to the rank of serjeant. He was sent to France in January last and had been in the firing line since then. Whilst on active service he was recommended for a commission by his officer. Unhappily, this was not to be. He was killed on the 21st July whilst in the act of rescuing a wounded comrade. With the true spirit of an English soldier, he met his death, bravely, laying

[16] 1914-1918 Invisionzone, The Great War Forum.
[17] 1st August, 1917. Taunton Courier and Western Advertiser from British Newspaper Archive.

down his life to save a friend; all honour to his memory. The heartfelt sympathy of a host of Taunton friends goes out to the young widow and her infant son (aged 18 months); also to the bereaved mother, sisters and brother. Mr Willie Clode is on service in the R. N. A. S. [18]

Remembering Percy Alfred Clode

School Obituary

Serjeant P. A. Clode

Killed, July 1917.

Percy Clode, eldest son of Mrs Clode, of Taunton, entered the School in May 1900, at the age of eleven, leaving July 1905. Gifted with a wonderful voice he early took part in the musical and dramatic performances of the School, and many will remember his brilliant rendering of the solo parts of the "May Queen" and his successes as "Puck", "Feste" and "Bassanio". At cricket he was good in the field and a certain run-getter, gaining his colours for the 1st XI. On leaving, he joined the firm of Messrs. Goodman, chartered accountants, of Taunton. He has often visited us since he left School, playing some wonderful games on our ground both in football and cricket. In his last letter to Mr Corner, he wrote: "I hope I shall be spared once more to wield the willow in the dear old School field". We extend our deep sympathy to his widow and mother in their sad loss.

Clode is buried in Dozinghem Military Cemetery in Belgium.

Clode's wife chose his gravestone inscription:

**IN THE MIDST OF LIFE
WE ARE IN DEATH**

[18] 8th August 1917, Taunton Courier and Western Advertiser from British Newspaper Archive.

110716 SERJEANT
P. A. CLODE
ROYAL GARRISON ARTILLERY
21ST JULY 1917 AGE 28
UBIQUE

Army Service Records

Percy Clode is one of the few soldiers whose Army Service Records are still available to read, most having been destroyed by German bombing in WW2. Here the various forms, service history and correspondence are stored in one 'folder'. Clode's service records give some insight into the long and sometimes arduous process that the next of kin went through in both trying to retrieve their loved one's personal effects and secure, in this case, the 'widow's pension'. Slow post, missed letters and bureaucratic forms all contributed to adding the stress to those still mourning their loss. Letters in the folder allow us to glimpse the pain and frustration of Percy's wife as she had to prove her marriage and the birth of their son.

For Clode's wife, the return of the personal effects was paramount and there are certain items which she longed to have back. In November it seems she was sent the personal items Clode had on him when he died. His wife's correspondence and photos are listed first. It must have given her some comfort to think that she was with him in some small way when he went into battle.

A postcard sent to Mabel from Percy gives us a poignant sense of the man, his love for his family and the huge sacrifice going to war meant for both himself and his family.[19]

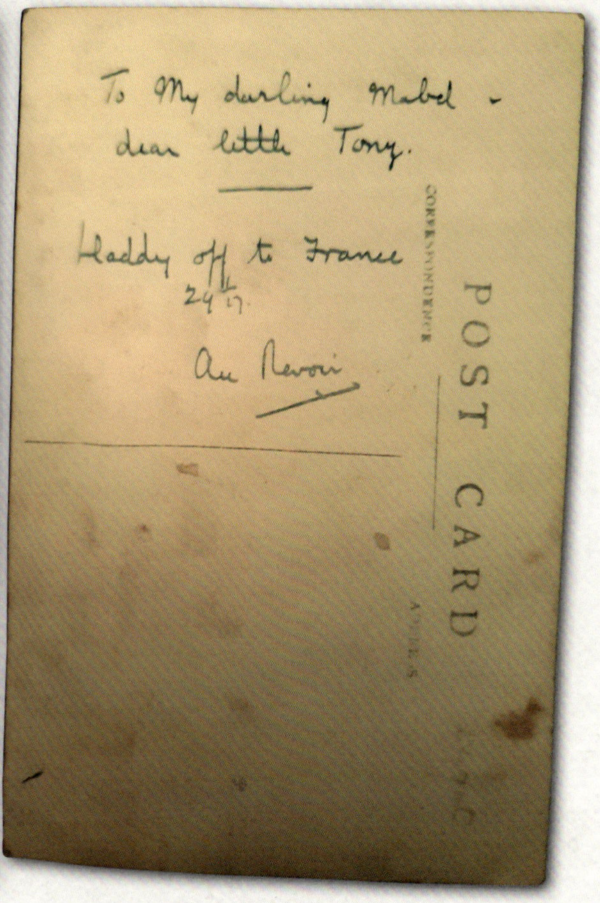

Clode's associations with Wellington School are deeper than many realise. His wife was the aunt of Frank Gillard, another famous old Wellingtonian.

[19] With kind permission of Clode's grandson.

Wellington Memorial Chapel - Letter to George Corner

Though we don't have a letter from Mabel, Clode's mother wrote to George Corner on October 15th, 1929.

Dear Mr Corner,

I have been away from home or should have replied to your letter before. I regret not being able to say the place where Percy fell, he was at the time somewhere near Arras. The only record we have is date when killed, cemetery where he is buried and nearest railway station as below.

Sgt. Percy Alfred Clode 110716, 244 Siege Battery, Royal Garrison Artillery fell 21st July 1917. Age 28. Buried at Dozinghem Military Cemetery. West Vleteren Belgium. Nearest station – Poperinghe [sic].

I fear this is of no use for your requirements.

My very best wishes to you and Mrs Corner,

Yours sincerely

E. Clode

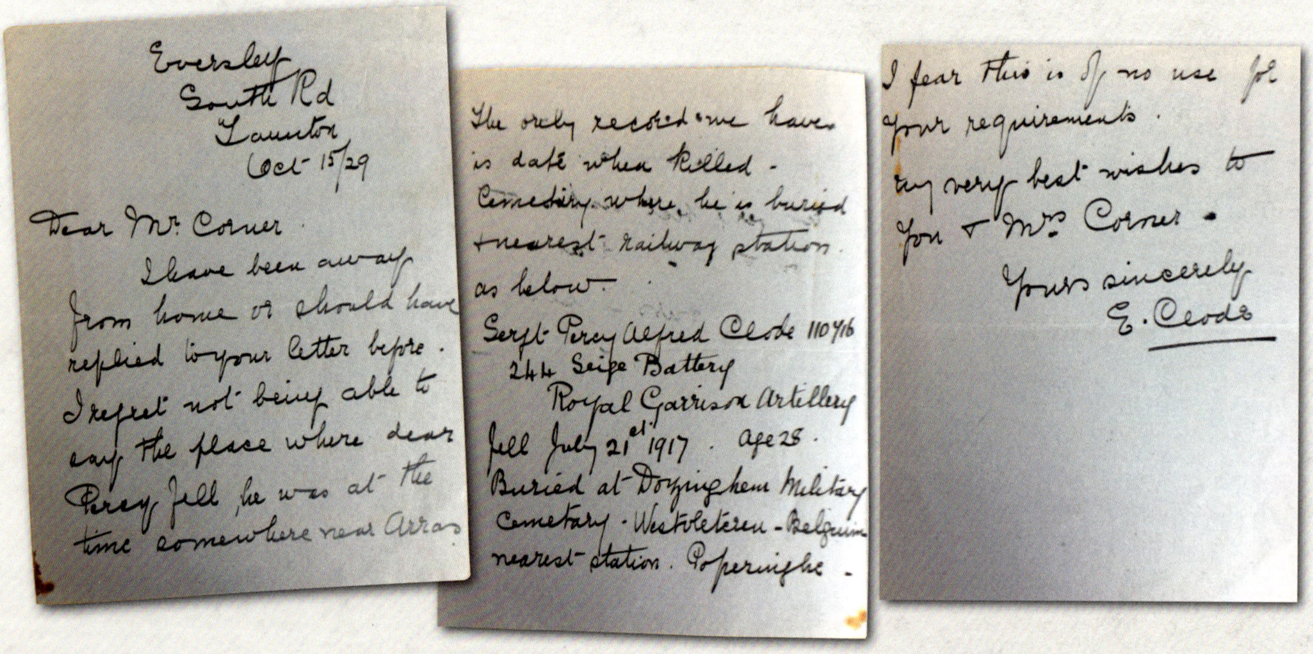

Eversley
South Rd
Taunton
Oct 15/29

Dear Mr Corner
I have been away from home or should have replied to your letter before. I regret not being able to say the place where dear Percy fell, he was at the time somewhere near Arras

The only record we have is date when killed - Cemetery where he is buried & nearest railway station as below.
Sergt Percy Alfred Clode 110716
244 Seige Battery
Royal Garrison Artillery
fell July 21st 1917. Age 25.
Buried at Dozinghem Military Cemetary. Westvleteren - Belgium
nearest station. Poperinghe.

I fear this is of no use for your requirements.
My very best wishes to you & Mrs Corner.
Yours sincerely
E. Clode

Clode's mother refers to him falling at Arras yet he is buried in Belgium over an hour's drive away. This shows, perhaps, the difficulty the families had in getting correct information about their loved ones. The sheer number of casualties must have made it very difficult for the correct information to be passed on.

2ND LIEUT. E. F. CORNER,
8th Batt. East Kent Regiment (The Buffs),
Killed in action near Hulluch, Sept. 26th, 1915.

2nd Lieut. Edward Franklin Corner

b. 1895 – died 26th September 1915, aged 20

'2nd Lieutenant E. F. Corner was first reported 'Missing believed killed', but we deeply regret to record that there appears the slenderest hope that this promising young officer has survived the fierce fighting of Sept. 26th.'

Edward Franklin Corner is Remembered with Honour on the Loos Memorial. He was also remembered by Darks House on November 11th 2007 and flowers were placed in Chapel in his memory.

Edward Franklin Corner was the only son and eldest child of Edward Corner and his wife, Jane (nee Bailey). The couple married in 1894 in Wellington. Edward Franklin Corner was also the nephew of George Corner.

In 1901, the family was living in Wellesley Park, Wellington where Edward listed his occupation as a Brick and Tile Manufacturer. The family consisted of Edward, aged 36, Jane, aged 32, Edward Franklin, aged 5, Norah Franklin, aged 4, Janet Franklin, aged 1, and Margaret who was only 4 months old. Tragedy struck the family before the next census when Janet died, aged 10, in 1909. She was buried in Wellington Cemetery. By the next census in 1911, most of the family had moved down to Cornwall. Edward Franklin Corner was at The County School. Further tragedy followed when Jane Corner, Edward's mother, passed away on 23rd February 1915, in Eastry, Kent. She was also buried in Wellington Cemetery.

School Life

Edward Franklin Corner was a 'high achiever' and there are numerous references to him throughout the Magazines covering the years he was at School.

Virtue Functi More Patrum Duces

Corner – entered May 1905, left April 1914. Form VI.

Prefect, Jan 1913; Senior Prefect, Jan 1914; 1907 Cambridge Preliminary; 1908 Cambridge Preliminary, 3rd Class Honours.

1910, Cambridge Junior 2nd Class; 1911, Cambridge Senior 3rd Class; 1912 Cambridge Senior 3rd Class; O.T.C. Col-Sergt. Certificate A, Nov 1912; Qualified Signaller 1909, 1910, 1911, 1912, 1913; 2nd XI Football Colours, Oct 1911; 1st XI Football Colours, March 1914; 1st XI Cricket Colours, June 1912; Vice-Capt. Cricket, 1913; Fives Capt. Jan 1914; Address: Bell Hotel, Sandwich.

Edward Franklin Corner's War

In April 1914 the Magazine reports that E. F. Corner has become a 2nd Lieutenant East Kent Regt. (The Buffs), South Down, Shoreham.

2nd Lieut. E. F. Corner, 8th Service Battalion, The Buffs, writes on Aug. 15th from Farnborough:

I shall suppose we shall soon be shifting. We were inspected on Tuesday by Lord Kitchener and he was quite satisfied with everything. I have got the job of machine gunner and have just had three weeks at Hythe. We begin firing the guns tomorrow.

2nd Lieut. E. F. Corner writes on August 30th:

We are off now in a day or so for France. We shall get up in line just about a year after joining I guess.

The 8th Battalion of The Buffs mobilised in France on 1st September 1915.

The Last Letter We Received From 'Teddy'

Sept. 11th 1915

Dear Uncle George,

We have been out here some days now and I have been sent up here on a week's course. We have not yet heard when we shall go up the line, but it won't be long I expect. We are billeted in a small village, miles from anywhere and no one can speak a word of English. We can hear the guns occasionally when the wind is right. The crossing was very good, and only one or two were ill.

Please excuse this scrawl but I have the only pen of the place.

The country is not much different from England except in the arrangement of the trees.

I saw the Prince of Wales a day or so ago; he was sweating up a hill on a push-bike.

Our address is 8th Buffs, B. E. F.

We get the job of censoring our men's letters. They are very quaint and are quite amusing, but we are not allowed to discuss them.

It is quite warm out here and if we get much marching the men will feel it very much with their full packs, as they carry everything with them.

I should be glad if you could write occasionally. We do get papers but except here, they are two days late, and letters are very welcome.

When does Harold expect to come out?

It is likely that because Teddy was George Corner's nephew he had greater access to the correspondence sent to his brother in the light of Teddy's death. Edward took it very hard and spent months trying to ascertain exactly what had happened to his son. Over time, the picture became clearer but the pain of losing an only son did not diminish. To think that the exact fate of his son was unknown was extremely hard to accept and there was always a tremor of hope that maybe, just maybe, good news would be found.

Remembering Edward Franklin Corner

School Obituary

2nd Lieutenant E. F. Corner

8th Batt. East Kent Regiment (The Buffs)
Killed in action near Hulluch, September 26th 1915.

2nd Lieutenant E. F. Corner was first reported "Missing believed killed," but we deeply regret to record that there appears the slenderest hope that this promising young officer has survived the fierce fighting of Sept. 26th.

We publish three letters, one from his Company Sergt-Major A Company of his battalion, one from the Capt. (Anthony Hamilton) and one from General Mitford, all addressed to the young officer's father, Mr E. Corner. They speak eloquently for themselves. These letters also give a brief but vivid picture of the terrible fighting in this portion of the line – surely men never had to face a hotter conflict.

2nd Lieutenant E. F. Corner was the only son of Mr E. Corner and nephew of the present Headmaster of Wellington School, where he received his education from the age of ten until the outbreak of the war. He enlisted in the first month of the war and was at once given a commission in the 8th Battalion Buffs (East Kent Regiment). At School he held many of the chief posts and won many prizes, being for some time senior prefect and receiving his colours for both cricket and football. A boy of lovable nature he will always best be known as 'Teddy Corner,' diligent, unassuming, and always ready to help those around him. He will be remembered by many old public-school signallers as a most reliable signaller, for he was able when still at school to take his place with a signaller of the Regular Army, and indeed often did so with credit, being often commended by the O. C. Signals at Rugby, now Headmaster at Bradfield. He matriculated whilst still at School, and also obtained a Certificate 'A' O.T.C.. He promised well as an engineer and has left several specimens of his work at his old school which are still in constant use.

France, 13th October 1915

Dear Sir,

I am in receipt of your letter addressed to Private Ballard, who I am sorry to say is missing, in which you ask for information regarding your son. The news that I can give you, I am sorry to say, will not help in the request you ask, and I only wish that I could give you good news. A better lad or officer we could not have had, being respected by all and one to study his men.

On the night (Saturday) the 25th September, he took over this platoon when ordered to attack a village; after completing this movement we retired back to the German trenches which were captured the day before with very few casualties. On Sunday morning the 26th, we had orders to attack Hill (deleted by Censor), and your son was detailed to take a Brigade Machine Gun with its complement of men from the Buffs. We made our advance exactly at 11 a.m. and from the time we left the trenches until we received orders to retire we were under the most severe fire that any troops could stand. Your son was at work with his gun on our left. The last time I saw him he was dashing up the Hill (deleted by Censor) with his team, after that, I saw no more of him. None of his gun team returned, his sergeant was wounded and taken prisoner; that is the only one we have any news of. With reference to the battalion, on Sunday, the 26th, out of 1,000 men who made the advance only 350 returned. My company, A, only had 60 men left and no officer. I don't think that we can strike another quarter so hot, so in conclusion, I hope that your son is safe, and by the time you receive this letter you may have better news. If I should hear anything regarding him, I shall only be too pleased to communicate the news to you.

Yours truly,

Company Sergeant-Major, 8th Battalion. The Buffs

France, October 10th, 1915

Dear Sir,

I am writing to you as our Commanding Officer is away. I will tell you all I can about your son but would first like to say how much everyone liked him and appreciated him. Speaking as one of the older men, I can tell you what an example he was to some of the other boys, always as keen as mustard and ready for work at any time. He was with the Brigade Machine Gun Officer (Curtis) who was also killed. I fear all the party suffered very heavily so it is impossible to get any definite news. We never found your boy's body and as they were some way back fighting most gallantly, we feared the worst. Still, the work of sending through names is very slow. I fear, however, that he must have been fatally hit.

Will you accept my most sincere sympathy in losing such a son.

Yours sincerely,
Anthony Hamilton, (Capt.)

Ps. The first time I saw our General after the fight he particularly mentioned him with great regret.

Brigadier General Mitford, writing on October 22nd, to Mr E. Corner, said:

"I regret very much that I can hold out no hope whatever of your gallant son being alive. I knew him and have watched him at his work for the last three years or four months and had a high opinion of his abilities, his keenness, and of the way in which he carried out his duties. Consequently, I asked especially about him during the afternoon of the 26th, when collecting and reorganising what was left of the various battalions of the Brigade after their gallant advance up to the 3rd line trenches. From what I learnt I think there is no doubt that your son was killed instantaneously by a shell which burst only a foot or two over him, as he was lying alongside his machine gun. All his team were killed or wounded and now prisoners. His death is a loss to the regiment, as well as to those of his own kith and kin, and I sincerely offer my condolences and sympathy to you and yours. He died a death any soldier would be proud to die – in action for his King and Country."

"The General's address to his Brigade, dated October 3rd, states that on the previous Sunday it went into action for the first time, only a year after the men came forward at their country's call, and though they had to retire their advance was not a failure, as they caused 16 of the enemy's reserve battalions to be brought into their area, and taken from the French just south of them, thereby enabling the French to make an appreciable advance. He should like all of them who knew the relatives of those now not with them to make known to them how gallantly they fought and how nobly they served their country in whose service they fell, and what prestige they brought to the names of the regiments to which they belonged. He felt it a great honour to have the chance of commanding such troops on service and he should never forget the ground about the village of Hulluch."

E. F. Corner's name has recently been added to the War Memorial in Wellington Park along with that of J. N. Treble and 31 other Wellington soldiers who lost their lives in WW1. He is featured in the publication ***Our Other Boys*** by Mike Perry and Ray Hitchcock

Letters from Edward Corner to George

The sense of hopelessness and grief is palpable in the correspondence from Edward. Not knowing exactly what happened to his son is tortuous, particularly following on so soon from the death of his wife. When Edward writes to George he is, of course, writing as a brother so the tone is more intimate than in many of the parents' letters.

My dear George,

Thank you for your letter. I cannot write about Ted yet, the blow is too severe. I am making every effort to get news. I send you all I have. Elizabeth found a wounded Buff in hospital at Shrewsbury. He saw Ted at 5 am. Sept 26th. Later they charged and this man was one of the final to fall, shot through stomach. The following is from his description. He was quickly patched up and sent away. He knows no more. As Ted was with the Brigade guns I am afraid the Buff officers cannot tell much. I am writing to Lord Mitford who knew Ted, asking him to have enquiries made.

I wish he had survived this final battle. I feel sure he could have got on well. How he would have liked to help in the good repulse of a few days ago.

You will remember the Germans retook Pit 8 on 26th – 27th and held it until I think Oct. 4th when it was again taken by us – see Lord Mitford's report Oct 6th or thereabouts.

Your affectionate brother,
Edward

Ps. I shall be glad if you will show all this to Annie Bailey (?) and anyone else you think proper.

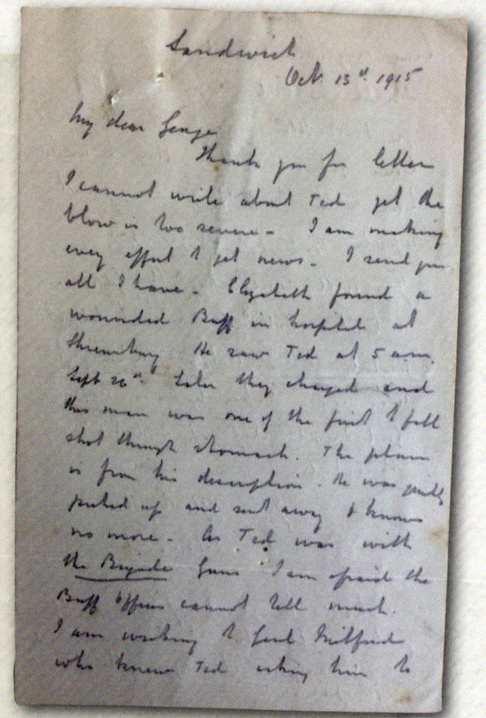

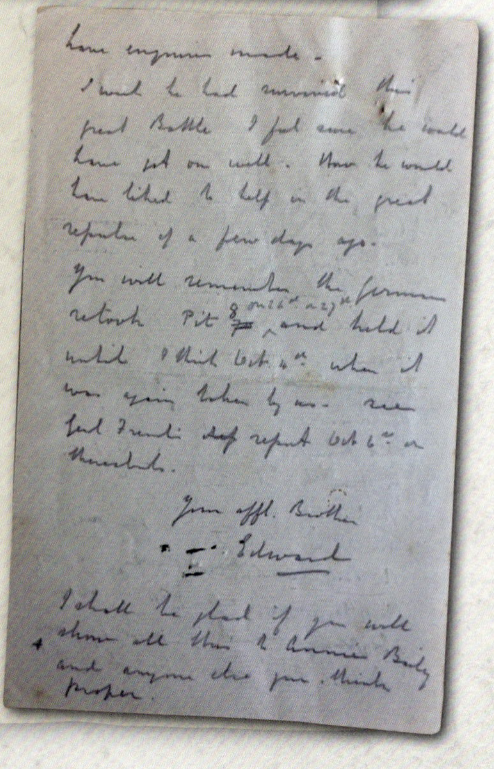

However, there was clear pride when he received a message from Buckingham Palace.

October 12th, 1915
Buckingham Palace 2.15 pm

To E. Corner Esq, Sandwich Kent
The King and Queen deeply regret the loss you and the army have sustained by the reported death of your son in the service of his country. Their majesties truly sympathise with you in your sorrow.

Keeper of the Privy Purse.

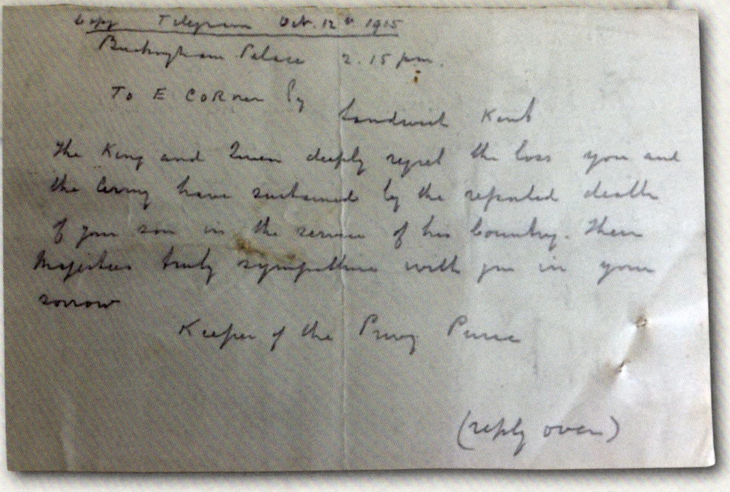
Copy Telegram Oct. 12th 1915
Buckingham Palace 2.15 pm.
To E Corner Esq
Sandwich Kent
The King and Queen deeply regret the loss you and the army have sustained by the reported death of your son in the service of his country. Their Majesties truly sympathise with you in your sorrow
Keeper of the Privy Purse
(reply over)

To: Keeper of the Privy Purse Buckingham Palace
Please express to their majesties my humble thanks for their gracious message of sympathy in the loss of my Boy who has done his duty also assurance of my personal devotion.
Edward Corner

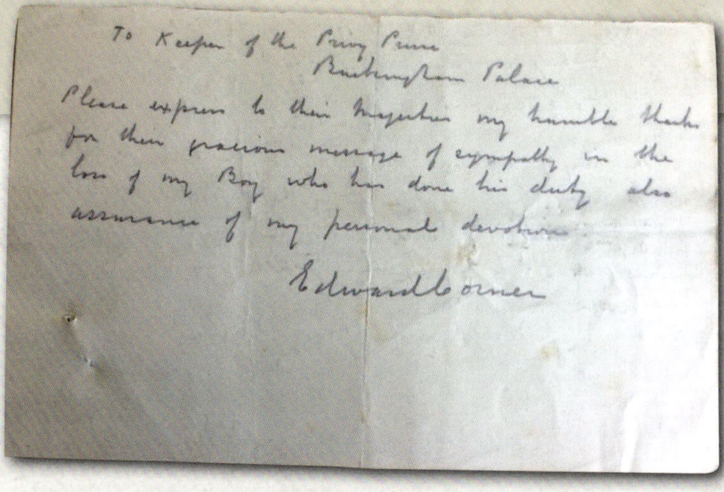
To Keeper of the Privy Purse
Buckingham Palace
Please express to their Majesties my humble thanks for their gracious message of sympathy in the loss of my Boy who has done his duty also assurance of my personal devotion.
Edward Corner

P. FARRANT, died on training.

Cadet Percy Farrant

b. 1890 – died 30th June 1916, aged 26.

"He was a boy of good ability and a hard worker, remarkable for his willing disposition and unfailing good nature." School Obituary

Percy Farrant is Remembered with Honour in Hemyock Cemetery. He is the only one of our Old Boys to be buried in England. In November 2009 he was remembered by Lights House and flowers were placed in Chapel in his memory.

Percy Farrant was the fourth son of Samuel (b. 1850) and Mary Farrant (nee Pringle) (b. 1853). Samuel was a farmer and the family lived in Hemyock.

In 1891, the family was living in Westown Hemyock. They had three sons living with them, but it is apparent that their son, Robert, was born in 1885 and died two years later in 1887. The eldest son was Samuel John (b. 1879), then Edward (b. 1881) and lastly, Percy, (b.1890).

In 1901, the family was still together, and the two older boys were listed as being a Farmer's son and a Dental Student respectively. Percy was a schoolboy and only 11 years of age.

By 1911, all the Farrant boys had left home and Samuel and Mary were on their own apart from their servants. Samuel (known as John) had married Sarah and was living with his two children and wife. John Bright Farrant was 3 years old and Samuel Farrant only 1. Edward had also married in 1910 and was living in Wellington. His wife Ellen Victoria (nee Clist) had given birth a month previously and their son was recorded as Infant Farrant. He later became Robert Edward Clist Farrant.

In 1911, Percy was recorded as being the guest of George Medway and his family at Hill Farm, North Curry, Somerset where he was a 'Pupil to Auctioneer and Surveyor assisting to Land Agent'.

School Life

Farrant's Virtue Functi More Patrum Duces is printed in the 1906 magazine:

Percy Farrant – entered September 1901, left Easter 1906. VI Form. Prefect, Sept. 1905, Football Colours, Xmas 1904, 3rd Class Honours Cambridge Junior, Xmas 1904-1905.

Percy Farrant's War

An account in the following publication tells us what befell Farrant. He never made it to frontline action and was in training when he 'fell'. It is interesting for many reasons but especially for giving some information about the often overlooked nurses.

From *The Upper Culm Valley Before, During and After the Great War*

On November 3rd 1915, just a few weeks after his marriage to Ethel, and at the age of twenty-five, Percy enlisted in the Inns of Court Officer Training Corps (OTC) at Lincoln's Inn, London, as part of the Territorial Force. Sadly, Percy's military career was relatively short-lived. Just over two months into his service, he contracted scarlet fever, which hospitalized him until February 22nd. Having recovered, he then suffered acute appendicitis for which he was taken to Aylesbury Military Hospital in Buckinghamshire, now known worldwide as the Stoke Mandeville Hospital. Unfortunately, it was too late. Percy died on June 30th, 1916. He was engaged with the Territorial Force for a total of 241 days, training to serve his country during that time.

A nurse before the war, Ethel also signed up to become part of the Territorial Force, joining the Nursing Service. She enlisted on October 27th, 1914, and amended her details following her marriage about a year later. During her time as a military nurse, she was based at 14 General Hospital on the north coast of France in the town of Wilmereux, near Calais. She would have known Dr John McCrae, the writer of the famous lines quoted in the Foreword. She spent just over two years as part of the Territorial Force Nursing Service, resigning on February 13th, 1917, a few months after the death of her husband and a few weeks before John Lutely arrived at the same hospital.

Ethel received a widow's pension of ten shillings a week commencing on January 1st, 1917. Initial correspondence was sent to an address in North Curry where the couple had met but, a few months later, Ethel moved to Station Road, Hemyock, to be close to her husband's family. Born in Devizes, Ethel later moved to her home county of Wiltshire and died aged 80 in Wootton Bassett in 1963. She had been a widow for 47 years, having lost her husband Percy after just nine months of marriage.[20]

Percy's Death

The Western Times reported Percy's death in the Hemyock section of the paper. It speaks of the tragedy being enhanced by Samuel's failure to reach his son before he died, even though he was on his way. According to the paper, he was five minutes too late.

Deep and widespread sympathy is felt with Mr and Mrs Samuel Farrant, of Westown whose youngest son, Lieut. Percy Farrant passed away at Aylesbury on Friday afternoon from appendicitis. The young officer was taken ill about a week previously, and an operation was performed. He became worse, and his father was telegraphed for. Mr Farrant at once set out but arrived about five minutes after his son had breathed his last. Prior to the war, the young officer was with Messrs. Morris, Son, and Peard, of Taunton, and later was appointed a Government valuer under Mr Lloyd George's scheme. He was of fine physique, and of a genial disposition, and was married last October.[21]

[20] 'The Upper Culm Valley, Before, During and After the Great War, by Blackdown Archives, 2014.
[21] The Western Times, 7th July 1916 from the British Newspaper Archive.

Remembering Percy Farrant

School Obituary

Cadet Percy Farrant

June 30th 1916.

Percy Farrant, youngest son of Mr Farrant, of Westown, Hemyock, entered the School in Sept. 1901, leaving in April 1906. He was a boy of good ability and a hard worker, remarkable for his willing disposition and unfailing good nature. He played in both elevens, won his 1st XI Colours for Football, and in his last years was a Prefect and Captain of Football, and of the Dark Blues. After leaving School he was one of the staff appointed to carry out the Land Valuation Scheme for the Government, and when released for O.T.C.. On completing his training, he was to have taken a commission offered him in the West Somerset Yeomanry, but unhappily contracted a serious illness which proved to be fatal, dying at the Military Hospital at Aylesbury. Deep regret is felt by all who knew Percy Farrant's useful and kindly life and all the greatest sympathy is extended to his widow, parents and family, who have the consolation that he gave his life for his country's cause.

F. H. FORD, missing since August, 1915 (believed killed).

Trooper Frederick Henry Ford

b. 1895 – died 21st August 1915, aged 20

"Freddie" Ford was devotedly attached to his old School and followed its doings with constant interest. He served in the fighting in Egypt and was reported as missing in August 1915." School Obituary

Frederick Henry Ford is Remembered with Honour on Helles Memorial. In November 2018 he will be remembered by Grange House and a poppy will be placed in Chapel in his memory.

Freddie was the eldest son of Robert Frederick Ford and Diana Elizabeth Ford (nee Wells) of North Newton, Wiltshire. Robert was a corn merchant. In the 1901 census, the couple had three children: Frederick Henry (b. 1896), Robert Charles (b. 1897) and Reginald Frank (b. 1899).

Two more sons were born: Wilfred Percy (b. 1901) and Harold Christy (b. 1904), but the family experienced a profound tragedy when Robert Charles died aged 7 ½ on 18th October 1904. The death was recorded on 22nd October in the 'Wiltshire and Trowbridge Times'. Quite how Robert died, we don't know, but we can guess his death had a profound effect on the family. By the census of 1911, the family appeared to have disintegrated. Robert, the father, was living at Fairview House, Bottlesford, N. Newton, Pewsey, with no other family members. Diana was living in Chirton, Wiltshire with Harry (aged 7) and had written 'separated wife' on the census form. Reginald (aged 12) and Wilfred (aged 9) were both boarding at The County School. Frederick, aged 15, was a boarder and working as an apprentice corn merchant in Egham.

Freddie must have signed up to fight in the war quite early; as did Reginald. There is a record of a Reginald Frank Ford joining the Prince of Wales Volunteers of the South Lancashire Regiment in 1915. Although we are not sure if this is our Reginald, his father is cited as being Robert Frederick Ford, so it does seem likely.

School Life

In the **Virtue Functi More Patrum Duces** Ford's short but important School career was summarised as follows:

F. H. Ford entered Sept. 1908, left July 1910. 2nd XI football colours, October 1909, Lance Corporal O.T.C. Summer 1910.

Frederick Henry Ford's War

Before the war, Freddie Ford worked as a corn and seed merchant's clerk. In the 'List of Old

Boys Serving Their Country', printed in the December 1914 edition of the School Magazine, Ford is shown to have joined up almost as soon as war was declared:

Ford, F. H. Trooper A Squadron, 3rd Troop East Berks. Yeomanry. 2nd South Midland Mounted Brigade, Churn Camp, Acacia Lodge, Wokingham, Berks.

1/1st Berkshire Yeomanry

The regiment was mobilized with its brigade on 4th August 1914 upon the outbreak of the First World War. Initially, it concentrated in Berkshire and on 5th August 1914 joined the 1st Mounted Division. On 2nd September it was transferred to the 2nd Mounted Division and in mid-November 1914 it moved with its division to Norfolk on coastal defence duties.

In April 1915, the 2nd Mounted Division moved to Egypt arriving at Alexandria between 19th and 21st April and was posted to Cairo by the middle of May. Here, Ford wrote to George Corner:

We came out here in April and spent a week under canvas at Alexandria: now we are at Cairo in barracks doing garrison duty. I have been to the Pyramids which are about six miles from our barracks.

On May 14th he says:

We are still in barracks. For me, this is a lovely climate to live in, although from 9 a.m. to 4 p.m. it is very hot, so much so that there is very little work to be done between those hours except by the natives.

May 22nd. As you can guess we are rather cut up by not having a chance to do a little, but from appearances, it looks as though we shall be with the lads right amongst it in a few weeks. Of course, there is a chance of the Arabs rising, but I think it is very remote, for although very ignorant they seem quite happy under our protection. I hear Italy has at last declared war and America would have done so long before, but they are a nation for Dollars and not for blood.

Berkshire Yeomanry Archive

Ford comes across as quite an opinionated and eager young man, keen to do more and be 'right amongst it'. He seems bored with the more touristy activities and looks forward to having more of a purpose than doing little in the heat.

The regiment was dismounted in August 1915 and took part in the Gallipoli campaign. It left squadron headquarters and two troops (about 100 officers and men) in Egypt to look after the horses.

They landed at 'A' Beach, Suvla Bay on 18 August and moved to bivouacs at Lala Baba on 20 August. On 21st August they advanced to Chocolate Hill via Salt Lake and Hetman Chair and took part in the attack on Scimitar Hill. Due to losses during the Battle of Scimitar Hill and wastage during August 1915, the 2nd Mounted Division had to be reorganised.

Ford's date of death on the 21st August would fit with him being killed in the attack on Scimitar Hill. Details remain sketchy, however.

In the July 1915 Magazine, Ford is 'reported as missing':
Freddie Ford was reported 'missing' from the Dardanelles in August. We have no news of him since.

Remembering Frederick Henry Ford

School Obituary

Trooper F. H. Ford

August 1915 (believed killed).

F. H. Ford was the eldest son of Mr Ford of Woodborough, Wilts, and entered the School in Sept. 1908, leaving in July 1910. 'Freddie' Ford was devotedly attached to his old School and followed its doings with constant interest. He served in the fighting in Egypt and was reported missing in Aug. 1915. It was hoped that news of his safety might have been received, but unhappily his family have reluctantly given up their fruitless endeavours to obtain any information as to his fate. His parents and brothers have received great sympathy in the painfully sad circumstances which leave no doubt of their loss.

Berkshire Yeomanry

In October 2010, a project was begun to install a permanent memorial to commemorate those who fell serving in the Berkshire Yeomanry. Inspired by the bravery of the only V.C. from the Berks., Trooper Potts, the statue was finally unveiled on 4th October 2015, just over 100 years after the fighting in Gallipoli. Frederick Ford is remembered here, and his name is on the memorial.

Wellington School Memorial Chapel - Letter to George Corner from Robert Frederick Ford

In 1929, Robert Ford writes from Bottlesford:

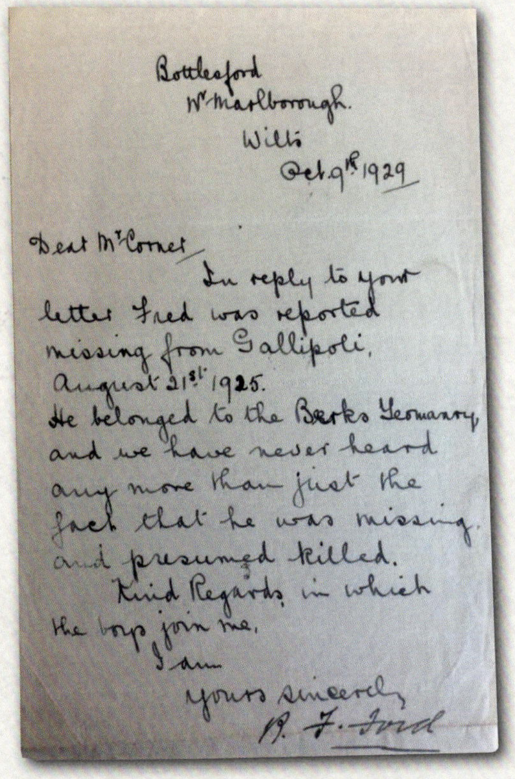

Bottlesford
Nr Marlborough.
Wilts
Oct 9th 1929

Dear Mr Corner
In reply to your letter Fred was reported missing from Gallipoli, August 21st 1915.
He belonged to the Berks Yeomanry and we have never heard any more than just the fact that he was missing and presumed killed.
Kind Regards in which the boys join me.
I am
Yours sincerely
R. F. Ford

Like so many other families, the Ford family had only limited information about their son and the circumstances of his death. The above letter is dated 1929, just over 14 years since Freddie was listed as missing believed killed; fourteen years of no information and no real idea of what happened must have been very hard to live with. What is more, there was no grave or headstone to give a sense of closure. Freddie Ford is commemorated with twenty thousand other men on the Helles Memorial.

J. H. GENT, 13th Hussars (died on active service).

Pte. John Henry Gent

b. 1895 – died 1st November 1918, aged 23

"Mr and Mrs Gent received many letters from Jack's comrades, telling of his pluck and his bravery, and one close friend who was with him at the last in Meerut wrote to Mrs Gent in these touching words, "Dear Jack fought magnificently, and his friendship was as true as steel." School Obituary

John Henry Gent is Remembered with Honour in Meerut Cantonment Cemetery and on the Delhi War Memorial. On November 11th 2007 he was remembered by Willows House and flowers were placed in Chapel in his memory.

John Henry Gent (b. 1895) was the second son of Frederick Gent, a farmer (b. 1864) and Emily (nee Blackmore, b. 1857). The couple had married on December 15th, 1891. In 1901, the family was living at Moss Hayne Farm in Broadclyst, having spent time living at West Monkton. John Henry, known as Jack, had two siblings: a brother, Fred (b. 1896) and a younger sister, Elizabeth Sealy (b. 1898). In the 1901 census records, Henry Gent, Frederick's father, was visiting the family. He was listed as a widower.

In 1911 Jack was a boarder at Wellington School and is recorded on the School's census.

John Henry Gent's War

The 'List of Old Boys Serving Their Country' in December 1914 records that Gent is a Trooper 4th Class for A Squadron, 11th Hussars and is based at 31 Camp Aldershot.

Records show that he arrived in France on 17th August 1915 as part of the 13th Hussars. The Meerut Brigade served in the 2nd Indian Cavalry Division and saw action on the Western Front in France and Flanders for the next two years.

The regiment fought in their mounted role and in the trenches for some time but in July 1916 they moved to Mesopotamia forming part of the 7th Indian Cavalry Brigade. They saw action here including Kut Al Amara and the capture of Baghdad in March 1917. Gent fought in many actions until April 1918 when he became ill, having to be hospitalised.

John Henry Gent's death was announced in the Exeter and Plymouth Gazette on Friday 22nd November 1918 – eleven days after the Armistice. This news, coming when the country was 'celebrating' the war's end, must have been even more distressing for his family.

Remembering John Henry Gent

School Obituary

Jack Gent

13th Hussars (died on active service) 1st November 1918.

John Henry Gent, younger son of Mr and Mrs F. Gent, of Mosshayne, Pinhoe, Exeter, entered the School in May 1907, and with his elder brother Fred. He left in April 1911, and during those four years of School life, he was loved by all for his delightful nature and sterling qualities. He was in the Devon Yeomanry and at the outbreak of war was stationed at first in Ireland and then at Aldershot, with 13th Hussars. Here he stayed for nearly a year training officers, as he was a fine horseman and a crack shot. A commission was offered to him, but he would not accept it and he was sent to France, where he served for a time. Then came the order to proceed to Mesopotamia, where he saw much heavy fighting and was one of the first to enter Baghdad. He was engaged in many battles until April 1918, when his health gave way under the hardships and the climate. He was then sent to Bombay to recruit his strength and from thence to various hospitals. Finally, he moved to Meerut, where he died, to the unspeakable sorrow of his parents who were counting the days to his return home, where he might, they hoped, be restored to health. Mr and Mrs Gent received many letters from Jack's comrades, telling of his pluck and bravery, and one close friend who was with him at the last in Meerut wrote to Mrs Gent in these touching words, "Dear Jack fought magnificently, and his friendship was as true as steel." One can add little to such a tribute. His memory will always be very dear to those who knew him.

Gent is also remembered on the Broadclyst War Memorial tablet inside the Church of St. John the Baptist in Broadclyst.

2nd Lieut. C. G. Gordon,
3rd Battalion Gordon Highlanders.
Killed Mametz Wood, July 1st, 1916.

2nd Lieut. Colin Graham Gordon

b. 1891 – died 1st July 1916, aged 25

'Indeed, Colin Gordon was greatly beloved by all who knew him... But most of all he will be remembered for his true impersonation of Henry V in the School Play of 1909.'' School Obituary

Colin Graham Gordon is Remembered with Honour in the Gordon Cemetery, Mametz. In November 2018 he will be remembered by Hardwick House and a poppy will be placed in Chapel in his memory.

Colin Graham Gordon was the only son of Henry Gordon and Bessie Laura Gordon (nee Swaffield) and was born in 1889. The 1891 census shows him living with his parents and three sisters in Portville, Bothenhampton, Dorset. His father was a civil engineer and secretary and manager to a water company and aged 37. His mother, Bessie, was 43. Colin's sisters were all older than him: Mabel Irene (b. 1880), Agnes Mary Gordon (b. 1881) and Gladys Emily (b. 1885).

By 1911, two daughters had moved away. Agnes was living with her parents (aged 29) at 48 West Bay Road, Portville, Bridport. Bessie's mother, Anna M H Swaffield, was recorded as being a visitor at this time. Colin was recorded as living at 28 May Flower Road, Clapham Road, SW. where he was boarding whilst training to be a solicitor.

School Life

Colin Gordon entered the School in 1903, but the first real mentions of him are in the Magazines from July 1906. Every school has pupils who seem to shine and create a larger than life legacy, and Gordon was one of these. He seems to have excelled in all he did and, more importantly, was very much liked and respected by all. He was a contemporary of W. J. C. Brown and they were great friends, Corner writes of them dying only three months apart.

The April 1909 edition records Gordon's legendary performance as Henry V. The production also saw Corner, Bowerman, Brown, Bilton, Kidner, Gent, Shapland and Ford on the stage. Of Gordon's performance we read, '***the dominating part of the play, that of Henry 'the mirror of all Christian Kings', 'the star of England' was ably sustained by C. G. Gordon, who won constant applause and delighted all by his elocution and acting, which were perfectly natural and dignified.'***

At the Athletic Sports on Saturday 10th April 1909, Gordon presented Miss Gill with a beautiful bouquet of flowers and then called for cheers which were 'given with enthusiasm'. He also won the 100 Yards in a time of 10.8 seconds, a School record.

Colin Graham Gordon's War

In the December 1914 Magazine a 'List of Old Boys Serving Their Country' was printed. Gordon was on this:

Dec. 1909 Gordon, C. G. Lance Corporal H. Co. 1550, 14th County of London and Scottish, No. 2 General Hospital (39), St Mark's College, King's Road, Chelsea, S. W.

The London Scottish were involved in action early in the war and Gordon arrived in France on 15th September 1914. Here he saw firsthand the horrors of war. Printed in the early editions of the School Magazine, Gordon's letters from the front give us a real picture of what is happening, but he does so with ironic humour and wit. He clearly is a character.

Lc-Cpl. C. G. Gordon writes also on November 1st, 1914:- (published after longer Dec. letter)

God knows why I am alive today. We fought the Germans yesterday and lost heavily; their losses were greater.

How I got out of it was a wonder. I, with half a section, got cut off and had to fight through the German lines. The fellows fought like fury and did very well. Never has the shelling been so great. It all seems a horrid dream. My friends are killed or wounded. Those that died, died well. We have, so they say, made a name that will last forever. I am now among the many wounded. It is too horrid to write about.

Lc-Cpl. C. G. Gordon, of the London Scottish, writes on December 12th 1914, as follows:

You will be sorry to hear that I have been sent home to England with my poor old knee crocked up. It seems to do me in everything. Well, this time it nearly did for me, for it went out as I was retiring from the Germans and had it not gone back almost at once, ten to one the dogs would have done for me as they killed our poor old doctor.

I guess you will like to know how I got on out there. I will not tell you all about what I did before the great Hallow E'en at Messines for it would fill up pages and pages and no doubt you have read of the doings of the great London Scottish in the papers. We were rather sick at the rot the papers have been talking about – we all know that it is for the benefit of the slackers still unarmed, but it was a bit too much. We did our duty and I trust we did it well.

As I have said already, I will not tell you all about how we went to Le Mans, Orleans, Villeneuve, Abbeville, St. Omer, and Ypres before the action at Messines.

Well, this is my story:-

We went to Ypres in motor buses, London ones painted with a kind of dark green, and passed through the town and slept the night in deserted cottages; or rather we tried to sleep, but we were too near the firing line and troops were passing too often for much sleep. We got up at 12 o'clock only to find we had to go to bed again, but finally got up at 4 o'clock and waited for a little time in the road. Most of us sat down in the mud.

We spent most of the early morning wandering in and about the woods. "Jack Johnsons" fell near and often but did us no bodily harm.

As I arrived at the trench a regular cheered me up by saying, "We have just had a 'Jack Johnson' in the trench, it buried four of us, I guess they have our range." I was soon of the same opinion. But the snipers were the worst; they came so close and the bullets whistled past within an inch of your head and if you tried to spot the dog you got another. We were lucky in that we had fairly well-made trenches, while the chaps behind seem to have been for two or more hours in a gutter.

The aeroplanes were always flying over and giving away our position. I have learnt to hate them.

After dark, we dug at our trenches and put straw in the bottom of them. The Germans advanced two or three times before twelve, but the rifle fire was too great for them. Before dark, I had only about a couple of dozen shots at the "dogs" but after dark, we were kept busy.

The Germans set fire to many houses and farms all about the place. Their bands were playing.

I got a little sleep about twelve when the firing seemed to subside greatly on both sides. At about two the Germans made a general advance and then it was I believe the charge at Messines took place. I wish I had been there, but Messines was almost a mile away from where we were. We could see the Germans advance on our right in masses and we had plenty of fun in the way of shooting. They advanced and passed. By now the little farmhouse was on fire.

The captain with us ran back and soon returned to say that we had to retire as quickly as we could. So off we went and soon got scattered. I ran past the burning house, bullets keeping up with me all the time, jumped two ditches (my poor old knee thought of going out at both), and ran to the right away from the Germans, who I believe, were just down the road, towards a crowd of what I thought were Tommies. When I was about fifty yards from them a regular came rushing up and said, "For Gord's sec, don't 'e run into them – them be Germans." I took him to be a worthy man and true, so thought I would not trouble to go and see.

I doubled round the flank and just after this my knee does its little trick. "My number is up," thinks I, but it was not so; before I had walked or dragged myself a dozen yards, it went back. I might tell you my knee has a trick of going out and staying out for hours, in fact once or twice a whole day, not like at school when it was in as soon as it was out.

Well, the rest of my story is unromantic. I quite lost myself for a time and wandered about with some fellow, whom, I know not; a regular I believe – and came at last on a little crowd of Scottish and others by a windmill. I took a chap, wounded in the mouth, poor fellow, to the field hospital (I hear the poor fellow – one of our company – is now dead). I went into a hospital a mile or so on and rested there for the night – knee goes out badly again on the way. Next morning the doctor tells me it is no good returning to the firing line with my knee, so I am sent to Versailles and I am now here.

Well, so much for that.

"He who fights and runs away will live to fight another day."

All I can say to the German dogs is "Just you wait a wee bit."

My knee, I hope, will be operated on shortly, but I want to be with the Scottish. I long for the end of the war more than anything.

Lieut. Male is calling to see me tomorrow or Sunday. My word! How these kids grow."

Gordon's injury required surgery, and this took him out of the war for some months. In 1916 he received a commission from The Gordon Highlanders and went back to France a few weeks before he was killed. On the 1st July 1916, near Mametz, Gordon led his men into battle. Along with tens of Gordon Highlanders, he was killed in what has now become a battle synonymous with the waste and destruction of the war – the first day of the Battle of the Somme.

In the Editorial to the July 1916 Magazine, Colin Graham Gordon's death is announced: *We deeply regret the addition of another name to the Roll of Honour – C. G. Gordon, who was killed in action on July 1st, will be remembered by many who read these pages.*

Remembering Colin Graham Gordon

School Obituary

2nd Lieutenant Colin Graham Gordon
July 1st 1916.

C. G. Gordon, only son of Mr H. Gordon, of Bridport, entered the School in April 1903. By his winning personality and devotion to the games, he rapidly became very popular amongst his schoolfellows. Indeed, Colin Gordon was greatly beloved by all who knew him. He was Colour Sergeant in the Corps in 1908-1909, and he also made his mark in many other ways. He was the finest sprinter the School ever turned out, establishing the record in the 100 yards. He obtained his Football and Cricket Colours, and in 1909 he captained one of our most successful cricket elevens. But most of all he will be remembered for his true impersonation of Henry V. in the School Play of that year. After he left, he worked in London and there he joined the London Scottish; and soon after the outbreak of war he went to France with his battalion and was in charge at Messines. In this fighting, he damaged a knee which had always given him trouble, but he decided to undergo an operation to render himself fit again, and when this was successful he was given a commission in the Gordon Highlanders. He had been in France only a few weeks with his new battalion and was killed near the Somme during the advance on July 1st.

His last letter to Mr Corner was written from the trenches on June 30th:

"Here I am with whizz-bangs falling all around. Guess in a few days I shall be back again in the old country if I am not very lucky. Hope all are well at the old School – my best love to it. How I should love to be there today. I guess you are having a match this afternoon. I have been out here just about a month now and have been in the trenches most of the time. They have been quiet, but things are working a bit more now.

Kind regards to Miss Corner.

I must pay a visit to the old place when next I am in England. Since July 1915, I have spent nearly all my time in Aberdeen. One month at Troon.

Good luck to Wellington."

The colonel of his regiment wrote to Mrs Gordon as follows: "He was shot through the head leading his men gallantly – a fearless soldier whose loss we all mourn. He has been buried in a little cemetery with five other officers who fell on the 1st. inst., by the road near Mansel Copse, leading to Mametz. The graves have all been wired in and a cross put up over each grave. I assure you I deeply deplore his loss and you have all my sympathy, but you will know he died the death of a brave and fearless soldier."

Colin's last visit to the School was on the occasion of the Break-up Supper of Christmas, 1912. Profound sympathy has been felt for his parents and sister in their great and irreparable bereavement.

2nd Lieutenant C. G. Gordon was buried in the Gordon Cemetery, on the road to Mametz. A note written in the Visitor's Book at Gordon Cemetery contains an extract from the diary of a stretcher bearer attached to the Gordon Highlanders as they entered the Battle of the Somme on the 1st July 1916 and it states that all in the Gordon Cemetery are from the 2nd Battalion and the burial of all took place on 3rd July 1916.

The inscription on Gordon's grave reads:

SAFE IN THE ARMS OF JESUS

Gordon Cemetery, on the road to Mametz

The Gordon Cemetery

*"A little further south-east along the road from the Devonshire Cemetery is another beautiful and very moving cemetery - **Gordon Cemetery**. On the 1st of July 1916, the 2nd Gordons attacked to the right of the Devonshires, so these two cemeteries, close to one another, represent their respective attacking fronts; the bodies of those who were killed being buried very near to where they had fallen. The War Office describes the place of burial as 'Behind grave in '67 Support Trench'. Despite the casualties, the attack here was successful, with gains made right through to the north of Mametz."* [22]

There are six graves in a row at the front of the cemetery and these mark the actual burial places of 6 Officers killed on 1st July. Colin G. Gordon is the furthest on the left as you look at the wording of the grave. The rest of the gravestones do not mark actual graves but rather the general place in the cemetery, 'Believed to be buried in this cemetery'. Almost all of the stones cite the date of death as 1st July 1916.

[22] From the website http://www.ww1battlefields.co.uk/somme/mametz.html

F A HEMBROW

Pte. Frank A Hembrow

b. April 1894 - died March 24th 1918, aged 24

"He was one of the simple, cheerful, unobtrusive heroes of the rank and file, whose work was so wonderful in just the daily toils of war."

Frank A Hembrow is Remembered with Honour on the Pozieres Memorial, on panels 25 and 26. In November 2018 he will be remembered by Lights House and a poppy will be placed in Chapel in his memory.

Frank Albert Hembrow was the eldest child of Albert Clement Hembrow (b. 1865) and Ellen Martha Hembrow (nee Smith, b. 1867). He was born in 1894.

In the 1901 census, the family was living at Bridge Close Farm, Hardington Mandeville, where Albert was a farmer. Frank was 7, Kathleen was 5, and Thomas was 2. By 1911, the living arrangements had changed. The family was now farming at Oath, Borobridge, Bridgwater. The boys were still at home, with Frank, now 17, helping on the farm and 12-year-old Thomas attending school. Kathleen was a boarder at a school in Dartmouth, aged 15, and she was with her younger sister, Edith, who was only 9 years of age.

Frank Albert Hembrow's War

Hembrow joined the West Somerset Yeomanry on the outbreak of war. He transferred to the 7th Battalion of the Somerset Light Infantry and went to France in 1916, although it is not clear exactly when. We cannot be sure what exact part Hembrow played in the following battles, but he must have seen much action as part of the 7th Battalion.

The 7th Battalion of the Somerset Light Infantry was part of the 61st Infantry Brigade of the 20th Light Division and was involved in a great deal of action. In 1916 it took part in the Battle of Mount Sorrel (2nd June), the Battle of the Somme including the Battle of Delville Wood (21st August), the Battle of Guillemont (3rd September), the Battle of Flers-Courcelette and the Battle of Morval (27th September), and finally, the Battle of the Transloy Ridges (1st October).

In 1917 it was involved in the German Retreat to the Hindenburg Line (14th March), action on the Hindenburg Line (26th May), the Battle of Ypres including the Battle of Langemarck (16th August 1917), the Battle of Menin Road Ridge (20th September) and the Battle of Polygon Wood (26th September). It also took part in the Battle of Cambrai – the Tank Attack (20th November), the Capture of Bourlon Wood (23rd November) and German Counter-Attacks (30th November).

In 1918, when the Germans began their major offensive, Operation Michael, on 21st March, the 61st Brigade was involved in The Battle of St. Quentin (22nd March) and actions at the Somme Crossings (24th March). Here the British front line was broken, and 23rd March is regarded as one of crisis in the British Army as the Fifth Army withdrew across the

River Somme, in one instance up to eight miles:

Heavy casualties suffered by the Fifth Army's brigades reduced the strength of the divisions to a fraction of their original; men from the engineers, pioneers and even cooks were drafted into the front line. The town of Peronne was evacuated as the British line broke up; a gap of almost 40 miles opened up.

By 24th March, the Germans had crossed the River Somme and despite some 'last man, last round of ammunition' actions, Third Army continued to withdraw as it attempted to regain and maintain contact with the Fifth Army. That evening Bapaume was evacuated and many enemy troops took Le Transloy and Combles as British troops retired over the previous year's Somme battlefields to take up positions ordered by General Byng along the line of the River Ancre.

Haig issued Byng with an order to "Hold the line....at all costs" and this is where the stand would be made by the 20th (Light Division) in XVIII Corps, Fifth Army, who had been in Corps Reserve when Operation Michael began.[23]

We do not know the exact circumstances of Hembrow's death, but it is likely to have been as a result of fighting here. He died on 24th March 1918 in what appears to have been an allied retreat.

Although not named in despatches or gaining particular mention, Hembrow would have seen more action on the front line than perhaps any of our Old Boys. He took part in the key battles of the war and yet little is known about him. There are no letters, no newspaper accounts or family words to help give us an insight into the man he was.

Remembering Frank Albert Hembrow

Obituary

Frank Hembrow

March 24th 1918.

F. A. Hembrow entered the School September 1909 and left in July 1910. On leaving he adopted farming as his career and enlisted in the West Somerset Yeomanry at the outbreak of war, in October 1914. After his training, he was transferred to 7th Somerset Light Infantry and sent to France in September 1916. He acted as Signaller in that regiment until he fell at St. Quentin on March 24th, 1918. At School he was a boy of steady and consistent effort; he left too early to rise to leadership as it is generally known and yet of him, it may be truly said that he led by his record of work well and conscientiously done. He was one of the simple, cheerful, unobtrusive heroes of the rank and file, whose work was so wonderful in just the daily toils of war.

St Andrews Parish Church, Curry Rivel

Frank Albert Hembrow's parents were keen to remember their son more publicly and, as can be found on the site 'Some Memorials of the War in the County of Somerset':

The architect Frederick Bligh Bond was the designer of the oak Litany Desk in the parish church at Curry Rivel given at a cost of £40 and probably broken hearts by the parents of Signaller Frank Albert Hembrow. The inscription concerning his death in France in March 1918 and the badge of the Somerset Light Infantry is incised in the desk top.[24]

[23] Forces War Records.
[24] https://sites.google.com/site/sswm001/in-the-cause-of-humanity-that-honour-might-live

Pte. Norman Jeffery

b. 1890 – died 11th September 1918, aged 28

"He died doing his duty, bravely and well, and his loss is a great blow to those of his comrades who pulled through. From a personal view, he was all that one could wish."

Colonel of Oxon and Bucks L. I.

Norman Jeffery is Remembered with Honour in Hermies Hill British Cemetery. In November 2010 he was remembered by Overside House and flowers were placed in Chapel in his memory.

Norman Jeffery was born in 1890 in Old Sodbury, Gloucestershire. He was the youngest of four siblings: Frances (b. 1881), Margaret (b. 1883), John (b. 1887) and Norman (b.1890).

In 1901, both John and Norman were enrolled at what became Wellington School. Norman was 10 and his brother, 14. In the census of 1911, Mary Ann was still living with her mother and sister. John was a single man living at 13 Belmont Place, Exeter and Norman was boarding at 6 Carlton Terrace, Station Road, Taunton. Both brothers were working in auction houses.

Norman Jeffery's War

We do not know much about what Jeffery was doing during the years between leaving School and entering the war. In 1911, he was living in Taunton, but the Oxfordshire and Buckinghamshire Light Infantry records show he lived in Launceston, Cornwall at some point. In fact, records suggest he joined the Duke of Cornwall Light Infantry around January 1916, transferring to the Oxford and Bucks. Light Infantry in July 1916.

The 2nd Battalion of the Oxford and Buckinghamshire Light Infantry was part of the 61st (2nd South Midland) Division. An account of its movements from 1916 is given on the Oxford and Bucks. Website. The winter of 1916 was bitter and the troops of the 2nd Battalion suffered from a lack of shelter. This meant that escape from both the shelling and the weather was difficult. In addition, cooking facilities were poor and the health of the battalion deteriorated. Many men could not fight because of trench feet and frostbite.[25]

The Battalion took part in the pursuit of the Germans retreating from the Hindenburg Line and then was sent to Arras in 1917. It saw action at Cambrai, Bourlon Wood and Bapaume.

On March 13th, 1918, Bdr. J. Jeffery, Norman's brother, wrote to George Corner, *"My brother has been in France for over two years, and has been fortunate enough to escape injury up to the present."* Sadly, six months later, Norman Jeffery was killed in action in France.

On 11th -12th September 1918 the Battalion fought at Canal du Nord and it was here that Norman Jeffery fell.

[25] https://oxandbuckslightinfantry.weebly.com/1st--2nd-battalions-in-the-great-war.html

Remembering Norman Jeffery

School Magazine Obituary

Pte. Norman Jeffery

September 11th 1918.

Norman Jeffery, son of Mrs Jeffery, of Rockbeare, Exeter, entered the School with his elder brother, John, in September 1900, leaving in 1908. During his eight years of School life, he had made numerous warm friends by his unfailing good humour and was ever ready to do a good turn quickly and quietly. Old boys of his time well remember his ready wit in emergencies and his humorous way of dealing with them when they arose. He was always a sportsman but was not robust enough to shine in the games. After going through a course of training he joined the Oxon and Bucks L. I. and was on active service in France for more than two years. In September 1918, the Germans made a violent attack on the Canal du Nord and on the 11th of that month, Norman fell, gallantly facing certain death. It is with sad satisfaction and appreciation that one reads the pathetic letter from the Colonel of the Oxon and Bucks L. I to Mrs Jeffery, Norman's bereaved mother – "It is with the deepest regret that I have to inform you of the death of your son. He died doing his duty, bravely and well, and his loss is a great blow to those of his comrades who pulled through. From a personal view, he was all that one could wish. Many hours has he assisted in the Coy. Concerts and afforded untold pleasure to scores of his comrades. He has always been the same Norman and during the two years he has been with me, I have never found a more willing or better soldier. The Coy. joins with me in sending their deepest sympathy and hope that you will bear your great loss knowing that he died the bravest of deaths unflinchingly for a Just and Noble Cause." One can only add to such a tribute the complete assent of those who knew him in his School and home life. He was a devoted son.

Norman Jeffery is buried in Hermies Hill British Cemetery. He was reburied here, identified by his Numerals and his identity was confirmed in 1920. His stone has 'Believed to be' at the top.

The inscription on Jeffery's gravestone reads:

ALL HE HAD HE GAVE

When the idea of a School Memorial Chapel was broached to Old Boys, Mrs Jeffery wrote to George Corner,

"I have much pleasure in enclosing you £5 for your War Memorial scheme and hope you will be successful in getting the sum you require."

96053 PRIVATE
N. JEFFERY

F. E. KENT
(killed at Ypres, Sept. 11th, 1917).

Gunner Frank Eric Kent

b. 1898 – died 11th September 1917, aged 19

'In his short life, he showed what can be done by determination and self-forgetfulness. At School, he was zeal itself.' School Obituary

Frank Eric Kent is Remembered with Honour in Duhallow A. D. S. Cemetery. On November 11th 2007 he was remembered by Beech House and flowers were laid in Chapel in his memory. He was also remembered by Willows House in 2017.

In the 1901 census, Frank was 3 years old and living with his parents and two brothers in Church Knowle, Dorset. His father was a farmer and the family had a governess and two domestic servants living with them. In the 1911 census, only Frank's twin brother, Claud, lived at home. Frank was a pupil boarding at a school in Bournemouth but Frederick's whereabouts are unknown.

Frank Kent attended Wellington School for only a short time, arriving in May 1913 and leaving in July 1914. He clearly threw himself into School life whilst he was a pupil. The School Magazines record his abilities in the classroom and in the swimming pool. A contemporary of Wilfred Baker and Eric Zealley, Kent and Baker are often recorded next to each other in an array of swimming races, polo matches and academic prizes. The July 1913 Magazine tells of Kent being the first swimmer to compete in the newly built swimming pool and Corner's obituary alludes to his prowess at swimming and diving. He was a keen engineer and it was this he turned to upon leaving school.

Frank Eric Kent's War

Kent joined up as a Gunner in the R.F.A. in late 1916. A letter to George Corner tells us what he is doing:

F. E. Kent writes from Cosham, Hants., December 3rd, 1916:-

I thought you might like to know that I have joined up. I went to the Inns of Court O. T. C. headquarters in London and could have got taken in that as an infantry officer, but I wanted to get in the artillery, so I didn't join it but went to Dorchester and joined as a gunner in the R. F. A.. They sent me up here where I have been for three weeks next Friday. We have quite a decent time here, and we do foot drill, rifle drill and gun drill with dummy guns, but I have done most of it in the O. T. C. at Wellington and find it easy. They put me out of the recruits' squad in two days. Five hundred of the R. F. A. are round here and have just been transferred to the infantry, but I hope I shall be lucky enough to stay in the R. F. A. as the work is much more interesting and we get a much better time all round.

If you have time to write to me one day I should be very glad if you could send me a list of the boys who have joined up from Wellington if you have one.

There is only one lieutenant in charge of us here and he swears like anything but is a very decent sort all the same and is always doing something for the men. We have had two whist drives and a concert since I have been here. I was very surprised to find I had first prize at one whist drive and had the choice of a card case or a pipe and tobacco pouch and tobacco. I chose the card case, as I don't smoke.

We are usually trained for three months in the R. F. A. before we go to the front, but the time is often altered.

With best wishes for the welfare of the Old School.

It is not entirely clear what Kent's experiences of war were but through looking at his Battalion we can, perhaps, get a glimpse of the fighting he may have taken part in and what part he played. Kent was part of 'B' Battery of 290 Brigade Royal Field Artillery

This was part of the 2/1 City of London Brigade and joined 58th Division on 25th September 1916. It moved to Salisbury Plain for final training. Here the artillery received their 18 pounders and 4.5-inch howitzer. The Brigade was assigned a number and became CCXC Brigade (290 Brigade). The batteries were re-designated A-C, a howitzer battery was added and became D battery and the brigade ammunition columns were abolished. The division began embarking for France on 20th January 1917 and CCXC Brigade first went into action in February at Bienvillers. The brigade remained on the Western Front for the rest of the war.[26]

In 1917, CCXC Brigade supported 58th Division in the following actions: German Retreat to the Hindenburg Line, (17th-28th March); Battle of Bullecourt, (4th -17th May); Actions on the Hindenburg Line, (20th May – 16th June); Third Battle of Ypres inc. The Battle of Menin Road Ridge (20th-25th September) and the Battle of Polygon Wood (26th-27th September).

Frank Eric Kent died on 11th September in the Third Battle of Ypres.

[26] Wikipedia https://en.wikipedia.org/wiki/City_of_London_Artillery

Remembering Eric Frank Kent

School Obituary

Eric Kent

September 11th 1917.

F. E. Kent, son of Mr and Mrs Kent, of Bournemouth, entered the School in May 1913, to work hard at engineering as a special study. He was a fine swimmer and diver. He left in July 1914, and at once began his chosen career as a practical engineer. At the earliest moment, he joined up and received his final training at Cosham Camp. In January 1917, refusing a commission, he was attached to 290th Brigade R. F. A., which was acting as a Flying Column. From his cheery and spirited letters, we gather that he must have endured many hardships – continually moving the guns by night, sleeping on the ground and suffering many privations – but always cheerful and bright with never a grumble or murmur. In September the enemy began to send over gas-shells outside Ypres and on the 11th of that month, one of these fell into young Kent's gun pit. There had been no time to put on gas-masks and the men fell, stunned. Eric was badly gassed and died in the Ambulance when it was on its way to the Dressing Station without regaining consciousness, at the early age of 19 years. He lies in the Cemetery at Ypres. His Major, in writing to his stricken parents, said of him that he was a tremendously keen gunner and a great favourite in the Battery. In his short life, he showed what can be done by determination and self-forgetfulness. At School, he was zeal itself.

Kent was buried in Duhallow A. D. S. Cemetery in Belgium.

The inscription on Kent's grave reads:

THERE IS A GLORY THAT SHINES UPON OUR TEARS

Kent is mentioned on the website 'War Memorials at St James The Greater, Pokesdown', which provides a detailed account of his life, service and death. He is also mentioned in the publication *Tig's Boys* ed. David Hilliam[27] which commemorates the fallen of Bournemouth Grammar School.

[27] Hilliam, David. Tig's Boys: Letters to Sir From the Trenches Gloucester, The History Press, 2011

184060 GUNNER
F. E. KENT
ROYAL FIELD ARTILLERY
11TH SEPTEMBER 1917 AGE 19
UBIQUE
QUO FAS ET GLORIA DUCUNT
THERE IS A GLORY
THAT SHINES UPON OUR TEARS

PRIVATE J. M. KIDNER
(15th Battalion). Died of Wounds.

Pte. James Merson Kidner

b. October 14th 1893 – died 7th May 1915, aged 21

'An old Dark Blue, and a keen member of the O.T.C. in which he was a Lance-Corporal, he was a conscientious boy, and in an emergency, he could be depended on to do the right thing. He will always be remembered by those who knew him for his unvarying good temper.'

School Obituary

James Merson Kidner is Remembered with Honour in Alexandria (Chatby) Military and War Memorial Cemetery. In November 2018 he will be remembered by Oak House and a poppy will be placed in Chapel in his memory.

James Merson Kidner was the fifth child of John Kidner and his wife Mary Elizabeth Merson. John, a farmer, married Mary in 1883 in Tiverton, Devon. The couple had seven children: five boys and two girls.

In 1901, the Kidner family was farming at Castle Farm, Ilchester. Six of their children were living at home: Ethel Mary was 14, Dora Mary, 12, Simon, 9, James, 7, George, 4, and Edward, 3. The eldest son, Francis John, was a boarder at The County School, Wellington.

In 1911, little had changed. Francis had moved back to help out on the farm and was 25 years old. George was a boarder at Faster's School, Hound St., Sherborne and was 14 but apart from these changes, everything remained the same. Ethel, Dora, Simon and James were all employed on the farm, whilst Edward was at school.

Family life was changed in 1912 when John Kidner died in Yeovil at the age of 66. At some point, James left to go to Australia where he was to work as a Station Hand.

Simon Kidner fought with the Dorset Yeomanry in the war and Edward with the Somerset Light Infantry. James Merson Kidner fought with the 15th Battalion of the A. I. F.

School Life

Kidner's Virtue Functi More Patrum Duces states that he entered the School in January 1908 and left in Easter 1910. He had become a Lance Corporal in the O. T. C. in December 1909, where he also won Colours for the 2nd XI Football.

James Merson Kidner's War

Kidner was working as a station hand in Australia when war broke out and on 5th October he enlisted in E Company of the 15th Battalion of the Australian Imperial Force (AIF). The Unit embarked from Melbourne, Victoria on boat Transport A40 *Ceramic* on 22nd December 1914. Before boarding the ship they had marched through the streets of Melbourne. Initially intending to sail to the Western Front, overcrowding and poor conditions in the training camps in the UK resulted in them being sent to Egypt instead.

On 10th April 1915, the 15th Battalion moved by train to Alexandria where it embarked upon the troopships *Seeang Bee and Australind*, bound for Gallipoli. The 15th Battalion landed at Anzac Cove on the afternoon of 25th April.

As the Ottoman defenders checked the Allied advance inland, on arrival the 15th Battalion was rushed into the line on the left flank of the beachhead. As the advance inland stalled, the battalion became isolated and threatened with destruction until Cannan withdrew his force to a more tenable position. Later, they helped shore up the line before occupying positions around 'Pope's Hill' and 'Russell's Top', where they joined an attack on 1st May. After that, they occupied 'Quinn's Post', and defended it against a strong Ottoman counter-attack on 19th May.[28]

James Merson Kidner received a gun-shot wound to the shoulder on 7th May 1915. He later died from his wounds.

News of Pte. J. M Kidner's Death

Kidner was the second Old Boy to die in the War. The July 1915 edition hastily put news of his death in the Editorial:

"As we write we have heard of the loss of J. M. Kidner, who died of wounds received in the Dardanelles, the first O.T.C. boy to lay down his life for his country's honour – the news is all too meagre thence.'

This term has brought us the sad news of the death of the first of our Old Boys to fall for his country in the present war. J. M. Kidner, who left us five years ago, died early in May of wounds received in the fighting at the Dardanelles; and the deepest sympathy of us all will go out to his mother and brothers in their loss.'

Remembering James Merson Kidner

School Obituary

Private James Merson Kidner

Born October 14th, 1893 - died May 7th 1915, age 21.

In Memoriam

With the deepest regret, we have to tell of the sad death of J. M. Kidner, who died of wounds at the Dardanelles on May 7th. An old Dark Blue, and a keen member of the O. T. C. in which he was a Lance-Corporal, he was a conscientious boy, and in an emergency, he could be depended on to do the right thing. He will always be remembered by those who knew him for his unvarying good temper.

Roll of Honour

Private J. M. Kidner, of Ilchester, will be remembered by many as one of our early Engineers in the Powerhouse where he did very well. He was affectionately known as "Gee". We regret that we have but meagre news of him. He left the Old Country soon after leaving School and went to Australia to a sheep farm, where he was one of the first to answer the call.

[28] Wikipedia https://en.wikipedia.org/wiki/15th_Battalion_(Australia)

We are indebted to Mrs E. J. Masson, Brewlaw, Catterline, Stonehaven, Scotland for such news as we have. He took part in the immortal Anzac Landing.

Appended is Mrs Masson's touching letter to Mrs Kidner.

July 12th 1915

In my son's notebook, J. M. Kidner is frequently named and his address given. As far as I can gather from my son's notebook, he met your son for the first time at Church Parade on March 14th in Egypt and the last time he mentions him is on April 23rd when he writes. "Just had an argument with Kidner as to whether the Turks would be benefited by finding the date on which we left Melbourne, if this book should fall into their hands: Kidner says they would, I say they wouldn't."

The next entry is April 25th. "Commenced landing. Heavy fighting." And that is the last, so they had been near each other and may have both been wounded at the same time. My son was in the 15th Battalion and I only had one postcard from him after he left Egypt. In his notebook, he says they left Egypt on 11th April and arrived in Lemnos Bay on 13th and anchored alongside Oleka with the 6th and 7th Battalion of the First Australian Force – over 100 troopships and men-of-war anchored around.

He also wrote part of the address made to them by their General before they landed... "Soldiers of the King, before you lies an adventure unparalleled in Modern History. We have got to effect a landing on a shore hitherto held to be impregnable, but with God willing and the help of the Fleet, we hope to succeed. Soldiers of Australia now is the time to make a name for yourselves."

My son was never able to write after he was wounded, his right shoulder was shattered. He was landed at Gibraltar as they knew he would not live to reach England. He was able to give the Chaplain and Nurse my address and ask them to write to me. An officer of the R. G. A. sent me his watch and chain and all the little things he had in his pockets.

Australian Service Records show that these things were the sort of things everybody would have. Kidner's personal effects, outlined in his Army Service Records, consisted of small, normal everyday items such as clothes brush, hair brush, comb, handkerchief, keys, pencil, 2 Austs, a piece of wood, 2 booklets and photo. There were packaged up and sent to Kidner's mother in Ilchester. It must have seemed very little to mark twenty-one years of life.

Kidner was buried in Alexandra (Chatby) Military and War Memorial Cemetery. There was no personal inscription on his gravestone.

754 PRIVATE
J. M. KIDNER
15TH BN. AUSTRALIAN INF.
7TH MAY 1915

E. G. J. KNIGHT, Hants. Regt. (*killed*).

Pte. Edward George James Knight

b. 1897 – died 20th September 1917, aged 20

"We tried to get information from every possible source but heard nothing beyond the fact that Edward went over the top with the Regiment on September 20th and was never seen afterwards."

Edward's mother in a letter to George Corner

Edward George James Knight is Remembered with Honour on the Tyne Cot Memorial on panels 88 to 90 and 162. On November 9th 2008 he was remembered by Beech House and flowers were laid in Chapel in his memory. He was also remembered in 2017 by Grange House.

Edward George James Knight was the eldest child of David Knight and Rose Louise Knight (nee Hill). The couple were married in Bedminster in 1893 and had six children. In the 1901 census, the family was registered as living in Bratton Somerset. David was a farmer and 32 years old. His wife, Rose, was 34. There were three children: Edward (aged 4), David (aged 2) and Percy (aged 1).

By the 1911 census, the family was registered as living in Wydon, Minehead, Somerset. There were now six children: Edward (14), David (12), Percy (11), Gladys (9), Louise (8) and Thomas (5). Only Thomas is not at school.

School Life

Edward was a pupil in the School for only a year. He joined in 1911 and left in 1912, we think to help his father in managing the farm. There are no records of him in the School Magazines.

Edward George James Knight's War

Little is known about Knight's war other than he was in France in 1917 where he transferred to the Hampshire Regiment. It is likely that he would have taken part in the Battle of Pilckem Ridge (July) and the Third Battle of Ypres and the Battle of Menin Road Ridge (20th – 25th September). He died on 20th September, a casualty of the Battle of Menin Road Ridge.

Remembering Edward George James Knight

School Obituary

Edward Knight

September 20th, 1917.

Edward Knight was the eldest son of Mr and Mrs Knight, of Wydon, Minehead. He entered the School in 1911 and left in September 1912, to assist his father in the management of his farm. He was a plodder, doing his duty in work and winning esteem from his fellows. In 1916 he joined the West Somerset Yeomanry and trained with them at Winchester and on the East Coast, until in July 1917, he was sent to France. He was then transferred to the 15th Hants. Regiment, which proceeded at once to the firing line – in fact to the first line of trenches. Mrs Knight, in replying to a letter of enquiry about her son, replied in these words, which speak for themselves and cause one to realise the terrible struggle so vividly – "We tried to get information from every possible source, but heard nothing beyond the fact that Edward went over the top with the Regiment on September 20th and was never seen afterwards. The O. C. and some of his comrades said the Regiment was holding the line just outside St. Quentin at the time of his death." Thus, manfully fell a true soldier, in his 21st year, whose loss brought poignant sorrow to his bereaved parents: another good Somerset yeoman.

Newspapers show that the possibility of losing three sons was too much for the Knight family and they appealed to overturn Percy's conscription. Edward was dead, David was fighting and if Percy went to war, running the farm would be extremely difficult. Percy was 19 years old at the time. This appeal was denied by a military service tribunal.

Research

The Wartime Memories Project is a website where people are invited to share information about loved ones who served in WW1. It is a site that contributes to the on-going project to remember all the individuals who served and died. Members of Knight's family have posted about him:

> **Pte. Edward George James Knight**
> **British Army 15th Battalion Hampshire Regiment**
> **from Wydon Farm, Minehead**
> **(d. 20th Sep 1917)**
>
> *My great uncle on my father's side, Ted Knight, was a member of the 15th Hampshires. He was killed on 20th of September 1917 at the Battle of the Menin Road Ridge (Ypres). His remains were never recovered, and his father David always questioned his death. I was able to find his name on the Memorial at Tyne Cot. His unit was the 15th (2nd Portsmouth) Bn of the Hampshire Regiment. Ted had 2 brothers (David John, and Percy) who also served in WWI and survived the war. David J Knight was my grandfather. Ted grew up on Wydon Farm in Minehead, and his family still owns the farm. I have attached a copy of his memorial. Also, my father David Edward Knight was nicknamed "Ted" in honour of his uncle.*

Unfortunately, my Father passed away last Summer. I do know that the War devastated the Knight family, so much so, that my Grampa (David John) emigrated to Canada (and then the US) shortly after the war.[29]

Edward George James Knight *(with the kind permission of the family)*

[29] Conversation with David Knight, Edward's Great-nephew.

Pte. Herbert Thomas Manley

b. 1895 – died 24th September 1917, aged 22.

A comrade of Manley's wrote

"He was a fellow in a thousand. It's not only my opinion but that of the whole platoon. Everybody liked him. It was impossible to do otherwise, owing to the unselfish and upright character of his life."

Herbert Thomas Manley is Remembered with Honour on the Tyne Cot Memorial, panels 14 to 17 and 162 and 162A. In November 2017 he was remembered by Lights House and a poppy was placed in Chapel in his memory.

Herbert Thomas Manley was born in 1895 in Wellington to Thomas Manley (1865 – 1927), a foreman in a wool-merchants, and Annie Manley (b. 1866?). In 1901 the family was living in Birch Villa, High Path. Manley had one sister, Winifred, who was 2 ½ months old in the 1901 census. Though the address is the same, the family had very much changed in the 1911 census. Thomas Manley was now a widower, so it is clear Annie Manley had passed away, but we have yet to find out exactly when. Winifred was not living with her father and brother in High Path.

Herbert Manley's War

Herbert Thomas Manley is mentioned in the December 1915/April 1916 edition where it is noted under *'Old Boys Jottings'* that he has *'joined the Public Schools Battalion of the Royal Fusiliers Oxford'.*

He went to France and whilst there transferred to the (Queen's) West Surrey Regiment, 1st Battalion in November 1916. He was wounded and sent home, returning to the front line in July. It is likely that he would have been involved in Operations on the Flanders Coast as well as fighting on the Somme. On 24th September he took part in the Battle of the Menin Road Ridge. He was killed by a shell on the first day of this battle.

Remembering Herbert T. Manley

School Obituary

H. T. Manley

September 25th 1917.

Herbert Manley, son of Mr Manley, of Wellington, entered the School in September 1909, leaving in July 1911. He proved to be a sound worker and was noted for his readiness and activity in School life, being also a very keen Cadet, noticeably in camp work. He joined the Fusiliers – Public Schools Battalion – in January 1916, and in the following November was sent to France, where he was transferred to the Royal West Surrey Regiment (The Queen's). He was wounded and sent home, but returned to his regiment again in July, being engaged on the Somme line, where the fighting was for so long so deadly. Here he was killed by a shell on September 25th, to the unending sorrow of his family and friends. His Platoon officer wrote to Mr Manley the following heartfelt words – "I shall feel his loss greatly. He was a fine soldier. There was nothing I put to him that he did not carry out and I could rely on him for anything." A comrade wrote of him thus – "He was a fellow in a thousand. It's not only my opinion but that of the whole platoon. Everybody liked him. It was impossible to do otherwise, owing to the unselfish and upright character of his life." Sometime after Herbert Manley's death, his father was travelling in Scotland where he met the friend whose words are given above and who told him how bravely Herbert had upheld the reputation of his School. Amongst other memories, he said that when they were encamped near the Somme two soldiers who were bathing were seen to be drowning in the river. Many of those standing by felt powerless to attempt a rescue because of the very great swiftness of the river, but Herbert, who was in camp, ran down and without even removing his boots dived into their assistance. He brought the men out but was very cut up because they could not be revived. His officer reported this to the O. C., who warmly commended him and said he would be recommended for the D. C. M.. This recognition he did not live to receive. This fine record of a short life, for he was but 22 years of age when he fell, is indeed a proud remembrance for his father and many friends, and his old schoolfellows.

Manley is also featured in the publication *Our Boys* by Mike Perry and Ray Hitchcock.

Pte. Harry James Martin

b. 1872 – died 16th October 1915, age 43

"If these lines meet the eye of anyone who can help we trust he will communicate with the Editor. We do, however, feel that the brave Australian forces have by their deeds written for themselves an epitaph which is more eloquent than any words, and Harry Martin was a member of those forces." School Obituary

Harry James Martin is Remembered with Honour at Beach Cemetery, Anzac, Turkey. On November 8th 2014 he was remembered by Overside House and flowers were placed in Chapel in his memory.

Harry James Martin was the third son of Thomas James Martin (b. 1842) and Julia Anna (nee Turner, b. 1840). Thomas seems to have hailed from Guernsey and Julia from Tavistock. They married in Tavistock in 1864.

By 1881 the family had moved to 95, Haines Hill, Taunton. The children living at home included Lilian, aged 13 – a scholar, Ernest, aged 11, Harry (Henry) James aged 8, and Kathleen Maud, aged 3. Thomas's sister, Rachel, and his nephew, Walter, also appeared at the property. Reginald T Martin, the oldest son, was recorded as living at 210 Balmoral, Holdenhurst, Christchurch, Dorset and working as a Draper's Assistant. He was 15 years of age.

By 1891, the family moved to Osbourne House, Trull Road, Taunton. Thomas was recorded as a 48-year-old Draper and Valuer. Julia was 50. Only the girls lived at home. Lilian was 23 and Kathleen, 13, a scholar. The whereabouts of Reginald and Harry in 1891 is unclear. They do not seem to appear on a census, so it is possible that they travelled abroad. Ernest is recorded as Head of his household in 2 Edward Street, Brighton. He is a veterinary surgeon in the Army.

Ernest Edmund Martin

Ernest Edmund Martin was a Colonel in the Army Veterinary Corps and spent a great deal of time in India. He died in 1925 as a result of appendicitis, at the age of 56. We know that Ernest married Alexine Aimee Samuelson in 1913 (Oct-Dec), in Kensington. They do not appear to have had children – Alexine was 37 when she married.

Harry James Martin

Harry attended Wellington School between 1887 and 1888. It is unclear whether his brothers also attended.

Though his whereabouts up until 1912 are unclear, he is recorded as marrying Margaret A. M. Graham in 1912 in Steyning, Sussex. In the summer of 1914, his daughter, Violet Beryl Martin was born in Steyning. Yet only six months later, Harry boarded the ship *Osterley* and sailed for Melbourne, Australia on 18th December.

Harry James Martin's War

Harry enlisted and joined the 23rd Battalion of the Australian Imperial Force on 31st March 1915. He was in A Company and he was 42 years old when he enlisted. He stated his occupation as 'Labourer'.

The Unit embarked from Melbourne, Victoria on board HMAT A14 *Euripides* on May 10th, 1915. It arrived in Egypt on 12th June 1915 where its advanced training would be completed.

As part of the 2nd Australian Division, the 6th Brigade landed at ANZAC Cove in early September. The 23rd Battalion was soon involved in manning one of the most dangerous and intense parts of the front line – Lone Pine. *"The fighting here was so dangerous and exhausting that battalions were relieved every day. The 23rd manned Lone Pine, alternating with the 24th Battalion, until they left Gallipoli in December 1915."* [30]

Though the 16th October 1915 doesn't seem to have been a particularly bad day for casualties, Harry James Martin was killed by shrapnel penetrating his chest. Though he was taken to the field hospital, the wound was so severe that he later died of his injuries. He was 43 years old. The School Obituary says he died on almost his first day, but it is likely he saw action from September 1915.

Remembering Harry James Martin

School Obituary
Pte. H. J. Martin – 1915

H. J. Martin was at School in 1887-1888 and was, therefore, one of Mr Beuttler's old boys. Mr Beuttler, alas, is no longer with us and we are not able to gather all the details that we could wish. What we do know is that Harry Martin was one of the immortal A. N. Z. A. C. and perished at Suvla, almost the first day of his service in Gallipoli. His regiment was the 23rd Battalion A. I. F. His wife had all details sent to her, but she did not long survive her husband. We may be able to glean some news from his brother, Colonel E. E. Martin, now stationed in India, but we have been unable to get in touch with him as yet. If these lines meet the eye of anyone who can help, we trust he will communicate with the Editor. We do, however, feel that the brave Australian forces have by their deeds written for themselves an epitaph which is more eloquent than any words, and Harry Martin was a member of those forces.

Harry James Martin was buried in Beach Cemetery, Anzac, Turkey.

He is featured on the Australian War Memorial Roll of Honour where his name is located at 99 in the Commemorative Area of the Australian War Memorial. Every 6 weeks or so his name is projected onto the exterior of the Hall of Memory. This is done for every member of the Australian Forces who gave up their lives in war.

[30] https://en.wikipedia.org/wiki/23rd_Battalion_(Australia)

If there is a story which presents the terrible and long-term suffering caused by a soldier's death in the war, it is that of Martin's family. Records kept in the Australian National Archive give us a glimpse into the gruelling battle to keep a family together. As has already been stated, Harry Martin married Margaret A. Mundell Graham in 1913. It would appear that she had two children already and Harry adopted them although there are no records to confirm this. Together they had one daughter, Violet Beryl, born in 1914. In 1917, at the age of just 31, and less than two years after Harry died, Margaret passed away, leaving three children orphaned. Violet and her siblings appear to have been split up. Violet, it seems, was adopted by Harry's brother, Ernest. She would endure further tragedy when she was 11 years old with the sudden death of her Uncle in 1925. The adopted children, Hubert Lewis and Muriel Graham, were looked after by their grandmother, Margaret's mother, Annie Mundell Graham.

Records show that Annie struggled to look after Hubert and Muriel. Grieving the loss of her daughter in 1917 and the death of her son, E. M. Graham, a private in the Royal Sussex Regiment, on 29th July 1918, Annie's mental and physical health declined. The children were absent from school too often and concern was raised when it was found that Annie shared a bed with 14-year-old Muriel. Lodgers were taken in to help pay the house rent, but a year's delay in the Commonwealth deciding whether to grant an allowance meant that Annie was behind on her payments and had incurred a debt of £30 for missed school fees. *"Would it be possible for the Commonwealth to grant me the £30 owing as I am, not in a position to pay it?"* she wrote in 1923. The inspector found her *'weak and nervous'* although *'there is no doubt of her affection for the children. They get the best of attention and treatment she is capable of giving them, but she is an elderly woman, very often ill.'* Placed in an impossible situation with ill health causing the children to be absent from school and the educational grant allowance forfeited, Annie must have wondered how she could go on. The stress may well have contributed to her frequent bouts of Bronchitis and general anxiety. In May 1923, Annie's application for an educational grant for Muriel was turned down on the grounds that it would *'be useless her undertaking a commercial course'* as her academic results were too poor, *'A trade, or course of domestic economy would be more likely to provide her with a means of livelihood.'* Annie was told to reapply but, given her poor state of health, it is unclear whether she did.

Annie died in June 1923 leaving her grandchildren alone once more. Hubert, aged 15, sailed to Australia almost as soon as his grandmother died to begin a new life but the fate of Muriel is unknown. Army Service Records show that Hubert was desperate to find out information about his father, seeming to not even know his regiment or where he fell. Whether this was information that was kept from him or whether in 1915, at the age of 7, he had been too young to really process all that was happening, he seems to know almost nothing about Harry J. Martin. We have no knowledge of what happened to Muriel when her brother left. She would have been about 13 years of age with no obvious adults in her life to look after her.

Wellington Memorial Chapel – Letters to George Corner

In answer to George Corner's letter to the families of the Old Boys who were killed in WW1, it seems that Alexine, Ernest's wife, wrote to Corner. There is no mention of either Violet or Muriel.

> *Dear Sir,*
>
> *My sister-in-law Mrs Stenlake has asked me to reply to your letter asking for particulars as to the death of her brother in Gallipoli. His Christian names were Harry James and his age at the time of his death was 43 years. I am sorry I cannot tell you the exact date on which my brother- in-law fell, as the only information my late husband had was as follows – 'despatches received indicate that Private H. J. Martin, 23rd Battalion A. I. Force has been killed in action at the Dardanelles."*
>
> *This was written from the Commonwealth of Australia and dated November 9th, 1915. Hoping that this information will be of use to you for the Commemoration Tablet.*
>
> *Believe me,*
>
> *Yours truly, Alexine A Martin*

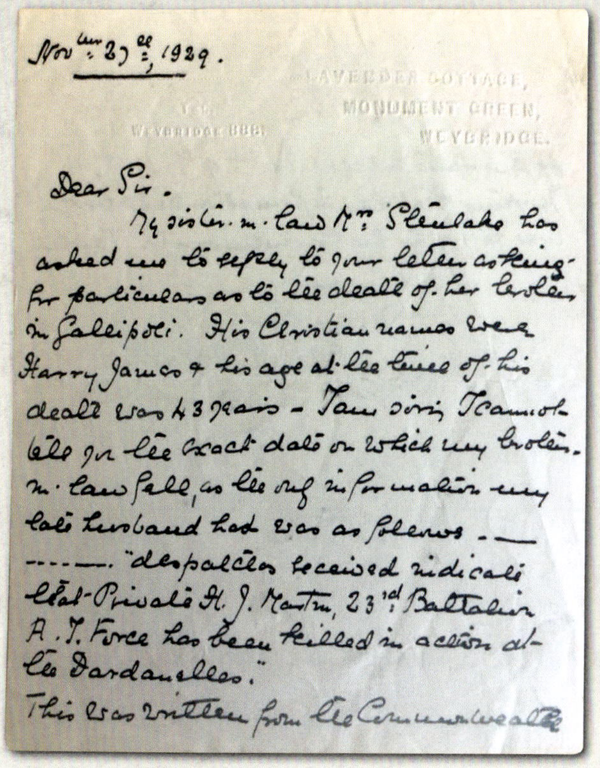

Novber 27th, 1929.

Lavender Cottage,
Monument Green,
Weybridge.
Weybridge 888.

Dear Sir.

My sister-in-law Mrs Stenlake has asked me to reply to your letter asking for particulars as to the death of her brother in Gallipoli. His Christian names were Harry James & his age at the time of his death was 43 years - I am sorry I cannot tell you the exact date on which my brother-in-law fell, as the only information my late husband had was as follows.—

———. "despatches received indicate that Private H. J. Martin, 23rd Battalion A. I. Force has been killed in action at the Dardanelles."

This was written from the Commonwealth

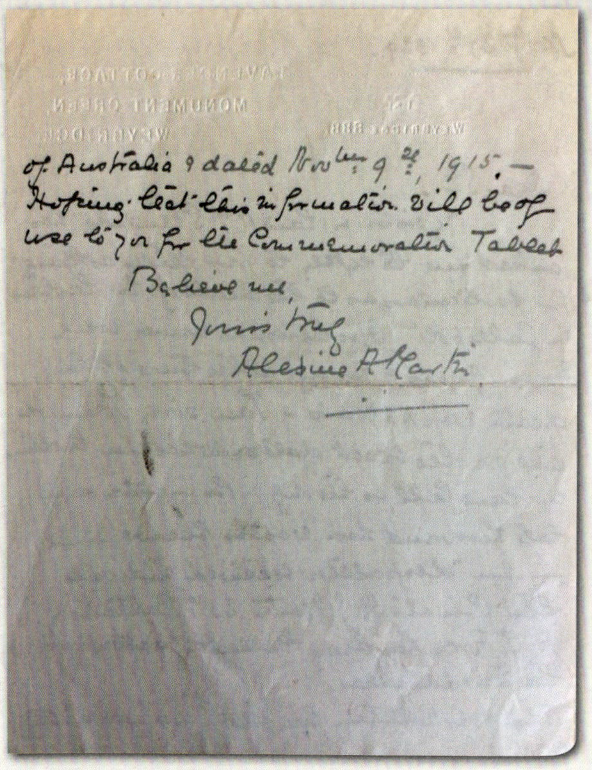

of Australia & dated Novber 9th, 1915.—

Hoping that this information will be of use to you for the Commemoration Tablet

Believe me,

Yours truly

Alesine A Martin

Lance-Corporal William John Miles

b. 1886 – died 14th January 1916, aged 29 years

'Jack Miles is down with rheumatism – he is a really good chap.' Sergeant Spear

L-Cpl. William John Miles is Remembered with Honour in Alexandria (Chatby) Military and War Memorial Cemetery, Alexandria, Egypt. In November 2018 he will be remembered by Overside House and a poppy will be placed in Chapel in his memory.

William John Miles was known as 'Jack' and was one of eight children born to William Miles and Elizabeth Duckett. Though they moved around, the family was living in Dipford Road, Trull in 1911. 'Jack' was 25 years old and helping his father on the farm. For years the family lived at Hill Farm, Kingston St Mary, which was opposite the Swan pub. It has now been converted into residential dwellings.

William John Miles's War

Miles joined the West Somerset Yeomanry and served for five years, leaving around 1912/13. Local newspapers report he was back in Kingston in 1913 and 1st January 1915. He was discharged as a result of ill health and subsequently worked on his father's farm. These do not seem to be the easiest of years and Miles got into a little trouble with the courts through drink. In November 1914, he re-joined the Yeomanry as part of the 1/1st West Somerset Yeomanry. He travelled to Turkey, arriving in Gallipoli on 9th October and was attached to 11th (Northern) Division (digging trenches). In November it was in the firing line, attached to the 2nd Mounted Division and 53rd (Welsh) Infantry Division. On 19th December, it was evacuated to Imbros.

In December 1915, the regiment landed in Alexandria to help defend Egypt.[31]

Those not directly involved in the war received snippets of information and 'updates' from certain soldiers. For the Taunton Courier and Western Advertiser, Sergeant Spear kept the people of Kingston and Taunton up to date with the men who were serving. Here he writes about Jack Miles's illness.

[31] Wikipedia https://en.wikipedia.org/wiki/West_Somerset_Yeomanry

Taunton Courier and Western Advertiser, 29th December 1915 [32]

WITH THE WEST SOMERSET YEOMANRY
SERGEANT SPEAR FROST-BITTEN
NEWS OF TAUNTON AND KINGSTON MEN

We (the Yeomanry) have had something to go on with since we left England. I hope to be spared to tell you a little about it. There were about six left of my Troop of 37 when I was brought away from Gallipoli. We have seen some terrible sights. There is a poor fellow in this ward who is just going to have both legs amputated for frostbite. The weather is lovely and warm here at Malta. The last I heard of Alfred Biffen he was in hospital at Cairo with dysentery. It has taken off quite a lot of our fellows. Tom Greed is getting on fairly well, also Cyril Bowering. Jack Miles is down with rheumatism – he is a real good chap. Jerry Hann has had dysentery very badly, Cyril Sparks as well, but both are much better. I cannot write any more now as I am feeling a bit done up."

And the worst news.

Taunton Courier and Western Advertiser 26th, January 1916 [33]

KINGSTON
DEATH OF TROOPER MILES

DEATH OF TROOPER MILES – Great regret was expressed with Mr. and Mrs. Miles and family, of Hill Farm, when it became known that they had on Saturday received a message from the War Office informing them that their only son, Trooper Jack Miles (of the West Somerset Yeomanry), had died of rheumatic fever, contracted while serving with his Regiment in the British Mediterranean Expeditionary Force. Prior to enlisting in the Yeomanry, the deceased soldier, who was over six foot in height, had served in the 2nd Life Guards. Of a genial disposition, he had made a large circle of friends, both at Kingston and Trull, where he formerly resided with his parents. On December 25th we published in our columns a letter from Sergeant Spear, who wrote of the deceased as follows:- "Jack Miles is down with rheumatism. He is a real good chap." A memorial service will be held in the Parish Church on Friday afternoon.

[32] The British Newspaper Archive Online.
[33] The British Newspaper Archive Online.

Remembering Lance-Corporal William John 'Jack' Miles

William John Miles was recorded in the Du Ruvigny Roll of Honour.

MILES, WILLIAM JOHN, L.-Corpl., 1st West Somerset Yeomanry (T.F.), s. of William Miles, of Hill Farm, Kingston, Farmer; *b.* 8 March, 1886; educ. Wellington County School; was a Farmer; served for five years in the West Somerset Yeomanry; enlisted in the Life Guards, but was discharged owing to ill-health; rejoined the West Somerset Yeomanry 28 Nov. 1915; served with the Mediterranean Expeditionary Force in Egypt, and died in the General Hospital, Alexandria, 14 Jan. 1916, from rheumatic fever contracted while on active service. Buried in Chatby Military Cemetery, Alexandria. One of his officer's doctors wrote: "He had done very well during the time in the trenches, and I was very sorry to lose such a good soldier." He was a keen Rugby football player and played for Taunton for three seasons; *unm.*

He is commemorated on the Kingston St Mary memorial plaque. Here he is remembered as John William Miles although it is almost certainly the same man.

Miles was buried in Alexandria (Chatby) Military and War Memorial Cemetery.

Wellington School Memorial Chapel – Letters to George Corner

William Miles, Jack's father, wrote to George Corner on October 30th, 1929. Though the letter is quite direct, the family's grief is clear. Miles's medals are framed and the mention of the photo of his grave gives us a sense of a family desperate to keep hold of his memory. It is unlikely that the family would have been able to go and visit the grave so a photograph would have been a very special item. Jack was William's only son.

Dear Sir,

Many thanks for your letter. Our poor dear son John was taken down in Rheumatic and had double pneumonia. He died in hospital at Alexandria, January 14th, 1916. We have his 4 medals framed. He was buried at Chatby. He joined up as soon as the war broke out. He was in the West Somerset Yeomanry. He got promoted to Lance-Corporal. We also have the photo of his grave.

With kind regards

Yours sincerely,

W. Miles

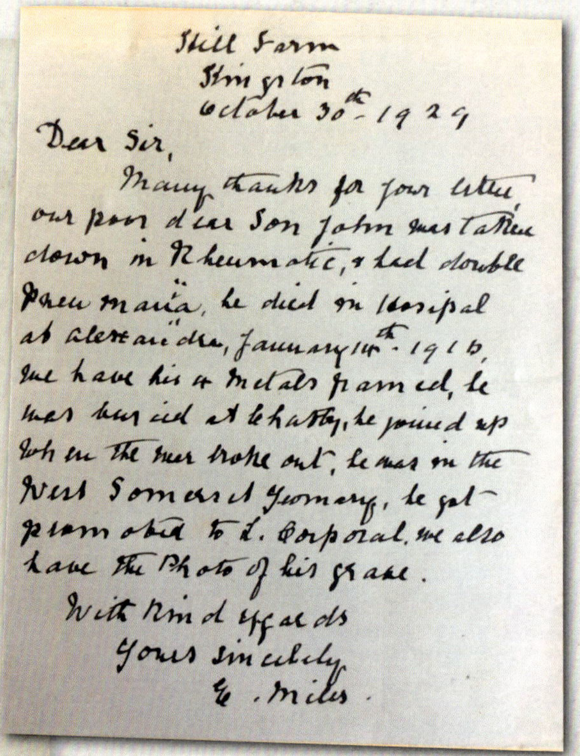
Hill Farm
Kingston
October 30th 1929

Dear Sir,

Many thanks for your letter, our poor dear Son John was taken down in Rheumatic, & had double pneumonia, he died in Hospital at Alexandria, January 14th 1916, we have his 4 medals framed, he was buried at Chatby, he joined up when the war broke out, he was in the West Somerset Yeomanry, he got promoted to L. Corporal. we also have the Photo of his grave.

With kind regards
Yours sincerely
W. Miles.

WEST SOMERSET YEOMANRY
1387 L. CPL
W. J. MILES
WEST SOMERSET YEOMANRY
14TH JANUARY 1916 AGE 29

Captain Waldo Alington Gwennap Moore

b. 1876 – died 31st October 1914, aged 38

'He served in the South African War, 1899-1900, receiving the Queen's Medal with five clasps and the King's medal with two clasps.' School Obituary

Waldo Alington Gwennap Moore is Remembered with Honour on the Ypres (Menin Gate) Memorial. On 8th November 2009 he was remembered by Willows House and flowers were placed in Chapel in his memory.

Waldo Alington Gwennap Moore was the second son of Colonel John G. D. Moore and Mary Catherine Johnstone. He had one older brother, Herbert Tregose Gwennap Moore (b. 1875) and a younger brother, Wilfred C. G. Moore (b. 1878). He was born in 1876 in Launceston Cornwall. In 1881, the family was living at 265 Tamar Terrace. John G. D. Moore's occupation was listed as Land Agent. In 1881, the family welcomed a fourth son, Hartley Russell Gwennap Moore.

In 1891, Waldo Moore was listed as a boarder at Kelly College, Tavistock. Herbert was a pupil at a school in Bucklebury, Berkshire. Charles and Hartley were boarders at The County School, Wellington. John and Mary had moved to Trewithen House in Probus, Cornwall.

In 1907, both Waldo and Herbert were married. Waldo married Hilda Charlotte Phillips and together they had a son, Charles Anthony Gwennap, who was born in 1913.

Waldo Alington Gwennap Moore's Career

Moore was a soldier by profession and by the time he was fighting in WW1 he had already seen many different battles in many different countries. There are newspaper articles outlining his experiences in South Africa. In one we read, 'Mr Waldo has a very low opinion of the Boers, *"The life and habits of the quiet pastoral Boer are,"* he says, *"disgusting."*

At the outbreak of war, the 1st Division of the Welsh Regiment was stationed at the Aldershot Old Barracks. It was a permanent Regular Army division. It was mobilized in early 1914 and was one of the first divisions to be mobilized for action in France. The Division crossed the English Channel, concentrated near le Nouvion and served on the Western Front in France and Belgium for the duration of the War.

In 1914 the Division, and it is likely Moore too, saw action at the Battle of Mons (23th Aug.); the Retreat from Mons (24th Aug.); the Battle of Etreux (27th Aug.); the Battle of the Marne (6th Sept.); the Battle of Aisne (13th Sept.); Actions on Aisne Heights (20th Sept.); Action of Chivy (26th Sept.); the Battle of Ypres (19th Oct.); Battle of Langemarck (21st Oct.) and Battle of Gheluvelt (29th Oct.)

Moore was killed on 31st October. An account of his death is as follows:

The Death of Captain W A G Moore[34]

Eventually what remained of the 1st Gloucesters and the 2nd Battalion Welsh Regiment were forced back to the line of the 54th Battery where stragglers were collected and some sort of order restored and a new line taken up, the sight of the guns in action acting as a rallying point to the disorganised infantry falling back. The Battery was about 800 yards from the Westerly edge of Gheluvelt village, just to the North of the Menin Road. Captain W.A.G. Moore, Captain Rees and Lieutenant Colonel Morland were standing in the shallow trench discussing the situation when a shrapnel shell burst in front killing Captain Moore and mortally wounding Colonel Morland. Captain Rees wrote later "I never saw him the slightest degree upset by anything that happened. He remained to the very end cool and collected as if he was on parade at home."

Colonel Morland was carried off on a door to the 1st Division's dressing station outside Ypres on the Menin Road where he died and was buried in Ypres Town Cemetery. Captain Moore has no known grave.

In summary, three officers were killed on the 31st October 1914, Lieutenant Colonel Charles Morland being buried in Ypres Town Cemetery (plot E1.11) and Captain Walter Ferrar being buried near to him in Ypres Town Cemetery (plot E1.14). Captain Waldo Alington Gwennap Moore has no known grave and is commemorated on the Ypres (Menin Gate) Memorial.[35]

One can only imagine why it is that Captain Moore has no known grave, especially when the others he was with were recovered. The brutality of the fighting, even this early in the conflict, is clear.

Remembering Captain Waldo Alington Gwennap Moore

School Obituary
Captain Waldo Alington Gwennap Moore

Capt. Waldo Alington Gwennap Moore, Welsh Regiment, who was killed in action on October 31st, 1914, was 38 years of age and got his first Commission in 1896. He served in the South African War, 1899-1900 and took part in the actions of Driefontein, Vet River, Zand River, Diamond Hill, Belfast and Colesburg, receiving the Queen's Medal with five clasps and the King's Medal with two clasps. He was the second son of Mr and Mrs Gwennap Moore, of Grampound, Cornwall.

Captain Moore left the School in 1888.

[34] The Death of Captain W A G Moore from Colonel Charles Bernard Morland's account World War 1 War Graves http://www.ww1wargraves.co.uk/ww1_cemeteries/charles_bernard_morland.asp
[35] http://www.ww1wargraves.co.uk/ww1_cemeteries/charles_bernard_morland.asp

A. H. W. PALFERY, Warwick Regt (*killed April 15th*, 1918).

Pte. Alfred Harold William Palfery

b. 1892 – died 15th April 1918, aged 26 years

"To his bereaved mother, Harold Palfery was all in all and the most widespread sympathy was felt for her in her irreparable loss. In his School life, he was cheerful serenity itself." School Obituary

Alfred Harold William Palfery is Remembered With Honour on the Ploegsteert Memorial. On 8th November 2009 he was remembered by Beech House and flowers were placed in Chapel in his memory.

Alfred Harold William Palfery was born in Wellington in 1892 to Alfred C. C. Palfery, a rail worker (b. 1863), and Sophia Palfery (1863 – 1944), a teacher. Tragedy struck the family in 1893 when Alfred, Harold's father passed away. A single mother, Sophia turned to teaching and in 1901 she was recorded as living in Langford Budville with Harold. In 1911, Harold appeared to have left home and was an elementary school teacher, boarding at 67 Station Road, Romsey, Hampshire. Sophia had also moved and the census recorded her as living in Baltonsborough, near Glastonbury, and working as a Headteacher. A death registry notice appears for a Sophia Palfery, who died in 1944 in Wells, Somerset. This is likely to be Harold's mother.

Life After School

We don't know a great deal about Harold's life once he left Wellington that isn't recorded in his letter of 1916 or in the School Obituary. In 1911 he lived in Romsey, Hampshire. This may explain why he is reported as enlisting in the Huntingdon Cyclist Battalion. Further research found that this A. H. W. Palfery was the same as ours, although quite how he got to join this is unclear. The Huntingdon Cyclist Battalions seem to have been a cavalry on bicycles and were known as 'the Gas Pipe Cavalry'. They were made up of men from Romsey and the surrounding villages of Huntingdon.

Alfred Harold William Palfery's War

Palfery enlisted in the 8th Royal Warwickshire Regiment in 1915. He spent time training before going to France for a short time but was then sent home for a year with illness. He re-joined the 1st Battalion Royal Warwickshire Regiment in June 1917 and went to France for the second time.

The 1st Battalion Royal Warwickshire Regiment was involved in the following battles in 1917 and it is therefore likely that Palfery was involved in some of these, if not all: the Battle of Ypres – Battle of Polygon Wood (28th Sept.); the Battle of Broodseinde (4th Oct.); Battle of Poelcapelle (9th Oct.); the First Battle of Passchendaele (12th Oct.) In 1918 the regiment fought at: the First Battle of the Somme – First Battle of Arras (28th March) and Battle of the Lys – Battle of Hazebrouck including Defence of Hinges Ridge (13th April). Palfery was killed on 15th April so it is likely that he was in this last confrontation.

Palfery's Letter

Although the magazines did not seem to record much of Palfery's School life, a letter from him to George Corner was published. The letter is dated June 23rd 1916 and is written whilst Harold is in hospital in Salcombe:

I have just received the School Magazine. Please accept my best thanks for the same. I was very glad indeed to get some news of the Old School. It also reminded me that I have not yet joined the O.B. Association, which I shall endeavour to do at the earliest opportunity.

I was sadly reminded by the photographs of those who have given their lives in this war. It is cruel to think that such splendid fellows as Wilfred Baker and 'Teddy' have passed to the great unknown. I was also very grieved to hear about Mr Treble.

I know you are always interested in the doings of "Old Boys", so I will tell you a little of my experience.

After spending five years as Assistant Master, I went to College to be trained for a headship.

I applied in the first instance to enter Culham, where Mr Treble went after leaving you. As it was closed to men students owing to the war I was accepted at Saltley College, Birmingham. When the circular issued by the Board was received by the Principal, respecting the enlistment of students, I joined the 8th R. Warwick Regiment. I was for some time training at the barracks in Birmingham.

We soon were moved to Clevedon, where we underwent very hard training. After a short training of three months, I was sent to France with a draft.

I was only there a short time as I developed 'nephritis'. I was taken into hospital at Le Havre and afterwards sent to England. I have now been in hospital for four months and have had a very painful time. I am glad to say that I am now convalescent, and I hope to be discharged shortly.

I should like to be able to obtain a commission, but I hardly know how to do so. Do you think that I should stand any chance? Unfortunately, I was only in the O. T. C. one term owing to illness. I went through a special course of musketry whilst in training but was sent to France before an examination was held. Being a teacher, I know all the Swedish Drill and am accustomed to giving words of command. Whilst in College I received instruction in military drill and gymnastics. I know how greatly you have helped Old Boys in this matter, therefore, I venture to ask your kind assistance on my own behalf.

I am glad to hear that the O. T. C. is flourishing. May it continue.

From this letter, the only one published from Palfery, we get to glimpse a little of his character. Clearly, he is keen to get back to the war, gain a commission and continue fighting. His four months in hospital suggest he may not be in the best of health after such a serious illness but that does not stop him from wanting to return to France to do his duty. He would have known full well what awaited him, yet he does not falter. He has faith in George Corner and hopes that Corner will be able to help him as he has helped others. Palfery's condolences on hearing of S. W. Baker, E. F. Corner and J. N. Treble suggest the strong community spirit, but also the full awareness that what happened to other Old Boys could equally happen to him. He is a brave man.

Remembering Alfred Harold William Palfery

School Obituary

A. H. W. Palfery

April 15th, 1918.

A. H. W. Palfery, son of Mrs Palfery, of Baltonsborough, was born at Wellington and entered the School in Sept. 1906. He was a diligent worker and his desire was to take up the profession of teaching. He joined the Royal Warwickshire Regiment whilst at Saltley College and in April 1916, sailed for France. Never too robust, severe illness invalided him for a year and then at his own request he was sent out again in June 1917. He served in the trenches for nearly a year and in May 1918, was reported as wounded, later as wounded and missing, and then for many months, no further news was forthcoming. Finally, through the medium of the Red Cross, a comrade of his was discovered in hospital who had been in the terrible struggle in which Palfery fell. Pte. Oliver Hyde wrote to Mrs Palfery as follows – It happened on the afternoon of April 15th, about 6 o'clock, when we had gone over the top at a place called Hinges, near the La Bassee Canal, up to which the Boches had advanced a few days previously. Palfrey was in my section and we were together the whole time. We advanced till we reached a spinney, where we were held up by rifle fire and machine gun fire from a house when an officer came along and asked for volunteers to rush the house. About 20 of us, including Palfery, myself and the officer crawled up to some wire, where we made a charge. This proved very costly as by the time we reached the hedge in front of the house there were only 15 of us left, the others being killed by rifle fire on the way. When we reached the hedge, we could neither go forward nor back and had to take cover as best we could. This proved our undoing – one after the other was killed by deadly fire. At last, there were only three of us left alive, as I glanced at him he turned his head to say something to me and was instantly killed by a sniper's bullet. At last, by the mercy of Providence, I managed to crawl back to our starting point, where we dug ourselves in for the night. I must say that Palfery was one of the best and liked by all his comrades, and from when I first knew him we were always the best of chums." This account is one of the many records of utter self-sacrifice for honour and country. To his bereaved mother, Harold Palfery was all in all and the most widespread sympathy was felt for her in her irreparable loss. In his School life, he was cheerful serenity itself.

Palfery is featured in the publication *Our Boys* by Mike Perry and Ray Hitchcock. He is also commemorated on the Baltonsborough War Memorial.

Lieut. J. V. R. PASTFIELD
(*killed Sept. 9th, 1918*).

Lieut. Joseph Victor Robinson Pastfield

b. 1898 – died 9th September 1918, aged 20

"He was always conspicuous at School for his 'grit' and strong originality and for his disdain of little trouble."

School Obituary

Joseph Victor Robinson Pastfield is Remembered with Honour in Pernes British Cemetery. On November 8th 2009 he was remembered by Avenue House and flowers were placed in Chapel in his memory.

Joseph Victor Robinson Pastfield (known as 'Victor') was born in 1898, the third son of John Robinson Pastfield, a Chief Inspector of Life Assurance, and Elizabeth Olive Pastfield.

The whereabouts of the Pastfield family in 1901 is unknown but the family was living in Exeter in the 1911 census. There were several children and some of the older children were still living at home (Florence and Joseph lived elsewhere). Listed are: John Robinson (aged 22, student of theology), Gladys Mary (aged 21), James Thomas (aged 19, and a student of Oxford University), Olive Hilda Sarah (aged 17, a scholar), Catherine Mildred (aged 15, a scholar) and David Barnabas Edward (aged 6). In the 1911 census, Joseph Victor was a boarder at The County School, Wellington. He was 12 years of age.

James Thomas Pastfield joined the Middlesex Regiment and fought in WW1. He was killed in action on 21st December 1914 in France. He is commemorated on the Le Touret Memorial, Pas de Calais.

David Barnabas Edward Pastfield set sail for Adelaide in 1938 at the age of 33. At some point, he joined the Australian Army Canteens Service where he was serving when he was killed on 25th June 1943, aged 39. He is buried/commemorated in Adelaide River War Cemetery, but further details are not known.

Of the four Pastfield brothers, three died in war. It seems brutal that one family should suffer such loss.

Joseph Victor Pastfield's War

Pastfield joined the Middlesex Regiment in 1915 and served with both the 5th and 13th Battalion. In August 1915, his regiment joined the 1st Garrison Battalion Essex Regiment and had sailed to Egypt by the end of the month. Records show he entered the 'Theatre of War in Egypt' on 6th September. He would only have been 17 years of age.

Some of Joseph Victor Pastfield's letters were published in the School Magazines during the War years so we are able to get a sense of his voice and his experiences at this time. The first mention comes in the 'Jottings from Old Boys' in the December 1915/ April 1916 editions. Here some old contacts had met Victor. H. F. Marks reports Kenneth Goffe wrote, *'I met Victor Pastfield 'mirabile dictu' out here about two months ago. He was attached to the Essex Regiment for the time being.'* And in the same edition, *'J. V. Pastfield, who has met K. H. Goffe, at Lemnos, got his Xmas card from the School safely.'*

Pastfield wrote many letters to George Corner informing him of his exploits. His wry sense of humour is seen, particularly when he describes the effects of living in very hot weather and prickly heat, '*Boils and all kinds of complexion spoilers have arrived. No wonder the ladies keep away.*'

2nd Lieutenant J. V. Pastfield writes from Tenedos, Jan. 10th 1916:-
I feel I must write to thank you for the Christmas card. I got last April's Magazine about two weeks ago. Funny where it does get to. I enclose my cheque for my yearly subscription. Having concluded my business task, I will give an account of my experiences in short.

We were all called from our various stations to form the 1st Garrison Battalion Essex Regiment, a composite battalion of all regiments, at short notice. After the usual wait, all ready to go at a moment's notice, we eventually got sailing orders on August 25th, and we sailed on the 27th from Devonport. I tried to drop a note from the train as we passed Wellington, but it evidently got lost. After an uneventful voyage, we arrived at Lemnos and disembarked on a sweltering day, September 7th. I was not very much impressed with the place. No – or little – water available, awful heat, myriads of flies. It is my idea of perfection as regards discomfort. At Lemnos, we began to split up and many found their way to Anzac and Suvla. I remained for a while, and eventually, 4 months (approx.) after landing at Lemnos embarked for Tenedos. It is at present in French hands, and that is as much as I can say for the present – the evacuation of Helles is on. We get less news here, 14 miles from the Cape, than you do in England. We see large monitors, mounting 15" guns, behind Rabbit Island, firing on the Turks – often into Asia Minor, and so we often hear shells going over our heads. The French are all very good to us. We came here without anything except our kit. No tools and few dixies[36], so we had to depend on the French. All very happy.

Luck to all at the old School.

P.S. – I am aware that subscriptions should be sent to the Treasurer, but not knowing who he is, or where, I should be much obliged if you would forward my cheque.

I have met K. Goffe, but have not been able to find Major Aplin, Lieuts J. Baker and C. S. Ogilvie, although they have all been at Lemnos while I was there. Major Aplin and Lieut. Baker are both in the Salonica expedition to the best of my knowledge. I am very sorry to hear about Lieut. S. W. Baker. Hope the news concerning Lieut. E. F. Corner is false. It is rotten to think of so many Old Boys being lost.

In December 1916 the Imperial Camel Corps was raised as part of the Egyptian Expeditionary Force and at some point, Pastfield joined it. It is likely he would have seen action in the First Battle of Gaza (March 1917), the Second Battle of Gaza (April 1917) and the Battle of Beersheba (Oct/Nov. 1917).

J. V. Pastfield writes us the following interesting letter from Khartoum, May 31st, 1917:-
Not much time to write nowadays, but I mustn't forget my yearly subscriptions. This I make my excuse for writing. I'm rather out of the way down here and it is just as hot, only in a different and less dangerous way, as in France.

Last year I wrote from the pretty little isle of Tenedos, just at the mouth of the Dardanelles. This time it is 2000 miles south, where one's greatest ambition is to feel cool for a minute or so on end. I came here from Lower Egypt to join the Camel Company. The work is very interesting

[36] A dixie was a British Army camp kettle.

From the School Magazine

but so very safe. If any of you contemplate going to the Sudan be forewarned. It is a case like Dante's Inferno, or Ruhleben, of 'Abandon hope all ye who enter here.' I might have transferred when in Egypt to a scene of activity. However, I said I'll do the voyage up the Nile and then transfer. I didn't know of the hopelessness of it then. One learns perforce that procrastination is the thief of time. There is still a ray of hope, though. The war won't be over this year, and next Christmas we leave for Egypt again. No one stays more than one year in Khartoum except as a punishment. Once a certain regiment mutinied – or at any rate became mutinous. I think they stayed two years or more. They might have shot them for pity if nothing else. In winter it isn't a bad place though. In peacetime, it would be delightful. There are many English residents now and many more would be here in peacetime.

The last two weeks the plagues have made their appearance. I mean the two worst. (i) 'Habboubs' ie. sand cyclones, sometimes two miles long, a mile deep and 1-2000 ft. high. They have a core the centre of which is a vacuum, I believe. The storm moves with the core, which is capable of 40-60 mph. Only yesterday a steamer 300 miles up country was capsized, and two English people and four natives drowned. A colonel and his wife were saved and sat on the bank all night. Cheerful, or what? (ii) Locusts and other insects. The locusts are so thick – well, it's impossible to describe them. Scorpions, tarantulas, and all manner of insects have arrived. (Wood is used as fuel, and they come up from country with the wood.) Prickly heat has come. Boils and all kinds of complexion spoilers also have arrived. No wonder the ladies keep away. I must hump it over to the camel lines now for paying out and other jobs. Doctoring camels is very amusing. Tie three legs, and he'll often rise 2ft. clear of the ground. Their bite is awful, but they are seldom very vicious when they know you. Salaams to the present boys, not forgetting the Head and Miss Corner.

Ps. I met Wilcox in Alexandria last year.

Mrs Pastfield writes on December 6th, 1917

"The Imperial Camel Corps took part in the fight for Gaza and Beersheba. Vic says the bullets were as thick as hail and it is a marvel how anyone escaped in the restricted area. I see from an official report that the Imperial Camel Corps was in action last Friday. In his last letter (15th October 1917) he says, "No more news for an indefinite period as we shall have our hands full keeping the Turks on the run."

This appears to be the last mention of Victor before news came of his death in September 1918. The Imperial Camel Corps was disbanded in June 1918 due to the change of terrain as the EEF went into Palestine. Pastfield transferred to the Western Front having re-joined the Middlesex Regiment, although we are not sure exactly when, and it was here that he was killed. He had fought for over three years and died just two months before the war ended.

Remembering Joseph Victor Robinson Pastfield

School Obituary

Victor Pastfield

September 9th, 1918.

J. V. R. Pastfield, third son of Mr and Mrs Pastfield, of Exeter, entered the School in September 1910 and left in July 1913. He proved himself a steady and resolute boy of considerable ability and played an energetic part in all the activities of the School. He joined the Army in 1915, receiving a commission in the Middlesex Regiment, and was on active service in the Dardanelles, Egypt and Palestine. Here he was in the Imperial Camel Corps and was present at the taking of Beersheba and fought from thence to Jerusalem. He then re-joined the 5th Middlesex and was transferred to the Western Front, where he was engaged in heavy fighting on the front line, combating night attacks and raids. On the night of September 9th, when visiting his outposts, he was suddenly surrounded by Germans who were armed with stick-bombs. Despite heroic resistance, Victor and many of his men lost their lives. So fell this lion-hearted fellow in his 21st year – a terrible blow to his parents, who had lost an elder son near Bully-Grenay, Pas de Calais, in 1914. The Colonel of his Regiment, in writing to Mrs Pastfield, said: "Since joining my battalion he has made many friends and he will indeed be hard to replace." Mrs Pastfield, when visiting the battlefields after the war, met by chance at Bruges an officer under whom Victor had served and who gave her much sadly interesting information about her beloved son, saying how much he was liked "though but a boy." On the first page of Victor's pocketbook, he had written –

"Sunset and evening star,
And one clear call for me,
And may there be no moaning at the bar,
When I put out to sea."

He was always conspicuous at School for his 'grit' and strong originality and for his disdain of little trouble.

Pastfield was buried in Pernes British Cemetery in France.

The inscription on his grave refers to his brother as well and reads:

ALSO 2/LT. J. T. R. PASTFIELD
MIDDLESEX REGIMENT
KILLED 21ST DECEMBER 1914
THEY DIED THAT WE MIGHT LIVE

MIDDLESEX REGT
LIEUTENANT
J. VICTOR R. PASTFIELD
MIDDLESEX REGIMENT
SEPTEMBER 1918
R. PASTFIELD
REGIMENT
DECEMBER 1914
THAT WE MIGHT LIVE

Wellington Memorial Chapel - Letters To George Corner

Corner's letter to Mrs Furze-Morrish, Victor's eldest sister, was returned to him with the required details added. It shows his urgency to not only get the inscriptions right but suggests the need to do so quickly and gives us a glimpse of the letter he sent to parents.

The response to the letter most likely came from Reverend J. L. R. Pastfield, Victor's brother.

My brother was killed at Lens. If you are in Exeter any time visit St Thomas's Church; you will read on the 'War Memorial' just under the Tower inside the church all necessary details including an action in which many regulars have said he should have won the V.C.. J. R. Pastfield, Ingleside, Weybridge.

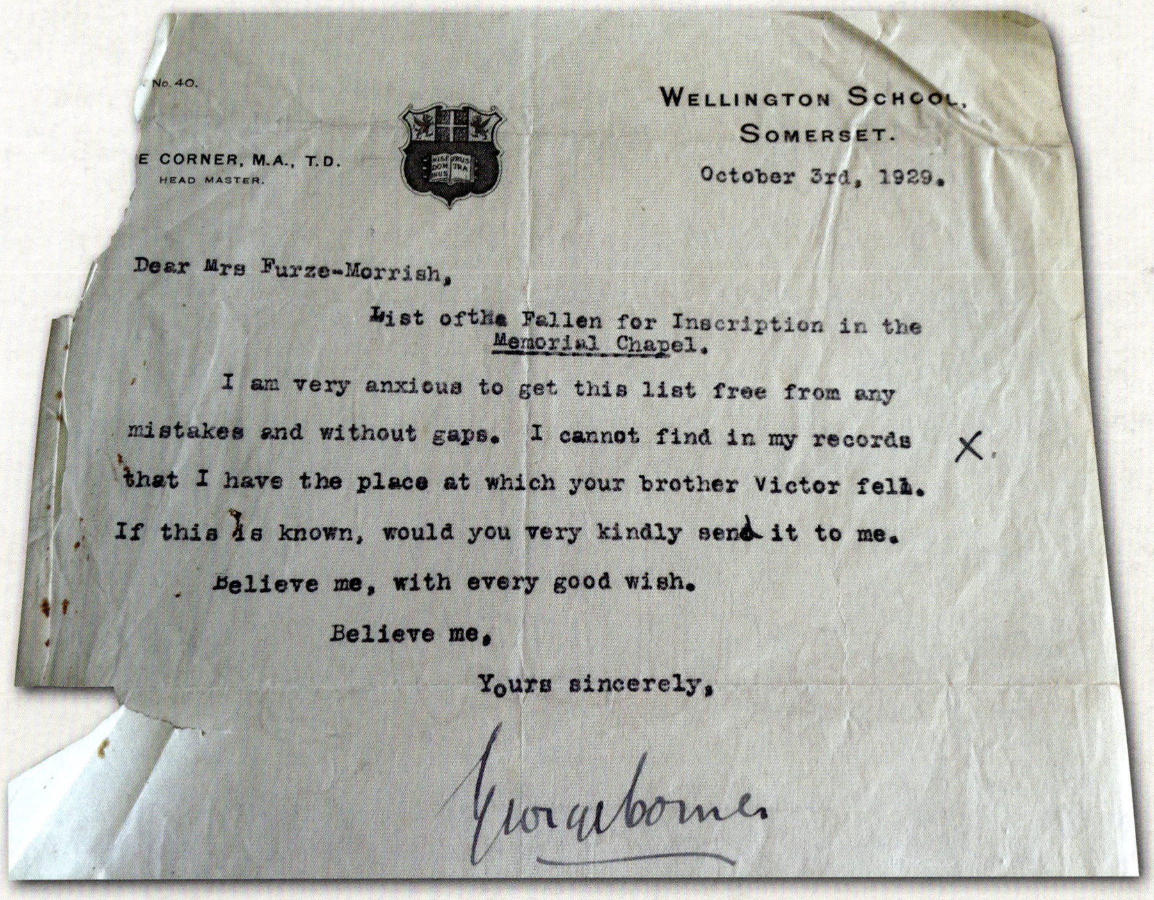

No. 40.

E CORNER, M.A., T.D.
HEAD MASTER.

WELLINGTON SCHOOL,
SOMERSET.

October 3rd, 1929.

Dear Mrs Furze-Morrish,

List of the Fallen for Inscription in the Memorial Chapel.

I am very anxious to get this list free from any mistakes and without gaps. I cannot find in my records that I have the place at which your brother Victor fell. X

If this is known, would you very kindly send it to me.

Believe me, with every good wish.

Believe me,

Yours sincerely,

George Corner

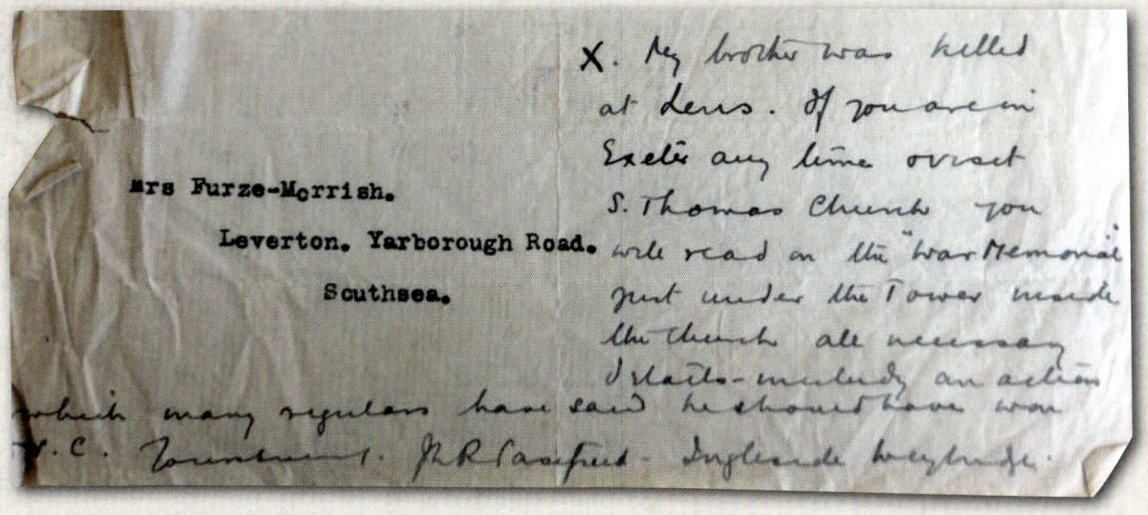

Mrs Furze-Morrish.
Leverton. Yarborough Road.
Southsea.

X. My brother was killed at Lens. If you are in Exeter any time or visit S. Thomas Church you will read on the "War Memorial" just under the Tower inside the church all necessary details – including an action which many regulars have said he should have won V.C. Townsend. J.R. Crawford – Inglesside Weybridge.

Letter from Florence Furze-Morrish, October 6th 1929

"Vicky is buried in Bully – Grenay Military Cemetery – Pas de Calais sector, but I cannot remember at the moment the name of the place that he fell, though I have visited it recently.

You may be interested in the enclosed ticket for Hill 60!!! I visited over 100 miles of the Ypres, Zeebrugge and Flanders area last month after leaving Wiesbaden and certainly, the little English cemeteries are beautifully tended.'

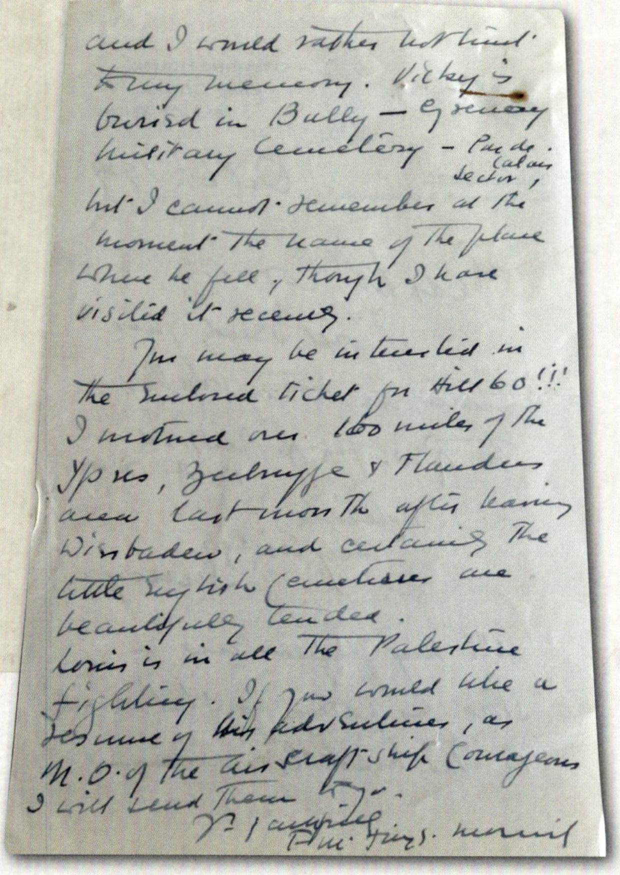

and I would rather not tire my memory. Vicky is buried in Bully – Grenay Military Cemetery – Pas de Calais sector, but I cannot remember at the moment the name of the place where he fell, though I have visited it recently.

You may be interested in the enclosed ticket for Hill 60!!! I motored over 100 miles of the Ypres, Zeebrugge & Flanders area last month after leaving Wiesbaden, and certainly the little English cemeteries are beautifully tended. Louis is in all the Palestine fighting. If you would like a resume of his adventures, as M.O. of the aircraft-ship Courageous I will send them to you.

Yrs faithfully
Flo. Furze-Morrish

G. W. POWELL, wounded and missing

Pte. George Winton Powell

b. 1898 – died 28th April 1917, aged 19.

"For a long time, his fate was in doubt and his parents suffered the terrible suspense of uncertainty for several weeks before they received the sad confirmation of his death. Winton was beloved by all who knew him."
School Obituary

George Winton Powell is Remembered with Honour on the Arras Memorial. In November 2017 he was remembered by Overside House and a poppy was placed in Chapel in his memory.

George was born to John Trevanion Powell and Margaret Mallon Powell (nee Showers) in April 1898. John and Margaret were both born in Taunton, Somerset: John in 1872 and Margaret in 1874. The couple were married in Taunton in 1895. George was born in 1898 in Lambeth, so the family obviously left the Taunton area at some point before this.

In the 1911 census, George was registered at The County School, and he appeared alongside such notable pupils as Pastfield, Tarbet, Bilton, Corner, Shapland, Gent and Dibble.

George Winton Powell's War

After leaving school in 1912, Powell moved to Bristol. In 1914 he was registered as a Railway Employee and in November 1915 it appears he was working in the Estates Dept. in Paddington.

In the July 1916 edition of the Magazine, George Winton Powell is recorded as visiting the School, so it is clear that he still has a connection to it. He joined up in 1916, trained through the summer and travelled to France in November where he moved to the 8th Somerset Light Infantry.

In the letter he wrote to the School on December 1916 he explained what he had been up to:

Winton Powell writes December 23rd, 1916, from France:-
I am afraid I've been awfully slack not having written before. During the summer I was training at Hursley Park Camp, Winchester, where I had quite a good time. Barrington – who perhaps you will remember – was in the same tent as myself, which was jolly. Orman was our Physical Instructor. In October we moved to Bournemouth and were billeted in large halls. In November I was put on an Egyptian draft and was taken off owing to be being a signaller. However, a week later on 23rd November, I was put on a French draft and left England on the 29th. As you will see by my address I have been transferred to the 8th S. L. I.. At present, we are

resting but expected to join in the fray very soon. The weather had been all sorts lately, cold, wet, rough and fine, and the mud – well, it reminds me of my country walks during the winter term at School.

While I was in a café the other day I happened to meet a fellow who was an engineer at Ford's, Wellington and helped to sink the well for the swimming bath.

How are you all? Quite well, I hope. I hope you will have a Merry Christmas
although I'm afraid this will not reach you by the 25th inst.

P.S.:- I should like the Mag. sent out awfully if it has not already been sent home.

As part of the 8th Somerset Light Infantry it is likely he would have taken part in the German Retreat to the Hindenburg Line (29th March 1917); the Battle of Arras – First Battle of the Scarpe (9th April); Capture of Monchy-Le-Preux (11th April); Second Battle of the Scarpe (23rd April) and the Battle of Arleux (28th April). Although reports of him being 'wounded' and subsequently 'missing' came through on this date, his death was not confirmed for some weeks.

In the July 1917 edition of the Magazine, news arrived of Powell's injury.

We regret we have to say that we have no news of Winton Powell, reported wounded on April 28th.

Remembering George Winton Powell

School Obituary

G. W. Powell, S. L. I.

April 28th 1917.

G. W. Powell, only son of Mr Powell, of Ealing, London, entered the School in Sept. 1909 and left in July 1912, when still in the IVth Form – Toro ii. and P. E. Dibble being contemporary with him. Winton was very popular amongst his fellows, being of a very modest and unassuming disposition. Fond of games, he began by playing Junior Footer against Ayshford School, as a forward, and was promising at Fives and Cricket. A keen Cadet, he was constantly to be found in the Armoury with Sergt. Allen, who saw in him the making of what he became – a brave soldier. He met his death in the hard fighting of April last. For a long time, his fate was in doubt and his parents suffered the terrible suspense of uncertainty for several weeks before they received the sad confirmation of his death. Winton was most beloved by all who knew him. We offer in all earnestness our great sympathy to his stricken parents.

Wellington School Memorial Chapel – Letter to George Corner

Mr Powell wrote to George Corner on the 5th October 1929. He and his wife would like to visit the school and see the Memorial Chapel for themselves. It is unclear whether they ever made the trip.

Dear Mr Corner,

In reply to yours, Winton was reported as being killed at *__Fampous__*, *E.N.E. of Arras.*

We have left London and above is our permanent address. Now we are nearer Wellington, Mrs Powell and myself would like to come and see the Memorial Chapel.

Perhaps you could give us a choice of afternoon that would not be inconvenient. I have not entirely given up business so am not absolutely free.

With kind regards,

Yours very truly,

J. T. Powell

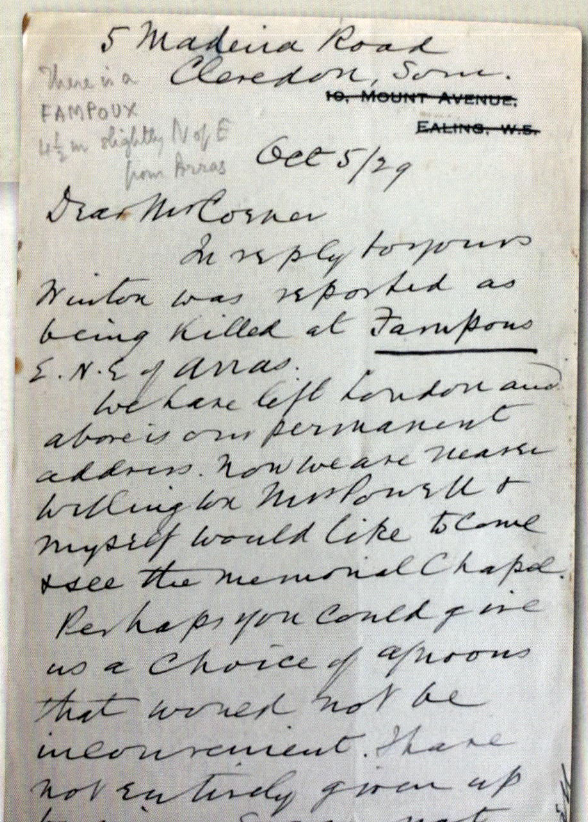

5 Madeira Road
Clevedon, Som.
~~10, MOUNT AVENUE,~~
~~EALING, W.5.~~

There is a FAMPOUX 4½ m slightly N of E from Arras

Oct 5/29

Dear Mr Corner

In reply to yours Winton was reported as being killed at Fampons E.N.E of Arras.

We have left London and above is our permanent address. Now we are nearer Wellington Mrs Powell & myself would like to come & see the Memorial Chapel.

Perhaps you could give us a choice of afternoons that would not be inconvenient. I have not entirely given up business so am not absolutely free.

With kind regards

Yours v. truly J T Powell

Sergt. HENRY PRATT
(*killed in action, Oct. 1st, 1918*).

Pte. Henry Pratt

b. 1888 – died 1st October 1918, aged 30

"In a letter to a sister, dated Sept. 30, the day before his death and never finished, he wrote, "I am looking forward to tomorrow, to be able to at last fight for dear old England." School Obituary

Henry Pratt is Remembered with Honour in Sancourt British Cemetery. He was remembered by Willows House on November 9th 2008 and flowers were placed in Chapel in his memory.

Henry Pratt was the second son of Charles and Ada Pratt of Tale House, Payhembury. He was born in 1888. He had four brothers and three sisters: Charles Camden (b. 1885), Eleanor (b. 1886), Henry (b. 1888), Edith (b. 1890), William (b. 1892), Ada (b. 1895) and John (b. 1896).

In 1901, the census showed that Charles, Ada, Edith, William, Ada and John were all living at home. Eleanor could not be found, but it is possible she was at school. Both Henry (aged 12) and Charles (recorded as Camden, aged 15) were boarders at The County School, Wellington. The same census record showed that William Miles (15), Percy Clode (11), John Jeffery (14) and Norman Jeffery (11) were also recorded as boarders in the School.

By 1911, Henry was in Canada. Charles was in New Zealand and it was possible that William was also in Canada.

William died in June 1915 whilst in the Candian Expeditionary Force. Eleanor and Edith moved with their parents to Hampshire and then Sussex. Charles died in October 1931 and Ada died in 1934, leaving her estate to her two daughters.

Henry Pratt's War

Pratt must have left the School in either 1905 or 1906 and attended a variety of Old Boy events before moving to Toronto with his banking job. In 1906 he attended the Annual General Meeting with Wadland, a fellow Canadian venturer. In 1909, the Magazine records that *'Henry Pratt writes to say he is getting on well in Toronto. He is in the Queen's Own Rifles and will probably come with them to England in their trip in the summer.'*

In September 1918, Henry finally got the opportunity to fight for 'dear old England'. He was killed in what is believed to be his first fighting on 1st October 1918. The Canadian Casualty record reads as follows: *'Private Pratt, 1st Battalion, Canadian Machine Gun Corps. 1.10.18. "Killed in Action" whilst taking part in operations East of Blecourt, he was wounded in the head and face by enemy bullets, dying before he could be taken to a Dressing Station."*

Remembering Henry Pratt

School Obituary

Henry Pratt

October 1st, 1918.

Henry Pratt, second son of Mr and Mrs Pratt, of Tale House, Payhembury, entered the School in September 1901. He was a remarkably bright and high-spirited boy and made marked progress in his work. On leaving School he took up banking as a career and at the outbreak of war was holding an important post in Toronto. In early childhood, he had the misfortune of injuring his left hand by a sudden accident with a machine, which in some measure hampered him. But he was eagerly determined to serve his country and joined the Canadian M. G. Corps, in which he received a commission. On arrival in England, he was stationed at Seaford and Folkestone and was engaged in drafting troops for three years. He longed to be engaged in active service but was rejected by the authorities as he was considered incapable of self-defence, owing to his weakened hand. He then took the step of resigning his commission, thus reverting to the ranks. This proves indeed the depth of his devotion to the cause he had at heart. In a letter to a sister, dated September 30th, the day before his death and never finished, he wrote, "I am looking forward to tomorrow, to be able at last to fight for dear old England." This letter was forwarded home marked "Picked up on the field of battle." The W. O. could only give the bare fact of Henry's death – killed in action, Oct 1st, 1918. Mr and Mrs Pratt had previously lost their third son, Willy, in action in France. In a pathetic letter, Mrs Pratt wrote: "It has been a heavy blow to have lost our two dear boys, but we would not have had them slackers." Henry Pratt's fearless devotion makes his old friends proud of so fine an Englishman. His determination to get out to action stamps him a brave man more than anything we can add.

Payhembury Memorial

Both Company Sergeant Major William Pratt of 3rd Battalion Canadian Infantry and Private Henry Pratt of the Canadian Machine Gun Corps are commemorated on the war memorial in the village of Payhembury. The memorial hosts the names of the six men of the village who died in WW1.

William Pratt, Company Sergeant Major, 9153, 3rd Battalion Canadian Infantry (Central Ontario Regiment) died on Saturday 5th June 1915 aged 23 years. He went to Toronto Canada at the age of 17. He was the son of Charles Pratt and Ada (nee Richards) then living at Tale near Payhembury. From the Payhembury parish magazine:- "He was bathing with other men in the canal after returning home from the trenches, and seems to have dived too strongly, and got his head stuck at the bottom. After going through so many dangers – on one occasion he returned with only seven men out of nearly 100 – it is remarkable that he should have met his death in this way". His grave is at Bethune Town Cemetery, Pas de Calais, France. Named on Payhembury and Tale War Memorials and Payhembury Roll of Honour 1914 – 1918.

Henry Pratt, Private 475183, 1st Battalion, Canadian Machine Gun Corps, a native of Payhembury. His parents Charles Pratt and Ada (nee Richards) had left Tale, Payhembury to live in Stockbridge, Hampshire. Henry died on Tuesday 1st October 1918 aged 30 years and is buried at Sancourt British Cemetery, Nord, France. Named on Payhembury and Tale War Memorials and Payhembury Roll of Honour 1914 -1918.[37]

Henry Pratt is buried in Sancourt British Cemetery.

The inscription on Henry's and his brother's graves is the same and reads:

THEM ALSO WHICH SLEEP IN JESUS
WILL GOD BRING WITH HIM
1 THESS. IV. 14

[37] http://www.devonhonour.org.uk/MoreInfo.aspx

2nd Lieut. Philip Henry Rowe

b. 1893 – died 17th September 1916, aged 23.

'Philip was a most amiable and vivacious boy, possessed it will be recollected, of a tuneful singing voice, which added to his general popularity.' School Obituary

Philip Rowe is Remembered With Honour in Serre Road Cemetery, No. 2. In November 2018 he will be remembered by Price's House and a poppy will be placed in Chapel in his memory.

Philip Henry Rowe was the youngest son of Mr Walter Paxton Rowe (b. 1852 in Bethnal Green, Middlesex) and Alice Louisa Chappell (b. 1854). Together they had six children: Thomas George (b. 1881), Alice Sophia (b. 1882), Charles Alfred (b. 1884), Clara Emily (b. 1884), Horace Sidney (b. 1891) and Philip Henry (b. 1893).

In the 1901 census, the family was living in Weston Super Mare at 62 Locking Road. Walter was a Commercial Traveller/Drapery Worker. Though 20, 19 and 17 years of age, Thomas, Alice and Charles were still living at home.

By 1911, the family had moved to Wellington and was recorded as living at 41 High Street. Only four of the children were now at home: Thomas, Alice, Clara and Horace. Philip Henry was recorded as living in the City of London at 6 Aldermonbury, 44 and 45 Farringdon, St. E C., where he was working as a Drapery assistant. He lived and worked with over 50 others. Charles was living in Westbury at Albion House, Market Place, Westbury. He married Jeanie McPhail Anderson on 19th June 1908 and was Head of his household. The couple would soon be joined by Thomas Chalmers born on April 23rd, 1912.

Philip Rowe standing on the right (with kind permission of the family)

Philip Rowe circled (with kind permission of the family)

Philip Henry Rowe's War

Though Philip Rowe left the School at the end of December 1906, he clearly still felt very strongly about it, visiting to attend the Break Up Supper in April 1911 as an invited Old Boy.

In December 1914 the 'List of the Old Boys Serving Their Country' was published and Rowe was on it.

Rowe, P. H. Pte. London Rifle Brigade, 130 Bunhill Row, London

Records show that Rowe joined the R.A.M.C (TF) in 1911, moving to the London Rifle Brigade in September 1914. As part of the Expeditionary Force, he went to France in March 1915.

Rowe wrote a letter to George Corner on June 17th 1915 detailing some of his experiences in France. The letter was printed in the Magazine:

Pte. P. H. Rowe, London Rifle Brigade, describing his experiences in the trenches in France, says on June 17th:

The regiment we relieved had been in for five days and had found things very quiet indeed: but we were met on the road up with terrible machine gun fire. Luckily all their shots were high and by lying flat down on the road we were more or less safe, at any rate, no one was hit. We got into the trenches alright then and had a fairly peaceful night, but at 4 o'clock the next morning they started shelling us and gave us a terrible time. They shelled us persistently till 11 o'clock when they quieted down a little, but they still peppered us pretty well all day long. To add to our troubles, it rained all day so that we were mostly soaked through and sitting in water. We were withdrawn that night and I am glad to say we have not been up since. We had very heavy casualties.

Wounded in July, he returned to England in December 1915. He transferred to the Middlesex Regiment and was given a commission on 13th December 1915.

He returned to France on 17th July 1916. The Regiment was involved in the Battle of the Somme, first of all at Ginchy (9th Sept.) and the Battle of Flers-Courcelette (15th Sept.)

There is some confusion as to whether he died on the 15th or 17th of September 1916. Rowe was initially reported as missing, but his death was then confirmed – he had been killed in action.

Remembering Philip Henry Rowe

School Obituary

2nd Lieut. P. H. ROWE

September 1916.

P. H. Rowe was the youngest son of Mr Rowe, of High Street, Wellington and entered the School in Jan. 1902, leaving in Dec. 1906. Philip was a most amiable and vivacious boy, possessed it will be recollected, of a tuneful singing voice, which added to his general popularity. Having served four years in the London Territorials he was gazetted as 2nd Lieut. to the 4/7th Middlesex Regiment and was slightly wounded before the second battle of Ypres, in which he took part. He was reported wounded and missing in September 1916, having last been seen when leading his men into action. The company was exposed to heavy shell-fire and, sad to relate, only some 28 men came out alive. His death at the early age of 23 is lamented by all who knew him. To his thorough training as a soldier, he also brought integrity and self-sacrifice, and his parents and family receive the deepest sympathy in their sad loss.

Rowe was also featured in the Du Ruvigny Register

ROWE, PHILIP HENRY, 2nd Lieut., 7th (Middlesex) Battn. The Duke of Cambridge's Own (Middlesex Regt.), *s.* of Walter Paxton Rowe, of Weston-super-Mare, co. Somerset; *b.* Bristol, 27 Jan. 1893; *educ.* Wellington School, co. Somerset; was in the firm of Crocker, Sons & Co., London; joined the R.A.M.C. (T.F.) in 1911, and the London Rifle Brigade in Sept. 1914; served with the Expeditionary Force in France from March, 1915; returned to England in Dec. 1915, and was gazetted 2nd Lieut. in the Middlesex Regt. on the 13th of that month; went back to France 17 July, 1916, and was killed in action at Leuze Wood, near Combles, 15 Sept. following. His Commanding Officer wrote: "He was a very gallant officer, and although he had not been with us long, we had all learnt his great worth as a soldier and companion," and a friend: "Everybody feels his death as a personal thing; he was so utterly single-minded and sincere and good, and I know how much you must have rejoiced in the continual evidence of such qualities. All who knew him so recognized the splendour of his nature that they must be thankful for having him at all in their lives." *Unm.*

Philip Henry Rowe.

ICH DIEN
ALBUHERA
MIDDLESEX REGT
SECOND LIEUTENANT
P. H. ROWE
MIDDLESEX REGIMENT
17TH SEPTEMBER 1916 AGE 23
HIS NAME IS NOT FORGOTTEN

Rowe's Grave

On the Graves Registration Report Form, it is noticeable that many of the men on the sheet are marked as 'Unknown Soldier' – only four, Rowe included, have been identified. On a Burial Return dated July 1930, Rowe's name has been handwritten over the top of a crossed out UNKNOWN BRITISH SOLDIER and it appears that Rowe's body has been identified recently. There is something shocking about the way that this identification has taken place, something that reinforces the physical brutality of the war that takes the life and leaves only the clothes, effects and body. On 18th July 1930, fourteen years after he died, the grave he was buried in at Combles was uncovered and a body exhumed. Hitherto it had been the resting place of 'An Unknown Soldier'. Quite why it was exhumed is unclear. Philip Rowe's body was identified by the engraving on the watch he was wearing. It is a simple engraving: 'P. H. R from G. S., Sept. 1914.' Who is G. S.? We will probably never know. Unlike the others who were identified by their discs, Rowe's 'Khaki shirt and trousers (or breeches), Officer's collar and tie (no tunic), Officer's Boots size 9' were recorded. He was reburied in Serre Road Cemetery, No. 2.

The inscription on his grave reads:

HIS NAME IS NOT FORGOTTEN

Sec.-Lieut. H. G. SHAPLAND
(*killed March 1st, 1918*).

2nd Lieutenant Herbert George Shapland

b. 1896 – 2nd March 1918, aged 21

"Herbert was a most able and determined worker – a splendid fellow to have by when we were up against a tough job. I feel that his death in action (tragic though it is and must remain) is of a piece of his character."

A colleague

Herbert George Shapland is Remembered with Honour in Rocquigny-Equancourt Road British Cemetery, Manancourt. In November 2014 he was remembered by Lights House and flowers were placed in Chapel in his memory.

Herbert George Shapland was the youngest son of George Webber Shapland and Mary Shapland (Elworthy). His father was a farmer and had married in 1883. They had two sons and four daughters.

In 1901, the family was living at South Bray Farm, Chittle Hampton, Devon. George was 45 and his wife 48. The children were all at home and are recorded on the census as follows: Mary Louisa (17), Lucy Helen (12), Christopher (8), Caroline Emma (6), Herbert George (4) and May Elizabeth (2).

In the 1911 census, the family appeared to have been separated. Herbert George was a pupil at The County School, Wellington; Caroline was a pupil at St Hilda's School, Exeter; and Mary Louisa was living with her husband, John Rawle, in Stoley Barton, Barnstaple. They had a new-born son, John. At the family home were George (55), Mary (58), Lucy (22), Christopher (18) and May (12).

Herbert George Shapland's War

The magazines tell us that Shapland visited the School in the spring term of 1915. War would have been underway but that doesn't stop him visiting again in the Easter term of 1916, July 1916 and November (ish) 1917. We read that Shapland failed to pass the doctor's inspection and was still in Cardiff in 1915/1916.

The July 1917 reports that '*2nd Lieutenant H. G. Shapland has had some hard experience in France like many more. We regret his last interesting letter came to hand too late for this Mag.*'

More than any of the other Old Boys who died in WW1, Shapland took time and pains to update George and Mary Corner on what he was doing. Perhaps many months of being unable to go the front led him to have more time on his hands than others, but there are several letters we can read to gain a picture of the experiences Shapland was having.

H. G. Shapland writes from Topsham Barracks, Exeter (July 1916):

At last, I am writing to tell you something of my doings at Exeter.

The course of instruction here is carried out in classes; A is the first class, then B, C, D, E and F. Each cadet is allowed to remain a fortnight in each class in ordinary circumstances, but at present, they are trying to turn us out in a much shorter time. I was one week only in each of classes A, B and C, and three weeks in D (really only a fortnight, as I was in hospital for one week with a cold – at least I was quite well the day after I went in, and why they kept me there a week I do not know). I am in E class this week. After the course is finished at Exeter, candidates for the R. F. A. proceed to Larkhill or Shoebury for a month's training there and then go to Okehampton for a week's firing. Provided you prove yourself fitted for a commission at the end of the course, indefinite leave is given you until you are gazetted. A few weeks ago, fellows only had a few days leave and were sent straight across. Now I believe a somewhat longer leave is granted. One is liable at any time to be sent to the ranks; they seem to drop upon one suddenly. We have three batteries in training here, probably about 600 cadets, so you can guess that a large number of artillery officers pass out from here. About 50 cadets go to Trowbridge from here every week for training in Siege Batteries, while another 40 go to Larkhill and Shoebury to complete instruction for R. F. A., heavies and anti-aircraft. I have chosen R. F. A., but those that are sent to Shoebury may possibly be taken for heavies whether you object or not.

We get very good food – coffee and biscuits first thing, breakfast 7.30, lunch 1, tea 3.45, dinner at 7. Reveille is at 6 a.m. and stables and everyone except for E class at 6.30. We finish at 5.30 and are then free to go anywhere within three miles.

I was home for last weekend (Saturday midday till Sunday night). I shall not get any more leave until I go to Lark Hill or Shoebury, which I hope will be in about three weeks' time. I must try and come out and see you then. Chris is at home on harvest leave at present, but I'm afraid they can't get on at all. We had about 90 acres down when I was home, so expect the corn must be growing out with so much rain. I wonder what you think of the war at this time. Things seem to be much more hopeful at present.

H. G. Shapland writes from France, September 27th, 1916:

We left Southampton three weeks ago yesterday at 8 o'clock in the evening and arrived at Havre 3 o'clock next morning. I'm not a good sailor and can't say I had a particularly happy time coming across; in fact, it took a day or two to recover! We were not allowed to leave the boat for several hours, it was 11 o'clock when we arrived at R. H. and R. F. A. Base Depot. We lived in canvas huts; no fire was to be found in the officers' mess; the food was very scanty; the weather was intensely cold; so, you will believe me when I say that everyone was anxious to leave Havre as soon as possible!

I received orders a week after my arrival at the Base to conduct a draft of men to my division, (2nd Div.) and to remain with the Division myself. We left Havre Station at 2.30 on the Tuesday morning, and at 9 a.m. detrained at a large French town, where we received instructions to march to the Rest Camp outside the town where we might be detained for several days. We stayed here until the following Sunday when we were ordered to continue our journey. At mid-day yesterday-week we arrived at Divisional Rail-head, and after a march of about six miles I handed the draft over to Headquarters, 2nd D. A. C.. I hope it will not be my luck to conduct a draft next time I come up the line from the Base, for it's a thankless job and a rotten sweat.

At Havre, I caught a bad cold, and the M. O., 2nd D. A. C., thought I was unfit to go about my work, as I had a high temperature; and was sent to hospital. Here I am in what was before the war an old French chateau. It is a nice quiet spot for a hospital, about 20 miles or so from the line I should say. I am nearly well again and hope to be back to my section in the D. A. C. in a day or two. I haven't seen much of the front yet – in fact, I haven't been right up yet. One thing I did see was mud – tons of it! The horses were simply plastered in it from head to foot. In spite of that, the horses in my section appeared to be in quite good condition.

Everyone here is rather excited at present. Startling news came down the line last night, and rumours continue to come. The Huns are evidently moving. Am anxious to see the papers, but they do not get here until this afternoon.

I don't know how long I shall remain with D. A. C. – not too long, I hope: I want to get to a battery.

2nd Lieutenant H. G. Shapland writes from Redford, Edinburgh, November 1916:

You will see from the above that I am now an officer. I was gazetted last Saturday week, and last Friday I received orders to report here on Monday. I left Taunton on Sunday night and arrived here at 10 o'clock the next day. I do not think I have written to you since I left Exeter. I was at Topsham Barracks for 9 weeks and then proceeded to Larkhill for a course of gunnery. The work there was much the same as at Exeter, only a higher standard was expected. They were very keen on map reading, and we had a lot of Battery Staff work and reconnaissance. We had our examination the last week we were there – a very easy one it was too – I got 99 per cent., so you can tell it wasn't very hard!

The Okehampton range is closed for the winter so we did our firing on the West Down range which is about 8 miles from Larkhill. We had to shift to another camp for this (No. 22 Practice Camp, about a mile from our first camp). We finished our firing in four days and returned to Exeter on the Friday to hand in our kit. We were told to proceed on indefinite leave pending gazettement and War Office instructions. We were also told that we should re-receive our posting orders 10 days before we had to report. I'm sorry I did not come out to see you, but I was going about all the time I was home and also helping with the threshing and intended to ride over after I received my posting orders (expecting to have 10 days' notice). As it turned out, I did not get the notice as promised and had no chance to come out. I thought of coming out on Friday afternoon, but the weather was terrible, snowing and raining all afternoon. However, I shall see you the very next chance I get.

I suppose you know that Chris is at Cambridge at Cadet School. He was home for last weekend and travelled back as far as Bristol with me on Sunday night. I hear that they are asking for volunteers for the "tanks," and Chris has given in his name, but doesn't know whether he will be accepted. He wants to be, as he thinks it's a very interesting job. We do not get a bad time here, the Colonel is very keen on riding, and will not pass you as efficient until you can ride perfectly. We did not have our first ride until this morning, as we have been waiting for other officers to arrive. There were about 25 of us riding and they kept us trotting and cantering around that school until we were all ready to drop off. I do not mind the jumping without stirrups and arms folded, but what causes trouble is riding around the school for about 20 minutes on end at a fast trot without stirrups! I was aching so much that several times I thought of falling off voluntarily! Only one chap fell off, and the Colonel complimented us at the finish by saying that hardly one of us had any idea of riding and that he expected us to be able to ride before! We have to vault and do all sorts of gymnastic tricks on horseback.

I was very sorry to see in the paper that J. C. Brown had been killed in action but pleased to see how Bown distinguished himself by winning the Military Cross.

I suppose you are having the Mag. for the Summer and Xmas terms, as I have not received one for the Summer term yet. I like having the School Mag. as that is the only chance I get of learning school news and the doings of Old Boys.

2nd Lieutenant H. G. Shapland writes to Miss Corner from France, June 27th 1917:-
Just a line to let you know how I'm getting on. I've now been sent out here for nearly 5 months, and during that time have seen a good deal of the war. I was in the Hun retreat down south and afterwards came up here for the Easter Monday show. We were supporting the Canadians.

Our present position is only a few miles from where we were then. Although we've had a pretty rotten time in our brigade and I think the 15th Battery has had its share of bad luck. There were 6 officers in the battery when I joined, of these 3 have been killed, or wounded, and one sent back to England with a bad foot, which I hear he will probably lose. I only came back from hospital a week ago having been there with mumps for more than a month. When I got back to the Division I found that 3 more officers had been posted to the 15th, and as there was no room for another I had to come to the D. A. C., for a time. My address is No. 3 Section, 2nd D. A. C., B. E. F. I hope to goodness I'm not here for long as I hate this job. I may say it is a pretty safe one, but when I'm out here I want to do some real work and not stay about 5 miles from the Germans most of my time. I saw the Colonel of my Brigade 2 or 3 days ago and he said he hoped to get me back again in a month or two. I was expecting to go home on leave next week, but I've just heard that I've been selected to attend a course at the Army Artillery School, so suppose I shall not get leave till after the course. I'm looking forward to the course very much and was only saying a short time ago how much I should like one. It will be a good opportunity for learning new things and also revising what I have learned.

I saw Harold Pound-Corner about 3 months ago. I shall never forget that day. It was during the retreat of the Germans. We were suddenly stopped from going further and ordered to move out of action and get ready for our march north. That was when I met Harold. He was laying 6 miles of cable, and at the time didn't know how he would get on owing to shortage of wire. The road was blocked with traffic for about 2 miles, and we were held up at this point for 5 hours on a cold winter's day – that is why I shall ever forget it! He passed me again later on his way home.

I wonder when the next School Mag. is coming out, as I haven't seen one this year. I was sorry to hear that Bilton had been killed – Geoff Dibble wrote and told me. By the way, I must have been near to G. W. D. when he was wounded. We have been supporting his Division for about 2 months now, but I didn't know he was in this Division at the time.

The weather is still good, just a shower now and then which is all that's wanted. I went to the Army Sports on the 25th. The Duke of Cornwall Connaught and Prince Arthur of Connaught visited the showground during the afternoon. There were some fine turn-outs of every description – horses, harness and vehicles got up in the most marvellous style.

Hoping to see you all soon.

2nd LieutHerbert Shapland writes from France, Dec. 5th, 1917:-
I've been frightfully busy since I returned from leave. At that time we were on a very quiet front and remained there another six weeks. Since then we've had a terribly exciting time. I wish I could tell you of all our experiences, but for obvious reasons, I cannot. One thing it would take too long to tell you everything, so that I may as well wait until I come home and make one job of it. At the present moment our division is very proud of itself (I will tell you why later).
I am due for leave but shall not put in for it for at least a fortnight probably, so am afraid my chances of being home for Xmas are very poor. Did I write and thank you for the School Mag.

- in case I didn't I do so now. Was so glad to hear all the news; it was a fine big Mag. and must have taken you an awful time to piece together. I haven't come across any Old Boys for a long time – 'twould be quite exciting to see someone I know. We're having very cold weather at present – hard frost, very nice – much better than rain at any rate.

The last mention of Herbert comes in a letter from Ivan De La Bere, written in France on January 1st 1918:

Last week I ran into Jago and H. G. Shapland and had a long talk of about two hours with each of them. Jago has got a job as Divisional Claims Officer and was just off on leave. Poor old 'Shags' was just returning, but in spite of it looked very cheery and fit.

Remembering Herbert George Shapland

School Obituary

Herbert Shapland

March 1, 1918.

Herbert G. Shapland was the younger son of Mr and Mrs Shapland, of Deane, Fitzhead, and entered the School in 1909. Naturally studious, he did well and took his Senior Cambridge Exam, successfully in 1912. He was not of a robust physique, but nevertheless a true sportsman and took part to the full in all School activities. The best of pals, his presence was always welcome and his influence with the younger boys in or out of School was as splendid as it was remarkable. As a Prefect he left nothing to be desired, being always ready and thorough in his duties. "Shags" was loved by everybody. On leaving School he entered an office in Cardiff and won esteem and attachment from his chief and colleagues – one of whom wrote to Mrs Shapland as follows – "Herbert was a most able and determined worker – a splendid fellow to have by when we were up against a tough job. I feel that his death in action (tragic though it is and must remain) is of a piece with his character." After joining he received a commission in 48th Division R. A. and in his letters from France to his Parents and friends gave very interesting accounts of the life and the fighting in which his battery was engaged. In his last letter, Feb. 16th, he says, "I've just come back from a forward gun – quite a good walk and one could see miles in the sunshine. Am enclosing cutting from the Daily Mail which gives the story of a great battle. You will see that the 2nd Division (who were between the other two divisions mentioned) were attacked heavily all day. Our infantry was magnificent and only about 200 yards were lost during the whole of the day and all this was retaken. Captain Stone and Lieut. Benzeeny of the rearguard got the V. C. and D. S. O. respectively. Although I myself didn't happen to have any dangerous job I was down at the wagon line when the Huns launched their first attacks and from the first, there was no doubt about their objectives. Gun teams were harnessed up and hooked into the limbers and I took them at a trot to within 400 yards of the Guns, where I waited for the rest of the day. There was no need to pull the guns out, however, as the Boche attacks completely broke down. When I started off with the limbers I was wondering who would get the guns first, myself or the Germans, however, I won! Things didn't half hum, wagon loads of ammunition pouring up from all directions, various officers galloping about goodness knows where and the fight in the air was tremendous. The whole sky was full of them and I believe about 7 German planes were brought down just on our part of the front." On March 1st an action was proceeding at Beaucamp and Herbert was in a dug-out just outside the lines, when a splinter from a stray shell wounded him badly in the head and though at once attended by the doctor and removed to a hospital, all attempts to save his life were useless and he died the next day, aged 21, his last words being to send his love to all in his beloved home. A brother officer wrote that he was buried in the Rocquiguy Road Cemetery and a cross was put up with his name on it. "I can't tell you," he continued, "how deeply we feel his loss and how much he is missed in the Battery." The Chaplain, Rev. F. Holden, wrote thus to Mrs Shapland, "I am writing to express my deepest sympathy with you in the loss of your son. As a member of the same mess, I feel the loss as a personal one. Moreover, I too am a Somerset man. None of us can realise that he is gone from us. May God comfort you in your sorrows and may they one day be changed into joy." Regrets at the loss of one who had so deeply impressed all those associated with him cannot be expressed. His memory will ever remain.

"Birthless and deathless and changeless,
Remaineth the Spirit for ever.
Death hath not changed it at all,
dead though
The house of it seems."

The inscription on his grave reads:

TO LIVE IN HEARTS WE LEAVE BEHIND IS NOT TO DIE

SECOND LIEUTENANT
H. G. SHAPLAND
ROYAL FIELD ARTILLERY
2ND MARCH 1918 AGE 21
UBIQUE
QUO FAS ET GLORIA DUCUNT

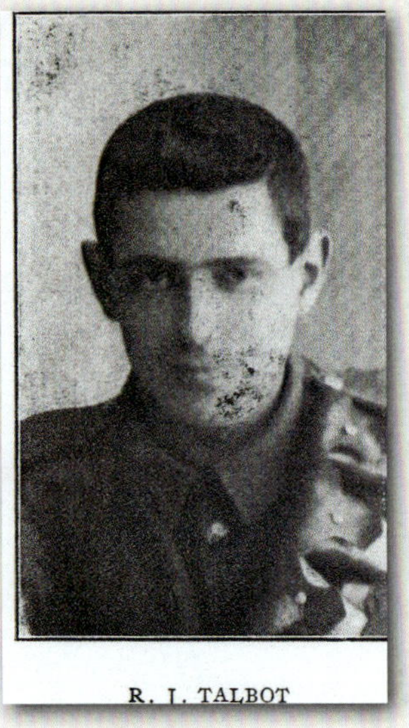

Gunner Robert John Talbot

b. 1894 – died 22nd November 1918, aged 24

'His early death was a heavy blow to his parents and his family, yet their grief at his loss has mingled with it the enduring recollection that he died for his country's sake. We remember him at School as a boy of singular promise.'

School Obituary

Robert Talbot is Remembered with Honour in Ramleh War Cemetery. On November 13th 2011 he was remembered by Willows House and flowers were placed in Chapel in his memory.

Robert John Talbot was the second son of Robert Talbot, a master baker and confectioner, and Emily Jane Wood. The couple married in 1886 in Wellington. In 1887 the couple had their first child, Ernest John. In 1891, the family was living at 32 Mantle Street. They had two children: Ernest, aged 3, and Gwendoline, aged 2. Tragedy struck the family when, in 1892, Ernest died aged only 5. By 1901, the family had moved to 42 Mantle Street. Robert was still a baker and employed a live-in apprentice. There had been more children: May, aged 8, Robert John, aged 7 and Charles Edwin, aged 5. Gwendoline was twelve years old and still at home. Further tragedy struck the family in 1906 when May died, aged 14. By 1911 the family appeared once more at 32 Mantle Street. Gwendoline was 22 years old and an elementary school teacher. Robert (17) and Charles (15) were both bakers.

The next significant event for the family was the marriage of Robert John to Louisa Bennett at Wellington Baptist Church in October 1916. Robert had enlisted to join the Army and was soon deployed overseas. On 6th May 1917, Louisa gave birth to a son, Thomas Reginald Talbot. It is not certain that Robert John ever saw him.

Robert John Talbot's War

Talbot enlisted on 6th December 1915 but wasn't mobilized until the 13th March 1917.

Records show he was approved for the Royal Garrison Artillery on 16th March 1917. He spent a week at the Military Hospital in Catterick Camp between 7th April and 13th April and it appears that ill health was to dog his military career.

On the 30th March 1917, he was posted to the 12th Mountain Battalion. He left England in January 1918 and finally made it to Alexandria on 16th February, having re-embarked at Marseilles. Records show he was admitted to hospital in May and then again in October. He was reported as dangerously ill on 3rd November and sadly passed away on 22nd November – eleven days after the Armistice was signed.

145122 GUNNER
R. J. TALBOT
ROYAL GARRISON ARTILLERY
22ND NOVEMBER 1918 AGE 24
UBIQUE
QUO FAS ET GLORIA DUCUNT
UNTIL WE MEET AGAIN

Remembering Robert John Talbot

School Obituary

R. J. Talbot

November 22nd, 1918.

Robert Talbot entered the School in September 1905, remaining until July 1908. He was a bright and steady boy and did highly creditable work. He joined the Army in February 1917, and was under training at Plymouth, in Yorkshire and finally on Salisbury Plain. He was sent to Egypt in January 1918, on Transport work, but soon fell ill of a fever and dysentery, which left him very much reduced in strength. However, on recovery, he was attached to the R. G. A. Mountain Battery and shared the progress through Palestine. When he reached Nazareth, he was again laid low by fever and died there on November 22nd, aged 24 years. His early death was a heavy blow to his parents and family, yet their grief at his loss has mingled with it the enduring recollection that he died for his country's sake. We remember him at School as a boy of singular promise.

He is featured in the publication *Our Boys* written by Mike Perry and Ray Hitchcock and commemorated on the Wellington Memorial.

Robert Talbot was buried in Ramleh War Cemetery in Israel and Palestine.

Louisa decided that the inscription on his grave should read:

UNTIL WE MEET AGAIN

Talbot's Service Records

Robert Talbot's Service Records are available online and in them, we can see not only his illnesses and hospital stays but also the communication from his wife and brother in trying to secure the safe passage of his personal effects. The records are not the best quality but particularly in Louisa's letter, it is easy to see the pain and desperation to have something to hold on to of her husband's.

Dear Sir,

I am writing in respect of my husband's personal effects which I have not received yet. It's three months ago since his death and I think I ought to have received them by now. Will you please let me know at your earliest convenience as I shall like ....[like to have them].

Though this letter was dated 24th February and the receipt was stamped 26th February 1919, Louisa had still not been sent Robert's things by May so her brother-in-law wrote on her behalf. It is hard to imagine how frustrating it must have been to know that the personal effects were sitting in an office, perhaps even lost, and had been for nearly three months. Only the grieving can impose a value on the items themselves and though Talbot's things may not have seemed to have much value, their significance to Louisa was huge. Eventually, the parcel did arrive. The records are in poor condition and not everything is legible but his personal effects include, 'photos, letters, watch, metal matchbox with crest, bible, Devotional Pack, cap badge, pocket knife, cigarette pack in a case.'

Sec. Lieut. V. TARBET
(killed in action, Oct. 4th, 1917).

2nd Lieutenant Victor Tarbet

b. July 1887 – died 4th October 1917, aged 20

"We put on one another's equipment at 3 a.m, and then shook hands. At 6 o'clock we went over the top, after which time I never saw him again. You have lost a good son and I have lost a good pal.' Pinnington

Victor Tarbet is Remembered with Honour on the Tyne Cot Memorial. In November 2018 he will be remembered by Richards House and a poppy will be placed in Chapel in his memory.

Victor Tarbet was the youngest child of William Henry Tarbet (b. 1860), a solicitor and freemason, and Annie Tarbet (b. 1860). Victor was born in July 1897 in St. Thomas, Exeter. In 1901 the family were living at 3 Victoria Terrace, Exeter. William and Annie were both 41; Mabel Harriett was 14 (b. 1886); Louisa Marguerite, 13 (b. 1888); Annie, 11 (b. 1889); Montague, 6 (b. 1895) and Victor aged 3 (b. 1897).

In 1911 the family had moved to 4 Baring Crescent in Heavitree, Exeter. Victor was now boarding at The County School (Wellington School), aged 13. Mabel had married and lived with her husband, Charles Arthur Besley, and young son, Charles William Phillip Besley at 32 Orlando Road, Clapham Common, S. W.. Louisa, Annie and Montague were all living with William and Annie.

Tragedy struck the family in January 1914 when William died, aged only 53. The local newspaper carried a long account of his funeral – he was clearly an important figure in the community.

School Life

Victor only attended the School for two years, but he managed to achieve a lot during this time and is mentioned in several Magazines. He has a place in School history as the first pupil to *'use the new sick room'* having broken his leg and dislocated his ankle playing football at Queen's College. The April 1913 magazine records events, *'He proved a model patient and recovered very quickly, we are glad to be able to say at the time of going to press, that he is walking about again.'*

Though Tarbet left in 1914, he is still mentioned in later editions of the Magazine. In the December 1915/April 1916 editions news is carried of his joining the Artists' Rifles, hoping to obtain a commission. He also visited the School in the Easter Term.

Victor Tarbet's War

After he left School, Tarbet joined an architect firm and became a trainee. He joined the Artists' Rifles early in 1916. His letters give us some insight into what he was doing at this time.

Cadet Victor Tarbet, Artists' Rifles, Romford, Essex, writes (published July 1916):
I am so sorry that whenever I write I am always asking you to do something for me, but as you can see I am applying for a transfer to an Engineering Cadet Unit and it is, therefore, necessary for me to get these signed and returned as soon as possible. I should be extremely obliged if you would sign them for the last 2 years I was with you.

The Cadet Schools are rather a nuisance but of course are very good.

I am getting on very well and am sure I should have been nowhere without my training in the old corps.

I must thank you very much indeed for the School Magazine which I received and am very glad it is up to the old standard. I was very interested to know you had succeeded in having a band, and am sure it is a jolly good idea, and I only hope you are able to keep it together.

I am longing to come down and see you but am afraid I shall not be able to for some time, however, when I am down that way I will certainly look in and see you.

We have nearly 3,000 in the camp, or not quite so many now because a school went away last week. They are all jolly good fellows and we have a very good time, but I don't mean we don't do any work because we do work very hard.

Victor Tarbet writes from Home, September 24th, 1916:-
I was so sorry at having to bother you about my papers a third time, but I am glad to say I shall not have to ask you again. I am going to the Cadet School here on Monday week and it will probably be a three months' course. I am, I must say, at present well up in the elements of most of the tactical subjects we do such as field engineering, map reading, and the elements of field warfare, and the course in the school ought to bring me well within reach of most things which I shall be called upon to do.

We had a beautiful view of the Zepp here last night and also the one the time before, and it was a sight I wouldn't have missed for anything.

Tarbet entered the Theatre of France on 20th June 1917. He received a commission from the 4th Battalion Devonshire Regiment but seems to have fought alongside the 8th Battalion at the time of his death. In early October 1917, the 8th Devonshires found themselves near Passchendaele, 'enduring the worst of the Third Battle of Ypres'.[38] 2nd Lt. Victor Tarbet was killed on 4th October 1917.

News Breaks of Victor Tarbet's Death
Mrs W. H. Tarbet of St. John's Road, Exeter, has been notified by the War Office that her son, Second Lieut. Victor Tarbet of the Devons was reported missing, believed killed, on the 4th October. Some time since his brother, Lieut. Montague Tarbet of the Dorsets was severely wounded and lost his left hand. Mr Victor Tarbet a son of the late Mr W. H. Tarbet, was an articled pupil with Mr J. Archibald Lucas, Exeter, and joined upon the outbreak of the war.[39]

Widespread regret will be felt at the news.

And later:

Mrs W. H. Tarbet was officially notified by the War Office on Friday that her son, 2nd Lieut. Victor Tarbet was killed in action in France on October 4th. His death was officially announced a day or two ago.[40]

[38] www.keepmilitarymuseum.org
[39] Times, 12th October 1917, British Newspaper Online Archive.
[40] Western Times, 15th October 1917, British Newspaper Online Archive.

Remembering Victor Tarbet

As the war progressed, news of the death of friends, schoolfellows and comrades was met with less shock and more sadness. Here, one of Victor's school friends took time to convey his memories of Tarbet to George Corner. The last line, *'please remember me to any of my old school pals, if there are any left,'* suggests, perhaps, the feelings of despair and bitterness that the war was taking so many and so much was being lost.

Clifford Ogilvie (minor) writes from Perthshire, January 15th, 1918:
How sorry I am to hear about the death of Vic. Tarbet, it seems only the other day he and I were playing football in the dark blue dormitory and got two drills each from Mr Baker.

Please remember me to any of my old school pals, if there are any left.

School Obituary

Victor Tarbet

Oct. 4th 1917.

Victor Tarbet, the youngest son of Mr and Mrs Tarbet, of Exeter, entered the School in September 1910 and left in December 1912. His bright, open manner, readiness to do a good turn at all times, and his keen sense of fun made him an immense favourite. He soon became a dashing forward at Football and though a lightweight, was noted for his pluck and tenacity, gaining his 1st XI colours in 1912. He was, too, a very promising cricketer. As a Prefect he endeared himself to all by his unselfishness in every-day life: his diligence and high sense of honour in daily duties and O. T. C. work were known to all with whom he had to do. On leaving School, he became articled to an architect and at the outbreak of war joined up. After a period of training, Victor received a commission in the 8th Devonshire Regiment and soon was noted as a conscientious and hard-working officer, always keen on his work and his men, during a terribly trying and anxious period of the war. On October 4th, 1917, the enemy made a furious attack in which the 8th Devons suffered heavy losses. Of the eight officers in Victor's company, not one was left. His great friend, Pinnington, wrote to Mrs Tarbet from Hospital, as follows – 'We put on one another's equipment at 3 a.m. and then shook hands. At 6 o'clock we went over the top, after which time I never saw him again. You have lost a good son and I have lost a good pal." Capt. Lock, D Coy. 8th Devons wrote: "Your son led his platoon and successfully reached his objective and it was whilst he was consolidating the captured ground that he was killed. In the battle, he set his men a fine example of bravery and fearlessness. Both officers and men feel his loss tremendously and send you their most sincere sympathy." His contemporaries at School will ever keep Victor in memory and regret the loss of one whom it was good to have known. His age was 21. He was the light of his home.

Wellington School Memorial Chapel – Letters to George Corner

The archive holds this letter sent to George Corner by Montague Tarbet in response to the correspondence regarding the Memorial Chapel. Montague feels the matter would upset his mother and chooses not to tell her of Corner's letter. Victor's death, although 13 years before, clearly still has huge impact on the family.

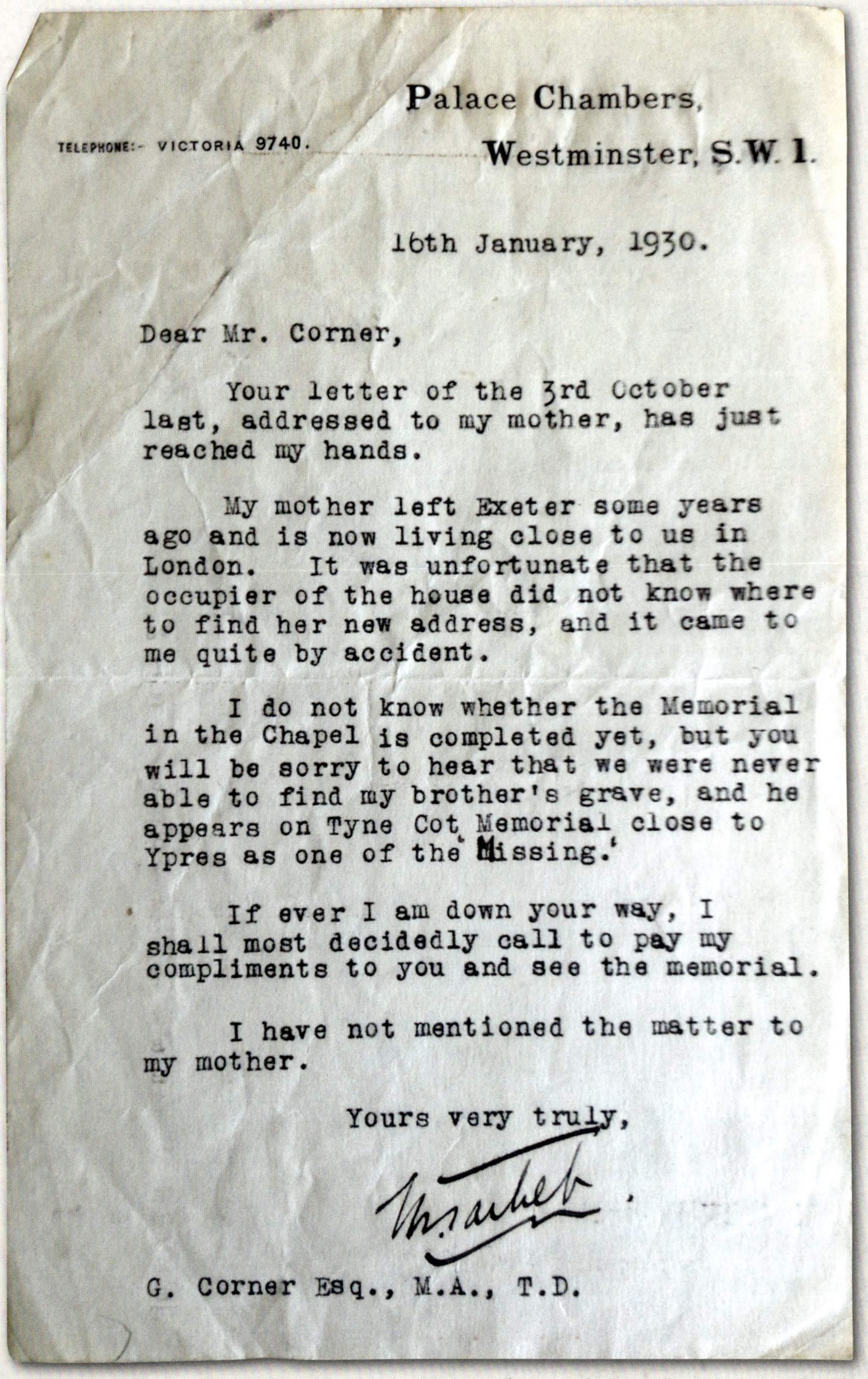

Palace Chambers,

TELEPHONE:- VICTORIA 9740. Westminster, S.W. 1.

16th January, 1930.

Dear Mr. Corner,

Your letter of the 3rd October last, addressed to my mother, has just reached my hands.

My mother left Exeter some years ago and is now living close to us in London. It was unfortunate that the occupier of the house did not know where to find her new address, and it came to me quite by accident.

I do not know whether the Memorial in the Chapel is completed yet, but you will be sorry to hear that we were never able to find my brother's grave, and he appears on Tyne Cot 'Memorial close to Ypres as one of the 'Missing.'

If ever I am down your way, I shall most decidedly call to pay my compliments to you and see the memorial.

I have not mentioned the matter to my mother.

Yours very truly,

G. Corner Esq., M.A., T.D.

Captain James Noel Treble

b. 1883 – died 18th October 1915, aged 32

'He made a host of friends in School and was beloved by boys and master alike. The loss of a man of his parts is irreparable to his country and friends. It is one more example of supreme sacrifice nobly given.'

School Obituary

Captain Treble is Remembered with Honour in Hebuterne Military Cemetery. In November 2018 he will be remembered by Willows House and a poppy will be placed in Chapel in his memory.

James Noel Treble was the youngest son of James Treble (b. 1854) and Mary (nee Lumley) (b. 1851). The couple married in 1876 in Hexham, Northumberland and had six children. James was a schoolmaster, a profession that James Noel followed.

In 1911, James Noel was 28 years old and Second Master at The County School, Wellington. He joined the School in 1906 and left to attend a new post in 1911. In July 1908 Treble received a commission as Lieutenant in the Cadet Corps. He was clearly a popular teacher. When the boys cheered him on his departure in April 1911, Treble *'then replied to the repeated calls on his name in a severe – but brief, speech'.*

A Reconnaissance Bude Camp - Treble, Aplin, Child

J. N. Treble and George Corner c. 1908

James Noel Treble's War

Treble joined the 4th Oxford and Bucks. L. I., in August 1914, shortly after war had been declared. He arrived in France towards the end of March 1915 and was in regular trench duty until his death in October. He wrote several letters to George Corner during this time.

Captain J. N. Treble, 4th Oxford and Bucks. L. I. writes from France on June 21st, 1915:
We have been out here for exactly 12 weeks, and with the exception of the first 10 days have been engaged in regular trench duty. For the most part our programme has been 4 days in the firing trench and 4 days in support alternately, but lately, we have worked on a slightly different plan and have had 4 days in Divisional Reserve included. The last gives us a certain amount of time about 4 miles behind the firing line.

We were in the trenches the other day when a mine was blown up under the German lines about 80 yards away. Immediately afterwards every gun, machine gun, and rifle opened fire, and the general din was added to by grenades and trench mortars. This lasted for 1 ½ hours, and strange to say we did not have a single casualty.

Captain J. N. Treble's Last Letter – 17th October 1915

Written to Miss Corner the day before he answered the last call: a sad reflection

I have just heard that Teddy is missing and believed killed – you all have my deepest sympathy. I do hope though that the news is not accurate and that he will turn up all right. This horrible war is bringing gloom and sadness to a tremendous number of people and I do wish it was over.

We are still engaged in regular trench duty and have been ever since we came out 7 months ago. So far, we have not been in any attack and I sincerely hope we will not go into one: it is quite enough as it is. I was home on eight days leave some five weeks ago and thoroughly enjoyed the change.

The winter is now beginning to set in and it gets very cold in the early hours before day breaks. I fear that when really bad weather comes along we shall lose a lot of men through sickness. Personally, I keep very fit – the open-air life seems to agree with me and it is remarkable what one can stand without taking any harm.

Poor Mr Aplin seems to have been having a very bad time of it, but I was pleased to hear that his wound turned out to be slight. Jimmy (Baker) I have not heard from.

I hope you are well and that everything connected with the School is flourishing.

In December 1915, the magazine wrote about Treble's loyalty and bravery, particularly when looking after his 'men': J. N. Treble was in command of his section of trenches the day he met his death. His last acts were done in thought for his men.

Remembering Captain James Noel Treble

School Obituary

Captain J. N. Treble

Ox. And Bucks. L. I

October 18th 1915.

Captain J. N. Treble, Ox. and Bucks L. I., was killed in France on October 18th, during a severe bombardment of the trenches. A man of marked ability, during his residence at Wellington School as Second Master from 1906 to 1911, he won all hearts by the even geniality of his manner and was a beloved and valued colleague, his influence for good being felt by all. He was an admirable sportsman, excelling in cricket, and will ever be remembered by Old Boys for his style in bowling. At tennis too he was a finished player. He was Second Master and Senior Science Master during the whole of his stay at the School. He held his first commission in the School O. T. C., and he became a most keen officer: his power of discipline was remarkable and was attained without any conscious effort. He made a host of friends in School and was beloved by boys and masters alike. The loss of a man of his parts is irreparable to his country and friends. It is one more example of supreme sacrifice nobly given.

In later editions of the Magazine, memories of Treble are still fresh: *We had a very kind letter this term from Mr J. Treble. How often we think of J. N. Treble. We never had a better master.*

Captain J. N. Treble was buried in Hebuterne Military Cemetery. His gravestone does not have an inscription.

J. N. Treble is commemorated on many war memorials and memorial plaques around the country. A recent statement from Wellington Town Council states that he and E. F. Corner were among the new names that were added to the town memorial. There is a second edition of *Our Boys* called *Our Other Boys* that features both of the above.

He is also commemorated on a range of memorials around Gosforth, Durham and Bedlington, in addition to Wellington.

SO HE PASSED OVER
& ALL THE TRUMPETS
SOUNDED FOR HIM
CAPTAIN
J. N. TREBLE
OXFORD & BUCKS. LIGHT INF.
18TH OCTOBER 1915 AGE 32

Wellington School Memorial Chapel - Letter to George Corner

In reply to Corner's letter to all families of the Old Boys, James wrote the following:

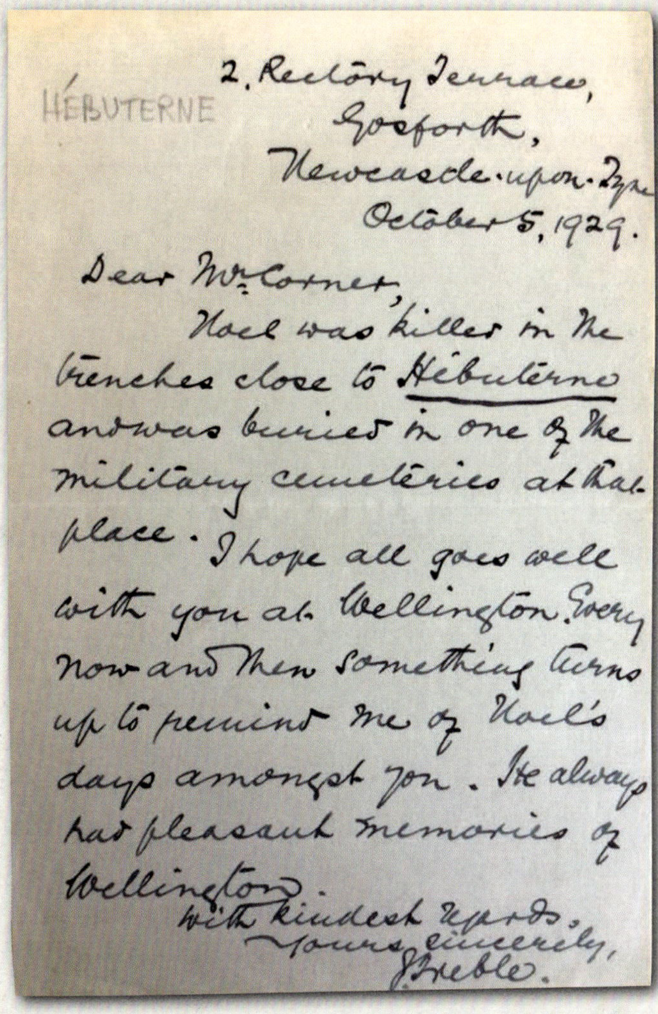

HÉBUTERNE

2, Rectory Terrace,
Gosforth,
Newcastle-upon-Tyne
October 5, 1929.

Dear Mr. Corner,

Noel was killed in the trenches close to Hébuterne and was buried in one of the military cemeteries at that place. I hope all goes well with you at Wellington. Every now and then something turns up to remind me of Noel's days amongst you. He always had pleasant memories of Wellington.

With kindest regards,
Yours sincerely,
J. Treble.

Henry Lawrence Wadland, pictured in uniform shortly before he was sent to the Western front.

Private Henry Lawrence Wadland

b. 1884 – died 10th November 1917, aged 33

'He was one of the yeomen of England, generous, straight and of great physical strength.'

School Obituary

Henry Wadland is Remembered with Honour in Etaples Military Cemetery. On November 8th 2014 he was remembered by Beech House and flowers were placed in Chapel in his memory.

Henry Lawrence Wadland was the eldest child and only son of Richard and Eliza (nee Vodden) Wadland. The couple married in 1883. Richard came from a long line of farmers and the couple moved to various farms around Devon and Somerset although the family plot rests in Roborough, Devon. By 1901, the family had grown and there were now a further three daughters. Henry was 17 and employed on the farm, May was 15, Winifred, 12, Kathleen, 10, Alice M, 8, Eliza Margaret, 5, and Elsie Hannah, 2. At the time, Eliza's sister and the governess were also living with the family.

On 20th March 1908, Henry Lawrence appears to have sailed for St. John, New Brunswick, Canada, from Liverpool, on the *Empress of Ireland.* This could explain why he does not appear on the 1911 census.

Over the years, the family had to face many struggles including Robert's strict farming methods which saw him in court, Henry's service in France and family illness. May was admitted to the County Asylum, Exminster, in the summer of 1915. She died on 5 January 1916, aged only 30. The family's mourning was compounded in 1917 when news broke of Henry's death following wounds received at Passchendaele.

School Life

Although he had left the school in 1900, Wadland visited it and involved himself in various Old Boys' activities. He attended the First Annual Old Boys' Dinner at the Squirrel Hotel, Wellington on April 17th, 1906 along with W. J. Miles. He is also recorded as attending the Annual General Meeting in December 1906 along with Henry Pratt.

Henry Lawrence Wadland's War

When war broke out, Wadland was living in Canada. He was very keen to serve and do his duty, so he returned to Britain on 13th September 1914, sailing from Montreal to Glasgow. He is recorded as being a labourer and 31 years of age. Unable to enlist because of his eyesight, it would seem he returned to Canada on 3rd December 1914.

Canadian Attestation papers show that he enlisted in the 16th Battalion (Canadian Scottish) of the Canadian Infantry on 14th January 1916. He spent time in England training and eventually made it to France in August 1917. He was wounded on 6th November at

Passchendaele and was taken to the St. John's Ambulance Brigade Hospital, Etaples where he spent four days. He passed away on 10th November 1917.

Wadland also received an entry in the Du Ruvigny's Roll of Honour.

Remembering Henry Lawrence Wadland

School Obituary

H. L. Wadland

Nov. 10th, 1917.

Harry Wadland was the son of Mrs Wadland, late of Aller Court, Langport, but now a resident of Dolton, N. Devon. He left School in April 1900 and had been also some time under the Headmastership of Mr Beuttler. During the time he spent under the present Head he proved himself a most reliable and plodding fellow who had great interest and pride in his School. In 1910 he decided to emigrate to Canada, but returned to England immediately war was declared, hoping to enlist in the North Devon Hussars. To his great disappointment, he was rejected – defective sight being the cause assigned. After a brief rest, he returned to Canada and joined the famous 226th Battalion at Russell, Manitoba. This Battalion was largely recruited from agricultural districts, the majority of them having been born in N. Manitoba. The "Men of the North", or the "Grizzly Bears" as they were commonly known, had the reputation of being physically superior to any Battalion at Camp Hughes. Their last camp in England was at Shorncliffe and to their deep regret they were not sent out as a whole but in sections. Harry was in the 16th and after only two months at the front was mortally wounded by a shell at Passchendaele on November 6th, dying in hospital at Etaples on November 10th, 1917. He lies in a military cemetery facing the Channel and the Homeland for which he gave his life. Mrs Wadland, in her letter to the Head, speaks of the maple leaf badge, of "which my dear, lamented son and the others were so proud" – the maple-leaf with a bear and crown surmounting it – "Men of the North" Overseas Battalion, 226, Canada. He was one of the yeomen of England, generous and straight and of great physical strength.

Henry Lawrence Wadland is commemorated on the memorial to the Manitoba Regiment in Canada. He is also named on his family's grave in St Peter's Churchyard in Roborough, Devon. There is also a commemorative plaque in the church to the six men who lived in the village and died in WW1.

The inscription on his grave reads:

HONOUR'D, BELOV'D AND MOURN'D

1000440 PRIVATE
H. L. WADLAND
16TH BN. CANADIAN INF.
10TH NOVEMBER 1917

Wellington School Memorial Chapel - Letter to George Corner

Eliza Wadland wrote to George Corner on 19th November 1929. The letter bears the calculations as to Wadland's age at the time of his death. We can assume the workings out are Corner's.

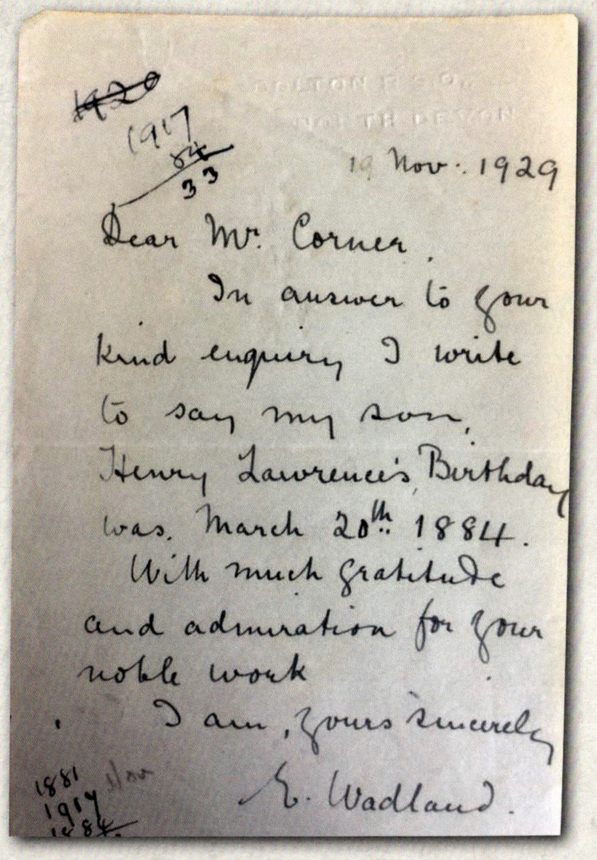

19 Nov. 1929

Dear Mr. Corner,

In answer to your kind enquiry I write to say my son, Henry Lawrence's Birthday was March 20th 1884.

With much gratitude and admiration for your noble work

I am, Yours sincerely

E. Wadland.

Our Miss Wadland

Henry's sister, Alice, became a much-loved and respected Headmistress in the village. Her life was recorded in a book an extract of which is written here. It details the pain caused by her brother, Henry's, death:

From ***Our Miss Wadland by Shane Wadland***[41] ***Sacrificed and Only 33.***

Many of Alice's attitudes and actions were typically Victorian. She was born during a decade when the British Empire was at its height, educated during the closing stages of the Victorian era, overlapping into the Edwardian years. With the outbreak of the hideous First World War (1914 – 1918) this was a turbulent time within the Wadland family. It has never been proven with absolute clarity, but local tradition had it that as well as Alice tragically losing her brother (known to the family as Harry) she had a boyfriend who also died in the war. The family also lost several other acquaintances, some of Alice's sisters had 'gentleman friends' who they also grievously lost, including one young officer who was gassed. Alice was very fond of her brother Henry, although there was eight years' difference between them. Henry was a most charming and peaceable individual, taking more after his mother's character, and he absolutely doted on his younger sisters.

On the outbreak of the war, Henry decided to join up, however, he failed his medical, thus denying him a place in the British Army. I believe the reason for this was that his eyesight was poor, and he had to wear glasses for reading. This did not perturb him, and he made it quite clear to his family that he would find some opening. So, he left England and sailed for Canada where he did manage to enter the army. He entered the Russell B Detachment as a private, training to become a member of the mounted yeomanry. His regiment was eventually sent to Europe, right into the horrors of the Western Front.

Obviously whilst on the continent, he corresponded with various members of his family, and in September 1917 he wrote to his sister Winifred. It is believed that this was the last time he wrote to a member of his family before he was seriously wounded in action on 6th November at Passchendaele, and four days later died of his injuries. The letter that he had sent to Winifred was found after Alice's death, amongst her treasured possessions and a transcript of it reads as follows:

[41] Wadland, Shane. Our Miss Wadland Bideford: Edward Gaskell Press, 1999 pages 29-31.

22nd September 1917

My Dear Winnie,

Many thanks for your letter which I received a week or two ago. Have been away about a month, your letter was forwarded on. Would like a pair or two of socks if you wish to send them. Please send them if you can by return post if it will not inconvenience you. Have just written to mother. Pt. H. L. Wadland 1000440 16th Canadian Scottish Batt., attached to 1st Canadian infantry Batt France.

We have been having good weather the last week or two, guess you are back in Leicester now till Xmas holidays. Well, I do not think I have much more news so will close with love to you and Elsie. From your loving brother.

Henry

Obviously, Henry's death at only thirty-three was of great devastation to his mother and sister, and none of them really recovered from the loss of their 'dearest Harry'. Years after his death, Alice would now and again reflect on her brother, and her eyes seemed to express the futility and pain of those torn years and the fact that she had lost something irreplaceable. However, the family kept their sanity and that was due to their faith. Alice had a very deep sense of the spiritual: and was the main strength for her mother.

Alice's mother was the recipient of the following letter. Nothing is known about the nephew who wrote it, not even his surname, as he was connected with Eliza's side of the family ie. the Voddens. One can only hope that his fate was kinder than his poor cousin's.

Sunday 3rd December 1917
9.30pm

My dearest Aunt Eliza

Yesterday evening brought me the worst tidings I have had for some considerable time.

I received a letter from the survivor informing me that my cousin Harry had been killed in action. He could not give me any details and I am now wondering whether the tragedy occurred on my front or elsewhere. I believe somehow that it is in our particular sector as I came across many men of the same regiment as the one to which Harry belonged but perhaps it was not his Battalion. At the time I was not in possession of mother's letter containing Harry's address. I expect I shall be receiving more details in the next letter.

It was only a few days ago I looked up Harry's address in my notebook and intended writing to him with the object of locating him. However, I am afraid I will never have the pleasure of realising my wish.

My dear Aunt, I can quite conceive how grieved you all must be, and I must admit I myself out here feel the pain very much indeed. You have only one consolation and that is of knowing he died as a hero, doing his duty nobly for King and Country. You have my more heartfelt sympathy and I share with you the grief in this sad bereavement.

How are Aunt Mary and all? I hope all right!

Pluck up the courage and be brave, the only way to lessen the pain.

With best love and kisses,
Your affectionate nephew,
George.

Will write again soon!

The military sent back Henry's belongings, including his Canadian Bible, and identity disc. Henry's mother was next of kin, and she was sent the silver Canadian memorial cross. The family also received the General Service and Victory medals, as well as the British Memorial Plaque, with the motto "He Died for Honour and Freedom", all of which I now have in my possession.

Sec.-Lieut. W. L. WARD, S.L.I., (*killed in action*).

2nd Lieutenant William Leigh Ward

b. 1898 – died 22nd December 1917, aged 19 years.

'He was liked by all because he knew his job and did it, whether in the line or out of it.' A Comrade

William Leigh Ward is Remembered with Honour in Voormezeele Enclosure No. 3. He was remembered by Beech House on November 11th 2012 and flowers were placed in Chapel in his memory.

William Leigh Ward was the eldest child and the only son of Harry Burge Ward (b. 1865) and Rosa Ward (nee Leigh) (b. 1875). In 1901, the family was living at 45 High Street, Williton. Harry was a newspaper office overseer having been born and grown up in Old Cleeve, Somerset. By 1911, the family had moved to Long Street, Williton although some records suggest Watchet. William was no longer an only child. The family had been joined by a daughter/sister, Kathleen Mary, b. 1910.

William Leigh Ward's War

William Ward left school in July 1913 and was working as a journalist like his father when war broke out. He was very keen to enlist straight away but he was too young. It is clear from a letter sent to George Corner how much William was looking forward to being old enough to join the war properly.

W. L. Ward, who is not yet old enough for service in the army writes an interesting letter dealing with his coastguard work from near Falmouth, Nov. 17th, 1915:

At present I am not serving in either branch of H. M. Forces, have been refused on account of my age on the outbreak of war. I was then Assistant Scoutmaster of the Williton troop of Boy Scouts, and I volunteered for Coastguard duty on being told I ought to wait at least a year before joining the army. I was appointed as second in command at this station, which is manned by eight ex-scouts, and three months ago I was promoted to the command. All the boys on the station are big, as in addition to an eight-mile patrol day and night, it is a boarding station, and all the vessels entering the Helford River have to be boarded, the boat's crew provided by the Scouts. The coast watching is carried on by three watches, each watch consisting of two coast watchers and one scout. One coastwatcher and the scout patrols the cliffs whilst the other coast watcher is stationed on a headland overlooking the entrance to the river. Each watch has six hours on and twelve hours off, the watches being relieved at 6 and 12. In addition to cliff patrols, one scout is always on duty by the telephone, this being a transmitting station from the Lizard section to the Falmouth section. The work of keeping the Station clean also falls on the scouts so that we have very little time to grumble, which is perhaps best, as there are only 9 houses here, 7 of which belong to the Coastguard, the nearest town being Falmouth seven miles away. Our pay is 10/6 per week, out of which we have to find everything except coal, light, doctor and boot repairs. We are billeted in one of the Coastguard houses, where we cook and do everything for ourselves. It is a very good experience for the boys, I should think, but the night watches are rather trying now, the coast being exposed in some places. I must close now as I am shortly going on duty, but I trust I have given you a little idea of how we live and what we are doing. Please remember me to Miss Corner. Wishing good luck to the old School and the O. T. C.

Having earned a commission he eventually made it to the Somerset Light Infantry 4th Battalion. He fought in France from August 1917. No doubt he was involved in the Battle of Passchendaele. On 22nd December 1917, he was killed in action.

The magazine of April 1918 prints a letter from Percy Dibble.

Percy E Dibble writes to Miss Corner from France, Jan. 10th, 1918

I was awfully sorry to see in the Somerset County Gazette, which I got last night, that W. L. Ward has been killed out here, he must be very young.

Remembering William Leigh Ward

School Obituary

W. L. Ward

December 21st, 1917.

Willie Ward, only son of Mr and Mrs Ward, of Williton, entered the School in September 1911, leaving in July 1913. He was at once noted as a boy of great promise and it was soon seen that he was of considerable ability. He was, too, immensely popular with all, as he took an active interest in sports and O. T. C. work – always ready to lend a hand and help – and he was so open and frank. On leaving School he joined his father in journalistic work, but on the outbreak of war, when the Boy Scouts were called upon to furnish patrols for coastal work, he responded at once, being still too young for actual military service. He was a Patrol Leader at an important look-out under the supervision of the Admiralty for a year, as a preliminary to joining the Inns of Court O. T. C. at Berkhamstead. After training there, he passed out – a splendid specimen of soldier – with a commission and was posted to the Somersets. Ward carried all his enthusiasm into his active service, which began in August 1917, and the next five months were full of the terrors of war. A comrade, who had been captured and sent to Germany, said to Mr Ward, on his return, "He was liked by all because he knew his job and did it, whether in the line or out of it." On December 21st the Somersets had to face a furious attack by machine guns, and after Willie had repelled an attack on his post and was about to see to another post, he was fired at and fell, living only a quarter of an hour. His O. C. wrote in the highest praise of him as an officer, saying – "We shall miss him very much in the battalion. I can only say that he died doing his duty and that perhaps is as fine an end as one can wish for." His death came as a crushing blow to his parents, who received the greatest sympathy in the loss of their only son, at the age of 19. Williton itself mourned him as one of her brightest and best and his memory will ever be treasured by all who knew him.

JELLALABAD
XIII
SECOND LIEUTENANT
W. L. WARD
SOMERSET LIGHT INFANTRY
22ND DECEMBER 1917 AGE 19

Ward is also remembered on the Williton Town Memorial on the Recreation Ground.
He was buried in the Voormezeele Enclosure No. 3 in Belgium.

The inscription on his grave reads:

GREATER LOVE HATH NO MAN THAN THIS

Wellington School Memorial Chapel – Letters to George Corner

Ward's father wrote to George Corner to explain all he knew about the death of his son. It is a short letter outlining the simple facts.

To Mr Corner,

In reply to yours of yesterday, my son fell on the edge of the Ypres – Lille Canal (dry at the time) near Hollebeke. He was about to visit some posts on the other side.

I am yours truly,

D. B. Ward

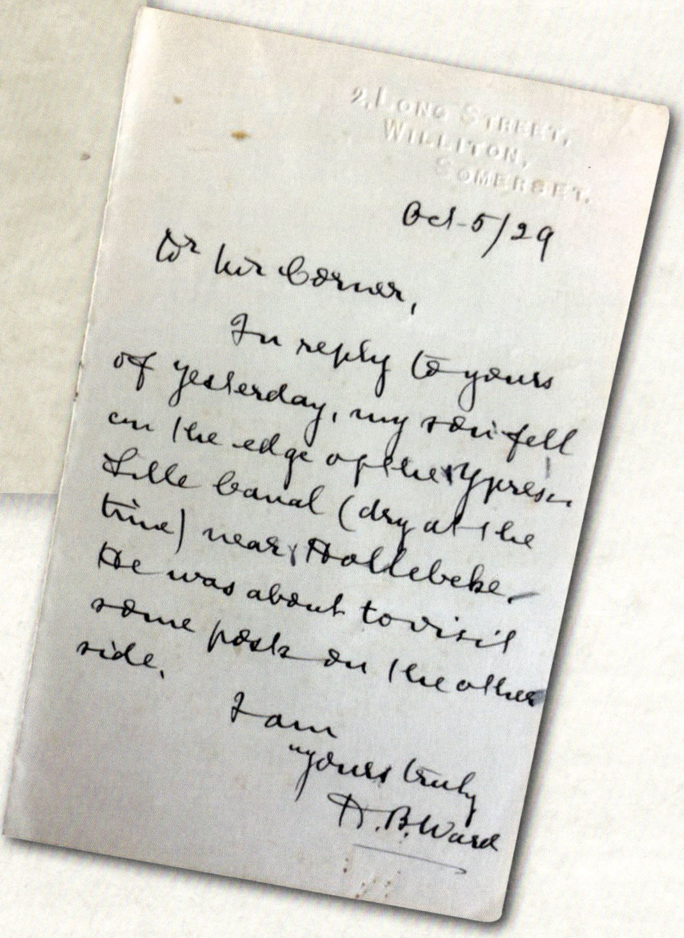
21 Long Street,
Williton,
Somerset.
Oct-5/29
Dr Mr Corner,
In reply to yours of yesterday, my son fell on the edge of the Ypres-Lille Canal (dry at the time) near Hollebeke. He was about to visit some posts on the other side.
I am
yours truly
D. B. Ward

2ND LIEUT. T. YANDLE, wounded, missing and believed killed. April 10th.

2nd Lieutenant Tom (Thomas) Yandle

b. 1882 – died 10th April 1917, aged 35

"My brother was serving in France but I cannot, unfortunately, give any further details' Robert Yandle

Tom Yandle is Remembered with Honour on the Arras Memorial. In November 2014 he was remembered by the boarding pupils of Wellington School, and flowers were placed in Chapel in his memory.

Tom Yandle was born to James Yandle a farmer (b.1838) and Verena Yandle (nee Follet). The couple were married in 1875 and had nine children.

In 1891 the family was living in Skilgate with their 8 living children: John (b. 1876), William (b. 1877), Verena (b. 1880), Tom (b. 1882), Francis (b. 1883), Henry (b. 1884), Robert (b. 1887) and Mary (b.1889). A daughter, Alice had been born in 1878 but passed away when she was two years old and is not mentioned on the census.

In the 1901 census, the family appeared to be living in different places. John, Henry, Mary and Verena were living with their parents in Skilgate. Francis was living with William in Upton, Somerset. William was farming and the head of his household. Tom was living in Bristol, Gloucestershire and was a Draper's Assistant.

The family lost their mother in 1902 and much had changed in 1911. Francis had emigrated to Australia, where he married Constance Emily Warr and died in 1958 in Narembeen, W.A. Robert was living in the City of London and working as an Assistant. James, Henry, Verena and Mary all appear to be at Skilgate.

School Life

Tom Yandle must have been a pupil before the reign of George Corner and we have no mention of him in any magazines. There are mentions in the war editions of a Robert Yandle, who must surely be Tom's brother. Robert Yandle was a very successful soldier and was awarded the M. C. He was wounded three times and returned each time to fight once more. He also achieved the rank of Captain.

Tom Yandle's War

In 1911, Tom Yandle is listed as being a Draper's Assistant living in Bristol. It appears that he joined the Public Schools Battalion in October 1915 and was gazetted as 2nd Lieutenant in the Royal Fusiliers in November 1916. He went to France in December 1916 and would have been involved in the Battle of Arras which began on the 9th April. He was reported as *'wounded, missing and believed killed'* on 10th April. The Forces War Records still have him as 'missing'.

CAPT. R. YANDLE, Wounded, Spring, 1917.

A local Bristol newspaper report gives us an insight into the things he enjoyed:

LOCAL OFFICER MISSING
His many friends in Clifton and Bristol will have seen with great regret the announcement that Second Lieut. Thomas Yandle was reported, "wounded and missing, believed killed". Mr Yandle, having attained the rank of sergeant in the Public Schools Battalion of the Royal Fusiliers, which he joined in October 1915, returned to Clifton in August, 1916, as a cadet in the 3rd O.C. B. He was gazetted as second-lieutenant in the Royal Fusiliers in November 1916 and went to France in the following December. Here, it is now feared, he lost his life. Mr Yandle was well known as an enthusiastic member of the Playgoers' Club and as Hon. Treasurer of the local branch of the British Empire Shakespeare Society, where his loss will be much felt. [42]

Remembering Tom Yandle

For some reason, there is no obituary in the School Magazine for Tom Yandle. There is no obvious reason for this omission although he was not one of Corner's boys. He is, however, included on the Chapel memorial plaques.

He is also commemorated in Skilgate Church where he is named on two plaques.

St Peter's WW1 War Memorial
A research project begun to find out more about the fallen remembered in St Peter's Parish (Bristol) discovered Tom (Thomas) Yandle. He was the oldest of the men on the memorial.

Wellington School Memorial Chapel – Letters to George Corner
We have no words of Yandle himself, but the archives hold letters from his siblings in connection to the names to be placed in the Chapel. On 25th November Verena wrote:

Your letter as hand this morning – my brother was registered Tom and christened Thomas as the clergyman refused after he had been registered Tom to christen him that as it was not a correct name. Please have put down which you think correct.
Believe me,
Yours sincerely,
V. F. Yandle

[42] Western Daily Press, Tuesday 8th May 1917 in British Newspaper Online Archive.

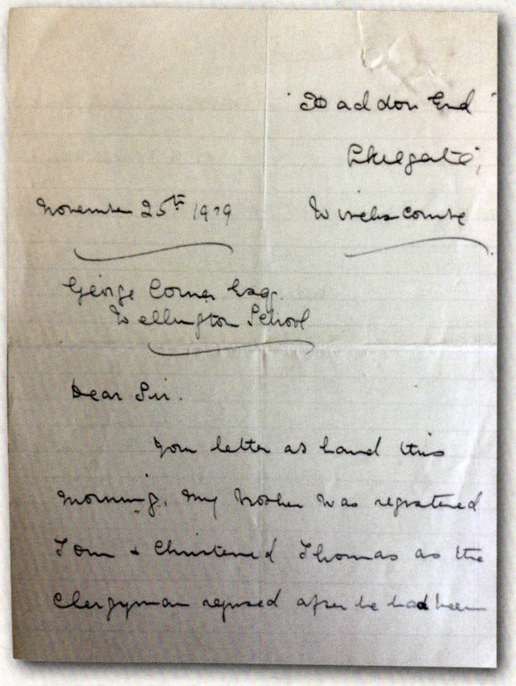

"Haddon End"
Chelgate,
Wiveliscombe

November 25th 1919

George Corner Esq.
Wellington School

Dear Sir.

Your letter at hand this morning. My brother was registered Tom & Christened Thomas as the Clergyman refused after he had been

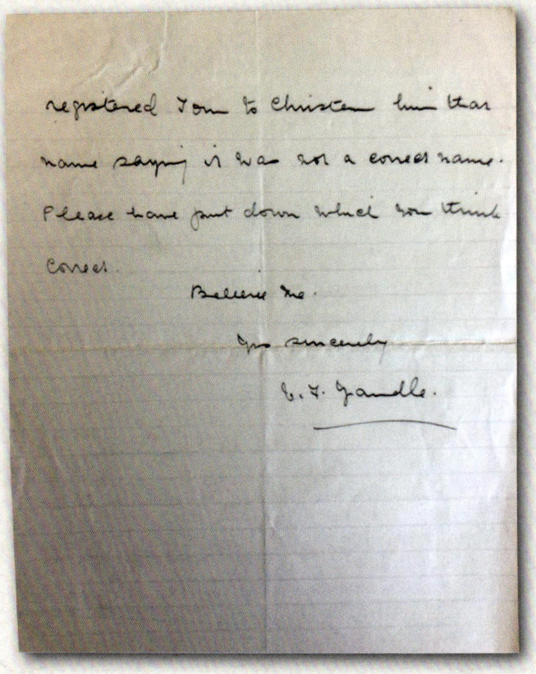

registered Tom to Christen him that name saying it was not a correct name. Please have put down which you think correct.

Believe me.

Yrs sincerely

E. T. Yandle.

CORPL. F. F. YEANDLE,

Corporal Francis Frederick Yeandle

b. 1893 – died 25th November 1915, aged 22

"His death was practically instantaneous. By his death the regiment has lost a good soldier, and, personally, I have lost a friend whose acquaintance I valued very highly." *Lieut. P. G. Carew.*

Francis Yeandle is Remembered with Honour in Lala Baba Cemetery, Turkey. In November 2018 he will be remembered by the Lower School and a poppy will be placed in Chapel in his memory.

Francis Frederick Yeandle was the eldest son of Frederick Yeandle (b. 1862) and Frances Edith Yeandle (nee Lutley) (b. 1865). The couple married in 1892 in Wellington. Frederick Yeandle was a farmer and from 1901 the family lived at Bidwell Barton, Thorverton, Devon. In 1901, Francis was recorded as living with his maternal aunt, Kate Ewens and uncle, William Henry Ewens. He was 7 years old at the time and lived with his cousins Alice (14), Kate (9), Henry (8) and 3 month-old Florence.

By 1911, Francis was living with his parents at Bidwell Barton, Bidwell Farm, Thorverton. He was 17 years old and his occupation was listed as farmer's son. He also had one brother, Edward Lutley who was a 13-year-old scholar. Frederick's brother-in-law, Ernest Edward Lutley was also living with the family and working on the farm. Visiting were Alice May Ewens and Henry Lutley Ewens.

Francis Frederick Yeandle's War

In the 'List of Old Boys Serving Their Country', published in the December 1914 Magazine, Yeandle appears:

April 1906 – Yeandle, F. F. Trooper A Squadron Royal 1st Devon Yeomanry. St. Osyth. Nr. Colchester, Essex.

Records show that the Royal 1st Devon Yeomanry had its headquarters in Dixie's Field, Exeter. It became part of the South Western Mounted Brigade in August 1914. In October 1915 it dismounted and moved to Gallipoli, withdrawing back to Egypt two months later. Francis Yeandle did not return to Egypt. He was killed in action on 25th November 1915.

Remembering Francis Frederick Yeandle

School Obituary

Corporal F. F. Yeandle

Killed in Action, 1915.

Corporal F. F. Yeandle was killed by shrapnel whilst on duty at the Dardanelles. He was greatly loved whilst at School but left early. We remember seeing him at a Break-up Supper two years ago. We append two letters received by his father, Mr F. Yeandle, of Thorverton, Devon.

Lieut. P. G. Carew, writing on behalf of the officers of A Squadron, to the deceased's father, expresses their deep regret at the death of Corp. Yeandle, and offers their sincere sympathy with the family in their sorrow. Lieut. Carew adds: "Yeandle has been in my troop ever since the regiment was mobilized 15 months ago, and I, and indeed, all his officers have always had a very high opinion of him, both for the way in which he has always carried out his military duties and his splendid behaviour in all circumstances, here and at home. His death was practically instantaneous. By his death the regiment has lost a good soldier, and, personally, I have lost a friend whose acquaintance I valued very highly."

The Rev. A. J. Child, Chaplain of the 159th Brigade, British Mediterranean Expeditionary Force, has written to Mr Yeandle. He says, "Yeandle was down at the base with a message when he was hit, and he only lived a very few moments. It happened close to my dug-out, and I said a prayer for him and commended his soul to God. A mate of his was wounded by the same shell. We are going to lay his body to rest at dusk in our cemetery here, as he was so very far from his own lines, and the 7th Cheshire Regiment are providing the funeral party. He died doing his duty, and I do not think he suffered at all."

Lieut. E. R. ZEALLEY
(killed August 30th, 1918).

Lieutenant Eric Ralph Zealley

b. 1897 – died 30th August 1918, aged 21

'As one of his comrades said, 'He died a hero's death, fighting for his King and the cause of freedom and justice.''

School Obituary

Ralph Zealley is Remembered with Honour at St. Pol British Cemetery, St. Pol-Sur-Ternoise. On 11th November 2007 he was remembered by Lights House, and flowers were placed in Chapel in his memory.

Eric Ralph Zealley was the only child of Andrew Zealley and his wife, Adela Ellen (nee Hecks). The couple married in July 1888 and Eric was born in 1897. The family seems to have been very settled, with residence in Court Mill, Wadeford, Chard, in the 1901 and 1911 censuses. Andrew, like his father before him, was a miller. He is listed as a corn/seed merchant/miller.

Adela (b. 1864) died in 1926, never, it seems, getting over 'Ralph's' death. Andrew (b. 1862) survived her by almost twenty years and died in November 1942.

Eric Ralph Zealley's War

Zealley left School in 1914 but the Magazines show he was a relatively frequent visitor in subsequent years. He had been on the O. T. C. Camp when war broke out and the camp was dispersed. In November 1915 he was gazetted to the King's Own Rifles (Lancs. Regiment).

Letters To George Corner

During the war years, three letters from Eric were published in the Magazine.

2nd Lieutenant E. R. Zealley, 10th Royal Lancaster Regiment, about to leave for France, writes on May 5th (1916?)

Just a few lines to let you know what I have been doing during the last six months. I should like to have been able to come down but am afraid shall not be able to this time, so I will endeavour to tell the tale on paper. After I got my commission, for which I am greatly indebted to you and the Wellington School O. T. C., which is still I trust in a prosperous condition, I was sent to a school of instruction at Yelverton near Princetown, about 2nd December 1915, under Colonel Swanton. There were about forty officers there at the school with me which lasted for about six weeks. After I passed out from there I was sent to my battalion at Wareham under Lt. Col. Bonomi, here I was given a platoon to look after which I found to be very interesting work.

On Feb. 22nd I was sent to a Y. O. C. at Swanage where I started in No. 4 Platoon carrying full pack and rifle for about three weeks then on to No. 3 and finally reached No. 1 about five weeks ago.

Whilst in No.1 Platoon we had a general inspection at which there were about ten officers picked out and their names sent to the War Office as being ready for service overseas. On the next morning, the Commandment called four of us up again and said our names had again been sent to the War Office to be struck off the former list to be kept as instructors in England and nothing more has been heard.

On the 26th May, all the Officers of the 'King's Own' were sent for to join their battalion, which news we were very glad to get as the camp was being moved from Swanage to Larkhill and we were quite tired of eating 'Bully Beef and Biscuits' which we got when the food supplies ran short.

When we got back to Wareham we were given platoons again and had our meals in the best Mess in the brigade, namely 'The King's Own'.

Last Wednesday ten officers had orders to hold themselves in readiness to proceed overseas at an early date and were given four days leave from Saturday, so I am now home until Tuesday when I have to return and get ready to start for France I expect about next Saturday.

Wishing the best of luck to the School and O. T. C.

Though he saw some action on the Somme in 1916, Zealley became ill and was hospitalised and eventually sent home to recover.

Lieutenant E. R. Zealley writes from home, December 28th, 1917:-

I am still in England and think myself very lucky to have been kept here so long, but although I have had a small taste of it I am quite ready to go again when they want me, which will be in the spring I expect.

I am still on the strength of "The King's Own (Royal Lancaster) Regiment" but attached to the R. F. C. now.

I left the King's Own at Harwich, on the east coast, in November, and went to Reading on a preliminary course for the R. F. C., where I have to return on Sunday. I have nearly finished the course now and I expect about a week more, when I get back, will finish it.

I like the work very much and find it very much more interesting than infantry work, although they don't give us much spare time, starting at 6.45 a.m. and finishing at 5.30 p.m., Saturdays included, and often exams on Sundays.

After we leave Reading we are sent to a squadron where we do our preliminary flying, which I am thinking will be much more interesting than all theory, and not just long hours, but I hope it will be a bit warmer by then.

I have not seen many of the Old Boys lately; I think the last I met was Chowins down at Plymouth. Townsend I think is in hospital after being slightly gassed, but I have not seen any of his people to know much about him.

The third was written roughly four weeks before he died.

Lieutenant E. R. Zealley writes August 3rd, 1918

Have received the P. C., which was sent home to be filled in for particulars of service etc. it has reminded me once again of the many times I have intended to write.

You will see by the address that I am in the R. A. F. now. I left "The King's Own" (Royal Lancaster Regiment) last November, and became attached to the R. A. F. where I am still in training as a pilot, but nearly finished, and expect to be flying overseas again before the month is out.

Flying is very interesting work, even in England, and I expect it is much more exciting overseas.

I have put in about 100 hours in the air now, so have some idea what it is going to be like. I have been extremely lucky in being posted to a "Bristol Fighter" Squadron, which everyone says has the best machines on the Front, as they can do almost everything a Scout can do, and at the same time, you have an observer to watch your tail.

We have here about six different kinds of Scout machines which are, in most cases, better than any Bosche Scout, and the Pilots always like to admit they have got all their work cut out to attack a "Bristol", and there are not many who would not be only too glad to transfer to "Bristols" if they had the chance.

Wishing the old School the best of luck.

Remembering Eric Ralph Zealley

School Obituary

E. R. Zealley

August 30th, 1918.

Ralph Zealley was the only child of Mr and Mrs Zealley, of Wadeford, Chard, and entered the School September 1912. He was thorough in his work and especially keen in his O. T. C. work – being great at detail. Ralph was an enthusiastic ornithologist and quite an authority on wild birds and their ways. Those who knew him well found him practical and diligent in all that he undertook, and it was opined that he would make an excellent man of affairs, prompt and farsighted. He left the School in July 1914 – he was in our Camp on Salisbury Plain when war broke out and the Camp suddenly dispersed. In November 1915, he was gazetted to the King's Own Rifles (Lancs. Regt.) and was sent to the Somme at the end of September 1916. When he got to the trenches he saw much fighting and fell ill with fever, having a long illness and being sent home from hospital to hospital and eventually home on leave. He soon reported and acted as an Instructor (P. T.) at Aldershot and Dovercourt for some time. He then was transferred to the R. F. C. and proved himself a very capable airman, passing his final examination with full marks. On August 24th he joined the 22nd Squadron at St. Pol and six days later, by a tragic error, an aeroplane crashed into Ralph's, and his fell, killing both him and his observer. As one of his comrades said, "He died a hero's death, fighting for his King and the cause of freedom and justice." Deep sympathy was felt for Mr and Mrs Zealley in the irreparable loss of their beloved son. He was but 21 years of age. He was a fine specimen of young British manhood. We lament him deeply.

Zealley is buried in St. Pol British Cemetery next to his observer.

The inscription on his gravestone reads:

DEAR HEART
I THANK MY GOD
UPON EVERY REMEMBRANCE
OF YOU

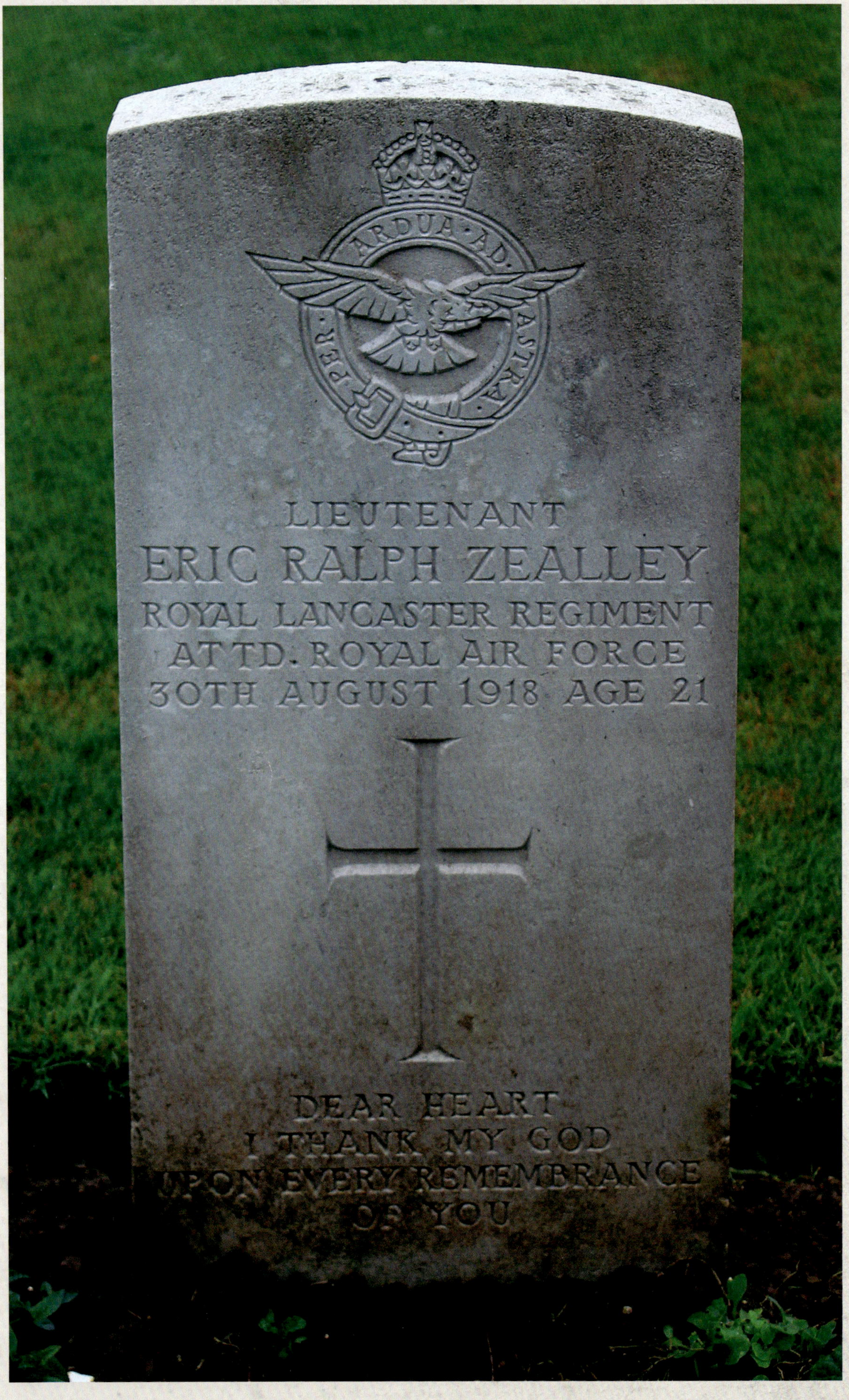
PER ARDUA AD ASTRA
LIEUTENANT
ERIC RALPH ZEALLEY
ROYAL LANCASTER REGIMENT
ATTD. ROYAL AIR FORCE
30TH AUGUST 1918 AGE 21
DEAR HEART
I THANK MY GOD
UPON EVERY REMEMBRANCE
OF YOU

Family Memories

Members of Zealley's family[43] were able to give information about 'Ralph' and the impact his loss had on his parents. The following comes from Ralph's second cousin.

"I have talked to my father, whose mother was the youngest sister of Adela Zealley (Ralph's mother). He doesn't remember ever meeting Ralph's parents but heard about the family from his mother, who was fond of Ralph.

- *They lived at Corn Mill and Andrew Zealley ('Uncle Drew') was shown in the censuses as a miller and corn/seed merchant.*
- *Ralph was an only child, so his death hit his parents hard and his mother never got over losing him.*
- *As a teenager, Ralph had stomach pain; the doctor came and diagnosed acute appendicitis and operated on him on the kitchen table with just the equipment he carried with him.*
- *"He died while on a training exercise when two planes collided."*

Another cousin (John Blofield, long since dead) wrote down his reminiscences about the Zealleys:

> *Adela Ellen and Uncle Andrew Zealley lived at Court Mills, Wadeford. Uncle Andrew was a miller. Their home was idyllic. It could be approached from the main road by a sloping lane to the cobbled frontage to the house; on the left-hand side, it terminated in one or two cottages in which Francis, the mill hand, and his family lived. On the side of the cottage was a small office of Uncle Drew's which was sacrosanct. Opposite as you faced the house was a small summer garden. Opposite the cottages was a walled kitchen garden. The house faced the end of the cottages. The second approach to the house and mill was further along the main road and backtracked the main road with a stream with a bridge of stone fording the road to Clayhanger beyond. The stream continued on under the bridge; it was crystal clear and clean and had watercress in it. It continued on, passing a small paddock or field which sloped up from the back of the house. Uncle Andrew only fished the trout once a year for Gran! I never saw any trout on Aunt Adela's table. Chickens free range in the paddock and bird life was abundant; moorhens used to come for the chicken mash and were shooed off. At the end of the paddock and house, the stream was diverted to the mill race which had a brick wall. The mill race was deep and quite wide, to channel the water to turn the water wheel at the side of the mill. The moss-covered water wheel was really large and beautiful. The surplus water which did not go into the race continued on its way through the orchard to a place called Pudleigh where its use was again made for a toothbrush factory (Kent?). One could follow the stream by footpath to Pudleigh; it was a haven of peace, with bird life – kingfishers and dippers – readily seen. I never went beyond the brush factory and now wonder into which the river the stream flowed.*
>
> *There were steps up to the mill with a platform to offload the grain in the middle of a large waggon house. It was very high and Ralph had a pigeon cote at the top.*
>
> *Aunt Adela was a very quiet, gentle person and when we stayed there during the school holidays I think we enjoyed every minute of the time. Uncle Andrew gave one the impression that he was a very taciturn and silent person. He did not appear to*

[43] Ralph's second cousin.

smile or express any emotions. He never remonstrated with us if he thought we had done anything amiss. Perhaps I am referring to the time when tragedy struck the family. Eric Ralph was the only son. He was educated at Wellington School and was recognised as a great ornithologist. At the outbreak of the First World War he enlisted and joined, I seem to remember, The Royal Lancashire Regiment and later transferred to the Air Force. He was killed in action on August 30th, 1918 and lies in the War Cemetery in St Pol in France. Some years later Uncle Drew sent me a photograph of his grave. Whether he made the journey to France I do not know. His pilot or gunner/navigator was Lieut. Partington who was killed with him. It revealed to me how, below that taciturn impression, lay deep emotions. Undoubtedly it affected him and Aunt Adela devastatingly. They both faced the loss with great courage. I cannot remember them mentioning Ralph in conversation, no doubt the loss was too unbearable. Had Ralph lived he would have inherited this lovely home and mill. Perhaps to forget this poignant loss they left Court Mills and retired to Colyton for Uncle Andrew's brother John (also a miller) lived at Colyford.[44]

Ralph's parents sent this 'return thanks' to those offering sympathy for their loss. To lose a loved, precious only child, as family relatives testify, affected them irrevocably; life was not the same and the home they kept with a view to passing it on to Ralph, as Andrew's father had passed it on to him, was perhaps too much a reminder of the future lost. When the note ends with the words inscribed on Zealley's grave, 'We Have Given Our all,' the immensity of their grief over Ralph's sacrifice is palpable; there was nothing left to give.

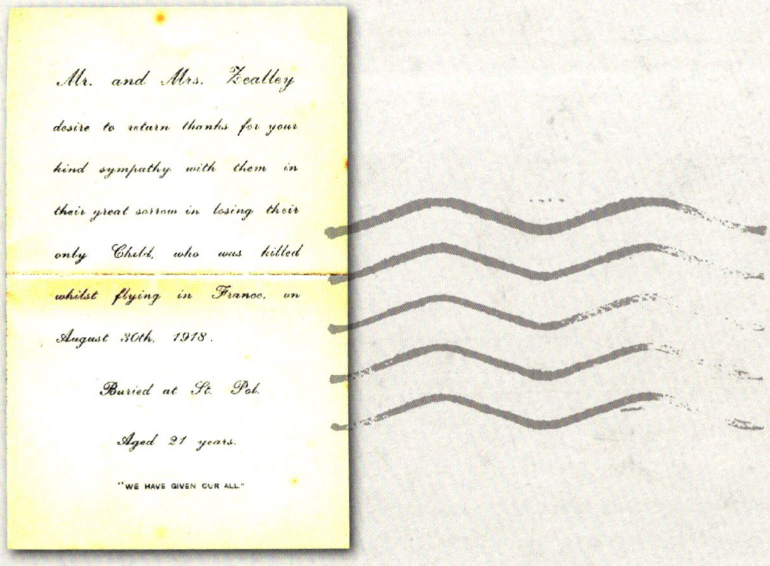

Mr. and Mrs. Zealley desire to return thanks for your kind sympathy with them in their great sorrow in losing their only Child, who was killed whilst flying in France, on August 30th, 1918.

Buried at St. Pol.

Aged 21 years.

"WE HAVE GIVEN OUR ALL."

[44] Information from family members.

Chapter 4

Building 'A Fitting Memorial'

As the School adapted to peace, Corner started to consider how best to commemorate the 37 Old Boys who had fallen in the war. His idea of a School Chapel had taken shape before he articulated his hope in his letter of 1919. In this letter, Corner talks of his *'deep-set hope'* that the Chapel would be a *'shrine'* as well as an *'incalculable benefit'* to the School and future generations; a building that would always stand to recognise the sacrifice of the past whilst *'healing'* the divisions of *'our fellow men'*. Its conception was, at heart, one of unity and community. Corner realised, however, that it could not ever happen without the dedication and commitment of the Wellington School 'family' and in this letter, he introduces his idea and asks his Old Boys to pledge what help they can. The language is powerful and emotionally charged, as was the placement of the Chapel Supplement shortly before the 'Recollections of the Fallen', the obituaries of the remaining Old Boys whose deaths had not been commemorated in previous editions. It is unsurprising that there are such passion and energy in Corner's words given the affinity and connection he felt to the 'gallant boys that fell'. His mission to create a fitting memorial is borne of wanting to create something to symbolise *'our reverence and love and our memory'*; to bring those who fell into the fabric of the School and to build something that would stand firm above the ebb and flow of time for the use of future generations of pupils. The Chapel Supplement carried with it an instruction/request for the reader to read the whole segment, which was sixteen pages in length. Coming before the 'Recollections of the Fallen', the readers would have been made aware of the exact 'dream' and still emotionally attuned when they read the distressing accounts of the remaining eighteen Old Boys. There would be no doubt in the reader's mind whose memory the Chapel would commemorate.

Wellington School,
Somerset,
January 1st, 1919

MY DEAR OLD BOYS.

You will be wondering if you are ever going to have news of your old School again. You shall shortly receive a big fat volume, being what we may call the second volume of your War Doings, in which you will find much news of your old schoolfellows.

I am sending you this letter chiefly with one object: – to ascertain what your wishes are with regard to the Proposed Memorial to those gallant boys who have laid down their lives for freedom and their country's honour.

The many plans which we are trying to mature in 1914 for the improvement of the Old Place have had to wait but they will all be resumed and carried, I trust, to such fulfilment that in the end, you may be truly proud of having helped by your schooldays to build up the foundation. These labours include the provision of University Scholarships, a Hall, more Classrooms, a Gymnasium, and a proper Library, amongst other things. These aims must wait, for there is added now this first and chiefest of duties, the setting up of a Monument in which can be enshrined our reverence and love of the spirit of our race and our memory of the gallant boys that fell.

Can we not build a commemoration School Chapel? I have a deep-set hope that such a shrine, besides being of incalculable benefit to the corporate life of this and future generations of boys, would prove a link to heal the transient and apparent divisions of our fellow men. It is a time for more unity of thought and there never was such a time before. Let us seize it.

The object cannot be obtained without the good-will and help of every single Old Boy and every friend of the School.

What seems difficult to a single one may, by the help and effort of all, become attainable. I look for your sympathy in this work.

What help can my Old Boys give me? This I must know if I am to make an appeal to the sympathy of others.

Will you write to me telling me what you think and giving me any promise you feel able to give of financial help. If the amount promised justifies our hopes I will at once take steps for you to select a comprehensible Committee of yourselves to put the matter in hand without delay and consult the School Governors.

If the site provided is not generally voted as the most suitable one to be obtained, I would willingly change my contribution to a sum of £150.

Believe me, with many good wishes,

Your sincere friend and old Master.

George Corner

The number of references to *'I', 'my', 'me'* and *'you', 'yourselves'* shows the extent to which Corner presents the idea as a community effort. He has the vision but vision without help is impotent. As he writes, *'what seems difficult to a single one may, by the help and effort of all, become attainable'.* Even with these motivational words, it must have appeared to the readers as an almost impossible feat. Such buildings took years to construct and proved extremely expensive; Wellington School was not a rich school. The supplement then published over eighty contributors and their initial promises and comments. Corner's idea was viewed to be a very good one and many expressed wishes about the Chapel, for instance, that the seating should be longitudinal and there should be a list of names of the fallen. Included within this number were family members of some of the Old Boys who fell:

> MR. BILTON (Teignmouth) writes: *"We think the idea of a School Chapel cannot be surpassed and hope that the money will be forthcoming to enable you to carry out your plans. We shall be pleased to subscribe ten guineas."*
>
> MRS BOWN (Yeovil): *"Your idea is excellent: Surely nothing could be more suitable as a Memorial to our honoured lads than a School Chapel. I do hope you will be able to carry it out."*
>
> MRS JEFFERY (Weston-super-Mare), writes: *"I have much pleasure in enclosing you £5 for your War Memorial scheme and hope you will be successful in getting the sum you require."*
>
> MRS. PALFERY (Glastonbury), writes: *"In memory of my dear son, A. H. W. Palfery, I herewith enclose £2 towards the building of a School Chapel."*
>
> MR. AND MRS. POWELL (West Ealing), in enclosing £5, say: *"If you let us know how the Memorial Chapel scheme develops we may be able to make a further contribution."*
>
> F. J. ROWE (Wellington) thinks that a School Chapel is the best possible suggestion.
>
> MR. SHAPLAND (Fitzhead), in writing for the family, says: *"We all think your proposal to erect a School Chapel in memory of the Old Boys who have fallen in the war an excellent idea."*
>
> MRS. ZEALLEY (Wadeford), in forwarding £5, adds *"I am quite willing for it to be spent in any way you may think best."*

Looking at these contributions it may seem as though offers of £2 and £5 were rather slight but in 1919 these amounts were worth much more. For example, £2 would be worth around £75 now and £5, £180.

The building of the Chapel was to preoccupy George Corner and those associated with the School for many years to come. At times, it looked as if there simply wasn't, nor would be, enough money to build the Chapel Corner had in mind. Economic hardship and lack of building materials, affected subscriptions. In these years, Corner had to continually motivate, inspire, cajole and directly ask the Wellington School community for help. It was a long, arduous and draining enterprise, but he never lost sight of what he was doing and why. Corner had a very clear sense of what he wanted the Chapel to look like, how it should be decorated inside, how it should be lit etc., and he helped, physically, as much as he could doing preliminary work on the wood. He never lost his faith both in the imperative need for the Chapel and in God's help to achieve it. He led by example and put much of his own money into the project. At the end, he was owed £6, 637 8s, which today is worth somewhere in the region of £332,000, but this figure had risen by the time he retired. There were, however, many bleak times where it seemed unlikely the Chapel would ever be finished.

In 1981, to commemorate the Chapel's jubilee, Mr J. Storr, the then Head of English, produced a play which dramatized George Corner's struggle in these years. Looking through the archives, Corner's own letters and official documentation, Storr was able to give voice to the Headmaster and the perspectives of those close to him as the physical demands of the 'dream' impacted on his health. Initially, the Corner presented in the play is a man fizzing with ideas and energy, sometimes frustrated that those around him lacked his verve. His drive and tenacity must have been exhausting for those close to him. But time and strain took their toll and though the vision never changed, Corner's letters begin to portray him as a tiring man, not that he was prepared to admit it. Many parts of the play show very well the 'journey' and extracts are shared here. The play was revised and produced in 1993.

The play opens with the letter Corner wrote to the Old Boys in 1919 asking for their help. The response as outlined previously in this chapter was immediate, but a long way from the amount needed. Corner's letter to his Old Boys of January 1922 encourages them to give more, recognising that the difficulties and hardships are what give the enterprise meaning. He reminds them that their fallen schoolfellows did not break apart but crossed the line together and that they must work together now to build the *'shrine to the past and inspiration to the future.'*

GC Well, Tom?

AM Yes, Headmaster. From some 300 Old Boys, the actual money received amounts to £415, 3 shillings and tuppence – without interest, of course.

GC Ah, jolly good (***motions to YB's who operate scoreboard).***

AM Er, if we add those, and allow for interest, we reach the total, (***calculating nervously)*** give or take a penny, of (***pause)*** NINE HUNDRED AND TWENTY-THREE POUNDS, SIXTEEN SHILLINGS AND TUPPENCE. (***applause from the cast. YB's correct scoreboard)***

GC (***rubbing hands)*** Excellent! Excellent! A very creditable sum, don't you know? (***looks around)***

AM But hardly enough to build a Chapel on, headmaster?

GC Whatyoumean? This is just the start. The money will come – the money will come. God will provide!

YB2 (***stage whisper to YB1)*** If George tells him to!

GC I'll write to them again... January 12th, 1922. My Dear Old Boys, ***(strongly),*** Your messages of support are stamped by certain sure and unmistakable characteristics – unanimity of feeling – buoyancy of hope – spontaneity of expression – a simple faith that banishes every difficulty – a faith that removes mountains and counts not cost nor effort. You have desired a Chapel to commemorate your fallen schoolfellows – I verily believe that you will achieve it. But faith – and effort – and sacrifice – are required for the work. There are, and will be difficulties: if there were none, effort and work would lose their meaning, and joy of achievement there could, and would, be none. ***(Pause. Leitmotif heard faintly through the next lines)***
(Cast stand by GC)
Side by side we live *(pause. Increasingly theatrical)* and side by side they fought and died in the trenches. In their death, they were not divided. Did they hesitate to cross the line together? No! Did they then part asunder? We answer –

Cast No!

GC Shall we then by constant division through life unfit ourselves for a common hereafter?

Cast No!

GC Our Chapel will be a right and proper adjunct of our School. Will anyone gainsay this?

Cast ***(loudly)*** No!

GC ***(triumphant)*** It will be a shrine of the past and an inspiration for the future! (sits down)

Though the drive behind the building of the Chapel was ostensibly Corner's, he had to continually ensure he had the support of those around him if he was to continue raising the funds. The constant worry about finances would have been stressful and, as the play suggests, Corner became frustrated by the apparent lack of commitment and action he felt from some of his past pupils. The tone of his letters changed in an effort to galvanise those who had yet to respond to his pleas.

Nar 2 At a meeting of our Old Boys held on Whit Monday, June 5th, 1922 the Headmaster out-lined the further progress made with the Chapel scheme and asked for their approval and authority to continue.

Narr 1 But by the end of 1924, £2,207 had been subscribed and £1200 was invested in Victory Bonds – and, provisionally, an architectural design had been adopted. ***(YB's change scoreboard)***

Narr 2 But a slightly querulous note was struck by the Headmaster, adding some irony to the School motto of Nisi Dominus Frustra.

GC *(slightly petulant, lecturing tone)* There is still a long way to go. We require between £4,000 and £4,500 before we shall venture to begin building and in all, we hope to raise £7,500.
I have an analysis in front of me of the numbers of subscribers of Old Boys before 1899 there are about four hundred and fifty – of those only some twenty have responded –

Cast (***disapproving)*** Shame! Poor show! Etc.

GC Of Old Boys since 1899 there are about one thousand and thirty: of these some 250 have responded –

Cast (***approving)*** Ah, that's better.......one in four....etc.

GC (***cutting in)*** Here too there is room for further awakening of zeal.

Cast ***(changing tune rapidly)*** Not good enough... Slackers... only 1 in 4.

GC There can be very few who cannot, from their memories of their schooldays, find at least one good reason for wishing to lend their aid to achieve this inspiring memorial. (**Cast** Hear! Hear! Agreed! etc.) As I write these words, in the quiet of Christmas holidays, alone in the Great Hall of your old School, there comes to me a certain feeling of assurance of your response.
With every good wish for the New Year.
Believe me, Yours sincerely, (***signs name)*** George Corner.

When the work finally started on the Chapel, everyone apart from Corner seemed surprised.

YB1 I say, what are those fellows doing over there?

YB2 Oh, they're just gardeners, aren't they?

GC ***(smugly)*** No – they are the builder's men. They're starting on the Chapel today! (**Cast** – ***react)***

AM But, Headmaster, you didn't say that ...

GC Didn't I? Parsons? Maybe not – nor I did. Well, see for yourself – the first brick (***produces brick***) will be laid on November 17th, 1927! (***Cast applaud***)

Nar 2 Yes, perhaps, after nine years of promises but no fulfilment, of frustrating inaction, there was some incredulity – but now things began to move.

Nar 1 The local firm of J. Twyford was to build the Chapel. The architect was Charles Biddulph-Pinchard, already known to the School through his design of Great Hall. And the interior work – the stalls and seating – was to be done in the School workshop, under the supervision of Mr Easterbrook and his young assistant, Sid Stephens.

Nar 2 February 20th, 1928 was a momentous day for Wellington School.

AM ***(addressing schoolboys)***
After prize-giving and speeches in Great Hall, our guests will proceed to the Chapel site. The prefects will tell you when to move, and you will assemble – noiselessly.

Once the foundation stone had been laid, work began in earnest on building the Chapel, but it wasn't always straight-forward, and problems arose that nobody had expected. These took both time and money to solve. Though funding still remained an issue, by 1929 the building had gathered momentum and various craftsmen and workers were employed. Corner's wish was to use local materials and craftsmen in building what he would later describe as *'one of the most notable [memorials] in the whole country, without any exception.'*

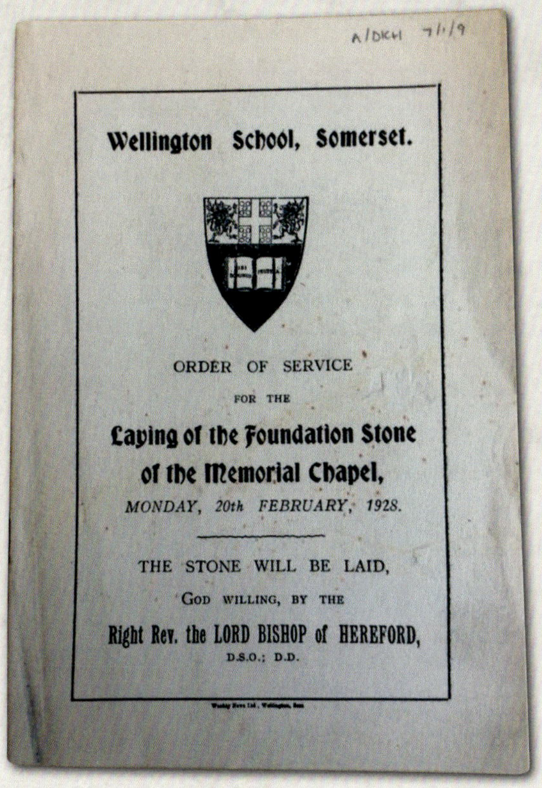
Wellington School, Somerset.

ORDER OF SERVICE

FOR THE

Laying of the Foundation Stone
of the Memorial Chapel,

MONDAY, 20th FEBRUARY, 1928.

THE STONE WILL BE LAID,

GOD WILLING, BY THE

Right Rev. the LORD BISHOP of HEREFORD,

D.S.O.; D.D.

Nar 1 The next three years were to be devoted to the Chapel project. From all quarters of the schoolboys, staff, parents and old boys – help came. Mr Twyford and his men discovered the foundations of a row of cottages burnt down about 1850. These were costly to remove. ***(Cast – noises of workers, hammering etc.)*** and, in addition, sand holes were discovered on the site. So, at a cost of an additional £200, it was decided to build on a raft foundation.

Nar 2 And, despite the efforts of so many, the total sum raised ***(YBs change total to £4987 15s 9d)*** remained some two and a half thousand pounds below the target shown on the board outside Great Hall. It should not be thought that only the men were busy with fundraising. Indeed, the Women's fund had been going on for some years, and, in 1928, Mrs Corner's Whitsuntide effort received a seven-page spread in the School Magazine.

Nar 1 As we move into 1929 more characters appear in this strange, eventful history. The Headmaster's step-son, Harold Pound-Corner took over the Chapel lighting scheme and conducted lengthy correspondence with the architect through letters and drawings.

Mr Biddulph-Pritchard wished to reproduce the type of 15th Century church decoration to be found in Somerset – at Carhampton, Bicknoller and Kentisbeare, for example. His idea was to create a glorious, radiant, happy Chapel. This involved a great deal of painting, and he employed two young girls to assist him with this.

Nar 2 Mr Francis Hunt, from Henlade, was a master-craftsman. He was responsible for carving the oak-work which is one of the Chapel's glories. Working in the old woodshop hut for over two years he produced intricately-carved bench-ends, and pews, and panels, and doors and figures.
And where was George? Everywhere, it seems: fitting out the Old Gym with saws and planes; working on his 'wonderful machine' which took out the deep ground-work in the oak panels before they went to the carver; issuing further appeals for funds; playing his beloved cricket.

Nar 2 Old Boy Edward Burrow very generously gave the stone from which the pinnacles on the Chapel roof were to be carved by Mr Hunt, and it was George who bored the stones in the Power House with a specially made twist drill ***(Cast drilling noises)***

GC ***(pleased)*** 130 feet of hole. Good. Right, you two – you can clean up now...

Nar 1 But memories had to be opened and old sorrows revealed when the Headmaster wrote to the families of those for whom the Chapel was being created, to confirm details of the names, and ages, and resting places, of the 37 who had fallen:

Woman 1 Dear Mr Corner, My son fell on the edge of Ypres-Lille Canal. He was about to visit some posts on the other side. I am, yours truly...

Man 1 You will be sorry to hear that we were never able to find my brother's grave, and he appears on the Tyne Cot Memorial, near Ypres, as one of the missing. ***(lowers voice)*** I have not mentioned this matter to my mother...

Woman 2 ***(Somerset Voice)*** Our poor dear son John was down in rheumatic and had double pneumonia. He died in Hospital at Alexandra January 14th, 1916. We have his four medals framed. He joined up when the war broke out. He was in the first West Somerset Yeomanry. He got promoted to Lance Corporal. We also have a photo of his grave. With kind regards...

Man 2 My son went right through the very heavy fire in the attack near Hulluch on 26th September, up to the German 3rd line. He was then ordered to take up a position with his gun team on the left of his brigade. All the team save one were killed by a shell which burst one or two feet over his gun while they were gallantly firing it...

Woman 3 I had notice from the Director of War Graves that [Clifford] lies at Bernafay Wood, near Albert. I've never had many particulars as to just where he fell, although I've written so many letters, asking for details...

Man 3 *(simple)* Your letter at hand this morning. My brother was registered Tom and Christened Thomas as the clergyman refused to christen him Tom, saying it was not a correct name. Please have put down which you think is correct...

Woman 4 [Eric] fell near Amiens and was buried at Allonville. What a splendid memorial to the boys in whom you took such interest. We parents will always feel so very grateful to you.

Nar 1 And the Headmaster still had in his possession a letter which he had received fourteen years before, written on October 13th, 1915 –

Man 4 My dear George, thank you for your letter. I cannot write about Ted yet, the blow is too severe. I am making every effort to get news. I wish he had survived this great battle – he would have got on well. How he would have liked to help in the great repulse of a few days ago. Your affectionate brother, Edward.

Nar 1 The spinney of trees to the west of the Chapel, on the corner of School Field, was created by George Corner and named Sanctuary Wood, to commemorate the place in France where his nephew died.

***(Music:** leitmotif gently, then silence)*

Still, some could not understand why the building of the Chapel was taking so long. One of the main reasons was the attention to detail that Corner had paid to every aspect of the build, from sourcing local craftsmen and material to the symbolic colours of the names of the fallen on the wooden panels inside. Another reason was financial – there was still not enough money to pay for some of the features Corner desired.

AM *(overhearing latter part)* It's taking so long to finish, Elliott, because the Headmaster doesn't tolerate shoddy work. He is a perfectionist, unlike you two. I'll show you what I mean. Run and turn the lights on, one of you. ***(Pause)*** Yes, it isn't really dark enough yet – but you can see that all direct light has been concealed, by using strip-lights behind the cornice – so that light is reflected off the panels and into the Chapel. Clever, eh?

Now examine the organ gallery which perfectly combines horizontal – Elliott? ***(YB2 hesitantly makes sideways line with hand)*** with vertical. The central panels have been emblazoned by Mr Ward from Taunton. In the middle are the Royal Arms, on the right the School Arms – ***(designed by the Headmaster)*** and on the left those of zummerzet. Then there are the commemorative panels where the names of those who fell are rendered in gold or red, symbolic colours. The panels follow in order the dates of the casualties, starting here in 1914 and following round to 1918.

Jim Easterbrook and Syd Stephens at work in the Chapel.

Look at the organ – that came from Osmond's of Taunton and cost one thousand one hundred and thirty-five pounds ***(YBs react – wow!)*** Examine the bench ends, the fine oak doors, the East window, the canopy stalls, the reredos behind the altar – carved from one piece of wood, and the cupola –

YB2 What's that, sir?

AM A cupola? Yes, funny-sounding word. It's Italian – meaning a dome or spherical vault on top of a building, a light-giving embellishment.

YB1 ***(looking around, with YB2)*** But where is it, sir?

AM Yes, well – it's going to go there – in the middle of the ceiling – eventually. It was part of the architect's original design – but, er, I think money's the problem, again. That's why the bucket's there – to stop our cupola overflowing, as it were: ha! ***(Boys groan)***

YB2 But who's paying for all this? It must be costing thousands of pounds.

AM Very true, Elliott. It is costing thousands of pounds – and the greatest contribution is from the Headmaster himself. He's very worried. I believe he's going to write to the Old Boys - again.

For Corner, the lack of money remained a constant source of strain and his next letter to his Old Boys suggests a more human and wearied tone. It is clear how much personal responsibility he has borne and phrases such as *'bear a heavy load', 'I tremble at my responsibility' and 'load...removed from my shoulders'* suggest a man allowing himself to entertain the fact his dream may not be realised. He admits he cannot do it alone, yet he has faith that *'the help of many'* will make the difference and lead to *'its ultimate happy outcome.'* This letter shows us that for once Corner seems aware of his limitations and the danger of committing himself too fully, *'but I dare not give the order for the remainder of the work unless I can see a (pause) reinforcement or help on a near front.'* The confident and strong voice of earlier letters seems to have quietened under the threat of defeat.

<u>GC</u> ***(writing)*** My Dear Old Boys,
I want to talk to you about Chapel matters. Let me explain what the task is. It is a great one – and often I tremble at my responsibility. ***(pause)*** But then I believe in the work and its ultimate happy outcome – with the help of many – and that makes all the difference. For the future, if the Chapel is to be dedicated next Whitsuntide, as we all hope it will be, finished, and with its organ. ***(looks up)*** and with its beautiful cupola, a further ***(changes figure)*** £2000 is required. ***(quicker)*** The work is all thought out and ready for the word 'go'. Personally, I bear the heavy load amounting to the difference between receipts and expenditure, but I dare not give the order for the remainder of the work unless I can see a (***pause***) reinforcement of help on a near front. ***(peruses letter, nods)*** If this load, whether through the instrumentality of the many, or the few, can be removed from my shoulders, I shall certainly subscribe (***pause***) £1000 to the opening of the Endowment Fund and shall count this the happiest day of my life.
Believe me, your sincere friend and old Headmaster, George Corner

The Auditors, Messrs J. and A. W. Sully, read out the receipts and payments account, February 1919 to March 1931. It made for difficult listening. Corner's vision had always been ambitious but perhaps he had exceeded his own personal limits. His sister, amongst others, began to worry that the strain was too great for him.

<u>Nar 2</u> Indeed, as so often, George chose to hide the true seriousness of the matter. The financial affairs of the Chapel account were critical – as the audit produced by Messrs J and AW Sully, chartered accountants, on April 23rd 1931 confirmed.
(Auditors read fast and very dryly, referring to ledgers throughout, rather smugly)

<u>Aud 1</u> Wellington School, Somerset. Memorial Chapel receipts and payments account, February 1919 to March 1931.
<u>Payments:</u> builder and heating apparatus/stonework and sculpture/oak and carving/ironmongery etc./electric fittings/rubber floor/casualty panels/wages etc./architect – gorgon (***pause, corrects)*** tut!

tut! organ, legal costs, bank charges, printing and postage, clerical assistance etc etc......TOTAL PAYMENTS – Eleven Thousand, One Hundred and fourteen pounds, seventeen shillings and fivepence.
Mr Sully, if you please –

Aud 2 Estimated Payments carver/carpenter/architect/reredos/coats of arms/ cupola/heating (***draws breath***) TOTAL ESTIMATED PAYMENTS – one thousand, eight hundred and ninety-one pounds, sixteen shillings.
RECEIPTS ***(sees spelling error, corrects it)*** That clerk will have to go, Mr Sully. RECEIPTS donations/bazaar etc./ women's fund/bank interest/ dividends on investments/income tax refund – TOTAL RECEIPTS – Five thousand, eight hundred and four pounds, one shilling and tuppence.

Aud 1 Balance due to Bankers Two hundred and ten pounds, nineteen shillings and two pence.

Aud 2 Balance due to Headmaster Five thousand and ninety-nine pounds, seventeen shillings and one penny.

Aud 1 and 2 ***(unison)*** TOTAL BALANCE TO BE RAISED Seven thousand, two hundred and two pounds, twelve shillings, and threepence.
(they turn to each other) Thank you, Mr Sully ***(shake hands)***

Mary C ***(she is always gentle and sweet, genuinely angelic)***
George. You have done so much for the School, and now all this financial worry. Don't you –

GC God will provide, Mary, God will provide. There's no need to worry. It's all been taken care of. Right to work:
The dedication of the Chapel will take place on May 25th, 1931. The Bishop of Bath and Wells is coming! Come on, you two, look lively (***YBs react reluctantly***)

The Chapel was ready in time for its dedication although all were exhausted, none more so than Corner. His sister, ever caring, even suggested at the end of the 'celebrations' whether he should consider taking things more slowly – he was not at all in favour of this as there were still so many projects he wanted to complete.

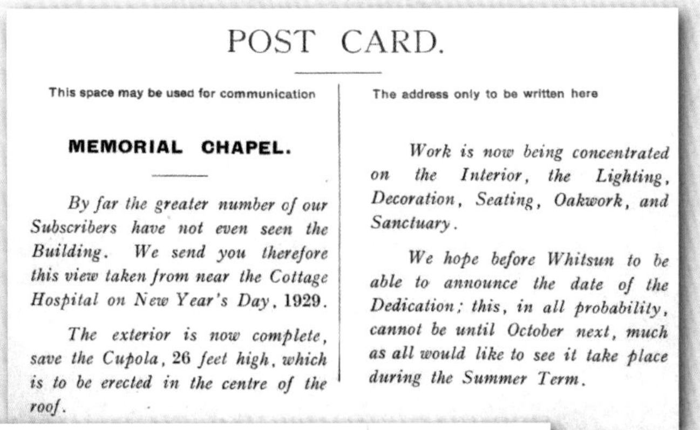
POST CARD.

This space may be used for communication | The address only to be written here

MEMORIAL CHAPEL.

By far the greater number of our Subscribers have not even seen the Building. We send you therefore this view taken from near the Cottage Hospital on New Year's Day, 1929.

The exterior is now complete, save the Cupola, 26 feet high, which is to be erected in the centre of the roof.

Work is now being concentrated on the Interior, the Lighting, Decoration, Seating, Oakwork, and Sanctuary.

We hope before Whitsun to be able to announce the date of the Dedication; this, in all probability, cannot be until October next, much as all would like to see it take place during the Summer Term.

Mary - The congregation were in their seats when my brother, George, looking very smart in his new suit, accompanied by officers of the O. B. A., the architect, senior masters, and boys of the School, preceded by the choir, entered by the sanctuary door and proceeded to the West door (although really, of course, it is the East door). At the conclusion of the hymn, 'From high'est Heav'n the Eternal Son' (chosen by Nancy, I believe), the Bishop of Bath and Wells, the Right Reverend St. John Basil Wynne-Wilson, knocked on the closed door three times (3 knocks heard) with his pastoral staff.

And George opened the door, saying –

GC *(theatrically)* Reverend Father in God, in the name and on behalf of the Old Boys and friends of the School, I beg you to dedicate this Chapel as a memorial to those Old Boys who fell in the Great War, and as a place of worship for the boys of this School.

Mary And the Bishop replied:

Bishop I am ready to proceed with the Dedication. Peace be to this House from God our Heavenly Father.

Mary And then the Bishop invoked God's blessing on the Chapel (as did we all, and none more vehemently than Nancy and I) and gave his thanks for the completion of his work. The candles of St. Michael and St. George (how appropriate) were lit, and while the choir sang 'Come Holy Ghost, Our Souls Inspire) we remained kneeling and added our heartfelt prayers to those of the Bishop.

Bishop In the faith of Jesus Christ, and in memory of those members of this School who laid down their lives in the Great War – in the name of the Father, and of the Son, and of the Holy Ghost –

Cast Amen. ***(music: leitmotif heard in background, continues for next para by Mary, quietly)***

Mary After George read the lesson, the Bishop dedicated each of the four commemoration tablets, and then he gave a truly inspiring address. I only wish you could have been with us, dear Lizzie. It was the culmination of all George's efforts for over twelve years. The Chapel was too small for all our visitors – so the Service was relayed to Great Hall.

On the Sunday we had a Sacred Concert – dear Margaret Balfour brought her husband – a very fine tenor I thought. The next day Sir Dennis Boles inspected the O. T. C., and then there was prize-giving and speeches, followed by the opening of the new Science Laboratories in Northside. Oh, and then we entertained some four hundred parents and friends to lunch in the Gymnasium – salmon and strawberries. In the evening, Doctor Armstrong gave a recital on the new organ – and that was followed by two plays in Great Hall by the Raban Society. And then, at last, it was all over. As you can tell we kept very busy. I hope now we can relax for a while. George is no longer a young man, although he likes to think he is. He's looking very tired –

Chapter 4 - Part 2

The Chapel Today

"It's a really special place and means different things to different people, I'm sure. As Director of Music, my work around the Chapel is, without doubt, the favourite part of my job and it's a pleasure and privilege to play a part in the continuing work of this beautiful iconic building. From regular daily assemblies to boarders' Sunday services, Carols to Commem., O.W. & staff weddings & memorial services, it has played and continues to play a vital role at the centre of the WS community, in both joy and sorrow. As someone's already said – its beating heart." Andrew Trewhella

The completion of the Chapel was Corner's personal mission and, in a sense, a gift to the 'school to come' from a community determined to make something positive out of the pain and trauma of war. When George Corner first considered a Chapel as the most appropriate memorial to the School's fallen in WW1, he saw it as becoming both a 'shrine' to the past and an 'inspiration' to future generations. As a Chapel, the memorial would have an active role in School life but would also stand strong as the inevitable ebb and flow of time changed the School; it would provide an eternal link with his present, which would become our past, and ensure that no matter what the year, the fallen of the School would be remembered. The Chapel seems so integral to the daily life of the School today. It is easy to forget that it hasn't always been there and to take the efforts of George Corner and the School community in the 1920s for granted.

There is no doubting that the Chapel is a beautiful and iconic building; many will have seen atmospheric pictures of it on cards and photos, but it is more than just a building. Though the fabric of the building remains very much the same as it was when it was built, the Chapel means so much more than Corner would, perhaps, ever have anticipated. For some, it is the 'beating heart of the School': a place where pupils gather together for shared worship, singing, prayer and contemplation; a place where pupils can enjoy musical and dramatic performances; a place to savour the music of the Chapel choir; and a place for personal reflection and quiet. For many pupils, their time at the senior school in Year 7 begins on induction afternoon with a meeting in Chapel and ends years later with the Leavers' Service on the last morning of the academic year. This service is one of reflection and celebration, marking the beginning of a new and exciting phase of life. This service is, perhaps, almost a rite of passage. Within the School year, the Chapel also hosts some of the most moving and enjoyable services such as the Easter Bonnet parade and Easter Service of the Prep School and the three carol services in the Senior School at the end of the autumn term.

For every member of the extended Wellington School community, the Chapel means something personal and different. For some, nowhere else on the School site represents the concept of the School as much as the Chapel. It is often the most requested place to visit when O.W.s return to look back around the School. Not everyone who feels so strongly about the Chapel is religious, but the connection is to something more 'spiritual' and essential. Many O.W.s choose to celebrate significant life events in the Chapel, as do the staff. There have been christenings, baptisms, weddings, civil marriage ceremonies, funerals and memorial services. In times of profound joy and sadness, the Chapel seems the most natural place to meet, commemorate and share these important life experiences. In recent times of tragedy, the quiet and stillness of the Chapel has been felt to be the most appropriate place to house the 'Book of Condolence'; inviting reflection, calm and contemplation.

Although the Chapel is much the same building it was when it was built, what it means to the School and how it meets the needs of the School community is not fixed. As society has changed, the School has changed, and as the School has changed, the Chapel has needed to adapt too. New services such as the Animal Thanksgiving service and the Family-Picnic service ensure that the 'Chapel' reaches out to all members of the School community, engendering feelings of openness, accessibility and warmth. Pupils are encouraged to use the Chapel as a place to recharge and gain 'thinking space,' to help themselves deal with the pressures and difficulties they sometimes face. People have said that the fact it is a 'Memorial Chapel' seems to add to its calm. Perhaps it is this sense of the past and the sense of purpose that drove its completion that helps people to see in the Chapel a more finely tuned and intense sense of what matters in life.

The Commemoration Service to mark 100 years since the beginning of World War One took place in the Chapel in November 2014. It was an extremely moving service with music, poetry, tributes to the fallen and acted scenes from 'A Fitting Memorial'. The service ended with the Roll of Honour read out by the Head Boy and Head Girl. People across the School community were invited to lay a card on the altar in memory of each of the 37 fallen. As the Last Post rang out from the balcony, the audience gazed at the altar to acknowledge and reflect on the sacrifices of our Old Boys, brought into Chapel for the first time. In this beautiful space, the rich colours brought out by flickering candlelight, we remembered.

Chapter 5

Remembering 'Your Old Friend and Master': George Corner

"100 terms is certainly a long time. I fear sometimes almost too long. There have been anxious times and troubled times – life is like that. But standing out above all is a feeling of thankfulness for work permitted to be done and for friendships made." [1]

The aim of this book was to find out about the men behind the names on the School's Roll of Honour for World War One. The School Magazines provided the starting point but reading through the early 1900s to the 1930s editions it soon became obvious that there was a very strong voice speaking from them. That voice was George Corner's. Impassioned, forthright and totally dedicated to his boys and his School, his story is inextricably linked to that of his fallen boys and the building of the Chapel. There is little doubt that without his personal commitment to fulfilling his 'dream', both in terms of motivation and money, the Chapel, or the building we know now, would never have been built. It is said that Corner paid nearly half the cost of the Chapel himself. His voice speaks to us from a different time, a different world but, nonetheless, the faith, pride, and vision it communicates are inspiring.

Though the last years of Corner's headship brought notable successes such as the celebration of his 100 terms as Headmaster and his election to the Headmaster's Conference, the purchase of Bulford Fields acted as a catalyst to inflame those who were losing faith in Corner's focus and vision. It seems there was a gradual division between Corner's vision for the School and the views of the parents and governors. This sense of 'irreconcilable differences' led to the Governors' seeking Corner's voluntary retirement. For a man who had given so much to the School, it must have felt like a betrayal by those close to him. Joe Storr's play conveys the ignoble decline of a great Headmaster very well. Even a man with Corner's energy and commitment could not fight the swell of thought that he was no longer the right man to lead Wellington School. In the play, Corner does not question the Governors' decision, but regrets that he was not the one to instigate notification of his retirement, *'still I grieve the initiative was not left to me. It would have come....'* Though Corner can see that a younger man *'should now be at the helm'*, the pressure of being steered into a life-changing decision before true readiness must have been keenly felt.

[1] Letter of George Corner from 'A Fitting Memorial' by Joe Storr.

Parkes Dear Mr Corner.
You ask me to write to you quite frankly, and I think it will be best to do so. I may say, in confidence, that I have been approached during the past year by several of your Governors to find out the Board's attitude towards your retirement, and enquiring about a full inspection of the School.

GC Dear Hugh Fox, I have had many painful reflections during the weekend. All considered it's got to be July, not Christmas. The question remains when in the interest of the School is it best to announce the thing?
You had a rotten job to do yesterday and I do not complain of the way you did it. I know you felt it as much as I – still I grieve the initiative was not left to me. It would have come.

Fox My Dear Corner,
It is absolutely essential that the Governors should be informed next Monday, the 4th, of your intention to retire at the end of the year. This should come from you rather than from me…. I know it will be a very painful occasion for you….

GC My Dear Frank,
It is with regret that I must ask you to lay my resignation before the Governing Board at their next meeting. I dare not attempt to give any reason for my decision as they are so many and so varied. Perhaps they are overshadowed by the feeling that a younger man should now be at the helm.

A Great Headmaster.

RESIGNATION OF MR. GEORGE CORNER.

38 Years Devoted Service to Wellington School.

LASTING MONUMENT TO NOTABLE LIFE WORK.

MR. GEORGE CORNER, M.A., T.D.

The news of Corner's intended retirement was reported as an exclusive in the Wellington Weekly News and was met with 'unfeigned regret'. He had been headmaster of the school for 38 years.

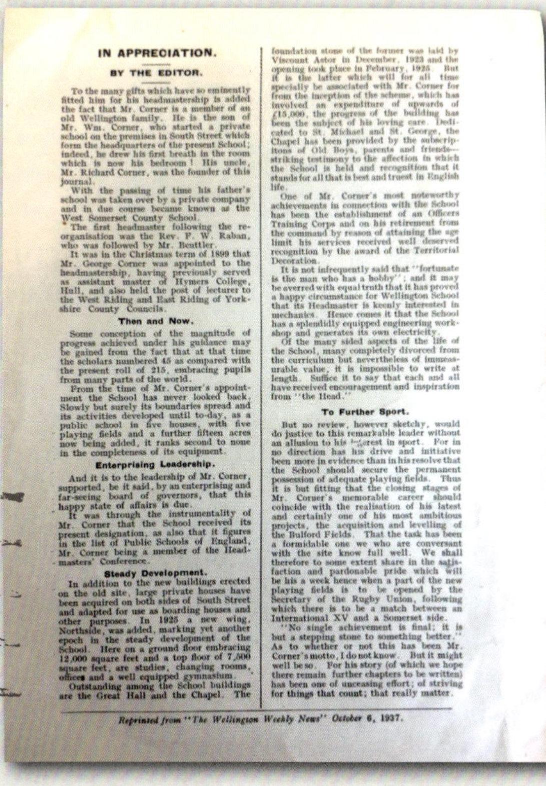

IN APPRECIATION.

BY THE EDITOR.

To the many gifts which have so eminently fitted him for his headmastership is added the fact that Mr. Corner is a member of an old Wellington family. He is the son of Mr. Wm. Corner, who started a private school on the premises in South Street which form the headquarters of the present School; indeed, he drew his first breath in the room which is now his bedroom! His uncle, Mr. Richard Corner, was the founder of this journal.

With the passing of time his father's school was taken over by a private company and in due course became known as the West Somerset County School.

The first headmaster following the re-organisation was the Rev. F. W. Raban, who was followed by Mr. Beattler.

It was in the Christmas term of 1899 that Mr. George Corner was appointed to the headmastership, having previously served as assistant master of Hymers College, Hull, and also held the post of lecturer to the West Riding and East Riding of Yorkshire County Councils.

Then and Now.

Some conception of the magnitude of progress achieved under his guidance may be gained from the fact that at that time the scholars numbered 45 as compared with the present roll of 215, embracing pupils from many parts of the world.

From the time of Mr. Corner's appointment the School has never looked back. Slowly but surely its boundaries spread and its activities developed until to-day, as a public school in five houses, with five playing fields and a further fifteen acres now being added, it ranks second to none in the completeness of its equipment.

Enterprising Leadership.

And it is to the leadership of Mr. Corner, supported, be it said, by an enterprising and far-seeing board of governors, that this happy state of affairs is due.

It was through the instrumentality of Mr. Corner that the School received its present designation, as also that it figures in the list of Public Schools of England, Mr. Corner being a member of the Headmasters' Conference.

Steady Development.

In addition to the new buildings erected on the old site, large private houses have been acquired on both sides of South Street and adapted for use as boarding houses and other purposes. In 1925 a new wing, Northside, was added, marking yet another epoch in the steady development of the School. Here on a ground floor embracing 12,000 square feet and a top floor of 7,500 square feet, are studies, changing rooms, offices and a well equipped gymnasium.

Outstanding among the School buildings are the Great Hall and the Chapel. The foundation stone of the former was laid by Viscount Astor in December, 1923 and the opening took place in February, 1925. But it is the latter which will for all time specially be associated with Mr. Corner for from the inception of the scheme, which has involved an expenditure of upwards of £15,000, the progress of the building has been the subject of his loving care. Dedicated to St. Michael and St. George, the Chapel has been provided by the subscriptions of Old Boys, parents and friends—striking testimony to the affection in which the School is held and recognition that it stands for all that is best and truest in English life.

One of Mr. Corner's most noteworthy achievements in connection with the School has been the establishment of an Officers Training Corps and on his retirement from the command by reason of attaining the age limit his services received well deserved recognition by the award of the Territorial Decoration.

It is not infrequently said that "fortunate is the man who has a hobby"; and it may be averred with equal truth that it has proved a happy circumstance for Wellington School that its Headmaster is keenly interested in mechanics. Hence comes it that the School has a splendidly equipped engineering workshop and generates its own electricity.

Of the many sided aspects of the life of the School, many completely divorced from the curriculum but nevertheless of immeasurable value, it is impossible to write at length. Suffice it to say that each and all have received encouragement and inspiration from "the Head."

To Further Sport.

But no review, however sketchy, would do justice to this remarkable leader without an allusion to his interest in sport. For in no direction has his drive and initiative been more in evidence than in his resolve that the School should secure the permanent possession of adequate playing fields. Thus it is but fitting that the closing stages of Mr. Corner's memorable career should coincide with the realisation of his latest and certainly one of his most ambitious projects, the acquisition and levelling of the Bulford Fields. That the task has been a formidable one we who are conversant with the site know full well. We shall therefore to some extent share in the satisfaction and pardonable pride which will be his a week hence when a part of the new playing fields is to be opened by the Secretary of the Rugby Union, following which there is to be a match between an International XV and a Somerset side.

"No single achievement is final; it is but a stepping stone to something better." As to whether or not this has been Mr. Corner's motto, I do not know. But it might well be so. For his story (of which we hope there remain further chapters to be written) has been one of unceasing effort; of striving for things that count; that really matter.

Reprinted from "The Wellington Weekly News" October 6, 1937.

His last letter to his 'Dear Old Boys' was written on 9th, November 1939 and addressed from Ruggin Court, his home upon retirement. Though long, it is an extremely powerful letter and shows the eloquence and sincerity that characterised his letters of wartime.

Dear Old Boys,

A few days before the outbreak of this second unhappy European War, I received from your Hon. Secretary, O. S. Hughes, a brief note enclosing a cheque for £282:2:6. He added that this was a portion of a Testimonial Fund, subscribed by Old Boys and friends of the School. Your president, Rudolph Hazzledine, also called, and with many kind words, explained that the gift was intended to mark the appreciation of the labours of myself, my wife and my dear sister, during our stay at the School.

This is indeed a very kind and generous act on your part and I wish now to thank you most sincerely. I have postponed my letter hoping that some occasion might present itself when I might meet some representative gathering of Old Boys and thank them personally for their kindness. But the opportunity for such a gathering has, amidst the present strain and stress of national and private difficulty, appeared to have receded further and further into a dim and anxious future. In a way, it would seem improper, at such a time, to trouble you with a letter; my only excuse is I do not wish to seem ungrateful.

Many of you are every day answering the Country's call, the call your fathers and your elders answered five and twenty years ago, either at home or abroad, on land, at sea or in the air – in the field, the factory or the office, and some are answering for the second time in their generation. We pray that you may be preserved and may be spared some at least of the horrors of 1914 –1918. Life at School was then a continual nightmare. May you all have the strength to bear the trials and hardships which the call of duty brings you.

Now that I am writing, there are other things I want to say, and it would be strange indeed if after such a long association it were not so. This is also a good-bye letter. I have sometimes felt that in these long 39 years I had perhaps outstayed my usefulness and some of you, not having a complete vision of the self-appointed task to which I had set my hand, may have shared that feeling. The work by which the tiny little country Proprietary School was to achieve the status of an Endowed Public School was long and difficult. Many obstacles had to be overcome. The work of development was intricate, difficult and manifold. I had realised for some time that after all a Headmaster is but a 'lodger', as it were in the abode of his work – others follow – they come and go. The School remains and grows. But I desired eagerly to complete the last of my works – to furnish the School with Playing Fields, adequate for its need, both now and in the future. A famous School has a great legend about the meaning of Playing Fields.

The distant fields of Pyles Thorne road were imperfect and dangerous of access. More than a decade ago I had purchased some 20 acres of meadow land immediately adjoining the School on the West. I felt that too long had the School relied on makeshift and rented ground. I handed the purchase to the Governors of the School – the fields are under the shadow almost of Wellington's Monument – they were glad to have them, but could not afford the work of levelling and development. I doubted (I hope not arrogantly) if the vision of Bulford Fields would ever be accomplished did I not follow up the task. My own attention and resources at that time were more than taken up in the completion of the Chapel and simultaneously the intricate development of Northside and the general work of the layout around the many new buildings. The fields had to wait their turn, much to the disappointment of all. That work is now finished. Some of you who read this no doubt will remember the effort of 1902 – 1903 when we levelled the Old School Field and fellows vied with one another in the work. We thought that a great work and so indeed it was in the days when mechanical aids were not to be had and pick, shovel and barrow were the only order of the day. Judged merely by the quantity of the soil handled this present work is just twenty-four times as great – in other words, 72,000 tons of soil and turf were moved.

I am now, as it were, a spectator at the end of a long picture gallery and as I retrace my steps from the far end – the early days – I view an almost never-ending series of events with the Actors: Boys, Parents, Masters, Governors and Friends who lived in and about those events. In thanking you all now collectively I feel once more how much I have owed to those I meet as I go along this long gallery, what courtesy, help, and forbearance I have encountered.

At the beginning in 1899, it was a tiny world to me after the bustle of a big Yorkshire School, but I found the right spirit there – J. O. Beuttler and his young lieutenant, E. C. Harries, had each brought something of Rugby and Shrewsbury with them and planted it there. The plant had fallen on good soil – there was keenness, not least on the field. Our games traditions – unbroken – can be dated to those early days.

Easily foremost then amongst the Old Boys who rallied to the School was

Howard Humphries, who gathered around him a band of zealous workers: the eldest DRAPES, T. L; the two SPILLERS, J. W. and R. G.; the two GARNEYS, E. and G. F.; ARNOLD HILL, HOWARD, TARRANT, CLAY and BURROW, all stalwarts in the formation of the O. B. A. and in fostering Schemes for the best interests of the School. Others who have passed the Great Divide, who did yeoman service, we meet as we go along, APLIN, RIDLER, DIBBLE, CAVALIER, TREBLE, HORNBY, FREDDIE LAW. Each wrought hard and left his mark.

Of those still with us one meets in succession a goodly company of Old Boys thronging past – captains, scholars, senior boys, and leaders – a long line of helpers – all in their day had played their part and each had laid his stone in the Building. To all these my thanks and gratitude are due – a list too long to name indeed but not one forgotten.

The days of School life, like the sterner days of later life, are full of light and shade, of joy and of sadness. Some days are boisterously happy and full of abounding life and energy – others are tempered by some adverse happening. There are joys of success in work or in games, as your old song says:

"In struggles keen, with book and pen,
In manful contests on the field
We'll put our mettle to the test,
And never drop the flag or yield." –

A prize, a gallant try, a glorious victory, a fine catch, a fifty scored – a difficulty overcome – a word of praise – these being a thrill in remembrance. There are the patches of shade – failure of effort, or it may be effort unrecognised, disappointment, a grouse, estrangement of a friend. These all are present in life, but it is the light of generous and happy doings that shines over the patches of disappointment and gives pleasure to all in recalling something of the days of their boyhood.

The Gallery is long and alive with pictures. Some actors there will be at one end in the distant past who do not know the present growth of their old School. Let them return and see. The new Head will welcome them. Others in the middle and nearer space have no knowledge of the early beginnings and the difficulties overcome. Let them rejoice.

I was deeply touched last spring by so many letters sent me, when I lost my greatest helper, my dear Sister, a buttress of the School and all that it stood for. None can ever judge the full part she played – she was the friend of all, boy and master, a faithful counsellor who enjoyed the confidence and affection of all, who never counted a task too humble or too difficult if it helped the life of anyone about her. My debt and the School's debt to her cannot well be measured. I trust all those letters, so kindly penned, were answered.

Some of you, no doubt, have been unable to join in this practical expression of thanks to me. To them, I would say without fear, every School must ultimately derive its strength from the goodwill and efforts of those who have been educated there. Many in the past have given of their substance to help in building up the School. Many have not done so. To these last, I would say, and I speak freely without fear, there is much still to be done that I had hoped to have done before I left. The Chapel is without its cupola – it is still open to the inclemency of the weather – the debt to the Architect and Carver is not fully discharged. The layout is only partly done. When quieter times come, I hope that the Old Boys will be found to set these works afoot. It should encourage all to know that from one source or another in the last 38 years no less than £50,000 have been spent in building up the old School, and of this sum, half has come from private sources.

There is hardly any School, if any, that in the last ten years has not had its time of strain. It is not easy to forecast the future, or what the upheaval of the present epoch may have in store for the Public Schools of this country, but this prophecy I will make, that neither this nor any other Public School will or can continue to exist if it does not enjoy the watchful care and help of the boys who have there received their upbringing; and this is as it should be. For so they strengthen and preserve what is in part their own possession and creation. Changes too, of Headmaster, are inevitable and necessary. Do not allow any change to abate one jot your devotion to the Old School, or your will to help. The School is there – the foundations are well and truly laid – it is for generations of Boys and Old Boys to build thereon.

This should mainly be a letter of thanks to you deep-felt and such I wish it to be, but it is also a good-bye and reminiscent letter and I cannot close it without acknowledging to the full the consideration and help I have always received from Parents and Old Boys, particularly in the last ten years of financial strain and stress of work, at times almost unbearable, caused by the final solving of the problem of the Playing Fields. As you know this work was consummated last Autumn and I rejoice and am proud to say that the event was coincident with a good examination result in July 1938 – indeed the best in the School's history, and one of which no School of our numbers need be ashamed. Briefly, the School attained the greatest number of School Certificates ever gained by it at one examination, namely, twenty-six.

For this happy event – this juncture of successes – I have to thank my old colleagues. For the work in School most particularly do I record my thanks to my old colleagues: FARRAR, THORP, HULME and NICOL, and to BAKER, SEAGER, DAWE RUSSELL and HUGHES for their untiring work both in and out of School. To Seager especially, as it was to me, it was an intense pleasure to record the brilliant and unique result of his old House Captain, at Sandhurst. Many fine results have been obtained in the past and about these you know, but about this one, most of you do not know and I feel you will like to know. My old pupil, INGALL, after being top in all three terms at Sandhurst, finally passed out last August Top, with the King's medal and Sword; the Norman Medal and the First Prize for Imperial and International affairs – here was an illustration of native ability, aided by will, industry, and determination. All honour to him. He is now in India. His old Prep. School Master, L. C. STEVENS, also an Old Boy, will be especially glad to know.

Once more please accept my thanks for your considerate and generous act, and

Believe me, with my kindest remembrances to you all, in which my wife joins,

Yours sincerely,

George Corner

It is sad to read at the end of this letter that Corner uses *'yours sincerely'* rather than the memorable, *'your old master and friend'* of the wartime letters. It signifies, perhaps, the recognition that the relationship with his old boys has irrevocably changed.

Ruggin Court was to provide a happy retirement for the Corner family for many years, but the death of Mary, followed by the deaths of Harold Pound (his brother in law) and his wife in the same month in 1941, brought a great deal of grief to Corner's last years. As we read in 'A Fitting Memorial':

Nar 1 *(gently)* The remaining years were spent quietly at Ruggin. There George enjoyed his garden and his horses, writing to Old Boys and entertaining many visitors. But there were grievous blows as those he loved passed on:

GC My Dear Hughes, The words you use my boy, are few and simple, but they show quite plainly how great was your regard and your affection for my dear sister, Mary. Her devotion was inspiring, and to me, her help was beyond words. Please thank all the fellows. *(Exit Mary).*

Nar 2 Two years later the Rev. Reginald Pound, Mrs Corner's brother-in-law died –

GC We are indeed a sad household. Mr Pound was so much a part of us. More than thirty years close friendship in all sorts of weather, and seven years at our table built up ties which when broken do grievous hurt. He was a fine type of character......(Exit Pound)

Nar 2 And this was followed, in the same month, with further loss:

GC My dear Farrar. Thank you so much for your kind little note – I know just what you felt when you wrote it. I am a stricken man (pause). I had hoped that I had nursed the dear wife back to something of her old self. The blow fell quite suddenly. I do not know in the least what I can or shall do, but I shall try to keep the garden nice – but Ruggin will not be the same. *(Exit Mrs GC)*

Even when dealing with his own grief and loss, Corner did not forget the men whose skills and craftsmanship had helped realise his dream for the Chapel. There were uncomfortable facts to face, mostly to do with the finances of the Chapel. Debts remained and money was still owed to those who had given so much of their skill to carve out the designs Corner desired.

Nar 2 The death of Charles Biddulph-Pritchard in 1944 inspired this tribute from George which appeared in the Wellington Weekly News –

GC His work was not only professional, it became a labour of love. An examination of the West end of the Chapel will illustrate what I mean. It is very beautiful and will compare with any oak-work of the same period. *(awkward pause)*

There is, I regret to say, a debt of £88 still owing to him on the Chapel work. If any Old Boys or other well-wishers of the School can assist in paying this sum to his executors, it would be a practical way of marking their appreciation of the great work Mr Pinchard has done for Wellington School. *(Exeunt B-P and others)*

Nar 1 Yes, some thirteen years after the Chapel was completed its finances remained in disarray. *(pause)*

Though Corner was able to fill his time with the things he loved doing, life away from the School and without his sister, wife, and brother-in-law must have been quite lonely.

He passed away in April 1947, at the age of 78, and was buried with his wife in the churchyard at West Buckland. His grave carries the Wellington School motto, 'Nisi Dominus Frustra' and reference to his headship, 'George Corner, Late Headmaster of Wellington School', marking in his death the very special feelings he had for the school. Mary's gravestone also carries this eternal connection, 'Mary Corner of Wellington School'.

As the play concludes, the narrator speaks:

(gently) George Corner died on April 6th, 1947. He lies with his wife and the Rev'd Pound in West Buckland churchyard. His grave is there, but 'si momentum requirat circumspiciat'. (pause). Look about you – if you wish for his memorial – a fitting memorial – it is here, in the building which was his dream, his creation, and his bequest to the School he loved so much – The Chapel of St Michael and St George.

'si momentum requirat circumspiciat'

In 1948 a tribute to George Corner was put in place above the doors before entering the Chapel. It was composed by Edward Snow, the then Head of Classics. The translation reads:

> ***You who enter this building, remember the energetic, loving and most-loved man of this school. George Corner. Thirty-eight years 1900-1938 was in charge of (the school) in a most distinguished way, died 17th April 1947. If you seek a monument for him, look around you.***

1996 – The George Corner Memorial Appeal

After prizegiving in July 1996, Frank Gillard unveiled the George Corner Memorial Statue. The statue is still in place next to the Chapel and opposite the Sunken Garden. It was the result of a designated fund-raising campaign to provide a more lasting memorial to the man. As Neil Copp's wrote in a letter to O.W.s, it was a very well-attended event with over 800 people watching as the statue was unveiled.

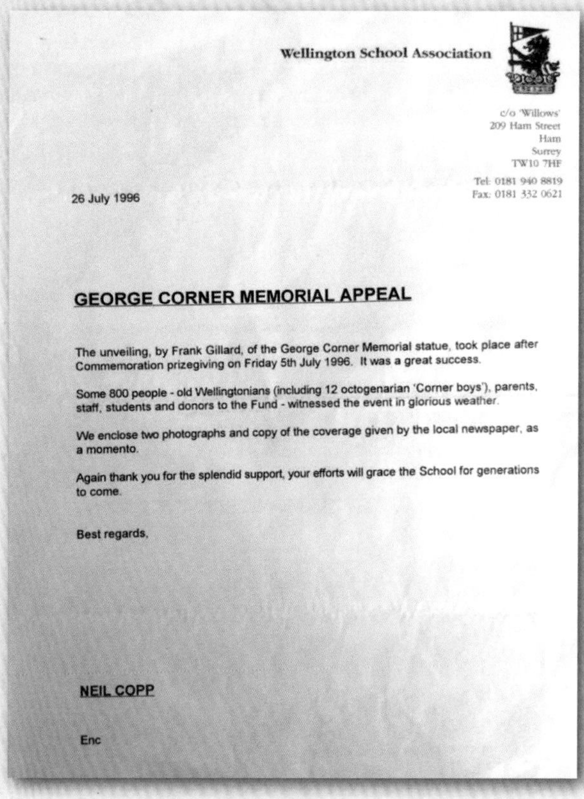

Wellington School Association

c/o 'Willows'
209 Ham Street
Ham
Surrey
TW10 7HF

Tel: 0181 940 8819
Fax: 0181 332 0621

26 July 1996

GEORGE CORNER MEMORIAL APPEAL

The unveiling, by Frank Gillard, of the George Corner Memorial statue, took place after Commemoration prizegiving on Friday 5th July 1996. It was a great success.

Some 800 people - old Wellingtonians (including 12 octogenarian 'Corner boys'), parents, staff, students and donors to the Fund - witnessed the event in glorious weather.

We enclose two photographs and copy of the coverage given by the local newspaper, as a momento.

Again thank you for the splendid support, your efforts will grace the School for generations to come.

Best regards,

NEIL COPP

Enc

Statue of George Corner outside the Chapel with sculptor Andre Wallace, O. W. and Frank Gillard O.W.

Conclusion

It is impossible to know where the School would be and what it would look like without George Corner's vision, dedication and action. He built the Chapel as a 'fitting memorial' to his 'Dear Old Boys' and it is here that the School feels his legacy most strongly. Yet his commitment to building the best school he could can be seen in Great Hall, Northside, the swimming pool, Bulford fields and Sanctuary Wood. Also, 100 years after they were written, his letters to his Old Boys and theirs back to him have gifted to us a very real sense of our School in a different time and the people who belonged to it and loved it. It is a story that deserves to be told and that is our 'fitting memorial' to 'our' men who died and the master who was determined they would never be forgotten.

Further Reading

There are many books that either feature our Old Boys or catalogue events that they were involved in but those listed below may be of particular interest.

Wellington School Chapel

Horwood, David ***Wellington School Chapel: from the beginning*** Revised 3rd edition 2012 Wellington: Wellington School, 1977

Isaac, L. F. ***The Story of Wellington School*** Wellington: The Friends of Wellington School, 1993

Pirt, Asher ***WSS Old Boys and The Great War*** Lulu: 2013

Wellington Town

Our Boys: The First World War Casualties Listed on Wellington War Memorial by Mike Perry and Ray Hitchcock Wellington: The Carly Press, 2014.
This book was published to commemorate the 'centenary of the outbreak of the Great War' and provides biographical information on all those listed on the town's memorial. It covers the 178 men named.

The Wellington School Old Boys featured in the book are: Silvanus Wilfred Baker, Arthur James Bowerman, William John Crofton Brown, William Edward Chave, Herbert Thomas (Bert) Manley, Alfred Harold William Palfery, Philip Henry Rowe and Robert John Talbot.

Our Other Boys: First and Second World War Casualties. Some local men not listed on Wellington War Memorial. By Mike Perry and Ray Hitchcock Wellington: The Carly Press, 2017.
This edition followed the first and features 32 men who were connected to Wellington and who lost their lives in the Great War, but who are not on the memorial. James Noel Treble and Edward Franklin Corner, both associated with Wellington School, are featured in this edition.

Individuals

The following books do not form an exhaustive list of books featuring our Old Boys and their units.

Lieutenant C. W. Bown

Any one interested in researching Cyril Walter Bown and his brother Herbert George Bown and the use of tanks in the First World War may find the following helpful.

Hickey, Captain D. E. ***Rolling Into Action*: *Memoirs of a Tank Corps Section Commander*** Sussex: The Navy and Military Press, 2007

Pope, Stephen. ***The First Tank Crews: The Lives of the Tankmen who Fought at the Battle of Fleurs-Courcelette, 15 September 1916*** West Midlands: Helicon and Company, 2016

Major Ernest John Brooks

The following book mentions Major Ernest John Brooks

Reed, Paul ***Somme: Courcelette*** Yorkshire: Leo Cooper, 1998

Sergeant Percy Alfred Clode

Although not mentioned by name, this book gives a very good account of the R.G.A. in WW1.

Severn, Mark ***The Gambardier: The Experiences of a Battery of Heavy Artillery on the Western Front During the First World War*** Lenaour: 2017

2nd Lieutenant Colin Graham Gordon

These books give an account of the Gordon Highlanders in WW1.

Falls, Cyril ***The Gordon Highlanders in the First World War 1914-1919*** Aberdeen: The University Press, 1958

Fraser, The Hon. William, ***In Good Company: The First World War Letters & Diaries of The Hon. William Fraser Gordon Highlanders*** Yorkshire: Pen and Sword Military Press, 1990 (reprinted 2016)

Gunner Frank Eric Kent

Kent is mentioned in this book which looks at the pupils of Bournemouth Grammar School and their Headmaster Dr Edward Fenwick, known as 'Tig'.

Hilliam, David ed. ***Tig's Boys: Letters to Sir, From the Trenches Gloucestershire: Spellmount, 2011***

Private Henry Lawrence Wadland

A biography of Wadland's sister, Miss Alice Wadland, Headmistress of her own private school in Dolton, Devon

Wadland, Shane ***Our Miss Wadland*** Bideford: Edward Gaskell Press, 1999

Laure Adler & Camille Viéville

THE TROUBLE WITH WOMEN ARTISTS

Reframing the History of Art

Flammarion

CONTENTS

INTRODUCTION

ARTISTS
AND PROUD OF IT

THE HISTORY
OF AN ONGOING STRUGGLE

Laure Adler

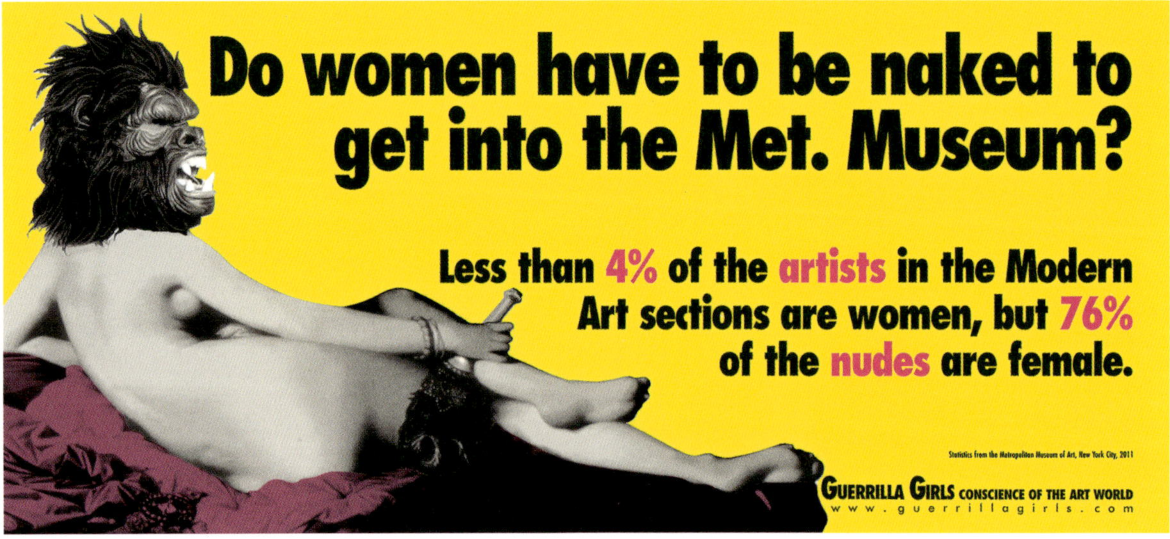

Guerrilla Girls
Do Women Have to Be Naked to Get into the Met. Museum?, 1989.

p. 6
Cindy Sherman
Untitled #224, 1990.
New York. Courtesy of the artist and Metro Pictures.

Since its beginnings, the history of art has been conceived, written, published, and taught by men for a primarily male audience (though some wives from the most privileged classes were sometimes allowed to enjoy, if not truly share in, their definition of beauty). The very idea of beauty has, for centuries, been constructed, shaped, and modified by the male gaze, and yet the feminine has been vital and necessary to the development of art, for, some might assert, there is no beauty without female attributes. Starting with the very first works of art created by the human hand, representations of the feminine have outweighed the masculine—Western art is teeming with depictions of Venus, to take just one example. Through art, woman emerged as a symbol and a representation of power: the power of nature, conception, divination, enchantment, and the taboo.

Woman and the image of woman seem, simultaneously, to have escaped definition and to have generated anxiety. Scholars, whether archaeologists, anthropologists, or art historians, have all observed this without engaging further discussion. The French anthropologist André Leroi-Gourhan, for example, in his analyses of the Paleolithic Venuses found throughout Europe, from southwestern France to Italy and to Germany, observed the ubiquity of female representations in caves but did not inquire into why this might be.

Are these representations mother goddess or fertility cult? Take, for example, the Venus of Willendorf, which defies every rule of representation, quite literally bursting free of them with its bulging sexual features. Is it evidence of the traces of a matriarchal civilization? This potent view of the female—one that is tied to fertility and power—contrasts starkly with the prehistoric representations of women promulgated by Victorian scholars, who developed and supported the theory of a bare-breasted woman in animal skins, condemned to live in her cave like a mother bear, children clinging to her, eyes downcast—while man left the cave to hunt, armed with his lance, his gaze turned skywards.

But the development of gender studies in the 1970s has allowed for other interpretations of female representations, both in prehistory as in other disciplines, and a reassessment of what had until then been the presumed "natural" reiteration of masculine domination. Gender studies enabled us to ask, what if woman left her cave? What if women could also gaze skywards? Without falling into the danger of rehabilitating the female at any cost, now is an opportune

Anonymous
Venus of Willendorf,
c. 30,000–25,000 BCE.
Naturhistorisches Museum, Vienna

time to revisit and reconsider in a new light those whose creative contributions have been overlooked due to an accident of birth—i.e. their gender—but who have fought to become and remain part of our shared history.

This reassessment is not tokenistic: these female creators will not be held up as (or even reduced to) icons, role models, or exemplars in the fight for women's rights. Nor will they be made legends, confined to the martyr role of woman-genius condemned to remain forever unknown. Rather the desire is to pay tribute to those women who have shared the same courage, the same determination, the same life force, and the same will to defy social, political, sexual, and psychological rules in order to answer their calling. In so doing they have left us symbols of their fervent desire to convey to the outside world that which resided deep within themselves.

Let us return to the cave and consider Plato and his allegory, in which emerging from the darkness of the cave exposes us to the possibility of being blinded. Being consigned to obscurity, as though by biological destiny, inspired some women to seek the outside world, even at the risk of getting burned. We must reconsider these women—their initial act of boldness, their exuberance, their necessity, the purity of their artistic approach—in order to integrate them into a shared history of art. Up until now, if they have been acknowledged at all, they have been merely *tolerated*, marginalized, or, for a very few among them, glorified—as though including a few brilliant outliers would suffice to placate those irritated at the dearth of recognized women artists.

The history of art is not a history of quotas or merit awards, and even less a history of representation, whether of sex, social class, or origins. Art does not give orders; it creates, and in so doing it transcends gender and class. But understanding the conditions in which the artistic gesture emerges requires an understanding of context and reality: in short, art arises within an environment. Clearly, one is not born an artist, but rather becomes one. And when you are born on the wrong side (in other words, on the side of those without rights), being an artist—proving it, gaining access, producing and exhibiting work, and continuing to remain an artist—is a perilous, never-ending fight, and physically, intellectually, and mentally exhausting.

A room of one's own is not enough. You need a workshop. You can draw with a pencil, but you can't paint. You need colors, brushes, and models. Where do you find the arrogance to ask for them? And whom do you ask? But above all, how do you defy the seemingly natural order of things and find the confidence to conceive a *representation* of the world outside yourself, when it seems as though nature has marked you out for reproduction and responsible motherhood? In other words, for remaining inside. To project outwards, to birth the vision of a world is a way of subverting the symbolic order.

This book is about those creative women: it reestablishes their strength of thought and conveys their perception of beauty, which continues to move us and inspire us despite the centuries that separate us.

This study is not exhaustive—nor could it be. Photographers and dancers, who deserve a book of their own, are not represented here. Questions of space obliged us to select from among many female creators, and many more women should appear here. As time goes on, recognition continues to grow for these and other women artists, thanks to the work of both male and female museum directors around the world, as well as the public's enthusiasm and growing interest in discovering unfairly neglected artists—many of whom are women. That is not to say the fight is over—sadly, as far as women's rights are concerned, every bit of progress is reversible. Visibility and recognition for women artists has not progressed as far as it may seem, despite the achievements of individuals: Alice Neel (see pp. 74–75) was celebrated in 2017 at the Van Gogh Foundation, in Arles; Annette Messager (see pp. 118–19) and Cindy Sherman (see pp. 138–39) were both awarded the prestigious Imperial Prize of the Japan Academy in 2016; while the UK's esteemed Turner Prize has, in recent years, been awarded to women—Laure Provost (see pp. 154–55) in 2013, Helen Marten in 2016, Lubaina Himid in 2017, and Charlotte Prodger in 2018.

Despite this, women artists remain less popular on the art market—which translates directly to their monetary worth; they are still outnumbered by men, and interpretations of their work too often circle back to gender-related

Niki de Saint Phalle
***Nana Assise* (Sitting Nana)**, 1968. Private collection.

discussions. The fact of their being women often means specialists examine only the psychological or psychoanalytical considerations of gender, instead of undertaking an analysis of the power of their artistic gesture. Would Goya, Picasso, or Duchamp ever be interpreted predominantly for their "masculinity"? Why is Niki de Saint Phalle (see pp. 104–5) always discussed in relation to her "Nanas" or Louise Bourgeois (see pp. 86–87) to her phallic figures?

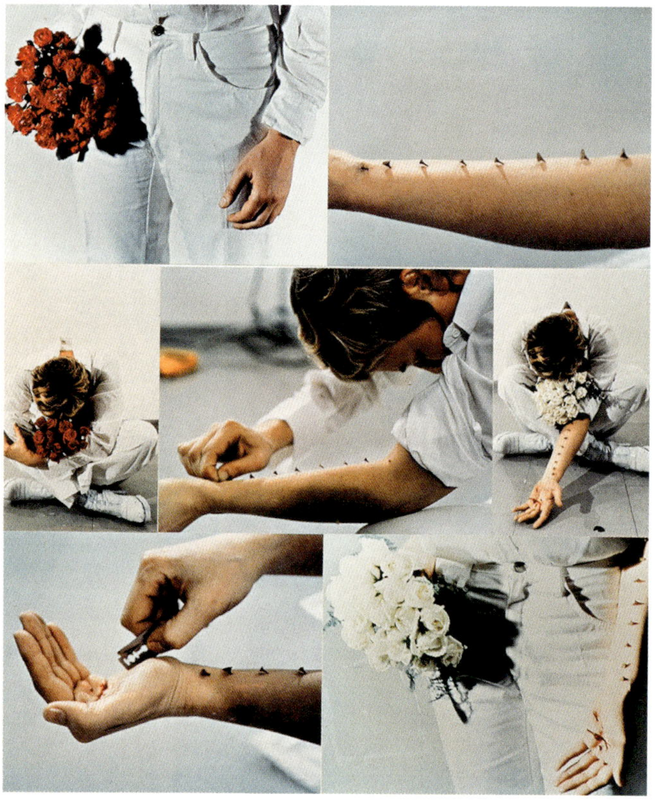

Gina Pane
***Azione sentimentale* (Sentimental Action)**, 1973.
Performance at the Galleria Diagramma in Milan.

Today, instead, we need to demand a kind of "neutral" criticism, free of excessive well-meaning or pleading. Expressions of admiration, no matter how well intended, can, in a different light, bear a dangerous resemblance to condescension. We can start by refusing to characterize these artists solely by their sexual identity, or to interpret their work based on their origins. In doing so we recognize their full and complete belonging to the artistic world by rejecting the clichés that are still so ubiquitous and in which women are still reduced to the role of wife, mother, or lover.

As John Stuart Mill wrote, "Everything which is usual appears natural. The subjection of women to men being a universal custom, any departure from it quite naturally appears unnatural."[1] That was in 1869, yet today there are those who see this as "natural"—and why, indeed, would those who benefit from it give up this supposedly "natural" order? As importantly, how can women themselves think beyond these so-called natural categories, in reality constructed by men who have everything to gain by maintaining them?

The very idea of being an artist, to claim such a title, to want to represent one's own vision of the world, to know that one is capable of doing so, implies considerable moral and mental strength. For this reason, artists—all artists, women and men alike—are dangerous, because they contain within themselves a capacity for disruption and revolution that rejects the legitimacy of the status quo. And the woman who creates—most often alone, without support of any kind, excluded from a community that does not permit her this form of accomplishment—is seen as an exception, an anomaly, or even a freak far more often than she is perceived as a genius.

Unlike the men who populate art history, there appear to be few female geniuses. What woman artist can compete with Michelangelo, Rembrandt,

Goya, or Picasso? No matter how talented they were, it was almost impossible for them to succeed, institutionally or politically. Women were excluded from the art schools, the system of apprenticeships, and the studios, and the heroic troupe of female artists that lingers in our memories was composed entirely of artists' daughters and/or lovers and wives of painters, at least until the nineteenth century. Time and again, their only option to create was through the masculine, and most followed in the artistic path of their father or lover. Before the mid-nineteenth century, few women enjoyed a creative process outside social norms. How would that even have been possible, when girls experienced only limited education? In Europe, women would have to wait until the late nineteenth century to earn the right to enroll in academies; and when they did so, it was with several restrictions, such as limited access to life drawing, for example. The United States appeared more forward-thinking, allowing women to draw from the male life model (modestly draped), but in all instances expectations for women were lower, both reflecting and creating the limited opportunities of their futures.

Despite these incremental advances for women, art remained a mental and political space where the immutable masculine continued to reign. Man contains the magical aura of the creator—what we admire as genius—not woman. It was as though woman, whose destiny is to create life, could not create a world from her own imagination, one shaped from material, color, and the invention of forms. As though to do so would be resisting her biological essence, creating an opposition between inner self and external world. It is no accident that many contemporary women creators—recognized and renowned—have made work that explores birth, being, endurance. Niki de Saint Phalle uses pistols to eliminate the very idea of the artist-painter in order to reinvent it; Louise Bourgeois creates a world that we'd like to inhabit; Annette Messager takes us back to childhood, where sorcerers and fairies cavort together. These artists invite us to celebrate the unconscious, to revisit our dreams, to destroy the divide between the real world and the dreamed world. They ease us into a state of extreme receptivity and help us to better understand what we experience deep down, hidden inside ourselves, as if they had clairvoyant powers, as if they were preforming a transference of symbols and signs, sleeping deep in our memory, that they know how to awaken. Are they healers? Witches? They are certainly warriors who have had to cross many lands, who have had to prove they could "make it" while never being satisfied with their achievements.

We think of them as sisters and we admire them as heroines because they managed to disrupt or even put an end to what Virginia Woolf called "the hypnotic power of domination."[2] They succeeded in making sure that men—fathers, brothers, lovers, or husbands—are no longer the only ones to enjoy creative pleasures. They freed us from the confines of the family home, where we have been shut up for millennia.

Indeed, how *does* one leave the family home? As a girl, how do you accept the gift and the desire to create? How do you claim it? Who can you trust with this secret? How do you learn to explore your full potential? How do you give yourself the permission to imagine realms other than the personal? The goddess, the huntress, the sorceress, the hysteric: we have been surrounded by these images of femininity since antiquity. Where do those who create find their strength? Do they reject the centuries of images that have been constructed around our sex? How does one carve out a place between virgin and seductress?

And yet, women painters have existed for millennia. According to Pliny the Elder, it was a woman who first had the idea to paint a wall, and there is evidence that women painters were very successful in ancient Greece: Pliny the Elder mentions Timarete, Irene, Aristarete, Lala of Cyzicus, and Olympia in his *Natural History*, though none of their works survives today. The first depiction of a woman painting appears on a vase in the Torno Collection in Milan. Yet, over the course of an ordinary day, ancient Athenians experienced women as art, not as artists. They saw statues of women keeping watch over cemeteries, gorgon faces with writhing serpent-hair decorating fountains, young girls in flowing robes on temple friezes, helmeted goddesses engraved on drachmas, and women lying in erotic poses on wine cups. They were glorified women, but they were excluded from city life. They were women as non-citizen slaves, as subjects of art, but women as objects, and thought of as such by the community.

It was through work that women had their skills recognized and would ultimately achieve emancipation. Women also began to represent themselves at work and in doing so left us traces of their activities. Let us honor those anonymous women whose work made them artists (though, like all early craftspeople, they were never considered as such), beginning in the Middle Ages with manuscript illumination, then throughout the centuries: all those women who sculpted stone, painted frescos and panels for churches, whose names were not written down in the history of art. Most women who had access to artistic practice were of noble background, and some chose to live in convents, the only alternative to a premature and/or often nonconsensual marriage. Within these convents, they wove, embroidered, created jewelry, made religious objects,

Attributed to the **Leningrad Painter**
The Caputi Hydria
(detail), c. 460–450 BCE. Torno Collection, Milan.

Guda
Homiliary of Guda (detail of an illuminated letter D, including a self-portrait of the illuminator), c. 1250–1300. Universitätsbibliothek Senckenberg, Frankfurt.

copied books, drew plants, invented bestiaries, illuminated manuscripts, and painted frescos. An inventory of these anonymous creations has yet to be undertaken. However, from this immense work, whose creators were destined to be forgotten, emerged a subtle change in the image of women in artistic representations: Eve, the bearer of original sin, was gradually replaced by the image of a woman endowed with reason, who could not be reduced to her physical appearance alone.

The agents of this change were women painters themselves. Through their determination and their choice of subjects, they changed not only the way we might perceive women artists, but also the representation of the eternal feminine. This moment in history began in Italy in the seventeenth century and continued into the nineteenth and twentieth centuries, starting with the few, rare men who allowed and encouraged their daughters, wives, or companions to engage in creative action.

The first women painters to live on in our shared history, albeit with difficulty and most of them only recently, are the daughters of artists. Among them is Artemisia Gentileschi (see pp. 28–29): at a very young age, she showed a gift for art, leading her father, Orazio Gentileschi, to teach her history painting. She demonstrated a mastery of anatomy and depicted heroines in large-format works. She seized power in her paintings, and through her choice of themes and colors, as well as her visions of mythology, she offered a radical reinterpretation of femininity, one that deviated from what many expected from painting: to gawk at women who offered themselves up to the viewer. Artemisia's heroines have powerful bodies, thoughtful poses, and intense gazes. They have agency: we can imagine them thinking and acting. She replaced the female victim with an image of superior female morality. Today, we have become reacquainted with just how well known Artemisia was in Europe. We know she signed her first painting at age nineteen; that at twenty-three she was the first woman to be admitted to the Accademia delle Arti del Disegno, in Florence; that she traveled throughout Europe, where she was fêted by princes; and that she opened a training studio in Naples. Today, it seems barely credible that she should have fallen into a black hole in the history of art and remained there, forgotten, for centuries. It took

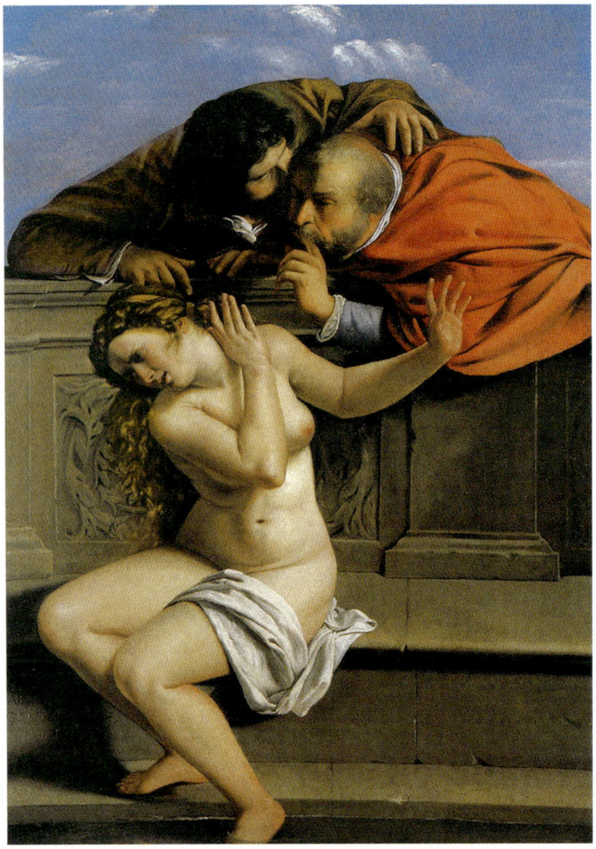

Artemisia Gentileschi *Susanna and the Elders*, 1610. Private collection, Pommersfelden.

the enthusiasm of Caravaggio specialist Roberto Longhi to rediscover, by accident, first her father and then Artemisia, and the fresh perspective of art historian Linda Nochlin to bring her back into the spotlight and spark a genuine enthusiasm for her work.

How many more women remain in the obscurity of storerooms and attics? Many. There are too many women whose names we don't know, or barely know, names forgotten long ago, like Elisabetta Sirani, Properzia de' Rossi, and Lavinia Fontana, who overturned masculine iconographic codes and gave us a different vision of woman. We owe thanks to women painters for giving us new ideas about women. As Leonardo said, "Women must be represented in modest attitudes, their legs close together, their arms closely folded, their heads inclined and somewhat on one side."[3] Centuries later, Angelica Kauffmann (see pp. 32–33) would overturn stereotypes of passive and sentimental femininity. Yet the history of women painters, like the history of women's opportunities in general, has never been driven irreversibly forward toward equal rights. Women painters returned to their inoffensive women's work. Once again they painted still lifes, landscapes, portraits of their children, and many, many bouquets. In fact, if they were tolerated in certain salons, it was no longer as painters but as "florists." That says it all.

In the early days, the women who were able to achieve self-expression and live free from self-imposed limitations often had the support of men in their lives: a father, a husband, a lover. This is not to say that they imitated or copied these men: consider Rosa Bonheur (see pp. 38–39), whose father was an artist, but who created a style of animal painting, a working method, and large-format paintings that have nothing in common with her father's style. In more recent history, fathers increasingly give way to boyfriends, husbands, and lovers. Many couples populate the history of modern art: consider Frida Kahlo (see pp. 80–81) and Diego Rivera; Dorothea Tanning (see pp. 84–85) and Max Ernst; Georgia O'Keeffe (see pp. 62–63) and Alfred Stieglitz; Sophie Taeuber-Arp (see pp. 64–65) and Jean Arp; and Sonia Delaunay (see pp. 58–59) and Robert Delaunay, among many others. Despite having shared projects and demonstrating mutual admiration, in most cases they inhabited independent artistic spaces. Museums and collectors were generally slower to recognize the women's work

Lavinia Fontana
Portrait of a Noblewoman, c. 1580.
National Museum of Women
in the Arts, Washington, D.C.

and did so to a lesser degree, aside from a few exceptions, like the couple Maria Helena Vieira da Silva (see pp. 78–79) and Árpád Szenes.

Must we undertake a "gendered" history of painting to overcome these injustices? Surely not; being a woman gives you neither a way of seeing nor of doing, nor a particular characteristic that is intrinsically "feminine." Neither does being female imply a connection to any mutual school or movement. What might unite Artemisia Gentileschi, Élisabeth Vigée Le Brun (see pp. 34–35), and Rosa Bonheur? Although impressionism was one of the first movements to welcome women, and surrealism often sang their praises, there is no pictorial feminism that shares a set of elements or an aesthetic movement. This does not prevent us from describing Chardin's painting style as "soft," "dulcet," and "feminine," or Corot's as "delicate." It is, however, more complicated to say that Rosa Bonheur's work is "charming" or that Georgia O'Keeffe's is "decorative."

The mind has no gender, said Poullain de la Barre.

Does the act of creating, which supposes transgressing boundaries, require us to think beyond sexual boundaries? Yes. But let us not forget that until the late nineteenth century women were forbidden to view the body. The trailblazers who enrolled in art schools had limited—if any—access to life drawing. Though a few women were tolerated in certain academies in the eighteenth century, they were expected to be "helpers," destined to draw flowers and plants or to copy famous works and make pastel drawings and a few portraits. When they began to exhibit at salons in the nineteenth century, they were hidden away in dark corners, and the prices their works fetched were nothing short of ridiculous. In any case, these women who created were considered somehow earthbound, without imaginative flair. Some had enough talent to dabble in floral compositions or touching paintings of their offspring, but it was a hobby, a distraction—like piano lessons or flower arranging. Women were not yet fully fledged citizens; at this time they were legally dependent on their husbands and (apart from in New Zealand) they would not have the right to vote until the twentieth century. Those who creaked open the doors to art school did so not as a hobby, but with the intention of learning just like their male peers.

In the nineteenth-century United States, the Pennsylvania Academy of the Fine Arts was at the vanguard of women's opportunities, allowing women to attend a ladies' life class (with women models only) in 1868 and, later, classes with draped male models. In France, women would have to wait until 1897 for the right to enroll at the École des Beaux-Arts in Paris; but even then, they only had access at specific times and were not allowed to attend classes or interact with men. In 1900, they gained the right to have their own studios, and in 1903 to enter the Prix de Rome. In the United Kingdom, the Royal Academy of Arts, established in London in 1768, numbered two women—Angelica Kauffman and Mary Moser—among its thirty-four founder members, but women would have to wait until the twentieth century for a single woman to be elected to the Academy again. How can one's full potential be achieved without access to a

Berthe Morisot
Eugène Manet and His Daughter in the Garden, 1881.
Musée Marmottan Monet, Paris.

complete education? Art is created, of course, but it is also learned, and momentum grew across Europe, where Natalia Goncharova (see pp. 54–55) and Sonia Delaunay symbolized this burst of avant-garde energy: women intended to be professional artists and would no longer tolerate being confined to the status of amateurs. They flocked to Paris to enroll in schools and academies and rent studios. Some of them joined movements, such as Berthe Morisot (see pp. 40–41) and Mary Cassatt (see pp. 42–43). Others developed collective ways of working, like Marie Bashkirtseff (see pp. 46–47), who paid homage in a painting to the young women who, like her, successfully entered the studio. Despite these new signs of freedom, the commitment of these women was not readily accepted by dealers, who considered their art a temporary pastime while they waited for marriage. Rosa Bonheur rejected such a future outright and dressed as a man, seeking to exercise her profession freely.

Some women, by subverting the imaginary and abandoning the idea of reproducing reality, opened whole new fields and finally earned recognition: when Sonia Delaunay painted her electric prisms in 1914, she invented a form of abstraction, giving painting an existence beyond the figurative. Borrowing from primitive, popular, and folk art, using fabric and furniture, she theorized and politicized what it means to be an artist: art must exist everywhere and speak to everyone. With her 1920 *Dada Head*, Sophie Taeuber-Arp created a woman-trunk with a fragmented face, freed herself from an idea of art that she judged “pretentious,” and went on to rethink the space in paintings as surfaces to be constructed, that could be divided into squares or rectangles.

Art no longer had to be figurative; it certainly didn’t have to be beautiful. These visionary women—Maria Benz, Meret Oppenheim (see pp. 88–89), Claude Cahun (see pp. 68–69), and Germaine Dulac in Paris, Frida Kahlo in Mexico, Toyen (see pp. 76–77) in Czechoslovakia, and many others—combined different materials, imagined radical works, created unidentifiable objects, and shifted the imaginary fields of our interpretation of art. Perle Fine, Shirley Jaffe (see pp. 96–97), Joan Mitchell (see pp. 98–99): each, in her own way, broke with all notions of realism and invented her own artistic world by creating new forms.

Aurélie Nemours
Tondo II, 1982.
Centre Georges-Pompidou –
Musée National d'Art Moderne, Paris.

Each one of them deserves to be internationally recognized for her boldness. So why is there still so much silence and invisibility?

"It is fatal for anyone who writes to think of their sex. It is fatal to be a man or woman pure and simple; one must be woman-manly, or man-womanly."[4] Virginia Woolf was right: women are just as capable of creating as men. It remains for society to accept the "masculinity" of their intelligence and allow them to get to work.

Gender theory, articulated by Judith Butler in the late 1980s, was preceded by many works by women who shaped their lives to avoid being reduced to their biological sex, and who forged a completely new identity, something between the virile Amazon and the effeminate dandy. Consider Romaine Brooks, Tamara de Lempicka (see pp. 72–73), and Gerda Wegener. Self-creation, metamorphosis, and sidestepping categorization according to biological sex all heralded a period in art, inaugurated in the 1930s, when the body would take on considerable importance: cross-dressing, existing as multitudes, creating fictional people—muddying the waters entirely. This approach continues today with Cindy Sherman (see pp. 138–39), Marina Abramović (see pp. 122–23), Sophie Calle (see pp. 134–35), and Nan Goldin (see pp. 132–33), and many others.

Yet it is impossible to categorize their work by school or movement. Each woman has her own personality and cannot and does not want to be confined to a definition. So it's each woman for herself? Joan Mitchell put it modestly: "Neither woman nor man, neither old nor young."[5] A painter, just a painter. Neither abstract expressionist nor postimpressionist. Joan Mitchell, who views the desire to invent as a masculine obsession, simply claims a right to paint, only to paint, and to continue to paint. There are many women like Joan Mitchell and Judit Reigl (see pp. 94–95) who ask for nothing, if only to spend their lives, to their very last breath, painting, not out of a need to demonstrate anything, but simply in order to live. This may also be why they achieve recognition late—if at all. Louise Bourgeois waited until 1982—she was born in 1911—for her first retrospective show at MoMA in New York. In 2018, Léa Lublin was honored at the Centro Andaluz

Romaine Brooks
Self-Portrait, 1923.
Smithsonian American Art Museum, Washington, D.C.

de Arte Contemporáneo in Seville, nearly twenty years after her death, while Paula Rego (see pp. 110–11), an incredibly visionary and powerful artist, enjoyed a retrospective at the Musée de l'Orangerie in Paris in 2019.

Do women artists have to wait for old age—Paula Rego was born in 1935—to gain recognition? Does the "double burden" still exist for female artists?

There are more women than men in art schools today, and an increasing number of curators and gallery owners are women. Major cultural institutions are contributing to changing our perspective, too, with exhibitions that not only feature more women artists, but that also seek to redefine the traditional story of art. This is long overdue: in the first editions of the "bibles" of art history—H.W. Janson's *History of Art* or E. H. Gombrich's *Story of Art*—not a single woman was featured. Revised editions are not much better. There are indications, however, that recognition, though slow to come, is growing. The world's leading museums are eager to show retrospectives of major artists like Paula Rego (not only at the Musée de l'Orangerie but also Tate Modern in London), Judy Chicago (at Miami's Institute of Contemporary Art), or Louise Bourgeois in both Europe and the United States. Etel Adnan (see pp. 100–101) has enjoyed late but magnificent success, while the UK's Turner Prize has, since 2013, been awarded to four women artists, including Lubaina Himid in 2017—the first Black female recipient of the prestigious art award. And that doesn't even include the new generation of women artists from France, Austria, Ireland, and the UK chosen to represent their respective countries at the Venice Biennale in 2019.

However, acknowledgment remains too timid and too careful. Who are the truly famous women artists and where are they? In how many major museums can their work be found? Museums are full of Picasso, Matisse, Miró—and we're not complaining—but despite their successes, artists such as Niki de Saint

Jenny Holzer
Untitled.
Installation at the Solomon R. Guggenheim Museum, New York, December 12, 1989 to February 25, 1990.

Elizabeth Catlett
Sharecropper,
1952, printed in 1970.
Museum of Modern
Art, New York.

Phalle and Louise Bourgeois are still considered exceptions in the history of art. And then there's the rapid but seemingly inevitable transformation of museums into cultural factories, where the already famous and spectacular are exhibited because they guarantee sell-out shows—what place do women artists have there? Some things are certain: women will no longer be prevented from creating as they were in the past; gender stereotypes—although they haven't disappeared—are continually changing, and approaches to the body taken by these living artists enable us to think about the world differently. That may be what is changing: we recognize the need for so much of what these artists give us. More than ever, through the emotions, reflections, and thoughts their creations provoke in us, they are the watchwomen for our unconscious, activists for our imaginations, and the unwitting messengers of our wildest desires.

1. John Stuart Mill, *The Subjection of Woman* (London: Longmans, Green, Reader & Dyer, 1869), p. 23.
2. Virginia Woolf, *Three Guineas* (London: The Hogarth Press, 1938).
3. Leonardo da Vinci, "The Practice of Painting," in *The Complete Notebooks of Leonardo Da Vinci*, p. 583.
4. Virginia Woolf, *A Room of One's Own* (London: The Hogarth Press, 1929), p. 87.
5. Catherine Gonnard and Élisabeth Lebovici, *Femmes/artistes, artistes femmes: Paris, de 1880 à nos jours* (Paris: Éditions Hazan, 2007), p. 424.

p. 25
Sonia Delaunay
Finnish Woman, 1908.
The Israel Museum, Jerusalem.

THE ARTISTS

Sofonisba Anguissola

(c. 1535–1625)

Sofonisba Anguissola transgressed many taboos surrounding her gender and status as a noblewoman of Cremona to become one of the first renowned female artists in history. Named after a particularly well-educated Carthaginian queen, she received a liberal education from a young age: she studied music, as was usual for a young noblewoman, but also literature and science—traditionally masculine fields—and, even more surprisingly, painting, which the aristocracy did not consider particularly respectable.

The talented Anguissola soon drew the attention of the greatest artists of the day: in 1554, she received advice and encouragement from Michelangelo and attracted the praise of the first Renaissance art critic, Giorgio Vasari, who contributed to her renown. For two decades, she made the Spanish court her preferred subject, after becoming lady-in-waiting to Elizabeth of Valois in 1559. It was only upon her return to Italy, after gaining much experience but mourning the death of the queen, as well as that of her father, and her first husband, that Anguissola dared to take up religious paintings, examining family intimacy with unprecedented attention in her paintings of the Virgin and Child or the Holy Family.

Though Anguissola mainly undertook self-portraits and portraits for reasons of propriety, they are nonetheless powerful demonstrations of her aesthetic ambition. *Portrait of the Artist's Sisters Playing Chess* (1555)—a game whose mastery symbolizes the siblings' education—is based on meticulous composition: the mischief in the subjects' eyes and the eloquent body language are combined with details of their grooming, set against a virtuoso landscape, which all attest to her painterly ambitions. The expressive faces and the familial closeness they convey was unusual for the time: it wasn't until the seventeenth century that genre scenes were developed and painters began to explore facial expression with more regularity. And Vasari, overturning the traditional stereotype of the virile, creative artist, pronounced, "But, if women know so well how to make living men, what marvel is it that those who wish are also so well able to make them in painting?"[1]

1. Giorgio Vasari, *Lives of the Most Eminent Painters, Artists and Architects*, trans. Gaston du C. Devere. Vol. 8 (London: Macmillan and Co. Ltd. and the Medici Society, Ltd., 1914), p. 48.

Self-Portrait at the Easel, 1556.
Muzeum Zamek, Łańcut.

Portrait of the Artist's Sisters Playing Chess, 1555.
Muzeum Narodowe, Poznań.

Artemisia **Gentileschi**

(1593–c. 1652)

Like many women born prior to the nineteenth century, Artemisia Gentileschi discovered painting through her father, a student of Caravaggio. Sensing a precocious talent, he taught her the secrets of his art, his recipes, and anatomy. In 1611 Artemisia Gentileschi was raped by a friend of the family; not long after she left Rome as a newly wed to settle in Florence for the winter of 1612–13. There, she quickly earned a reputation as a talented artist and became the first woman to enter the renowned Accademia delle Arti del Disegno. As her success grew, commissions poured in from across Italy and the European courts. She lived in Milan, London, and Naples, during a time when it was rare for women to work independently. Unlike Sofonisba Anguissola (pp. 26–27), who was limited to portraits and religious paintings because of her aristocratic background, Gentileschi had the opportunity to tackle a much broader and more daring range of subjects: mythological and biblical motifs, still lifes and portraits, all carried out in large-format compositions that also provided the artist with a means to demonstrate the full extent of her virtuoso talent.

Gentileschi was influenced by Caravaggio and painted works depicting a violence that was at times interpreted as purely personal and over-analyzed as representing the trauma she experienced as a young woman. However, her preference for powerful or virtuous heroines like Jael, Susanna, or Lucretia, which her patrons and collectors also appreciated, was real. She was particularly fond of Judith—the biblical figure who saved her people from the Assyrian invasion by decapitating Holofernes, the general of the enemy army—who became a symbol of the Catholic Church's victory over the Reformation. In this version, set in Holofernes's tent, Judith, her bloody sword in hand, appears to bid her servant Abra to be still and silent; the head of the soldier lies at their feet. While chiaroscuro serves to emphasize the elements of still life the artist so loved, here it especially contributes to underscoring the drama of the scene and endows these female characters with a remarkable presence.

Self-Portrait as the Allegory of Painting, c. 1638–39.
The Royal Collection, London.

Judith and Her Maidservant, c. 1625–27.
The Detroit Institute of Arts, Detroit, MI.

Mary **Beale**

(1633–1699)

Justice must be done for Mary Beale: though largely unknown to today's readers, she was the first female professional portrait painter in England, able to support her family through her painting. Though little is known about her education, it is quite likely that her father, a member of the Painters' Guild, taught her the basics of drawing. Her husband, Charles Beale, a hobby painter, specialized in mixing and making pigments, which he commercialized. The couple was friends with Peter Lely, a highly esteemed court painter and portrait artist, who lavished advice and encouragement upon the young woman. As her reputation grew, she was soon receiving many commissions, notably from the London middle classes, who were enthusiastic about portraits: merchants, doctors, politicians, scientists, and their wives, and clergy all willingly sat for her.

Mary Beale's studio in central London became the heart of the family business: Charles, assisted by their two children, among others, oversaw the preparation of colors and canvases as Mary undertook the portraits. This inverted division of labor—in an environment where women and girls traditionally played the role of assistant—enabled Mary Beale to attain the new status of professional artist while protecting her reputation as a respectable woman. Her *Self-Portrait*, painted around 1666, reflects this unique position. Dressed in a silk gown with delicate folds, she depicted herself as a painter—her palette in hand—but also as a mother, suggested by the sketch of a double portrait of her sons. Though Charles Beale does not appear in the painting, his presence is implicitly felt through his children and, no less symbolically, the delicate shades of pigment which he likely prepared. In an essay on friendship, Mary Beale defended marital equality; her success lies in this ideal she shared with a spouse who seemed to care little for convention.

Self-Portrait, c. 1666.
National Portrait Gallery, London.

Angelica **Kauffmann**

(1741–1807)

Like Artemisia Gentileschi (pp. 28–29) and Mary Beale (pp. 30–31), Angelica Kauffmann learned to paint from her father, the Austrian artist Joseph Kauffmann. She received an extensive education, studying languages with her mother, as well as music. But it was a precocious talent for painting that earned her recognition early on. During a stay in Italy, she was elected to the Accademia di San Luca in Rome, where women could be recognized, despite being unable to attend classes. She then settled in London, where her masterly style won over the royal family and the aristocracy. She was so successful that in 1768, with the consent of George III, she became one of the thirty-six founding members of the Royal Academy of Arts, along with just one other woman, Mary Moser.

After fifteen years in the British capital, Angelica Kauffmann returned to Italy. She executed portraits of the king and queen of Naples and received a commission from Emperor Joseph II for history painting, the most highly regarded pictorial genre at the time. In their house on the Pincian Hill in Rome, she and her husband, the painter Antonio Zucchi, hosted the great minds of their time, including Johann Wolfgang von Goethe, Johann Gottfried von Herder, and their friend Anna Amalia of Brunswick, duchess of Saxe-Weimar.

After her death, art historians lost interest in Kauffmann, although in her day she had been the most famous artist in Europe. Her work and its analysis had been overshadowed by a fascination with her personal life, romanticized countless times, and focusing instead on themes of freedom, fame, or suspected lovers. Nevertheless, a painting like *Self-Portrait of the Artist Hesitating between the Arts of Music*

and Painting reveals more than the fleeting glories of fame. Revisiting the decisive choice she was forced to make as a young girl between a career as a painter or a singer—the second was considered less respectable—she transposed the masculine iconography of "the Choice of Hercules"—the theme of the virtuous hero being very fashionable at the time—and elevated the female figure, which she embodied herself, to a similar level of nobleness.

Self-Portrait of the Artist Hesitating between the Arts of Music and Painting, 1791.
National Trust, Nostell Priory, West Yorkshire.

Élisabeth Louise **Vigée Le Brun**

(1755–1842)

The incredible recognition Élisabeth Louise Vigée Le Brun enjoys today is equal to her reputation under the Ancien Régime. The daughter of a pastel artist, she took a keen interest in painting as a child. After the death of her father, she worked in several studios, where she gained a confident mastery of portraiture. She married an art dealer, who was also a member of the Académie de Saint-Luc in Paris, and she used her connections to find commissions and support, to remarkable success: she became Marie Antoinette's official painter in 1778. Indeed, it was the queen's support that enabled her, in 1783, to enter the limited circle of women admitted to the Académie Royale de Peinture et de Sculpture. It was the ultimate recognition. But the French Revolution rendered this institutional acknowledgement dangerous and forced her into exile, first in Italy, then Russia, and finally Great Britain, where her style, considered typically French, was greatly admired. She returned to France permanently in 1802, and continued to receive prestigious commissions, while also working on her memoir, a unique record of the life of a female artist.

Vigée Le Brun's fame rested in large part on her capacity to render the spirit of the times in painting. Though her delicate aesthetic, which included an attention to fashion and an element of eroticism, presented a flattering portrait of her era, she left her true mark on the history of art in her transcriptions of certain major ideological shifts led by Enlightenment philosophers. In the late eighteenth century, Jean-Jacques Rousseau brought a new perspective to nature, childhood, and maternal love—henceforth perceived as instinctive. Vigée Le Brun endeavored to represent this new sentiment and painted her own affection for her daughter, as in this self-portrait with Julie (*Self-Portrait with Her Daughter, Julie*), a variation commissioned by Count d'Angiviller, general director of the King's Buildings, of a previous painting titled *Maternal Tenderness*. In it, mother and daughter, both wearing fashionable "Greek" outfits, tightly embrace, rendering the viewer an essential witness to their love.

Self-Portrait with Her Daughter, Julie, 1789.
Musée du Louvre, Paris.

Marie-Guillemine **Benoist**

(1768–1826)

Though French women could more easily enter the profession of painting towards the end of the Ancien Régime, most were either daughters or wives of artists—unlike Marie-Guillemine Benoist. Encouraged by her sister Élisabeth to follow an artistic path—now considered a mark of distinction for high-society young women like herself—she trained with Élisabeth Louise Vigée Le Brun (pp. 34–35) and then Jacques Louis David, one of the first male painters in the French capital to open his studio to women. Drawing on family connections and the contacts she made during her training, and through regular participation in the Salon de Paris, Benoist succeeded in pursuing a high-profile professional career, alternating between religious and genre scenes, history painting, and especially portraits. Her marriage to a former advisor to Louis XVI accused of counter-Revolutionary activities was detrimental to her work for a time, but her renown later increased under the Consulate (1799–1804), then the First Empire 1804–15), especially with *Portrait of a Black Woman* (1800), a statement in support of Black emancipation.

When she painted her *Self-Portrait Painting David's Belisarius* in 1786, Benoist was working under the supervision of her master, whose studio she had just entered. Jacques Louis David's *Belisarius Begging for Alms* (1781) is a milestone in the history of art. In it, David laid the foundations of neoclassicism: a cool aesthetic—as opposed to Jean-Honoré Fragonard's light and sensual style—inspired, like his subject, by classical antiquity. With her self-portrait, Benoist swore her fealty to David's style in copying his manifesto-painting, synonymous with renewal, and in her classical vestments. But she also declared her own status as a painter, appearing with brush and palette in hand, striking a subtle balance between submission and self-affirmation, signifying women's new place in the late-eighteenth-century Parisian art scene.

Self-Portrait Painting David's Belisarius, 1786.
Private collection.

Rosa **Bonheur**
(1822–1899)

Today, Rosa Bonheur first and foremost represents a legend—that of the virile woman-artist striding through animal markets and slaughterhouses in pants—one that she in part contributed to herself, as the pioneer of a new kind of marketing strategy. She was a rebellious child, and the only education she would accept were lessons from her father, who was a drawing professor. Passionate about animal art, she first exhibited at the Salon de Paris in 1841, presenting two paintings of rabbits and goats: this was to be the path she would follow henceforth. This specialty, as well as her style—unmoved by the siren song of modernity—brought her great success, but also, after her death, indifference, as her work was quickly overshadowed by the "Rosa Bonheur" legend.

Upon her father's death in 1849, Bonheur took over his position as director at the free school of drawing for young women, a role in which she was greatly appreciated. At the same time, commissions streamed in from Europe and the United States. She was supported by dealers, who took it upon themselves to commercialize her paintings, making them available as engravings. But in 1860, weary of a social scene at odds with her meditative personality, she withdrew to a small village in Seine-et-Marne, outside of Paris, with Nathalie Micas, her most loyal protector, and then a young American, Anna Klumpke, who would later record her memoirs. Despite her unconventional lifestyle, Rosa Bonheur succeeded in making her choices acceptable through the harmonious image she presented of rural life, untouched by social or political upheaval. Appreciated by those in power, she was the first woman to receive the French Legion of Honor in 1865.

Six years before Rosa Bonheur's death, her portrait was painted in her studio by Georges Achille-Fould, who, despite her masculine name (a pseudonym), was a woman. Bonheur appears with brush and palette in hand just as she did in photographs: with short hair, an open gaze, and wearing a simple blouse and her usual pair of pants—for which she had a prefectural authorization for "cross-dressing," as women were forbidden to wear pants at the time. Astonishingly, Achille-Fould asked her model to execute the animal paintings depicted in the studio, bowing to her unrivalled authority in the field.

Georges Achille-Fould and Rosa Bonheur,
Rosa Bonheur in Her Studio, 1893.
Musée des Beaux-Arts, Bordeaux.

Portrait of Berthe Morisot and Her Daughter,
1885. Private collection, Paris.

Berthe **Morisot**
(1841–1895)

Berthe Morisot's work was long dismissed as merely an expression of charming elegance. The fault lay with her time—the late nineteenth century was characterized by intense misogyny towards women artists generally—and with Morisot, specifically, or, more precisely, her talent as a colorist, full of charm. Yet, this girl from a good family—who as a child, along with her sister, asked to take outdoor painting lessons—was much more than that.

In 1860, Berthe Morisot began receiving advice about painting from Camille Corot and started participating in the Salon de Paris four years later. Soon she was involved in the "realist" circles that had formed around Édouard Manet, with whom she cultivated a strong artistic and intellectual relationship; she later married his brother, Eugène. In the early 1870s, she turned away from the official Salon de Paris to exhibit with her impressionist peers Claude Monet, Edgar Degas, and Camille Pissarro, ignoring the scandal provoked by their paintings. She painted landscapes, family scenes, and portraits in an increasingly bold style. Unlike most critics, who saw nothing more than loveliness in her work, the writer Octave Mirbeau astutely observed, "Berthe Morisot is disturbing [and] seems to paint with her nerves on edge, providing a few scanty traces to create complete disquieting evocations."[1] One of her self-portraits with her daughter Julie, carried out in 1885, is striking proof of this. On an unprepared canvas—a rare choice in the nineteenth century—she depicts her own face with precision, while her seven-year-old daughter's is barely sketched. In doing so, she successfully conveys the elusive nature of childhood, at once feverish, fleeting, and mysterious, both literally and figuratively. The rest of the composition leaves hatching and wide brushstrokes visible on the bare canvas. The painting, which the artist considered complete, proved to be extraordinarily alive and suggestive, with an innovative power that few of her contemporaries ever achieved.

1. *La France*, May 21, 1886, cited in *The New Painting*, ed. Charles S. Moffett (Seattle: University of Washington Press, 1986), p. 460.

Child among Staked Roses, 1881.
Private collection.

Mary **Cassatt**

(1844–1926)

The American Mary Cassatt, whose respectable middle-class origins would not have suggested an artistic career, discovered Europe with her parents when she was a child. Disappointed by the Philadelphia Academy of the Fine Arts, which she considered too academic, she succeeded in getting permission to study painting in France, escorted by her very Francophile mother. With her family's financial support, she entered the studio of a fashionable artist, but was again dissatisfied with that education; in the end, she chose to visit only the galleries of the Louvre, where she stubbornly copied the masters. In 1868, she began exhibiting at the Salon de Paris, but the Franco-Prussian War of 1870 forced her to return to the United States for a while, before setting off for Italy and then returning to Paris. There, she eagerly discovered the impressionists, who were newly reunited under the name *Société anonyme des artistes, peintres et graveurs* (Anonymous Association of Painters, Sculptors, and Engravers), and with whom she would exhibit multiple times. She soon became friends with Edgar Degas, who was very impressed with her work.

Mary Cassatt used her synthetic, vibrant style to paint almost exclusively child and female figures—most of them from her circle of friends—captured with a naturalism devoid of sentimentality. *Little Girl in a Blue Armchair* depicts a child of the upper class, not as a miniature adult, as in society paintings, but as an actual little girl next to her dog, who looks as rumpled as she does. The play between the patterns on the armchair and the flat areas of gray on the floor, as well as the restricted palette, create a pictorial space, inspired by Japanese engraving, that almost seems to float. This fondness for synthesis also comes through in her numerous engravings; in them, she enjoyed using positive and negative space to compose around the same themes. In 1893, a large retrospective of her work held at the gallery of impressionist dealer Durand-Ruel was a success, but she was slow to receive recognition in her native country, much to her chagrin. She gradually abandoned painting, preferring to advise American collectors, and to contribute to enriching American walls with numerous old and modern European paintings, from Titian to Manet.

Portrait of Alexander J. Cassatt and His Son, Robert Kelso Cassatt, 1884.
Philadelphia Museum of Art, Philadelphia, PA.

Little Girl in a Blue Armchair, 1878.
National Gallery of Art. Washington, D.C.

Morning Awakening, c. 1877–78.
Kunsthalle, Bremen.

Éva **Gonzalès**
(1847–1883)

The daughter of a successful writer and a musician, Éva Gonzalès studied with the academic portrait artist Charles Chaplin before receiving training from Édouard Manet, becoming his only student. Though Manet significantly influenced her work, the young woman still managed to forge her own path.

Despite being associated with impressionism—she had a habit of painting outdoors and using wide brushstrokes, a keen sense of color, and a preference for "modern" subjects and atmospheric variations—Gonzalès never participated in the group's exhibitions, preferring to present her work at the Salon de Paris, where she attracted the critics' interest. In May 1883, just weeks after giving birth to a son, conceived with her husband, engraver Henri Guérard, she was stricken by an embolism and died. Despite a retrospective organized by Guérard two years after her death, plus a significant sale of her paintings and pastels at the Drouot auction house, her work was partially forgotten until the 1950s, when it was gradually rediscovered.

Morning Awakening summarizes Gonzalès's explorations into representations of everyday life. Though the painting contains an element of sensuality, Gonzalès abandons the erotic dimension traditionally associated with the motif of the woman in bed. Taking her sister Jeanne, with whom she was very close, as a model, she preferred to depict the private space where both the everyday and the miracle of the sunrise are felt. She paid special attention to morning light, which caresses the young woman's round, golden arm and enables her to modulate the large white area formed by the sheets, the curtains, and the shirt, using a combination of yellow, mauve, and green strokes. The nightstand, painted more clearly, is the only element that lends structure to the composition. The artist painted a matching work, *Sleep*, in which the beautiful Jeanne appears, still sleeping.

Édouard Manet,
Éva Gonzalès, 1869–70.
The National Gallery, London.

Marie **Bashkirtseff**

(1858–1884)

Marie Bashkirtseff molded her entire brief existence into a work of art. Born into an aristocratic Russian family, she had a thirst for knowledge, eagerly studying languages, classical and modern literature, music, sculpture, and painting. After a brief stay in Nice, she settled in Paris, where in 1877 she entered the Académie Julian—the École des Beaux-Arts was closed to women at the time. She dramatized her life in her journal, which she began in adolescence (and which she hoped would be published after her death), her letters, her photographic portraits, and her painted self-portraits, revealing a pretty young woman as ambitious as she was talented, as well as brilliant, fickle, incredibly concerned with her self-image, and aware of her own mortality due to recurrent bouts of illness. Possessed of a keen political sense, she also published articles in the feminist paper *La Citoyenne* under the pseudonym Pauline Orell: "what we need," she insisted in the March 6, 1881, edition, "is the chance to work like men and not have to engage in incredible feats to obtain what men simply have. We're asked with an indulgent irony how many major women artists have existed. Hey! Gentlemen, they have existed and that's amazing, considering the enormous difficulties they encounter."

To paint the women's studio at the Académie Julian—located under the eaves, above the men's studio—Bashkirtseff chose a nude session, with a young man posing in the middle of a clutter of easels, sketches, and tubes of paint. The painting, which earned her notice at the Salon de Paris, illustrates the rivalry and emulation that reigned at the academy, through the way the figures eye one another. Proof that her preoccupation with death was ever present, Bashkirtseff depicts herself from the back, dressed in black, with a skeleton suspended overhead. She died of tuberculosis three years later and, in accordance with her wishes, the hundreds of pages of her journal were gradually published, making for a moving portrait of the young artist.

L'Académie Julian, 1881.
Ukrainian Fine Arts Museum, Dnipro.

Camille **Claudel**

(1864–1943)

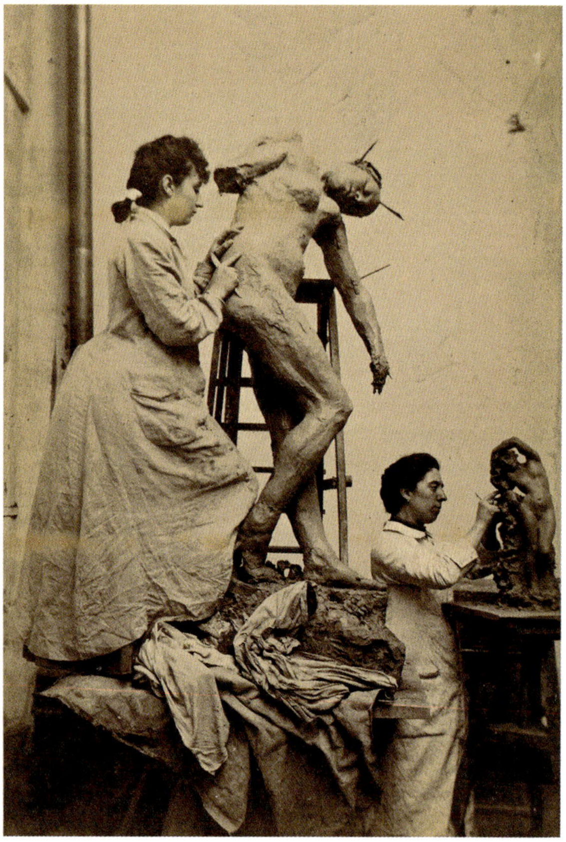

Camille Claudel's turbulent life; her beauty; her passionate affair with Auguste Rodin; her famous brother Paul; insanity, followed by internment in a mental institution; and a pauper's death are the many facets of a legend that, despite bringing her widespread popularity, has largely overshadowed her work.

Born into a middle-class family, Camille Claudel was convinced from a very early age that she would become a sculptor. In 1881, she entered the women's class at the Académie Colarossi in Paris, where she met Auguste Rodin. Soon after, she began practicing in his studio; they developed both a personal and artistic relationship based on artistic exchanges and mutual inspiration. Her aesthetic explorations partially overlapped with Rodin's, evidenced in *Crouching Woman*, c. 1885.

Though Claudel received an honorable mention at the 1888 Salon de Paris, she gradually tried to distance herself from Rodin's work. She turned to more prosaic and less literary themes, seeking more expressiveness, and attracted new supporters, including the writers Octave Mirbeau and Gustave Geffroy. After her split with Rodin, she continued to sculpt for several years in a more decorative style, before ceasing to produce altogether. She was committed to an asylum in 1913, where she spent the last thirty years of her life.

In *The Age of Maturity*, 1899, Claudel sought to represent Fatality—depicted as an old woman—tearing a man away from Youth with one inescapable movement. The composition's imbalance symbolizes the unequal struggle between life and death, while the gnarled appearance of the nude bodies reflects the subject's poignancy. The work, also one of the artist's most well known, provoked much commentary: in retrospect, many chose to see in it her split with Auguste Rodin—separated from the tearful sculptor by his lifelong companion, Rose Beuret—rather than recognizing the universal message, thus participating in the recurring discourse that constantly reduced her work to mere biographical interpretation, overshadowed by the master.

William Elborne, photograph of Camille Claudel and Jessie Lipscomb in their studio on Rue Notre-Dame-des-Champs, Paris, 1887.

The Age of Maturity, 1899.
Musée Rodin, Paris.

Adam and Eve, 1909.
Centre Georges-Pompidou –
Musée National d'Art Moderne, Paris.

Suzanne **Valadon**
(1865–1938)

At the turn of the twentieth century, few women from modest backgrounds managed to have an artistic career the way Suzanne Valadon did. Born in a village in the Limousin region of France, Valadon—her real name was Marie-Clémentine—grew up in Montmartre with her mother, a washerwoman. Self-taught, she began drawing while working as a seamstress and in a florist's. Soon, she was posing for artists, who were intrigued by her irreverence and her rebellious beauty. Moving in artistic circles, she became mistress to Pierre Puvis de Chavannes, August Renoir, then Henri de Toulouse-Lautrec, who dubbed her "Suzanne" in reference to the biblical theme of Susanna and the Elders, a common pictorial pretext for including nude women in a painting. She continued to learn drawing and also began engraving under the tutelage of her painter friends. She then married a stockbroker and for a few years led a quiet life raising her son, Maurice Utrillo, who would also become a painter.

But in 1909, Suzanne Valadon's encounter with André Utter, an apprentice painter barely twenty-three years old, changed her life: she felt an intense passion for the young man, who encouraged her to give up drawing for painting and to acknowledge her preference for the realism of Gustave Courbet, Paul Cézanne's use of color, and, above all, Paul Gauguin's synthetism. She began creating ambitious compositions (landscape, still life, bathers, genre scenes) and many portraits, including groundbreaking depictions of her lover—as Adam under the charm of an Eve–Susanna or as a muscular fisherman—that, for the first time, cast a female gaze on a man's nude and desirable body.

In the Montmartre studio, life revolved around the artist Utter (whom she married in 1914) and Utrillo, who was too ill to live alone. Following World War I, she continued to paint energetically, freeing her palette even more, and exhibited regularly, including at the Salon held annually by the *Société des femmes artistes modernes* (Society of Modern Women Artists). But her final years were spent in solitude: she died suddenly and alone in 1938, after marrying off her son and growing estranged from her husband.

Self-Portrait, 1898.
The Museum of Fine Arts, Houston, TX.

Paula **Modersohn-Becker**
(1876–1907)

Paula Modersohn-Becker was relatively unknown outside of her native Germany, but the recent re-evaluation of the role of women artists in the history of art has brought her international recognition.

Born into conservative German society under Emperor William I, Paula Modersohn-Becker negotiated fiercely for the right to study painting. She attended several private academies in England and Germany, as well as Paris, where she traveled for the first time in 1900, a journey marked by her discovery of Paul Cézanne. After that, she spent time at the Worpswede artists' colony—where "nature" and "rurality" were key concepts—and married one of its founding members, Otto Modersohn. She turned to landscape painting, still life, and portraits, using an increasingly minimalist style reflective of Paul Gauguin's synthetism and the Fayum mummy portraits, and which in some ways foreshadowed the emergence of expressionism. "A great simplicity of form is something marvelous," she wrote in her journal in 1899.[1]

In 1906–7, Modersohn-Becker spent many months in Paris working on nude female figures or children, one of her favorite subjects. She died prematurely from an embolism on November 20, 1907, several days after giving birth.

In *Child with Goldfish Bowl*, the little girl holds—one might say religiously—a plate of fruit; at her feet, the artist has depicted goldfish in a bowl. The body is rendered like a wooden statue and conveys a bold primitivist style. The background, patterned by the leaves of plants, reinforces the composition's decorative dimension. Some of the elements are part of a symbolic language that reappears from one painting to the next. Here, nudity represents a celebration of origins and lemons the proliferation of plants, while the fish's red scales convey growth and life; together they form a sympathetic portrayal of childhood, characteristic of the artist.

1. Quoted in *Voicing Our Visions: Writings by Women Artists*, ed. Mara R. Witzling (New York: Universe, 1991), p. 198.

Self-Portrait with an Amber Necklace II, 1906.
Kunstmuseum, Basel.

Child with Goldfish Bowl, 1906–7.
Neue Pinakothek, Munich.

Natalia **Goncharova**

(1881–1962)

Natalia Goncharova benefited from Russia's liberal attitude towards women's artistic education and was allowed to attend classes at the Moscow School of Painting, Sculpture, and Architecture alongside her companion, Mikhail Larionov. Early on in their careers, they both turned their attention to the cubist explorations of Georges Braque and Pablo Picasso, founded the avant-garde group the Jack of Diamonds, contributed to the futurist movement, and took a keen interest in popular engraving.

In 1914, during a trip to Paris, Goncharova created the sets and costumes for the Ballets Russes, the first in a long series of collaborations. She left Russia definitively in 1915 and settled in France with Larionov. The interwar years were marked by intensive theater work, as well as many forays into illustration, decorative arts, and fashion. Her motivations were not only financial: she also had a desire to break down the barriers between different art forms and destroy bourgeois hierarchies.

After World War II, the couple, who had obtained French nationality, encountered great financial difficulties, but in 1954 a major retrospective around the Ballets Russes sparked the interest of museums and paved the way for institutional acquisitions and many more exhibitions.

In *Cyclist*, Goncharova explores the possibilities of futurism, adapting its features to her own personal style. Hostile to progress and the idea of the domination of humanity by machines, she was nonetheless fascinated by mechanical movement, which in her opinion resembled human movement. In this work, she illustrates the alliance between man and machine—and their mutual shuddering along the cobblestones—against an urban setting symbolized by fragments of posters in the

background. Though she was interested in representing both the energy and the triviality of modern life, formally speaking she was less radical than the Italian futurists, for whom the human figure itself seemed mechanized; however, she cast an infinitely more critical gaze on the technical evolutions that emerged from the Industrial Revolution.

Cyclist, 1913.
The State Russian Museum, Saint Petersburg.

Marie **Laurencin**
(1883–1956)

Marie Laurencin, the illegitimate child of a maid and a politician, turned to easel painting after studying porcelain painting, encouraged by her friends Georges Braque and Francis Picabia. The writer and art patron Pierre Roché purchased her first works, and in 1907 she began exhibiting at Clovis Sagot's gallery. There, she met Pablo Picasso and the whole Bateau-Lavoir clique, including Guillaume Apollinaire, with whom she began a passionate relationship. Influenced by fauvism and cubism, she created many compositions using flat areas of color. In 1914, she married a German baron, acquiring his nationality just weeks before war was declared, which resulted in a long exile in Spain; she painted little during this period.

By the time she returned to France in 1921, her aesthetic had sharpened. Laurencin shaped her models—selected from among bohemian society—into the slender, elegant ideal she is known for to this day. During this period, she began working for the theater and had successful exhibitions in Paris, as well as London and New York, before turning to religion following World War II. If her art was avant-garde, her personal life was even more so, peppered with affairs with men and women alike. Upon her death, she was buried with Guillaume Apollinaire's letters held tightly to her breast.

Similar to Henri Fantin-Latour in his ambitious group portraits, in *Apollinaire and His Friends* Marie Laurencin includes the writer Gertrude Stein, Fernande Olivier—Pablo Picasso's companion, seated to the right of Guillaume Apollinaire—the poet Marguerite Gillot, the critic Maurice Chevrier, and, of course, the artist herself and her dog Fricka. This work celebrates

artistic and intellectual friendship and encapsulates the style Laurencin developed in the early days of cubism; although more mannerist than that of Picasso or Braque, it draws on a similarly earthy color palette. "Mademoiselle Laurencin's art," remarked Apollinaire in 1913, "is tending toward pure arabesque, humanized by an attentive observation of nature."[1]

1. *Apollinaire on Art: Essays and Reviews, 1902–1918*, ed. Leroy C. Breunig, trans. Susan Suleiman (New York: Da Capo Press, 1972), p. 292.

Apollinaire and His Friends (detail), 1909.
Centre Georges-Pompidou –
Musée National d'Art Moderne, Paris.

Electric Prisms, 1914.
Centre Georges-Pompidou –
Musée National d'Art Moderne, Paris.

Sonia **Delaunay**
(1885–1979)

Sonia Delaunay grew up with her maternal uncle in Saint Petersburg before enrolling at the Academy of Fine Arts in Karlsruhe, Germany. She arrived in Paris in 1906, where she discovered the chromatic brilliance of fauvist painting and participated the following year in a group exhibition along with Georges Braque, Pablo Picasso, and André Derain. She was influenced by fauvism and painted portraits in bright colors with loose brushstrokes. In Paris she met the painter Robert Delaunay, a decisive encounter that led to their marriage in 1910. When their first son was born in 1911, she began sewing blankets and dresses that recalled her first "simultaneous" paintings, the result of non-figurative explorations into color and movement undertaken with her husband. During World War I, the couple moved to Spain, where they opened Casa Sonia, an interior design store, in Madrid and began working for the theater.

Upon her return to Paris, Sonia Delaunay continued to paint vibrant, rhythmic paintings as well as to work in the decorative arts, including textile design, illustration, advertising, murals, etc. When Robert died in 1941, she became the custodian of her spouse's work, while promoting their joint role as pioneers in the history of abstraction. By the end of World War II, her reputation had spread worldwide. Her connection with Galerie Denise René brought her into close contact with the latest experiments in abstract art, and major retrospectives hosted by the world's leading museums confirmed her institutional recognition.

Electric Prisms is one of Delaunay's masterpieces. The work, painted shortly after a collaboration with Blaise Cendrars for the illustrated edition of *Prose of the Trans-Siberian*, bears the poet's influence—his name appears at the very center of the composition—and of his texts, which are veritable "mental photographs." Crammed with colored rings that recreate the effects of electric light and its refraction, the work is a monumental and cerebral ode to color, which Delaunay continued to celebrate in her paintings, dresses, and embroidery until her death.

Finnish Woman, 1908.
The Israel Museum, Jerusalem.

Hannah **Höch**

(1889–1978)

The search for a "new" and androgynous woman, free from the tethers of masculine domination, is central to Hannah Höch's artistic explorations; in works like *Das schöne Mädchen* (The Beautiful Girl), she relates each female figure to a mechanical element, in order to clearly illustrate the alienation provoked by the tyranny of beauty.

Born into a middle-class family, Höch attended the School of Applied Arts in Berlin, where she learned painting on glass, calligraphy, and embroidery, practices all considered acceptable by her social environment. This, of course, did not include her encounter with Raoul Hausmann and her subsequent involvement with Dada—she was the movement's only female member in Berlin. While working for a publisher, she experimented with photomontage and collage, at the time avant-garde media. But she also made good use of the disciplines she learned in school, creating compositions out of bits of fabric or lace and sewing patterns to convey her fierce criticism of the misogynist Weimar Republic. In a text on the modern embroiderer ("Die stickende Frau" [The Embroidering Woman], 1919), she entreated women to liberate their creativity and proudly engage in a practice scorned by men.

After the Dada group dissolved, Höch settled in The Hague with her companion, the writer Til Brugman, and participated in the activities of the Dutch Independent Group. Shortly after returning to Germany in the early 1930s, she began to experience pressure from the Nazi authorities, who considered her work degenerate; she would have to wait until the end of World War II to exhibit in Germany. She joined a number of artistic organizations, perhaps to forget the isolation she felt under the Third Reich, and turned to abstraction. She didn't make an overt return to women's issues until the 1960s: once again fighting against a conservative image of women, which this time emerged as Germany society began reconstruction.

Das schöne Mädchen
(The Beautiful Girl), 1919–20.
Private collection.

BMW
HH
1920

Georgia **O'Keeffe**

(1887–1986)

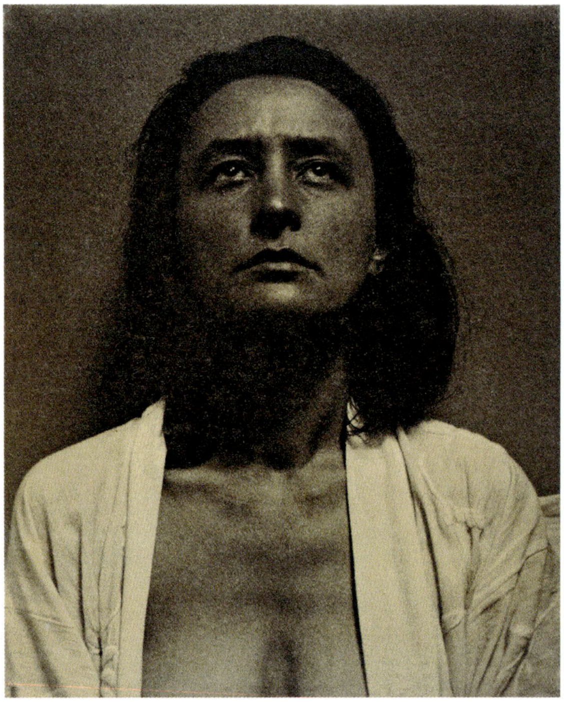

Georgia O'Keeffe was a pioneer of American modern art. As a child, she took many painting and drawing classes, and she would go on to become a professor herself. In 1916, she began a correspondence with the photographer Alfred Stieglitz, a leading figure of the New York avant-garde, who exhibited her works in his gallery. It was the encounter of a lifetime. O'Keeffe was already painting nearly abstract landscapes and soon she would paint her first large-scale flowers, rejecting the sexual interpretations immediately put forth by critics. She gradually began using a more diverse range of motifs, often painted in series: skyscrapers, arid landscapes, the low, rectangular facades of houses in New Mexico, and animal skeletons found in the sand together form an iconography shaped by the American imaginary. In *Cow's Skull: Red, White, and Blue,* a background of blue and red stripes evokes the flag of the United States, while the magnification of a blindingly white cow's skull—its crags and rough surface—is an evocation of the desert she so loved.

O'Keeffe was independent, splitting her time between New York, Lake George—215 miles north of the city—and New Mexico. She exhibited regularly and her reputation grew: in 1946, she was the subject of the first retrospective dedicated to a woman ever held at the prestigious Museum of Modern Art in New York. After Stieglitz's death the same year, she settled permanently in New Mexico, where the telluric landscapes continued to seep into her work, influencing a palette that oscillated between vibrant contrast and softness. In the 1950s, she began traveling around the world—to India, Egypt, Spain, Costa Rica—though she never considered leaving her desert and the immutable visions it offered her. She was nearly one hundred years old when she died in Santa Fe. "I know I cannot paint a flower," she wrote in a letter to William Milliken in 1930, "I cannot paint the sun on the desert on a bright summer morning but maybe in terms of paint color I can convey to you my experience of the flower. . . . Color is one of the great things in the world that makes life worth living."[1]

1. Quoted in Laurie Lisle, *Portrait of an Artist: A Biography of Georgia O'Keeffe* (New York: Washington Square Press, 1981), p. 128.

Alfred Stieglitz,
Georgia O'Keeffe, 1918.
Victoria and Albert Museum, London.

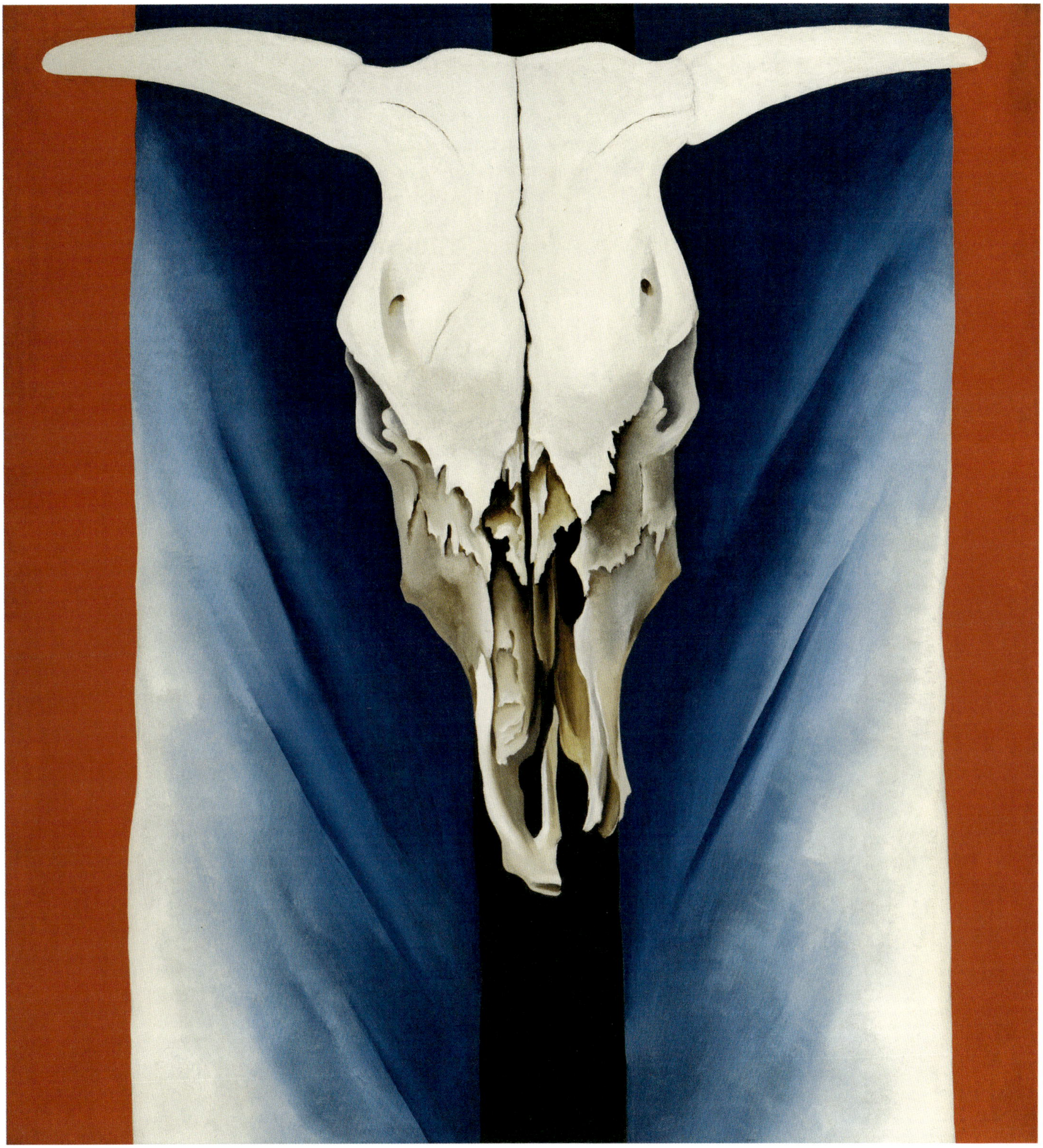

Cow's Skull: Red, White, and Blue, 1931.
The Metropolitan Museum of Art, New York.

Sophie **Taeuber-Arp**

(1889–1943)

Sophie Taeuber became a professor of textile design and embroidery in Zurich after studying applied arts. In 1915, she met the painter Hans Arp, whom she married and with whom she collaborated closely all her life, and participated in the Dada group. She brought a keen sense of color and abstract forms to sculpture, painting, and drawing, while also creating jewelry, handbags, fashion accessories, puppets, and theater sets.

In the 1920s, Taeuber-Arp added another feather to her cap when she created the interior design for several private residences, hotels, and entertainment spaces. She was living in France at the time, where she continued to paint, and soon joined the groups Cercle et Carré and Abstraction-Création, situated at the forefront of non-figurative painting. During World War II, Taeuber-Arp and her husband fled the occupied zone for Grasse. During a trip to Switzerland, she died from carbon monoxide poisoning, leaving Arp unable to work for several years.

In the 1970s, historians re-evaluating women's place in the history of art were troubled by her practice of sewing and embroidery, anxious not to reduce her output to traditional "women's work." Yet, it was through this new and often female-led approach—similar to Sonia Delaunay's (pp. 58–59)—that sought to eliminate the boundaries between fine art and craft, that avant-garde artists overturned the established order in the early twentieth century.

This *Dada Head* in turned wood is an example both of Taeuber-Arp's contribution to the Dadaist goal of making a clean break with artistic conventions and of her effort to deconstruct the entire portrait genre with humor. The facial features blend into geometrized volumes and areas of color that recall the artist's abstract paintings, as well as the tribal-inspired masks she created for the stage, revealing the deep connections between all of these practices.

↗ ***Dada Tapestry, Composition with Triangles, Rectangles, and Circles***, 1916. Centre Georges-Pompidou – Musée National d'Art Moderne, Paris.

→ ***Dada Head***, 1920. Centre Georges-Pompidou – Musée National d'Art Moderne, Paris.

1920
DADA

Marianne **Brandt**

(1893–1983)

Born in Germany to a family of art aficionados, Marianne Brandt began to paint under the influence of the expressionist movement. But in 1923, during an exhibition in Weimar, she discovered the Bauhaus and was so impressed by their work that she destroyed her paintings and decided to enter the school. She attended classes given by Wassily Kandinsky, Paul Klee, and Josef Albers and then, after much perseverance, she entered László Moholy-Nagy's metal workshop; in theory, the directors of the Bauhaus were in favor of women attending the school, but they preferred to see them in less sought-after classes, like embroidery. She took over the workshop in 1928 and successfully negotiated advantageous industry contracts.

At the Bauhaus, Brandt created stunning objects (teapots, ashtrays, lamps, etc.) inspired by cubism and constructivism, which made their mark on the history of modern design. She also practiced photography and made photomontages that scrutinize the status of women in contemporary society. Chinese-American actress Anna May Wong is the central figure in this collage from 1929, in which Brandt examines femininity and exoticism as spectacles of mass production delivered by Hollywood to sate the Western imagination.

In 1929, Marianne Brandt left the Bauhaus for Walter Gropius's architecture and design agency in Berlin, before taking over the design department at the Ruppel Werke company, which specialized in metal. She began painting again, but her professional situation deteriorated under the Third Reich. In hopes of acquiring funding and obtaining the right to exhibit her work, she became a member of the regime's "Department of Culture" (*Reichskulturkammer*), though she was never a card-carrying member of the Nazi Party. After World War II, she was elected to the Dresden Academy of Fine Arts before taking up, albeit modestly, her activities as an independent designer.

In the 1960s and 1970s, the first historical works about the Bauhaus led to a rediscovery of Marianne Brandt, one of the few women to have ever held responsibilities within the legendary institution.

↑ ***Tea Infuser***, 1924.
The Metropolitan Museum of Art, New York.

→ ***Untitled [with Anna May Wong]***, 1929.
Harvard Art Museums, Cambridge, MA.

Claude **Cahun**

(1894–1954)

Claude Cahun's work remained practically unknown during her lifetime, yet it heralded a disruption in genres that rattled the art world in the 1960s and 1970s, when she was rediscovered.

Lucy Schwob, a literature student and niece of the symbolist writer Marcel Schwob, chose the androgynous pseudonym Claude Cahun early on—her companion, the illustrator Suzanne Malherbe, chose the more masculine name Marcel Moore. Cahun began creating photomontages while also writing essays, critiques, and poems for the *Mercure de France*, the *Journal littéraire*, and the gay review *Inversions*, before publishing *Aveux non avenus* (*Disavowals*) in 1930, an autobiographical book she illustrated, prefaced by Pierre Mac Orlan. Self-portraits and portraits of her entourage, reappropriated objects, and landscapes were her preferred photographic motifs. She also had a keen interest in theater and esotericism, was friends with the writers Henri Michaux, André Breton, René Crevel, and Georges Bataille, and participated in surrealist activities.

During World War II, Cahun was engaged in the resistance with Malherbe on the island of Jersey, where they lived. She distributed anti-German tracts, some of them illustrated with photomontages and signed "The Unnamed Solider," which led to the women's arrest in 1944 by the Gestapo. They were given the death sentence, but their punishment was miraculously lifted. Following the Liberation, Claude Cahun's health began to deteriorate. She continued to write, however, and took up photography again, reconnecting with her surrealist friends.

This 1929 photomontage encapsulates Claude Cahun's explorations into the question of identity. With a keen interest in transvestitism, she posed variously as a young dandy with a shaved head, an Asian princess, a well-behaved student, and, as seen here, double-exposed and wearing a wig, her cheeks extravagantly rouged like a Russian doll. "Under this mask is another mask; I will never be done removing all these faces," she wrote, considering herself to belong to a third gender.[1] While her skill for metamorphosis may have been rooted in an intentional narcissism, it remained an extraordinary challenge to social, sexual, and aesthetic conventions, as well as to the dominant bourgeois culture, which Cahun masterfully rejected all her life.

1. *Disavowals* (London: Tate Publishing, 2007), p. 183.

Self-Portrait, 1929.
Centre Georges-Pompidou – Musée National d'Art Moderne, Paris.

Germaine **Krull**

(1897–1985)

Self-Portrait, 1922.
Museum Folkwang, Essen.

Germaine Krull is without doubt one of the most renowned photographers of the early twentieth century. After training in a photography school in Munich, she frequented anarchist circles and absorbed revolutionary ideas, traces of which appear in her engaged approach to art. After opening a studio in Berlin in the early 1920s, she moved to the Netherlands and then to Paris in 1926. Her work straddles reportage and the avant-garde, employing her keen sense of composition to depict modern architecture, factories, and the working class. She also practiced nude and portrait photography, with a preference for well-known female subjects like Sonia Delaunay, the writers Colette and Germaine Beaumont, the comedian Berthe Bovy, and the singer Damia. Her images appeared in many reviews, and she published monographic works, something few photographers did at the time. After joining the Free French during World War II, she covered the conflict as a war correspondent, then settled in Thailand and India where, using photography, she fought for the preservation of Buddhist heritage and Tibetans in exile.

In *Rue Auber, Paris,* Krull chose to take the photo from an unusual angle overlooking the street, behind a store sign. The lettering and its metal frame fill the foreground and form an abstract screen that gives this Parisian street scene a decidedly modernist aspect. The work can be compared to *Métal,* a portfolio Krull published around 1928, composed of a series of photographs of architecture and metallic objects; the work confirmed Krull's definitive role in avant-garde history during the interwar years.

Rue Auber, Paris, c. 1928.
Museum of Modern Art, New York.

Tamara **de Lempicka**

(1898–1980)

Tamara de Lempicka grew up in a wealthy and cosmopolitan environment. She learned painting at the Academy of Fine Arts in Saint Petersburg, then at the Académie de la Grande Chaumière and the Académie Ranson in Paris, where she moved with her husband and their daughter to flee the Bolshevik Revolution. During her exile, she chose to be a painter to support herself financially, while her husband firmly refused to work.

De Lempicka developed a style blending references to Italian Renaissance painting and post-cubist geometrization of forms, one that was in tune with the art deco aesthetic then in fashion. She was soon exhibiting across Europe and earned success with her worldly portraits, large-scale nudes, and New York landscapes. But in the early 1930s, a serious mystical crisis, combined with a deep depression during an economic recession, provoked a radical change in her work. Casting aside light-hearted subjects, she turned to representing religious motifs and peasants, and strove to give her work a more classical aspect. In 1939, she moved to the United States, where she mostly painted busts of young girls and still lifes. After World War II, she divided her time between the United States and Europe, and experimented with abstraction, while also copying some of her own paintings from the 1930s. Her early work gained new recognition in the 1970s, when art deco was rediscovered, and she was viewed as one of the movement's rare female icons.

In this portrait, the Duchess de La Salle, known for her beauty, strikes a confident pose in riding boots, modeling for her friend as a modern Amazon. Architectural drapery structures the composition, morphing into an urban landscape in the lower part of the painting where it forms a kind of backdrop for the figure. The portrait, typical of De Lempicka's style, depicts a strong and independent woman. She painted it at the very moment when a new feminine ideal based on a strong desire for emancipation was emerging in Paris: the garçonne.

Portrait of the Duchess de La Salle, 1925.
Private collection.

Alice **Neel**

(1900–1984)

Trained at the Philadelphia School of Design for Women, Alice Neel moved to Havana in 1925, before moving to New York two years later. Painting became a focus early on. Paying remarkable attention to her models' bodies—whether they were newborns, strapping young men, or tired nannies—she explored the boundaries between the public and private realms. She attached great importance to overall appearance, from the position of a foot to the folds of clothing, or to makeup, etc.—in other words, to a multitude of details with considerable expressive power.

In New York she lived in the impoverished neighborhood of Spanish Harlem, where she confronted poverty daily—her own and that of her neighbors. Her political engagement with communism is palpable in *T. B. Harlem* (1940), a portrait of her brother-in-law, who suffered from tuberculosis, and in *The Spanish Family* (1943). She was influenced by Diego Rivera and artists belonging to the Neue Sachlichkeit (New Objectivity), such as Max Beckmann and Otto Dix, for whom social critique was imperative.

At the turn of the 1950s, Neel moved into a sunny apartment on the Upper West Side, a cosmopolitan neighborhood near the University of Columbia popular with the New York bohemian crowd. At this point, her color palette became sharper, her interiors more luminous, and her brushwork freer. She rubbed shoulders with art historians, critics, transvestites (*Jackie Curtis and Ritta Redd,* 1970), and artists (*Andy Warhol,* 1970), who sat for her by turns. In *The Family (John Gruen, Jane Wilson and Julia),* she depicts the photographer John Gruen (1926–2016), his wife, the painter Jane Wilson (1924–2015), and their daughter, Julia (born in 1958), in a subtle composition, where the models' personalities and their misgivings about being painted are reflected with honesty. Alice Neel's portraits of pregnant women and mothers (*Ginny and Elizabeth,* 1975) demonstrate her steadfast interest in the status of women, and, towards the end of her life, caught the attention of young feminists. Though she did not agree with the younger generation's radical approach, she nevertheless agreed to be one of their role models, like a pioneer.

Franck Leonardo,
photograph of Alice Neel,
October 20, 1980.

The Family (John Gruen, Jane Wilson and Julia), 1970.
Museum of Fine Arts, Houston, TX.

Toyen
(1902–1980)

Trained at the School of Decorative Arts in Prague, Marie Čermínová adopted the pseudonym Toyen—likely derived from the French word *citoyen* meaning citizen—refusing to be seen only for her female identity. She brought this political awareness to the anarchist group Devětsil, which she joined with the writer Karel Teige and her closest partner, the painter Jindřich Štyrský. Like Natalia Goncharova (pp. 54–55) in Russia, she was interested in both the developments taking place in contemporary art and in popular engraving. She traveled to Paris in 1925 with Štyrský, where they founded artificialism, a sort of third way between abstraction and surrealism that gave full rein to imagination and memory. Still, she took an interest in André Breton's group and, in 1934 in Prague, rallied together the Czech surrealist group, which remained very active until 1938, when the Nazi Party became too great a threat. At this time, her often erotic painting became haunted by mysterious figures.

Toyen fled Czechoslovakia after World War II and settled once again in Paris, where she exhibited regularly and continued to participate in surrealist activities. She had always been interested in illustration, and in the 1960s she created book-objects, but, after the surrealist movement broke up in 1969, she gradually withdrew from society, before passing away in her adoptive city in 1980.

When Toyen painted *Le Devenir de la liberté* (The Gradual Growth of Freedom) in 1946, she was particularly attached to the metamorphoses and interplay between the real and illusionary. Some saw in this figure made of peapods the influence of mannerist artist Giuseppe Arcimboldo or the traditional costumes made of vegetation worn by the Dogon people of Mali, which were reproduced in the surrealist review *Minotaure*. As André Breton wrote of this painting and several others painted just after the war: "An optimism based on the theme of eternal germination makes its break-through."[1]

1. *Surrealism and Painting* (New York: Harper & Row, 1972), p. 213.

Le Devenir de la liberté
(The Gradual Growth of Freedom), 1946.
Private collection.

Maria Helena **Vieira da Silva**

(1908–1992)

Born in Lisbon and raised in a cultured environment, Maria Helena Vieira da Silva studied painting and drawing from an early age, before attending the Académie de la Grande Chaumière in Paris. Initially influenced by cubism, she gradually developed her own personal artistic language, recomposing space by combining large dominant lines and small fragmented squares of color in a combination that distorts form. Many critics saw in this style the traces of her native city and of its tangled architecture, others saw *azulejos*, the traditional Portuguese square glazed tiles. In *The Chess Game*, similar to Paul Cézanne's *The Card Players*—a work Vieira da Silva liked very much—the chessboard seems to overwhelm the room, as though illustrating the game's grip on the players' mental space. "I had an idea of what I wanted to do," explains the artist, "but there you have it—I made little squares and the players' appearance was unavoidable. They came from the background, from behind, and I was pleased. It wasn't what I had wanted, it wasn't what I had expected, but for once I was pleased because the painting seemed bigger, vaster than what I had imagined."

During World War II, Vieira da Silva fled to Brazil with her husband, the painter Árpád Szenes. Upon her return, she benefited from Parisians' enthusiasm for lyrical abstraction, with which her work was associated, despite being grounded firmly in the real. She exhibited regularly, took up engraving, stained glass, and tapestry, while also working for the theater and illustrating books. She took French citizenship in 1956

and in 1966 she became the first woman to receive the Grand Prix National des Arts, recently created by André Malraux. After her husband passed away in 1985, white became more important in Vieira da Silva's work, appearing as a brilliant eruption at the heart of the canvas.

The Chess Game, 1943.
Centre Georges-Pompidou –
Musée National d'Art Moderne, Paris.

Frida Kahlo

(1907–1954)

Kahlo was born to a Mexican mother and a German photographer father. As a child she suffered from polio, which meant she started school later than her peers, but she went on to attend the renowned National Preparatory School in Mexico City—she was one of the few girls accepted into the institution—with the aim of becoming a doctor. In 1925, her dreams of becoming a doctor ended when she was involved in a serious streetcar accident; she would suffer the painful consequences of the accident her entire life. She spent her convalescence drawing, but after two years of bed rest she joined the Mexican Communist Party and dreamed of an emancipated life. Her many self-portraits, influenced by popular art, represented her life, as well as her "Mexicanness"—expressed through her hair or her clothing—and her status as a woman in society, creating a vision that surpassed the autobiographical. In 1929 she married the mural artist Diego Rivera and the couple lived for several years in the United States, where Rivera received large commissions. Her time spent there inspired in Kahlo a growing rejection of that country, which in turn fed her nationalism (*Self-Portrait on the Border Between Mexico and the United States of America*). In the 1930s, the two artists were in close contact with André Breton and his wife Jacqueline Lamba. After a successful exhibition at the Julien Levy Gallery in Paris in 1939, Kahlo traveled to the French capital. The trip was not a success: she hated the city as much for its food as for what she considered the pointless discussions of its intellectuals, and she refused to be affiliated with surrealism. In the 1940s, her health began to deteriorate and, after undergoing several operations, each more disabling than the last, she died in July 1954.

In *Fulang-Chang and I*, Frida Kahlo depicts herself against a background of lush vegetation, as a Mexican Madonna, not with a child, but with one of her little domesticated spider monkeys. This self-portrait, in which a pink satin ribbon winds through her hair and the animal's fur, inspired Breton to say that Kahlo's art was "like a ribbon around a bomb."[1] When Kahlo gave the painting to her friend Mary Sklar, she attached a mirror in an identical frame so the image of the two women would be united. This surprisingly modern gesture allows every viewer to enter the work for themselves.

1. "The Talk of the Town," *The New Yorker*, Nov. 12, 1938.

Fulang-Chang and I, 1937.
Museum of Modern Art, New York.

Self-Portrait on the Border Between Mexico and the United States of America, 1932.
Manuel Reyero Collection, New York.

Dora **Maar**

(1907–1997)

Even today, Dora Maar's work remains overshadowed by her relationship with Pablo Picasso. To reduce her to the seductive role of muse is to forget that she actually collaborated with the Spanish artist, but more importantly that she was a committed photographer and a sensitive painter.

Raised in Argentina by Franco-Croatian parents, Henriette Theodora Markovitch took up painting upon her return to France in 1926, then photography with Emmanuel Sougez. She opened a photography studio under the pseudonym Dora Maar and received her first commissions for the newspaper press and advertising, with her austere fashion, nude, and reportage photographs appearing in numerous publications. Her involvement with surrealist circles in the mid-1930s paved the way for more experiments—montage, diversion, grattage, double exposure—centered around the imaginary. In *Untitled (Hand and Shell)*, she depicts an elegant female hand, like a hermit crab, emerging from a shell under a stormy sky; the resulting image is strangely troubling.

At the same time, Dora Maar became involved with the far left, joining the Union of Intellectuals against Fascism, the Association of Revolutionary Writers and Artists, and Georges Bataille's group, Contre-Attaque (Counter-Attack). It was during this period that she met Picasso; it was the beginning of a relationship as turbulent as it was fruitful. Maar became his model. She immortalized the different stages of *Guernica*—Picasso's masterpiece about the Spanish Civil War—and together they undertook astonishing photographic experiments. But their relationship deteriorated during World War II and they eventually separated. Dora Maar lived in growing solitude between Paris and Ménerbes, in the Vaucluse region. She continued photography, as well as painting, which she had taken up several years earlier, trying her hand at abstraction before making a number of paintings of the Lubéron landscape. For many years, her work was virtually obscured by her association with Picasso. It was rediscovered after her death when her studio was sold, several works were published, and two museum exhibitions were held, in Marseille and Paris.

Untitled (Hand and Shell), 1934.
Centre Georges-Pompidou – Musée National d'Art Moderne, Paris.

Dorothea **Tanning**

(1910–2012)

Dorothea Tanning's contribution to postwar surrealism has often been overshadowed by the work of her husband, Max Ernst. And yet her chimeras, headless women, mysterious children, and strange beasts in unreal architectural structures form a remarkably rich artistic world.

Born in Illinois, Tanning was self-taught, preferring to learn from visiting the Chicago Art Institute to classes given at the Chicago Academy of Fine Art, which she attended for a mere three weeks—and rightly so. In 1936, while working as a commercial illustrator in New York, she went to the exhibition *Fantastic Art, Dada and Surrealism* at the Museum of Modern Art, which shocked her aesthetically and had a decisive influence on her work. She couldn't have known that six years later she would meet some of the surrealists who had fled World War II for the United States, including Max Ernst. His wife at the time, gallerist Peggy Guggenheim, had tasked him with finding women artists for an upcoming exhibition: he was very impressed with *Birthday*, a self-portrait by Tanning. In this painting, which she described as a talisman, she introduces herself to the world. In a dreamlike atmosphere, colored with a unique eroticism, she declares her affiliation with surrealism loud and clear.

Soon inseparable, Tanning and Ernst, her "life companion," moved to Arizona shortly after their meeting, where they painted prolifically, while making regular trips around the United States and to Europe. But during the McCarthy era Ernst, born in Germany, lost his American nationality, which he had acquired several years earlier and the couple moved to France, dividing their time between Paris and Huismes—a small village near Tours—and Provence. In the late 1960s, Tanning renewed her practice and created textile sculptures with sensual, anthropomorphic forms. Following Ernst's death in 1976, she returned to the United States and began to write and draw extensively. Many exhibitions and retrospectives of her work followed. She died in New York at the age of one hundred and one.

Birthday, 1942.
Philadelphia Museum of Art, Philadelphia, PA.

Louise **Bourgeois**

(1911–2010)

Louise Bourgeois was one of the pioneers of postmodernism, and her constantly shifting work resolutely escapes any attempt at classification.

Born in Paris, she studied painting, then ran a painting gallery before following her American husband, Robert Goldwater, to the United States. She gave free rein to the creative impulse of her work, which was founded on an exploration of her unconscious and the images it produced. In the late 1940s, in the series *Femmes-maisons* (Women-Houses), Bourgeois combined two levels of form that were vital to her work: the corporeal and the architectural. Against a domestic backdrop, they serve as a framework for exploring her emotions, her memories of childhood, her stormy relationship with her adulterous father, and the love she felt for her mother, all of which she gave universal significance. During this period, she experimented with sculpture—as well as continuing to draw and paint—before trying her hand at engraving and embroidery, in memory of the hours spent in her parents' tapestry restoration workshop.

Interest for Bourgeois's work grew in the United States, then in Europe. By the 1960s, she was an active member of feminist groups. She explored increasingly sexual motifs, as in the world-famous *Fillette* (Little Girl), an imposing phallus that curiously erases the frontiers between masculine and feminine. She began to play even more with the plasticity of forms and their capacity for metamorphosis. At the turn of the century, she created large-scale installations, which she called "Cells"—*Passage dangereux* (Dangerous Passage), *Precious Liquids*, *Red Room*—worlds independent of the space in which the works were exhibited. During this same period, a new motif—the spider—appeared in Bourgeois's sculptural work, though it had been present in her drawings for the previous five decades. According to Bourgeois, the spider, a weaver, seen in a positive light, evokes her mother, the upholsterer. "Because my best friend was my mother and she was as intelligent, patient, clean and useful, reasonable, indispensable, as a spider."[1] In other words, a figure more capable than any other of repairing the childhood trauma that constantly resurfaced in her psyche.

1. Quoted in M. L. Bernadac, *Louise Bourgeois*, trans. Deke Dusinberre (Paris: Flammarion, 1996), p. 149.

↑ **Bruce Weber**, photograph of Louise Bourgeois, 1997.

→ ***Maman*** (Mommy), 1999. Guggenheim Museum, Bilbao.

M.O.
43

Meret **Oppenheim**
(1913–1985)

German-born Meret Oppenheim's first role model was her grandmother, Lisa Wenger, an artist, writer, suffragette, and one of the first women to attend the Düsseldorf Academy of Art. Under her influence, she took up the artistic path and revealed herself to be sensitive to feminist struggles, while subtly opposing the idea of "feminine art."

Having decided to become a painter, at the age of eighteen Meret Oppenheim moved to Paris from Basel, Switzerland, where she had been raised. She became friends with Hans Arp, Alberto Giacometti, Man Ray, and André Breton, who invited her to exhibit with them. Influenced by psychoanalysis—she consulted G. C. Jung in 1935—she explored her dreams as a main source of inspiration for her drawings, paintings, collages, assemblages, and *détournements*. But her rapid rise to success provoked a serious crisis that kept her partially estranged from creative work for many years. Then in the mid-1950s, reassured by a happy marriage to businessman Wolfgang La Roche, she set about completing projects that she had abandoned before World War II. Her *Spring Feast* or *Cannibal Feast* (1959) generated great excitement: this "happening," which featured a nude woman covered in food served to guests, was a celebration of fertility. She continued to explore new avenues in her art, and moved in artistic circles, often seen at the Café du Commerce in Bern, a hotspot for the European avant-garde. Major retrospectives soon followed.

Though Oppenheim was the creator of the emblematic fur-lined cup and saucer in 1936, which became a symbol of surrealism, she was often reduced to the role of muse by the surrealists themselves, who cast her as the woman-child archetype. In *Daphne and Apollo,* painted in 1943, she asserted the full power of a creative woman and explored the burden of beauty. She drew inspiration from Ovid's *Metamorphoses*, in which the nymph Daphne asks to be transformed into a tree to escape Apollo's advances: "A thin bark closed around her gentle bosom, and her hair became as moving leaves; her arms were changed to waving branches, and her active feet as clinging roots were fastened to the ground—her face was hidden with encircling leaves."[1] But in her interpretation, she inverses the danger, transforming the insistent lover into a tuberous plant that Daphne, in female form, stands over almost threateningly.

1. Ovid, *Metamorphoses,* trans. Brookes More (Boston, MA: The Cornhill Publishing Company, 1922), Book 1, lines 548–50.

← ***Daphne and Apollo***, 1943.
Lukas Moeschlin, Basel.

↑ ***Object***, 1936.
Museum of Modern Art, New York.

Leonora **Carrington**

(1917–2011)

Born into a privileged family in Lancashire in the north of England, Leonora Carrington had a patchy education due to her rebellious nature. She attended the Chelsea School of Art for a year, and then enrolled in the Ozenfant Academy of Fine Arts, founded by the artist Amédée Ozenfant in London. In 1936 she eagerly discovered surrealist painting at the group's international exhibition held in London. The following year, she met Max Ernst and the pair moved to Paris. Carrington began writing, while painting works populated by strange creatures and wild horses, doubles of herself, as in her unbridled *Self-Portrait* from 1937–38 in which she depicts herself in a dreamlike atmosphere wearing horse-rider's garb and sitting next to a hyena, her hair alive and streaming.

But World War II tragically impacted Carrington's life. Ernst, a German citizen, was detained by the French authorities. She secured his release, but he was once again arrested. Distraught at his arrest, she fled to Spain where she stayed in a psychiatric clinic after suffering from a serious breakdown. She then moved to Portugal, where she obtained the protection of the Mexican consulate through the support of the poet and diplomat Renato Leduc. Living in exile with him in the United States, she collaborated with the surrealist group that had taken refuge in New York, before moving to Mexico.

In 1946, Carrington married photojournalist Imre Weisz, with whom she had two children. During this period, still receptive to imagery from myths, the occult, and alchemy, she joined Mexican literary circles, befriended Octavio Paz, wrote plays and poems, and worked for the theater. In the 1960s, exhibitions of her work flourished in Mexico, France, and the United States, where she lived part of the time. She continued to create up until her death, giving her chimeras and dreamlike figures a new form in the 2000s by casting them in bronze.

Long defined by her beauty in her youth, in the early 1940s Carrington described how age freed her work. "I'm no longer the young, ravishing girl who passed through Paris, in love. I am an old woman who has lived greatly and I have changed—if my life has value, I am the result of time. . . . I will never be frozen in a youth that no longer exists—I accept the current, honorable decrepitude—what I have to say now is laid as bare as can be."[1]

1. Letter to Henri Parisot in 1943, quoted in *En bas. Précedé d'une lettre à Henri Parisot* (Paris: Eric Losfeld, 1973).

Self-Portrait, c. 1937–38.
The Metropolitan Museum of Art, New York.

Lygia **Clark**

(1920–1988)

Lygia Clark was born in Brazil, where she learned to paint with Roberto Burle Marx in Rio de Janeiro, then with Fernand Léger and Árpád Szenes in Paris. In the 1950s, she explored abstraction while seeking to escape formalism. After signing the Neo-Concrete Manifesto in 1959, she gradually abandoned painting and began creating her first modular sculptures. Her ambition was to create a profound disruption in the relationships between artist, work, and viewer, and to destroy the boundaries that have traditionally separated them. This ambition soon found her making objects that offered viewers a new experience of themselves and the world: she created masks and clothing that modified perception. At the Venice Biennale in 1968 she presented an installation entitled *The House is the Body*, a sort of intra-uterine voyage that aimed to "liberate inhibited instincts," according to the artist. In the early 1970s, Lygia Clark returned to Paris where she taught gestural communication at the Sorbonne. She established art-therapy sessions that demonstrated her fierce desire to bring art and life together, but that found little support in the psychoanalytical or medical fields. She returned to Brazil in 1976, where she continued her experiments up until her death.

In the late 1950s, with the series *Planos em superfície modulada* (Planes in a Modulated Surface), Clark deepened her reflection on abstract painting and the canvas as a three-dimensional object. She also deconstructed the relationship between the center and the border of the work through a pivotal movement from the center of the canvas outwards. In doing so, she developed a complex composition that suggests art's capacity to penetrate the world, foreshadowing her explorations into modular sculpture, as seen in 1962's *Bicho (máquina)* (Critter [Machine]).

Bicho (máquina)
(Critter [Machine]), 1962.
The Museum of Fine Art, Houston, TX.

Planos em superfície modulada no. 4
(Planes in a Modulated Surface), 1957.
Museum of Modern Art, New York.

Judit **Reigl**
(born 1923)

Judit Reigl's work, which has fluctuated between abstraction and figuration since the 1940s, is still not recognized for its true value. André Breton, albeit with a dose of misogyny, predicted as much, writing to her on July 5, 1954, "You have means that amaze me coming from a woman, and I see you capable of accomplishing immense things."

Trained at the Hungarian Academy of Fine Arts in Budapest, Judit Reigl spent two years in Italy on a scholarship, before arriving in France in 1950 after several unsuccessful attempts to flee communist Hungary. Soon after her arrival, she met the surrealists, who introduced her to automatic writing. In 1954, with Breton's guidance, she held her first solo exhibition at the gallery À l'Étoile Scellée.

However, Reigl moved away from surrealism towards abstraction, along with her friend Georges Mathieu. Immersed in themes of emergence and disappearance, she gave the gestural a key role in the series Éclatement (Outburst) and *Centre de dominance* (Center of Dominance). Reigl often placed her canvas on the ground and flung paint on it, engaging in a reflection on the notion of the mark, starting with the corporeal prints of her *Drap, décodage* (Drape/Decoding) and *Déroulement* (Unrolling), which reveal the smear left by her brush on the reverse of the canvas, to the body in free fall in *New York, 11 September 2001*.

In the 1960s, the figure re-entered Reigl's work in the form of almost exclusively male torsos and trunks that filled the canvas in the series *Homme* (Man). These indications of presence reflect the power of the human body and suggest Michelangelo's *ignudi* in the Sistine Chapel, muscular characters with glorified nudity that the young woman saw in Rome in 1947.

Homme (Man), 1967.
Centre Georges-Pompidou – Musée National d'Art Moderne, Paris.

Shirley **Jaffe**

(1923–2016)

Born in 1923 in Elizabeth, New Jersey, Jaffe studied art at Cooper Union in New York and in Washington, D.C., before heading to Paris where she settled in 1949 with her husband, a journalist for the France-Presse news agency. Her painting, in the style of abstract expressionism, began to be exhibited in Parisian galleries alongside works by her compatriots and friends Sam Francis, Joan Mitchell (pp. 98–99), and James Bishop. But in the early 1960s, tired of seeing her work poorly understood by critics who labeled it "abstract landscape art," she gave her paintings a more geometrized aesthetic. Soon, she was arranging forms according to a dancing rhythm, using a recognizable color palette that could be vibrant or muted. Certain elements reappear in each work, inspired by careful observation of a demolished building, an interior, a landscape: a half-circle, a spiral, a crenelated module, together form a surprising repertoire evoking jazz improvisation. Jaffe also took up engraving and in 1999 tried her hand at stained glass in the Gothic chapel of Saint-Jean-l'Évangéliste in Perpignan, southwest France.

Well liked by a young generation of painters that she enjoyed receiving in her Parisian studio, Jaffe worked nearly to the end of her life. "I am interested in non-centrality, coexistence, constant invention-making movements that are not repetitious but function together as a whole," she explained. "There is always an element of non-belonging that holds everything together in tension. I don't want a lyrical beauty. One could say I want to capture an unborn reality."[1]

1. Shirley Kaneda, "Shirley Jaffe," *BOMB*, no. 87 (Spring 2004).

Hop and Skip, 1987.
Museum of Modern Art, New York.

All Together, 1995.
Centre Georges-Pompidou –
Musée National d'Art Moderne, Paris.

Joan **Mitchell**

(1925–1992)

The daughter of renowned poet Marion Strobel Mitchell and a dermatologist and amateur painter, James Herbert Mitchell, as a child Joan Mitchell was fascinated by the work of Vincent van Gogh and Oskar Kokoschka. A graduate of the School of the Art Institute of Chicago, she frequented the New York avant-garde—the painters Willem de Kooning, Franz Kline, and Philip Guston, and the poet Frank O'Hara, whose writing had a deep influence on her work—and exhibited with the abstract expressionists. In 1955, she returned to Paris after a previous student exchange seven years earlier; from then on, she divided her time between France and her native country.

When her mother passed away in 1967, Mitchell bought land in Vétheuil, a small village on the Seine, northwest of Paris, where the landscape inspired her to paint many works. Poetry continued to play an important role in her work: she illustrated texts by her friends Jacques Dupin, J. J. Mitchell, James Schuyler, Pierre Schneider, and Chris Larsen. In the 1970s, she began to employ the all-over technique, which consists of addressing the pictorial space as a whole, abandoning the usual notions of "left," "right," "high," or "low." Mitchell achieved some institutional recognition and, in 1982, she became the first American woman to be featured in a retrospective at the Museum of Modern Art in Paris. Suffering from cancer, she rented a studio in Paris in order to continue working during her medical treatments and completed many pastels. Though she was very weak, she continued engraving until her death.

An outstanding colorist, Joan Mitchell took a strong interest in Paul Cézanne and his reflections on color. Her controlled approach to composition, despite appearing spontaneous, distanced her from the action painting popularized by Jackson Pollock. In *Ladybug*, she combines intense tones and

diluted pigments in a complex entanglement of drips and emphatic brushstrokes. As usual with Mitchell's work, this ladybug is as much the memory left by the insect as a representation of it. "Painting is a means of feeling 'living,'" she said in 1986.[1]

1. Quoted in *Theories and Documents of Contemporary Art*, ed. Kristine Stiles and Peter Selz (Berkeley: University of California Press, 1996), p. 32.

Ladybug (detail), 1957.
Museum of Modern Art, New York.

Etel **Adnan** (born 1925)

Etel Adnan is a major figure of the international artistic and literary scene. The daughter of a Syrian Muslim father and a Greek Christian mother, she grew up in Lebanon and dreamed of becoming an architect. At the time, however, the profession was considered inappropriate for a woman, so instead she pursued studies in literature and philosophy in Beirut, Paris, and the United States, where she began to forge an academic career and to paint.

The multilingual Adnan published essays, novels, and poems in English, French, and Arabic, expressing solidarity for Algerian independence or criticizing the Vietnam War, and developed an artistic language that was as unique as it was synthetic. Her paintings, created with a palette knife, are landscapes in luminous colors, so simplified in form as to be almost abstract. Many of these compact, architectural visions are inspired by Mount Tamalpais in California, which the artist admires, much like Paul Cézanne did Mont Sainte-Victoire or Hokusai, Mount Fuji. While her writings are characterized by a distinctly political interpretation of the world, her paintings reflect a more direct relationship to nature. "Painting expresses my happy side, the one who is at one with the universe."[1]

A collectively minded social activist enthusiastic about tapestry and craftwork, she tried to create a Lebanese Bauhaus—a project tragically interrupted by the civil war. Adnan typeset and illustrated several anthologies of Arabic, European, and American contemporary poets. She imagines these collections as genuine artist books, that, once open, form works in their own right; next to texts she writes by hand on sheets of paper, Japanese-style, compositions unfold in a new variation on the central ideal of landscape—an image of what she considers an unbreakable connection between art and nature.

1. Simone Fattal, "On Perception: Etel Adnan's Visual Art," in *Etel Adnan: Critical Essays on the Arab American Writer and Artist* (Jefferson, NC: McFarland and Co., 2002), p. 121.

Untitled [set of 9 inseparable paintings]
(detail), 2010.
Centre Georges-Pompidou –
Musée National d'Art Moderne, Paris.

Yayoi **Kusama**

(born 1929)

Born into a wealthy family in Matsumoto, Japan, Yayoi Kusama learned to paint against her parents' wishes. After experiencing hallucinations as a child, she began to incorporate dots into her drawings and gouache paintings, until they finally became a veritable leitmotif. Driven by a fierce desire for emancipation—both from her family and, more generally, from patriarchal Japanese society, which suffocated her—she began to exhibit her work in Japan, before leaving for the United States in the late 1950s. Through contact with the American avant-garde, she modified her approach and showed what she called her "infinity net" paintings at the Brata Gallery, in New York. These paintings are drawn from her childhood hallucinations and break free from their usual format to occupy the exhibition space. During the 1960s, she employed this process in many installations where sculpture—accumulations of phallic volumes—began to play a large role. She also created anti-capitalist and political happenings in the streets of New York. She grew increasingly successful and was friendly with artists Donald Judd, Eva Hesse (pp. 112–13), On Kawara, and Joseph Cornell. Upon her return to Japan in 1973, she began to write novels, short stories, and poetry. In 1977, she spent a month in a psychiatric hospital in Tokyo, and later chose to become a permanent resident, setting up her studio nearby. Since the 1980s, she has exhibited her work around the world and is thought of as a pioneer in the Japanese art scene.

At the crossroads of body art, minimal art, and pop art, Kusama's work takes on its full meaning in the iterative development of a practice that integrates painting, sculpture, environment, and performance. In the work *Dots Obsession*, Kusama creates a space entirely covered in dots, repeated endlessly by the play

of mirrors, in which the viewer, literally submerged, seems to drown, reaching the obliteration of the self, encouraged by the artist. "My life is a dot among thousands of other dots," she emphasized in 1960.

Dots Obsession, 1998.
Les Abattoirs, Toulouse.

Niki de Saint Phalle

(1930–2002)

Born to a French father and an American mother, Niki de Saint Phalle spent an unhappy childhood, caught between the Old World and the United States, and retained a sense of great anguish and depression from this time. At the age of eighteen, she married the poet Harry Matthews and, entirely self taught, started to paint. Hostile to the McCarthyism sweeping the United States, the couple moved to France in 1952, where Saint Phalle discovered Simone de Beauvoir's *The Second Sex*, which had a great impact on her. She began exhibiting her work and, in the early 1960s, she joined the new realist group, the only woman alongside Arman, François Dufrêne, Raymond Hains, Yves Klein, Martial Raysse, Daniel Spoerri, Jacques Villeglé, and Jean Tinguely, whom she married in 1971 after separating from her first husband in the 1960s. During this period, she made a name for herself with her series of performances known as *Tirs* (Shots): she fired a rifle at a board covered with plaster and pockets of paint to create exploded compositions. The violence of the process conveyed a similar violence inherent in the mental images that haunted the artist, as well as the contemporary world; more literally, it expressed the symbolic destruction of traditional easel painting.

In the mid-1960s, Niki de Saint Phalle created monstrous sculptures out of a mix of objects, a wild menagerie emerging from the shadows, contrasted by the first *Nanas* of the same period: sunny, sensual women made of papier-mâché, wire, fabric, or polyester, that offer a joyful and unbounded image of femininity. These figures blossomed in graphic prints as well, where the artist created a bittersweet world, as in the screenprint *Why Don't You Love Me?*. Fascinated by Antoni Gaudí's Park Güell in Barcelona and Ferdinand Cheval's Ideal Palace in Hauterives, France, Saint Phalle also explored monumental ensembles. The result was her Tuscan *Tarot Garden*, populated with strange creatures and fitted with a grotto covered in a mosaic of mirrors, bringing together two aspects of her work, one terrifying and furious, the other joyful and warm.

← Niki de Saint Phalle shooting. Film still from *Daddy*, co-directed with Peter Whitehead, 1973. Sprengel Museum, Hanover.

↑ ***Why Don't You Love Me?***, 1968. Musée d'Art Moderne et d'Art Contemporain, Nice.

Yoko **Ono**
(born 1933)

Yoko Ono was a pioneer of conceptual art, but her work was long overshadowed by her relationship with John Lennon.

Ono grew up between Tokyo and the United States, following her father's postings as a banker. She was the first woman philosophy student at the University of Gakushuin, Japan, where she discovered recent movements in Western thought, from Marxism to existentialism. Ono was a talented musician; she met John Cage through her first husband, the composer Toshi Ichiyanagi, mixed with the New York avant-garde, and created her first performance pieces, which she recorded as "event scores"—documents that replaced the physical artwork with a series of instructions for the spectator. Foreshadowing conceptual art, these performances earned her a first solo exhibition in 1961 at the AG Gallery, New York.

In the 1960s, Ono's performances focused on audience interaction, establishing her at the forefront of participative art. In *Cut Piece* (1964), the artist sat immobile, in a traditional Japanese seated pose, inviting each participant to cut a piece of her dress and take it with them, gradually revealing her body in a kind of self-offering. During this period, she also contributed to Fluxus, an international, interdisciplinary group of artists that explored the process of making art and the status of the artist and their relationship to society.

Ono's close relationship with John Lennon led to marriage in 1969. The couple participated in one another's creative ventures, one of which was a very public commitment to world peace. Ono collaborated with Lennon musically, contributing to the Beatles' *White Album* and founding her own group, the Plastic Ono Band, in 1969. A major exhibition of her work was held in 1971 in Syracuse, New York, and the following year, documenta in Kassel, Germany, showed some of her work. For the rest of the decade, Ono and Lennon withdrew from public life, returning in 1980 with an album, *Double Fantasy (A Heart Play)*, that met with great success. Following Lennon's assassination on December 8, 1980, Ono focused increasingly on making music and promoting peace, developing no new conceptual art projects until the 1990s. Since then, many retrospectives of her work have been held around the world. Continuing to be engaged with the contemporary scene, she has founded several prizes, including the LennonOno Grant for Peace and the Courage Award for the Arts.

Yoko Ono and John Lennon hold a campaign poster against the Vietnam War, London, December 1969.

WAR
IS
OVER!
IF YOU WANT IT
Happy Christmas from John & Yoko

Sheila **Hicks**

(born 1934)

Sheila Hicks was introduced to textile arts by Anni Albers, a former Bauhaus student and wife of Josef Albers, Hicks's painting professor at Yale School of Art. Thanks to a scholarship, from 1957 to 1959 Hicks was able to live and travel in South America where she discovered the local art of weaving. This had a decisive impact on her life, inspiring her to build a small loom and create her first textiles. At the same time, she taught drawing and color theory in Santiago, Chile, then in Mexico, where she soon began exhibiting her wool pieces.

In the 1960s, Hicks tried her hand at three-dimensional weaving, encouraged by the architects Luis Barragán and Felix Candela. She paid particular attention to dyes and color, as well as the traditional practices that inspired her. In 1964, she moved to Paris and founded the Atelier des Grands-Augustins where, to this day, she works at the crossroads of art and craft. Along with more personal works, she designs for an Indian textile manufacturer, a Moroccan carpet factory, and the contemporary furniture designers Knoll International. She also receives commissions for large tapestries and fabric sculptures from companies like Air France, the Rothschild banking company, and the Ford Foundation. In the 1980s, she undertook a more sociological exploration into textiles focusing on hospital sheets and military uniforms, and launched a specialized review, *American Fabrics and Fashion.* Though she never joined a feminist movement, she actively supports women, notably through her workshops. Today, she continues her research into volume and color, as evidenced in her monumental installation at the Venice Biennale in 2017. "Fibers have a memory

and can be sculpted in space," she explains. "The language of fiber is vast, it is universal."[1]

1. Clémentine Mercier, "Sheila Hicks, exercices textiles," *Libération*, September 25, 2016.

Escalade Beyond Chromatic Lands, 2017.
57th Venice Biennale.

Paula **Rego**

(born 1935)

Originally from Portugal, Paula Rego studied at the prestigious Slade School of Fine Art in London, where she settled permanently in the 1970s. A painter, engraver, and sculptor, she invented a world populated by monstrous beings, large-headed children, women with sturdy bodies and troubling gazes, and puppet men, inspired by both British literature (Charlotte Brontë, Lewis Carroll) and the painting of William Hogarth and Francisco de Goya, as well as the work of illustrators Gustave Doré and Benjamin Rabier. This cruel and grotesque world, which the artist says is fueled by Jungian psychoanalysis, conveys her critical view of the repressive policies of Estado Novo—the dictatorship that dominated her native country until 1974—the relationship between men and women, and women's status in society.

In her monumental paintings, Paula Rego depicts unsettling scenes where the role of the protagonists often eludes traditional morals. She reveals the ambivalence of human relationships, as in *The Family* (1988), one of her most famous works, which includes a disjointed, marionette-like man, a woman, and two young girls. A reflection of her own family situation—her husband, the painter Victor Willing, was dying of multiple sclerosis—the work is also a jeering evocation of Lazarus's resurrection, the last of Jesus's miracles: one girl dresses the impotent man while the second rubs up against him in the hope of bringing him back to life through sexual arousal, while the third prays for success, "in vain," explains the artist.[1] Violence and tenderness have rarely been so freely united. "No other artist has ever come close to capturing Rego's sense of the phantasmagoria that is female reality."[2]

1. Quoted by Mick Brown, "Paula Rego," *The Telegraph*, November 5, 2009.
2. Germaine Greer, "Untamed by Age," *The Guardian*, November 21, 2009.

The Family, 1988.
Courtesy Saatchi Gallery, London.

Eva
Hesse
(1936–1970)

Eva Hesse was three years old when she and her family fled Germany and the Nazi regime, first to England and then to New York. In 1946, her mother committed suicide, an event that left her traumatized. She studied at Cooper Union and the Yale School of Art, with Josef Albers among others, then returned to New York in 1959. She painted relentlessly and sold her first canvases, but they nevertheless left her feeling profoundly dissatisfied. In the summer of 1962, in Woodstock, New York, she created her first sculpture, in mesh and jersey.

In 1964, she had the opportunity to see her native country again, leaving for Germany with her husband, the sculptor Tom Doyle, at the invitation of a collector and patron. While there, she experimented with plaster and exhibited at the Kunsthalle in Düsseldorf, showing drawings and reliefs assembled from found materials. Upon her return to New York, she used rope, tires, balloons, and papier-mâché, fusing the organic and the industrial, the soft and rigid, all of which became central to her work. In 1967, she added latex and fiberglass, which enabled her to play with qualities of light. These experiments suggest a connection between Hesse's work and Robert Morris's antiform, which promotes the use of potentially perishable materials for their flexibility and imperfections. *Untitled (Seven Poles)*, created by Hesse when she was dying of a brain tumor, summarizes her explorations into the body, suffering, and existential pain, through visceral forms without equal.

Though women were increasingly visible in the art scene in the 1960s, inequalities between the sexes persisted. "Woman, beautiful, artist, wife, mistress of the house, cook, saleswoman, all that," wrote Hesse in her journal. "I can't even be myself or know who I am. I have to find something clear, stable, and peaceful within myself."[1]

1. *Eva Hesse Diaries*, ed. Barry Rosen (New Haven, CT: Yale University Press, 2016).

← ***Ringaround Arosie***, 1965.
Museum of Modern Art, New York.

↑ ***Untitled (Seven Poles)***, 1970.
Centre Georges-Pompidou – Musée National d'Art Moderne, Paris.

Nasreen **Mohamedi**

(1937–1990)

Although Nasreen Mohamedi remained relatively unknown during her lifetime, she was a pioneer of abstraction in India, where the male-dominated art scene was characterized by a conventionalism inherited from the British colonists. Born in Karachi (in what is today Pakistan), she attended classes at St. Martin's School of Art in London (now Central St. Martins) and lived for a while in Bahrain—where she discovered the immensity of the desert. A scholarship took her to Paris from 1961 to 1963, after which she moved to Mumbai. In 1972, she settled in Baroda and taught at Maharaja Sayajirao University until her death.

Mohamedi's art is founded on very strict discipline and extremely precise gestures; at the end of her life, though suffering from a degenerative disease that seriously affected her motor skills, she continued to draw by hand by imposing extraordinary control over her movements. If in the 1960s her work can be said to have belonged to lyrical abstraction, it was later characterized by meticulous research into the grid and the line—which has parallels with Kufic calligraphy (an Abbasidian writing often used to copy the Koran from the eighth to the eleventh centuries) and Islamic architecture, both of which the artist admired. She also practiced photography with the same exacting visual standards and succeeded in geometrizing the real in a series of very elaborate works.

Playing with the rhythm of line motifs and the luminous white of paper or, more rarely, of canvas, Mohamedi managed to create spaces at once spare and complex—genuine non-figurative landscapes—using little in the way of materials (as in *Untitled*, 1970s). Her approach to light calls to mind the *jali*, the sculpted stone screens that decorate the facades of Indian mosques and palaces. As the pages of her journal reveal, Mohamedi was also influenced by European abstraction, from Kasimir Malevich to Wassily Kandinsky, Piet Mondrian, and Paul Klee, classical Indian music, Rainer Maria Rilke's poetry, and Le Corbusier's architectural modernism in Chandigarh in northern India.

Untitled, 1970s.
Kiran Nadar Museum of Art, New Delhi.

Beatriz **González**

(born 1938)

Beatriz González, a major figure in Colombian art, has been creating highly political work since the 1960s. Incorrectly associated with pop art because of the use of bright colors, simplified forms, and mass culture, González's work is deeply connected to the history of Colombia and the events that have torn the country apart over the last few decades.

One of the first paintings González made upon graduating university, *The Suicides of the Sisga* (1965), was an expression of faith. Inspired by a true story—the suicide of two lovers instigated by the young man in the throes of a mystic hallucination—the work already contained elements of artistic maturity: a dramatic subject, a reappropriation of newspaper headlines, a color palette and formal qualities borrowed from folk prints, and finally, a reflection on social violence.

In the 1970s, González further explored the exaggerated beauty promoted by the advertising world, the cheap, mass-market images of the Grafica Molinari company (religious scenes, pin-ups, animals, landscapes, etc.), and copies of classical artworks that decorated many Colombian homes. With humor, she turned them into manufactured objects, such as curtains, furniture—as in *Naturaleza mesa viva* (Living Nature Table, 1971)—dishes (*Salomé*, 1973), or televisions.

The year 1985 was a major turning point in González's work, marked by the hostage-taking at the Bogotá Palace of Justice by the M-19 guerilla movement, which led to the death of twelve people. Abandoning irony, she approached the theme with utmost seriousness, representing the main figures of the tragedy in deconstructed compositions and darker tones. Corrupt leaders in *Los Papagayos* (The Parrots, 1987), anonymous victims of the civil war of 1948–1960, members of the paramilitary and drug traffickers in *Auras anonimas* (Anonymous Auras, 2009), not to mention her fellow citizens recently deported from Venezuela by Nicolás Maduro's government in *Los Dezplazados* (The Displaced, 2016), reveal the chaos that seems to continually destabilize Colombia.

Camilo Rozo, photograph of Beatriz González, 2015.

The Suicides of the Sisga, 1965.
Private collection, Bogotá.

Annette **Messager**
(born 1943)

Since the early 1970s, Annette Messager has been creating a mythology of the personal in a critique of women's status in society. Displacing hierarchies by using intentionally modest materials and techniques (everyday objects, popular imagery, embroidery), she questions cultural stereotypes in several series, including *Annette Messager Artist*, of course, but also *Truqueuse* (Trickster), *Femme pratique* (Practical Woman), *Colporteuse* (Peddler), and *Collectionneuse* (Collector). However, there's not a hint of sentimentality in her approach, which gladly opens the door to the shadows of the unconscious, as suggested by the poses of her stuffed sparrows in *Les Pensionnaires* (Boarders). "To be an artist," she says, "is to heal and reopen your wounds at every moment, in a single movement."[1]

In the 1980s, Messager continued her explorations with installations that gave the individual greater significance. In *Mes voeux* (My Vows) and *Mes trophées* (My Trophies), she assembled photographs of body parts—like votive offerings—to create a fragmented image of identity. She also began using stuffed toys—mutilated, torn, and dismembered—providing her work with a fantastic and familiar menagerie that formed, in her own words, "little cadavers of childhood that we remain very attached to."[2] She began to include movement within increasingly complex environments using parts of machines. In doing so, Messager added a dramatic dimension to her work, reflecting her enthusiasm for the work and special effects of Georges Méliès. *Articulés-désarticulés* (2001–2) activates anthropomorphic puppets in a drama that is simultaneously tragicomic, macabre, and sarcastic.

In *Les Interdictions* (Prohibitions, 2014), Messager reuses the puppet motif, which she combines with the pattern for sixty-eight prohibitory signs from around the world, collected during her travels or online. She draws attention to the normative powers that structure human society, mocking them through satire. It is perhaps a cruel irony that only one of these signs was entirely of the artist's invention: the one condemning prostitution.

1. Bernard Marcadé, "Messager, Annette (1943-)," *Encyclopædia Universalis* (http://www.universalis.fr/encyclopedie/annette-messager/).
2. Interview with Robert Storr, Musée d'Art Moderne de Paris, 1995.

← ***Les Hommes que j'aime, les hommes que je n'aime pas***
(The Men I Love, The Men I Don't Love), 1971–72.
MAC/VAL, Vitry-sur-Seine.

↑ ***Les Interdictions***
(Prohibitions), 2014.
Marian Goodman Gallery, Paris.

Barbara **Kruger**
(born 1945)

Born in Newark, New Jersey, Barbara Kruger took up sculpture, painting, and photography while working for fashion magazines. In the late 1970s, she began altering found images from mass culture, a practice that would make her famous. Armed with a keen sense for page layout acquired as a graphic design student at Parsons School of Design in New York, Kruger borrowed the visual codes of the Soviet avant-garde aesthetic: the exclusive use of black, white, and red, texts printed diagonally, simplified composition, etc. Faces with Hollywood beauty, chubby children straight out of 1950s advertisements, manicured hands, and sophisticated-looking smokers are overlaid with expressions or injunctions engraved in the collective unconscious. "The future belongs to those who can see it," "I shop therefore I am," and "Love for sale." The use of direct language encourages viewers' involvement and invites them to take a position.

Through these processes, Kruger questions stereotypes, particularly sexual and racial ones, as they are spread by the media, and reveals an often troubling subtext about power in the West today. She also casts a critical gaze on consumer society, which significantly contributes to disseminating these clichés. She pushes the deconstruction of media mechanisms as far as she can, widening the diffusion of her work beyond the traditional gallery and museum circuit to occupy city walls and the pages of magazines, as with *Untitled (Your Body is a Battleground)*, created for the abortion rights march in 1989 in Washington, D.C. "I never say I do political art. Nor do I do feminist art. I'm a woman who's a feminist, who makes art."[1]

1. Quoted by Christopher Bollen, "Barbara Kruger," *Interview Magazine*, March 2013.

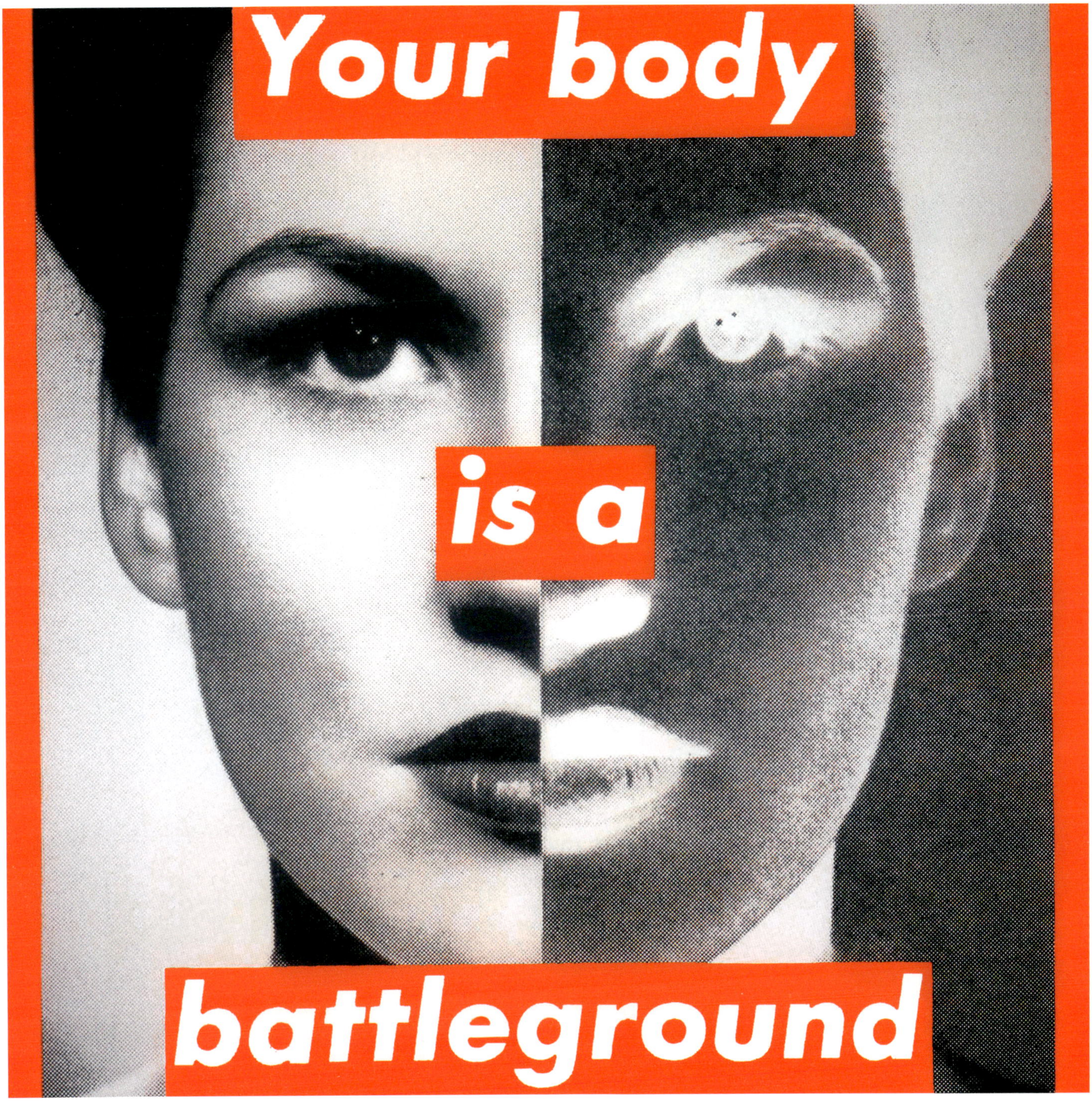

Untitled (Your Body Is a Battleground), 1989.
Poster.

The Artist Is Present, 2010.

Marina **Abramović**
(born 1946)

Trained at the Belgrade Academy of Fine Arts, Marina Abramović first engaged in painting and drawing before, in the 1970s, becoming one of the most active representatives of body art. She appeared, often nude, in intense performances, like *Art Must Be Beautiful* (1975) at the Charlottenburg Art Festival in Copenhagen, in which she filmed herself combing her hair with metal combs with increasing violence. She was particularly interested in physical endurance and mental strength, both challenged by a form of ritual that she reinvented with each work. The same year, Abramović met the German artist Ulay and together they began thirteen years of engaged reflection on gender equality. Space also played a large role in their actions, from *Relation in Space* (1976) in which they collided against one another with increasing force, to *Imponderabilia* (1977) in which, standing nude in a doorframe, they forced the viewer to brush up against them, up to their last joint performance on the Great Wall of China, where they met for a final goodbye after walking 1,200 miles (2,000 km), one from the Yellow Sea, the other from the Gobi Desert.

In the 1990s and 2000s, despite her noticeable presence at documenta in Kassel, Germany, (1992) and the Venice Biennale (1997), Abramović dedicated most of her time to teaching.

But the retrospective of her work at the Museum of Modern Art in New York in 2010 gave her the opportunity to present a spectacular new performance, *The Artist Is Present*. Day after day, during opening hours, she sat in one of the museum's galleries. Audience members sat down one at a time in front of her, for as long as they chose, from several minutes to several hours, in a silent face-to-face encounter. The first evening, her former companion Ulay joined the crowd of anonymous visitors and moved the artist to tears. "I test the limits of myself in order to transform myself, but I also take the energy from the audience and transform it. It goes back to them in a different way. This is why people in the audience often cry or become angry or whatever. A powerful performance will transform everyone in the room."[1]

1. Quoted by Sean O'Hagan, "Marina Abramović," *The Observer*, October 3, 2010.

Art Must Be Beautiful... Artist Must Be Beautiful..., 1975.

INTRODUIRE
5F
LE BAISER DE L ARTISTE
Doublé Peau
Très pratique
Combien Féminin
Grand Luxe
MERCI

ORLAN
(born 1947)

Since the 1960s, ORLAN has made her own body the site of extensive experimentation. "[A]s a female artist, the main material and recording surface I had to hand was my body, which I had to reappropriate because I had been dispossessed of it, in a way, by dominant ideology."[1] In her performance *The Kiss of the Artist*, presented at the International Contemporary Art Fair in Paris in 1977, she sold her kisses to visitors, haranguing the crowd like a market vendor: "5 francs for the artist's kiss. . . . A real artist's kiss for 5 francs, an honest-to-goodness artist's kiss! . . . It's a steal, get it now! Come on, come on, 5 francs, just 5 francs! . . . A conceptual work accessible to every wallet!" In becoming one with her work, she embodies her reflections on the place of the woman artist and emphasizes the extent to which the body—subjected to a host of personal, social, and religious pressures—is political.

Gradually, ORLAN began to focus more on the changes of a constantly evolving identity. The series of performances around surgery (1990–93) marked a turning point: in an operating theater-cum-studio she redesigned her physical appearance, shaping and sculpting it in the ultimate artistic gesture. She then began a vast work on the sum of cultures by way of hybridization: using the possibilities inherent in digital imagery, she combined self-portraits and aesthetic elements of pre-Hispanic and African peoples to better investigate the standards of beauty each are held to, but also to transcend questions of gender. Then, in the same spirit, she integrated biosciences into her work and practiced in vitro culturing of her cells mixed with that of animals or other people, to create an equally hybrid genetic patchwork *Harlequin's Coat*.

1. Bernard Blistène, *Orlan* (Paris: Flammarion, 2004), p. 190.

← ***The Kiss of the Artist***, 1977–2009. Centre Georges-Pompidou – Musée National d'Art Moderne, Paris.

↑ **Philippe Leroux**, photograph of ORLAN, 2002.

Sophie **Ristelhueber**

(born 1949)

After obtaining a degree in modern literature, Sophie Ristelhueber went to work for the photographic review *Zoom*. In the early 1980s, she laid the foundations of her work by investigating the destruction wrought by the civil war in Beirut, creating heady images of gaping holes left by the bombs and bullets in the Lebanese capital. Working at the crossroads of photography, installation, and video, Ristelhueber uses armed conflict to explore the question of territory and the traces it leaves on human lives, both literally—in the series *Every One* (1994), images of stitched wounds leave their imprint on bodies—and figuratively—in *WB* (2005), for example, photographs of blocked roads in the West Bank symbolize the political fragmentation in the region.

This approach, which in some ways resembles photojournalism, comes with a powerful aesthetic element: the artist uses photography as raw material. *Eleven Blowups* (2006), for example, emerged from Ristelhueber seeing televised images of the assassination attempt on the former Lebanese prime minister Rafic Hariri on February 14, 2005. The attempt, made with a car bomb, ripped an enormous hole in the streets of Beirut. Then she watched hours of footage of car bomb attacks. Singling out the craters formed by the explosions, she built ruined landscapes, at once real and virtual, using her own photographic archives amassed during travels to Turkmenistan, Syria, Iraq, and the West Bank. "After these suicide car bombs explode," she explains, "it's as if the earth had been sucked into its center. The idea of earth full of history swallowing itself is a concept that I find inspiring."[1]

Another aspect of Ristelhueber's work focuses on personal stories. In the series *Vulaines* (1989), she juxtaposes images of a family home, empty and abandoned, and photographs of children on vacation straight out of the 1950s. This apparently autobiographical account lets traces of the past filter through to the present.

1. "La mise à nu des choses : Entretien avec Sophie Ristelhueber," interview with the artist by Philippe Mangeot and Laure Vermeersch, in *Vacarme*, vol. 37, no. 4 (2006), p. 16.

Eleven Blowups, 2006.
Rencontres Photographiques
photography festival, Arles.

Untitled, 1985–88.
La Caixa Collection, Barcelona.

Rosemarie **Trockel**

(born 1952)

Since the late 1970s/early 1980s, Rosemarie Trockel has worked with various media—video, ceramics, weaving, installation, photography, etc.—radically freed from traditional aesthetic constraints. Her aim? A satirical demonstration of how unstable are the meanings of the images that shape our daily lives. This critical approach enables her to question the social order and its influence on the construction of identity, the ties between humans and nature, and the domination of a patriarchal culture, and to deconstruct sexual stereotypes, starting with the tyranny of beauty in the era of mass consumption and the reification of women's bodies.

Rosemarie Trockel made a name for herself in the 1980s with her woven works. Using a knitting machine, she reproduced motifs borrowed from popular culture, like the stylized yarn skein of the Woolmark logo or the Playboy bunny. When seen together, they appear to summarize the two main functions generally assigned to women: one domestic, the other erotic (*Untitled*, 1985–88). In the 1990s, she brought the animal and metamorphosis into her work, in a series on Brigitte Bardot and sea lions—"An interesting example of the contradictions and incoherencies of contemporary engagement,"[1] she notes—and the figure of the monkey as a symbol of the artist, as well as the anthropological experiments undertaken with her partner Carsten Höller (*House for Pigs and People*, 1997; *Prunelle*, 1999). More recently, Trockel has focused heavily on collage, a practice symbolic of the innovations of the early twentieth century and one perfectly adapted to her tendency to blend diversion and humor: in *Nobody Will Survive 2* (2008), she transforms Francis Bacon into a cyclops, his face eclipsed by a strange eye-nipple.

1. *Rosemarie Trockel*, exh. cat. (Munich: Sammlung Goetz, 2002), p. 23.

Mona **Hatoum**
(born 1952)

Born to a Palestinian family exiled in Lebanon, Mona Hatoum left Beirut, her native city, in 1975 to visit London. Due to the war, she settled there permanently, studying art at the Slade School of Fine Art. This rootlessness and her life in Europe became the main focus of her work, along with a reflection on female alienation. In the 1980s, she created her first performances, subjecting herself to harsh trials of imprisonment and immobilization (*The Negotiating Tale*, 1983; *Position: Suspended*, 1986). Hatoum would abandon this kind of performance for complex installations and diverted objects that engage the spectator's body both figuratively and literally. In a critique of domesticity, she created a series of children's beds in steel and wire (1993) and in glass cylinders resembling test tubes (1994)—a troubling image of maternity—cooking utensils bristling with menacing screws (1996), and a doormat made of thousands of brass needles with the ironic inscription "Welcome."

Cells (2012–13) incorporates a political analysis of the West, particularly the violence inherent in its institutions and urban and geographic organization. Using cages containing organic forms in blown glass, the work dramatizes control—symbolic, state, bureaucratic, police—which those in exile, and citizens more broadly, are subjected to in the democracies of Europe and North America. In this regard, *Cells* can be likened to the work on cartography that Hatoum has undertaken

for several decades. At times, it is open and fragile, as with *Map* (1999) in which marbles on the ground form a planisphere without borders that shifts with the movement of visitors' footsteps. At others it is brutal, as in *Hot Spot* (2006), in which neon tubes forming continental coasts glow red on a gridded globe. "The concerns in my work are as much

about the facts of my origins as they are a reflection on or an insight into the Western institutional and power structures I have found myself existing in for the last twenty-odd years," explains Hatoum.[1]

1. Quoted by Janine Antoni, "Interview with Mona Hatoum," *BOMB*, no. 63 (Spring 1998).

Cells, 2012–13.
Coproduction Marseille-Provence 2013, Arnoux-Industries, CIRVA, Galerie Chantal Crousel, Paris.

Nan Goldin

(born 1953)

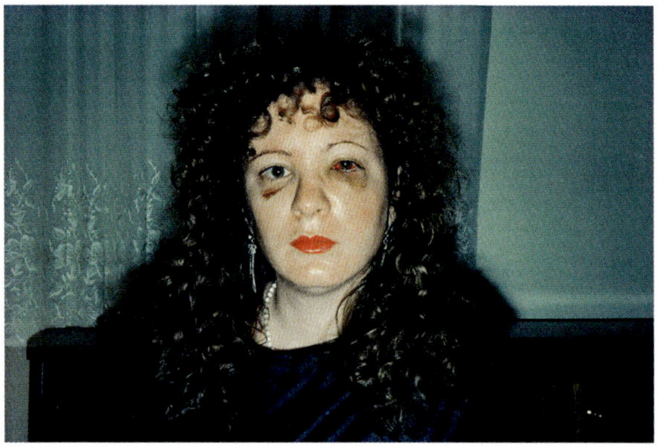

Nan Goldin—for whom intimacy and creation are so closely connected—photographs her everyday world and entourage, and nothing else. She turned to photography as a teenager, after her older sister committed suicide in 1964 and she realized with despair that she had kept so few photos of her. She was initially self-taught, but in 1972 she enrolled in the School of the Museum of Fine Arts in Boston. Her direct style evokes the immediacy of snapshots, while demonstrating a keen sense of composition.

Goldin was part of an underground scene and created an utterly novel portrait of marginalized youth, excluded, for better or for worse, from the American dream. Nothing escaped her lens: sexuality, violence, nightlife, illness—but also love and friendship. To share her photos with her friends, from 1979 to 1986 she created a series entitled *The Ballad of Sexual Dependency*; it was soon appearing in galleries and museums to a soundtrack that gave the project an almost cinematic narrative power. *Nan and Brian in Bed* (1983) is part of this collection. Appearing with her boyfriend in a half-lit room, Goldin conveys all the ambiguities of their relationship and the unavoidable distance that sometimes settles between two lovers.

In the early 1990s, Goldin witnessed the ravages of AIDS. She was one of the first artists to take extensive photographs of the era, all of them poignant and discreet. During this period, inspired by her trips to Europe, she brought her personal approach to new motifs, such as landscape or still life. Many retrospectives of her work were held throughout the world. In 2004, she created an ambitious installation, *Sisters, Saints and Sibyls*, drawing inspiration from time spent in a psychiatric hospital for substance abuse and depression, recalling the tragic death of her sister. "When I say that my camera has kept me alive," she says, "I mean that literally. My work is what I am."[1]

1. Quoted by Sean O'Hagan, "Nan Goldin," *The Observer*, March 23, 2014.

Nan, One Month after Being Battered, 1984. Tate Modern, London.

Nan and Brian in Bed, 1983.
The Metropolitan Museum of Art, New York.

ROOM 29

Friday March 6, 1981. 9a.m. I go into room 29. It seems vacant. The twin beds have not been used. The only sign of presence: the suitcase placed on the luggage rack. It is empty. A more careful examination reveals that the right bed has been occupied (a few short black hairs and a creased pillow) though without being unmade. In the bathroom, the first thing that I notice is the glass of water in which a handkerchief is soaking. On the edge of the sink, there is a small transparent toilet kit; it contains a rose hip soap still in its package, some tissue paper, a thermometer, a toothbrush (but no toothpaste), a knife, two small cases of Elephant and Power toilet water, a tooth mirror and finally two towels placed over the hotel ones. I go back to the room and open the wardrobe. No clothes hanging, but on the shelf a large number of miscellaneous objects that I place on the bed to photograph them better:

— a transparent case full of medicines and syringes
— a cardboard box sealed with scotch tape. I lift it. It is light. I am unable to guess its contents
— a hammer, and the following series of items, each obsessively separated in a plastic bag:
— a French Railways bed sheet
— a sponge
— some silverware
— two clothes brushes
— some sewing articles
— one glove and a cloth

Inside the opaque plastic bag, there are some products for cleaning wood, aluminum and a can of mosquito spray. Everything is ordered, wrapped up, sterilized. No cleaning to do here except for the necessary tidying up after my own search. It is my last day at the hotel C. I leave the guest of room 29 to the real chambermaid.

On Friday March 6, 1981 at 1 p.m., my duties at the hotel C. come to an end.

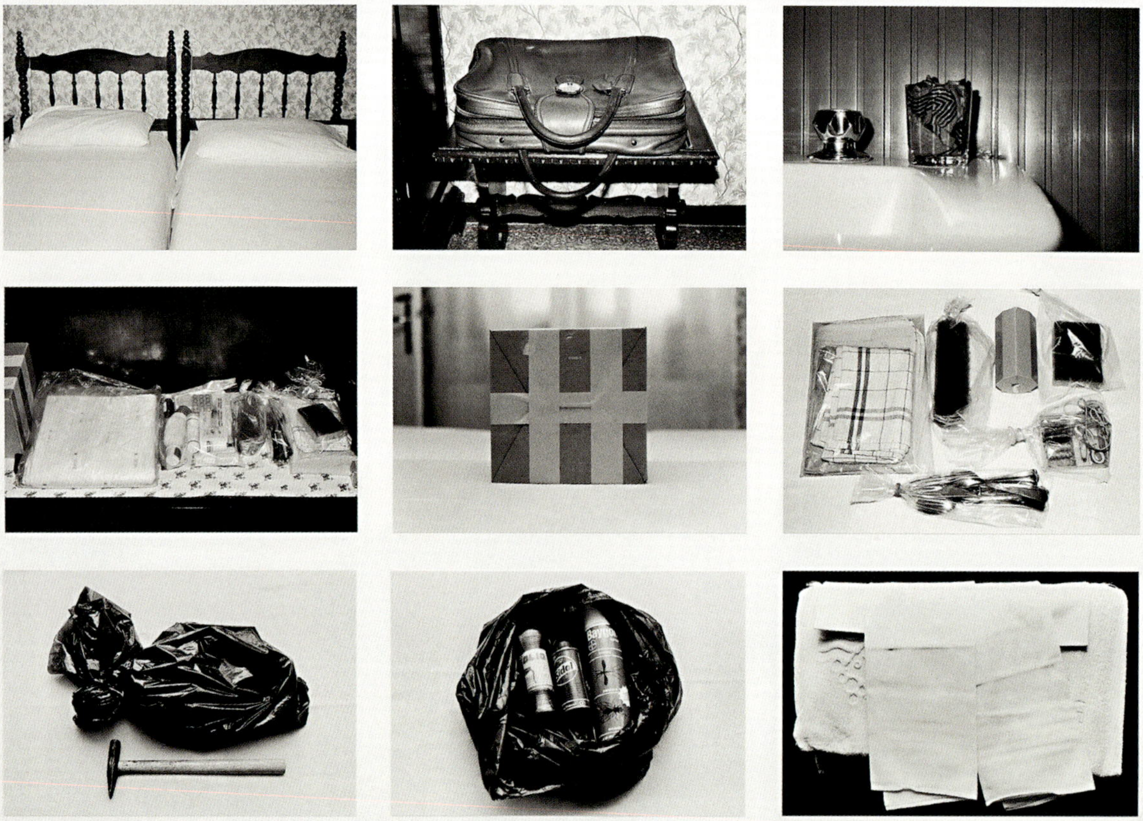

Sophie **Calle**

(born 1953)

Like artists Christian Boltanski or Annette Messager (pp. 118–19), Sophie Calle has been creating a highly biographical body of work since the 1970s—one that fuses reality and fiction.

Calle records everyday personal events using a narrative method, most often through stories and photography. Her work is shot through with themes of absence, memory, simulacrum, and traces: from *La Filature* (The Shadow, 1981)—in which a detective followed her through the streets of Paris, photographed her, and established a report—to *Douleur exquise* (Exquisite Pain, 1984–2003)—the summary of a painful breakup—as well as *Chambre avec vue* (Room with a View, 2002), in which, for one night, she installed her bed at the top of the Eiffel Tower where strangers told her stories to help her stay awake. Collaboration with the audience, as well as her exchanges with writers or artists, enriches these self-dramatizations and further tightens the connections between autobiography and story. After Paul Auster based Maria in his novel *Leviathan* (1992) on Sophie Calle, the French artist tried to carry out the actions dictated by the novelist. "I thought, things become more interesting," she explains, "when there is an exchange between realty and fiction, so I decided to carry out the rituals that Paul Auster imagined. So I bent to his rules of the game."[1]

In *L'Hôtel, Chambre 29* (1981–83), Calle recounts her experience working as a cleaner in a Venetian palace. Day after day, like an obsessive private detective, she meticulously described each alcove, photographed the occupants' belongings—clothing, toiletries, medication, books, letters—or the traces of their movements—an unmade bed, towels on the floor—rummaged through their appointment books and their trashcans, listened at doors. Nonetheless, this ambiguous voyeurism never manages to capture the essence of the people being observed, who remain invisible both to the artist and the spectator.

1. Quoted by Jean Max-Collard, "Sophie Calle," *Les Inrockuptibles*, September 9–15, 1998.

← ***L'Hôtel, Chambre 29***, 1981–83.
Centre Georges-Pompidou – Musée National d'Art Moderne, Paris.

↑ ***Des journées entières sous le signe du B, du C, du W. BB*** (detail).
Sophie Calle as Maria, the fictional character created by Paul Auster, 1998. Galerie Perrotin, Paris.

Carrie Mae **Weems**

(born 1953)

Carrie Mae Weems, a hugely influential artist in the United States, has been exploring cultural identities and their relationship to domination and power for nearly four decades. Influenced by Marxist thought, her work is a political engagement with and reflection on the stereotypes imprisoning African Americans. As an adolescent, Weems took an avid interest in theater and street dance, before turning to photography. In the series *American Icons* (1988–89), a documentary work, she enters American homes to create an inventory of knickknacks decorated with racist caricatures—trinket bowls shaped like laughing delivery men, a thermometer with a child's chubby-cheeked face, salt and pepper shakers modeled after a pair of tubby cooks, etc.—a manifestation of everyday racism that touches every facet of daily life.

Gradually, Weems moved toward a more conceptual approach, mounting her photos in panel form and often incorporating text or video. In *From Here I Saw What Happened and I Cried* (1995–96), she used portraits of Black men and women from the nineteenth and early twentieth century, some of them slaves, to emphasize how photography—as a conduit for the segregationist gaze—profoundly shaped the image of Africans and African Americans in the United States. Each photo is accompanied by commentary that gives the oppressed a voice and, in doing so, restores their humanity.

After Manet (2003), from the series *May Days Long Be Forgotten* (in reference to International Workers' Day, May 1), also contributes to this highly political critique. Weems questions the canons of Western history and art by having pre-adolescent children pose like the models in Édouard Manet's *Déjeuner sur l'herbe*. But a form of resistance to social stereotypes is also palpable in this representation of middle-class Black youth enjoying their leisure time in poses and against a background similar to the first photographs of the white bourgeoisie taken in the nineteenth century.

Untitled (Woman Standing Alone)
from the series *Kitchen Table*, self-portrait, 1989–90.
National Gallery of Art, Washington, D.C.

After Manet, 2003.
The J. Paul Getty Museum, Los Angeles.

Cindy **Sherman**

(born 1954)

Cindy Sherman turned a childhood fondness for dressing up into an entire body of work. In the mid-1970s, just after graduating from the State University College of Buffalo, New York, she began acting, in costume, made up, and masked, playing the role of both cinematographer and actress. Soon she began organizing these variations on identity into series. In *Untitled Film Stills* she investigates the female stereotypes produced by Hollywood on an industrial scale in the mid-twentieth century: the sexy student, the pin-up, the voluptuous housewife, the victim, the femme fatale, the dancer, etc. In the 1980s, artifice, which she had carefully concealed until then, became increasingly visible and gave the images a dark and troubling aspect. Sherman continued this serial work, focusing on troubling motifs like clowns or "landscapes" formed by decomposing leftovers, sometimes combining them with deformed figures (as in the *Disasters* series). During the same period, she turned to art history, revisiting the old masters from Raphael to Caravaggio. In *Untitled #228*, she appears as Judith, the biblical heroine who saves her people by decapitating the invader chief, Holophernes; this theme—a model of powerful femininity—has long been appreciated by women artists, among them Artemisia Gentileschi (pp. 28–29).

After tackling cinematic and artistic mythology, as well as monstrosity, Cindy Sherman turned to another aspect of contemporary mass imagery: pornography. Using accessories purchased in medical supply catalogs, she took her exploration of the limits of obscenity to the edge of absurdity. In the late 1990s, she created the series *Broken Dolls*, with disjointed and indecent bodies, which might be compared to Hans Bellmer's surrealist *Puppets*, before returning to her study of stereotypes perpetuated by literature and Hollywood (*Untitled #574*, 2016).

Untitled A, 1975.
Tate Liverpool, Liverpool.

Untitled #574, 2016.
The Broad, Los Angeles.

Kiki **Smith**

(born 1954)

The daughter of opera singer Jane Lawrence and sculptor Tony Smith, Kiki Smith grew up in South Orange, New Jersey, before settling in New York in 1976. There, she participated in the group known as Collaborative Projects or Colab, which brought together artists from all disciplines to work on collective projects. The body and its social and cultural representations became central to her work following the deaths of her father and sister in the early 1980s. "[M]y work isn't didactic," she says. "It's not like I'm trying to say, 'This is how the world should be.' I'm trying to synthesize my experience."[1]

Fascinated by the illustrations in medical textbooks and obsessed with the fragility of life, Kiki Smith produces anatomical motifs in a wide variety of media (sculpture, glass, engraving, photography, drawing). She endlessly revisits images of organs (*Possession is Nine-Tenths of the Law*, 1985; *Second Choice*, 1987; *Untitled [Kidneys]*, 1995), bodily fluid, breasts (*Untitled [Bosoms]*, 1994), limbs (*Las Animas*, 1997), and fetuses (*All Souls*, 1988). Through repetition she is able to emphasize both the universality as well as the intimacy of the human body.

In the early 1990s, nature took on a larger role in her work. Constellations, cosmologies, wild animals (including the she-wolf) enriched Smith's reflections on the human condition. In her drawings, large-format engravings, and installations, the world is a fairytale, primitive, violent, marvelous, and cruel, ambiguities that at first glance appear hidden behind a formal fragility (*Companion*, 2000). Smith also set about analyzing specific female figures that haunt the collective unconscious, like the Virgin Mary, Lilith, La Loba (the She-Wolf), Little Red Riding Hood, and Alice in Wonderland (*Pool of Tears*, 2000). In this way, the female body appears as one of the most powerful vehicles of legendary, phantasmagoric, and scientific tales in the Western imagination.

1. Quoted by Heidi Julavits, "Kiki Smith," *Interview Magazine*, 2017.

Nina Sublin, photograph of Kiki Smith, 2013.

Companion, 2000,
Pace Gallery, New York.

Outside #3, 1990–91.
The Metropolitan Museum of Art, New York.

Michal **Rovner**

(born 1957)

Born in Tel Aviv, Michal Rovner studied cinema, philosophy, and photography. In a multi-faceted body of work that includes drawing, photography, installation, and video, she explores history and territory, as well as the conflicts that have been destroying the Middle East since the mid-twentieth century. There are similarities between the formal beauty of her images—which she colorizes, manipulates, scrambles, and reframes—and pictorialism, as well as Edward Steichen's grainy photographs.

In her series *Outside* (1990–91), Rovner considers the versatility of perception and memory, and its relationship to reality. For two years, she photographed a Bedouin hut in the Israeli desert, then retouched each photo in order to create a spectral, shifting image of the modest structure isolated in an inhospitable setting. Then the Gulf War broke out. In New York, she photographed the television screen, which never left her sight, before reworking her Polaroids to isolate and blur the equally ghostly figures (*Decoy*, 1991); in doing so, she accentuated the real and symbolic distance effected by satellite retransmission.

In the mid-1990s, Rovner regularly turned to video. She filmed the border between Lebanon and Israel as a meeting place of documentary and fiction (*Border*, 1993–97) and depicted crowds of strangers and migrating birds (*Monoprints of Birds*, 1998). At the start of the new millennium, she collected old stones from various Israeli and Palestinian sites and built monumental constructions with the help of masons from both territories (*Makom*). More recently, she created the series *Night* (2016) in an effort to take a step back from these social questions: while absence and disappearance have long been central to her work, here she explores the troubling presence of jackals around her house, a metaphor for the primitive and impenetrable that lies within each of us.

One-Person Game Against Nature I #33, 1992. Guggenheim Museum, New York.

Rei **Naito**
(born 1961)

Rei Naito graduated from Musashino Art University and made her entrance on the international art scene in 1997, when she participated in the Venice Biennale with *One Place on the Earth*: a tent filled with small objects (leaves, seeds, wire, needles, etc.) and which viewers were only allowed to enter one at a time, to preserve the quiet atmosphere.

A loyal reader of the philosopher Simone Weil, Naito investigates the effect of our presence in the world, as something between a blessing and a curse. The work's relationship to the place where it is presented is vital to the artist, as is the notion of earth and of ground. Influenced by animism, she attaches great importance to the specific characteristics of environment—light, wind, colors, connections between interior and exterior, etc. Her collaboration with the architect Ryue Nishizawa at the Teshima Art Museum is one such example (*Matrix*, 2010). Within a completely open site with organic architecture conducive to meditation, she offers the viewer a unique experience in a form of reconciliation with living things; nature, represented by dripping water, plays a vital role. "I think I actually want to feel that I'm connected to the world, that my presence isn't unrelated to or divorced from it," she explains.[1]

In the early 2010s, following the Fukushima catastrophe, Naito dedicated her first work to her native city, Hiroshima, and the atomic bomb, and created a "meditation space," as she calls it, in the very heart of the city. In 2017, in Paris, she presented an installation on the same theme, *The Emotion of Belief*, juxtaposing irradiated objects and small sculpted figures symbolizing hope.

1. *ART iT*, no. 23 (Spring 2009).

The Emotion of Belief (detail), 2017.
Bottle from the Hiroshima Peace Memorial Museum collection. Maison de la Culture de Japon, Paris.

Matrix, 2010.
Teshima Art Museum, Teshima.

Agnès **Thurnauer**
(born 1962)

Agnès Thurnauer, a graduate of the École Nationale des Arts Décoratifs in Paris, has made painting and language the core of her work. In the early 1990s, she undertook the works *Big-big* and *Bang-bang*, two vast series structured around forms that are at once dual and anthropomorphic, and, as she sees it, timeless. Soon after, she began incorporating words—injunctions, puns, synonymy, and homonymy erupted in her work, as in *Olympia #2* (2012), in which the body of Édouard Manet's model is covered in pet names of varying degrees of affection ("my life," "my pet," "my fawn"). At times, the inclusion of the text is implicit. *Bien faite – mal faite – pas faite* (Well Made – Badly Made – Not Made, 2003), a series created using advertising from a famous lingerie brand, is a like a collage, with the slogan from the original images reduced to a white, abstract rectangle, like a yawning gulf of pure paint surrounded by headless bodies.

From *L'Exécution de la peinture* (The Execution of Painting, 2013)—the artist is depicted nude, painting a replica of Manet's *Bar aux Folies-Bergère* as photographers snap away at her—to the series *Prédelles* (in reference to the lower section of an altar, known as a predella, traditionally decorated in simplified iconographic motifs), Thurnauer explores painting as a historical medium and as a conduit for radicality in the contemporary world. In 2007, she began her *Portraits grandeur nature* (Life-Size Portraits), which have greatly contributed to her reputation. Not without irony, she transforms the names of great modern artists onto giant badges. Here, Marcelle Duchamp, Francine Bacon, La Corbusier, Jacqueline Pollock, and Joséphine Beuys—next to a Louis Bourgeois!—render the history of art surprisingly feminine. "It was simply a fact: there were no women in the history of art until the twentieth century. . . . I started going to museums when I was pretty young. And very quickly, I began looking at the names of artists only to find there were no female first names."[1]

1. Quoted in *Art présence*, no. 58 (April–May–June 2006).

Portrait grandeur nature (Marcelle Duchamp)
(Life-Size Portrait *[Marcelle Duchamp]*), 2009.
Centre Georges-Pompidou –
Musée National d'Art Moderne, Paris.

Olympia #2, 2012.
Artist's collection.

Yu **Hong**

(born 1966)

Yu Hong believes that "the macro-environment one grows up in largely determines individual fate. The only thing we can do is make a small adjustment between the two."[1] It is this fragile space that her work explores.

A graduate of the Central Academy of Fine Arts in Beijing, where she now teachers, Yu Hong is primarily interested in portraits. In painting after painting, she chronicles the lives of Chinese women. In the series *Witness to Growth* (begun in 2000), she depicts herself with her daughter, revealing here and there the sociological and economic upheavals that have shaken China since Mao's death. In the same vein, the series *She*, begun in 2003, depicts women in their homes and reveals a part of their inner selves and their everyday lives.

For the 2009 exhibition *Fresh Ink*, the Museum of Fine Arts in Boston asked several Chinese artists to each reinterpret a piece from its collection. For her *Spring Romance*, Yu Hong chose *Court Ladies Preparing Newly Woven Silk*, a twelfth-century silk painting attributed to the emperor-artist Huizong. She asked students from the Fine Arts Academy to pose for her, some in the same poses as the women in the painting, others in poses from Hong's own work. The overall composition borrows from the Song Dynasty masterpiece. In Yu Hong's version, the past, visible in its references to the Chinese pictorial tradition, and the modern world, embodied in the women in high heels and thick-soled boots, coexist. But in this feminist reworking, the expressiveness of the characters, their presence, and their vitality have replaced the figures who, in the original version, seem hopelessly unaware of their own existence.

1. Quoted by Queenie Li, "Home Is Where the Art Is: Yu Hong," cherwell.org (http://archive.cherwell.org/2017/03/02/home-is-where-the-art-is-yu-hong/), March 2, 2017.

Spring Romance, 2009.
Artist's collection.

Malala **Andrialavidrazana**

(born 1971)

Malala Andrialavidrazana, a professionally trained architect, explores the relationships between land, culture, and intimacy. She left her native Madagascar in the early 1980s for France. Her work seeks to dismantle the exoticism through which the Western world views its former colonies. In photographic series like *Ny Any Aminay* (2011) and *Echoes (from Indian Ocean)* (2011–13), Andrialavidrazana uses details—a bed, a bouquet of daisies, a few bottles of nail polish, a body lying down, hands on thigh—to construct a representation of Africa and Asia far removed from postcard clichés. Though the work firmly avoids miserabilism, it does not deny the weight of economic difficulties. The artist is also engaged in a critique of liberalism and globalization: in *Steel Life/ Still Factory* (2011), she photographs a South Korean former industrial complex, today nearly deserted in favor of Chinese sites and threatened with demolition by current urban policies.

Though Andrialavidrazana abandons photography in *Figures* (a series begun in 2015), she continues her reflection on the connections between representation, colonization, capitalism, and land. These digital collages—"digital embroidery," as she refers to them—combine maps, bank notes, old engravings, and even record sleeves from the 1970s–80s, opening the door to multiple interpretations. She uses them to deconstruct the myths about former colonies that saturated the European unconscious, while highlighting the ethnocentrism and domination of the colonizers. In *Figures 1861, Natural History of Mankind* from this series, she explores the role of women as guardians of a rich, pluralist culture symbolized by the ethnographic map of the African continent at the center of the image. But on another level, she also condemns the status of women, long confined to the domestic sphere. Andrialavidrazana concludes, "When you're an artist, to be a woman and African is a double burden when faced with the patriarchal Western hegemony."[1]

1. Quoted in Magali Lesauvage, "Nouvelles impressions africaines au Havre," *Libération*, October 24, 2016.

Figures 1861, Natural History of Mankind, 2016.
Centre National des Arts Plastiques, Paris.

Yto **Barrada**

(born 1971)

Yto Barrada, who grew up between Tangier and Paris, has made the Strait of Gibraltar the focus of her work. In her photographs, sculptures, and videos, the former student of political science carries out a critique of North–South relationships and analyzes what she calls "Western desire,"[1] which is sweeping Morocco. In an effort to document the situation in Tangier, and in Africa more broadly, she avoids exotic seduction, instead presenting the image of a city condemned to turn in vain towards a horizon—Europe—rendered inaccessible by the Schengen Agreement in 1990. She describes the terrible impasse gripping the city, far from the myth of cosmopolitan Tangier as it was perceived by the Beat Generation. The series *Dormeurs* (Sleepers) depicts men sleeping in public parks, their faces hidden, as though absent. *Iris Tingitana*, named for a local wildflower, explores resistance to encroaching urbanization as well as the city's deadly adaptation to mass tourism. Likewise, for the installation *Gran Royal Turismo* (2003), she created an urban circuit in which the scenery grows momentarily more beautiful as an official delegation passes. In *Autocars* (Buses) (2004), she focuses on the logos of bus companies bound for Europe that enable undocumented child migrants to identify their destination before hiding onboard, in hopes of crossing the border.

In recent years, Yto Barrada's work has taken on a more ethnographic dimension. For *Faux guide* (False Guide, 2015–16), a major

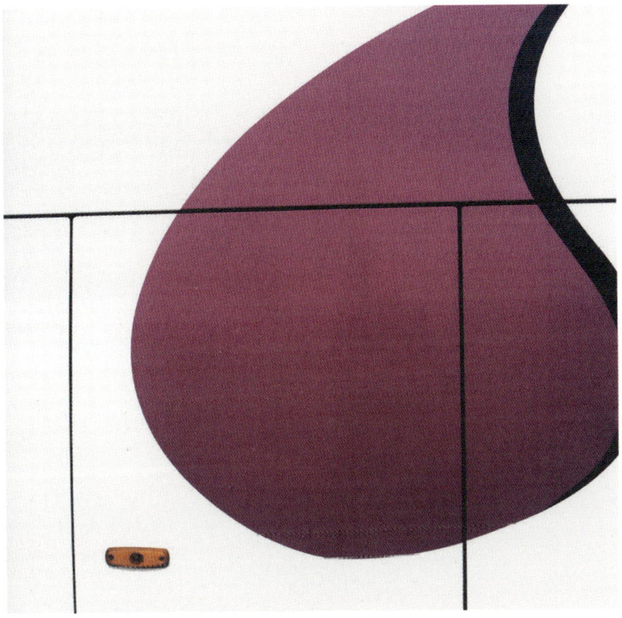

reflection on the notions of authenticity and archive, she photographed Berber children's toys in the Musée du Quai Branly collection in Paris and assemblages of pipes made by itinerant plumbers in Grand Socco, and assembled fossils, bones, drawings, and images of geological cross sections around monochromatic carpets from the Middle Atlas region; these were excluded from the inventory of Moroccan culture carried out in the early twentieth century under the aegis of Hubert Lyautey, the first Resident-General in Morocco under the French protectorate.

1. Quoted in Claire Guillot, "Yto Barrada photographie Tanger," *Le Monde*, April 3, 2006.

Autocars: Figures 1 à 4, Tanger
(Buses: Figures 1 to 4, Tangier), 2004.
Galerie Polaris, Paris.

Laure **Prouvost**

(born 1978)

Laure Prouvost, the first French woman to receive the prestigious Turner Prize (2013), centers her work around fiction and language, and their evocative power. Tall tales and crazy stories, and a fondness for the absurd and the utopian feed into her videos and installations. "Dream and reality, fiction and action, they are not separate. . . . Today, it seems to me that we are in much more linear narratives. . . . But I am certain there are still many stories to invent to make the world more fascinating—though it will not become any safer."[1]

In the early 2010s, Prouvost turned her imaginary grandparents into main characters (*Wantee*, 2013): a conceptual artist grandpa, supposedly friends with the Dadaist Kurt Schwitters (1887–1948), and a grandmother nicknamed Wantee, in homage to Schwitters's real-life companion, who was always saying, "Do you want tea?" One day, the grandfather digs a tunnel under his living room all the way to Africa and disappears; the elderly lady, like Penelope, overcomes domestic boredom by embroidering and making pottery.

Though Prouvost gradually moved away from the family fable, many of the elements appear in her recent works, such as the installation created for the Palais de Toyko in Paris in 2018, *Ring, Sing and Drink for Trespassing*. Set in a time marked by global warming and a wasteland ambiance that eliminates the border between illusion and reality, around a fountain of giant breasts, the viewer discovers plants, fruit, abandoned objects, puns, and videos, as well as—in an echo of the previous work with the "grandparents"—paintings, ceramic growths, and enormous tapestries; in other words, the encounter between heritage and the possibilities of the digital, which fascinate Prouvost.

1. Quoted in Ingrid Luquet-Gad, "Laure Prouvost, de l'autre côté du miroir [et au palais de Tokyo]," *Les Inrockuptibles*, June 13–19, 2018.

Wantee, 2013.
Tate Britain, London.

Camille **Henrot** (born 1978)

Camille Henrot likes fables and beliefs: ancient Greek myths, religious tales, the gut feelings that pepper the history of science, everyday fictions, and other stories feed into a shifting work (drawing, sculpture, video, installation, etc.) that she voluntarily describes as academic. It's an accurate description: Henrot likes to use literary and scientific references to more accurately express the difficulties of defining the real in a time of global information.

In this regard, the video *Grosse Fatigue* is an amazing feat. In thirteen minutes of tight editing, where the frame is divided into windows as though on a computer screen, Henrot invites a rereading of the history of the universe, from the void to death, including the birth of the gods, the creation of the Earth, and the invention of human knowledge. She offers a poetic synthesis of myths (Navajo, Shinto, Inuit, etc.) in a kind of inventory of beliefs. Images of ceremonies, ritual objects, zoological specimens, anthropological collections—which attest to a Western culture of conservation (museum, scientific) by destruction—are associated with other, more enigmatic images (froth, marbles representing the Big Bang, a cloud of colored liquid, strange animals, bare bodies, eye drops in an eye, scrolling Wikipedia pages, etc.). A text written in collaboration with the poet Jacob Bromberg is chanted by a spoken-word artist, heightening the dizzying effect of this series of images. This flux is precisely what fascinated the artist. "This dimension is what interested me, it's this excessive dimension, the way the universe overflows representation. The desire to capture the universe, though necessary, generates a profound solitude, a fatigue, a feeling of 'the after,' this fatigue that arrives after creation."[1] The film earned the young artist a Silver Lion at the 55th Venice Biennale in 2013, confirming her international renown.

1. Interview with Camille Henrot at the 2013 Venice Biennale, for the Biennale Channel.

Grosse Fatigue, 2013.
Museum of Modern Art, New York.

Lola
Gonzàlez
(born 1988)

Video artist Lola Gonzàlez graduated from the École des Beaux-Arts in Lyon in 2012. For several years, her films and performances have explored the resources and limits of the group identity and dynamic. Using her friends as models, she explores the dissolution of individuality within the collective, but also the power and the energy that it can generate. Often gathering in large houses on the Atlantic coast, these young adults engage in ordinary activities—eating, sleeping, smoking—and warrior or enigmatic rituals—shooting practice, physical training, long monotonous readings of first names, passing a snow-drop from hand to hand—in an atmosphere that feels distinctly end-of-days. Gonzàlez's work on narration, framing, editing, lighting, and photography reveal a cinematic approach to video art, despite the fact that she purposely seeks to dismantle certain customs (employing, for example, spare dialog, and music without illustrative purposes).

In *Veridis Quo*—the Latin-sounding title is borrowed from a Daft Punk song that suggests several meanings in English like "Very Disco" or "Discovery"—the artist depicts the mysterious life of several men and women in an isolated villa. "A group of individuals," she explains, "appear to be preparing themselves to lose their sight. They are also training to shoot without using their eyes. They wake up blind, and unsurprised by the fact, they are guided by two other members of the group to a creek, where they are left waiting, weapons in hand."[1] While it's tempting to apply a strictly political reading to this video, Gonzàlez insists on her right to make fiction: these blind figures, which she compares to crustaceans, represent an image of lost humanity that is as fierce as it is poetic.

1. Artist's website, http://lola-gonzalez.com/index.php/videoworks/veridis-quo/